DATE DUE

Joyous Greetings

Joyous Greetings

The First International
Women's Movement, 1830–1860

Bonnie S. Anderson

OXFORD
UNIVERSITY PRESS

2000

OXFORD
UNIVERSITY PRESS

Oxford   New York

Athens   Auckland   Bangkok   Bogotá   Buenos Aires   Calcutta
Cape Town   Chennai   Dar es Salaam   Delhi   Florence
Hong Kong   Istanbul   Karachi   Kuala Lumpur
Madrid   Melbourne   Mexico City   Mumbai
Nairobi   Paris   São Paulo   Singapore
Taipei   Tokyo   Toronto   Warsaw

and associated companies in
Berlin   Ibadan

Published by Oxford University Press, Inc.
198 Madison Avenue, New York, New York 10016

Oxford is a registered trademark of Oxford University Press

Library of Congress Cataloging-in-Publication Data
Anderson, Bonnie S.
Joyous greetings : the first international women's
movement, 1830–1860 /
Bonnie S. Anderson.
p.   cm.
Includes bibliographical references and index.
ISBN 0–19–512623–8
1. Feminism—History—19th century. 2. Women's rights—
History—19th century. 3. Feminism—International cooperation—
History—19th century. 4. Women's rights—International cooperation—
History—19th century. 5. Equality—History—
19th century. 6. Social movements—History—19th century. I. Title.
HQ1154.A6856   2000   305.42'09'034—dc21   99-14778

1 3 5 7 9 8 6 4 2
Printed in the United States of America
on acid-free paper

To my wonderful mother
Geraldine Scofield Sour
and to the memory
of my dear friend
Alice L. Miller

The Pioneers of human progess are like the Seagulls, they behold new coasts, new spheres of daring thought, when their co-voyagers see only the endless stretch of water. They send joyous greetings to the distant lands. Intense, yearning, burning faith pierces the clouds of doubt, because the sharp ears of the harbingers of life discern from the maddening roar of the waves, the new message, the new symbol for humanity.

—Emma Goldman,
about Mary Wollstonecraft

Contents

∽

Acknowledgments

~

Doing a project which crosses traditional national and chronological boundaries is daunting. From the beginning, I have benefited tremendously from the encouragement and support of colleagues in a wide variety of fields. They read the work in various drafts, supplied documents difficult to obtain, and cheered me on. It is now a pleasure to thank Harriet Alonso, Scarlett Freund, Linda Grasso, Dorothy Helly, Dagmar Herzog, Nancy Hewitt, Pam Hirsch, Jacquie Matthews, Maggie McFadden, Claire Moses, Karen Offen, Michèle Riot-Sarcey, Leila Rupp, Brita Stendahl, Jörg Thurow, Hugh Van Dusen, Jean Fagan Yellin, and Judith Zinsser. My fellow members of the German Women's History Study Group—Dolores Augustine, Maria Baader, Rebecca Boehling, Renate Bridenthal, Jane Caplan, Belinda Davis, Atina Grossmann, Amy Hackett, Deborah Hertz, Maria Hoehn, Young Sun Hong, Marion Kaplan, Jan Lambertz, Molly Nolan, Molly O'Donnell, and Nancy Reagin—read and commented on the first four chapters. Special thanks to Amy Hackett for help with translations from the German, and to this lively bunch for providing a long-lived and inspiring example of female support, critical attention, and productivity. Members of the Columbia University Seminar on Women and Society read and commented on an early draft of chapter 1.

Numerous librarians in this country and abroad made my research possible. They include Wendy Chmielewski at Friend's Historical Library, Swarthmore; Rosamund Cummings at Friend's House, London; David Doughan at the Fawcett Library, London; Anne Escott at the Glasgow Public Library; Dennis R. Laurie at the American Antiquarian Society, Worcester; Nancy Mackechnie at Vassar College; Kate Perry at Girton College, Cambridge, England; and Wendy Thomas at the Schlesinger Library, Cambridge, Massachusetts. Thanks also to the staffs at the Brooklyn College Library, the Bibliothèque Historique de la Ville de

Paris, the Bibliothèque Marguerite Durand, the New York Public Library, and the Ruhr-Universität Bochum.

My research was funded by three grants from the Professional Staff Congress Faculty Research program at the City University of New York, a summer stipend from the National Endowment for the Humanities, and the Wolfe Faculty Fellowship at Brooklyn College, which generously provided a year off at full pay. Throughout, I was aided and heartened by younger scholars of the next generation, who sent me their writings, tracked down references and illustrations, and provided me with reams of source material. They include Hagit Ben-Moshe, Lorely French, Toba Friedman, Hannfried von Hindenburg, Sattara Lenz, Nicola Matthews, Claudia Mogel, Ariana Speyer, and Kathryn Tomasek. Special thanks to my brilliant student, Theresa Ventura, for doing the picture permissions. Nadia Malinovich, my dear relation who is also a historian, provided help both personal and professional. My friend Jane Weissman generously supplied copying facilities and also read some early chapters.

The entire manuscript was improved by comments from my friend Stephanie Golden, a first-rate editor. I have also had wonderful editors at Oxford University Press, Thomas LeBien and his assistant, Susan Ferber. Both read and commented helpfully on the entire manuscript and did major editing on a far-too-long draft of the last chapter. Thanks also to my agent, Geri Thoma, for helping me to find a new home at Oxford.

The hard-working chair of the History Department at Brooklyn College, Philip Gallagher, gave me teaching schedules designed to facilitate my writing for many semesters and consistently supported my work. The equally hard-working and supportive chair of the History Department at the Graduate Center, David Nasaw, invited me to lecture and teach on this topic. All our jobs have been made far more difficult by the relentless and mean-spirited attacks and budget cuts visited upon the City University of New York during recent years.

Throughout bad times and good, I have been supported and sustained by a wonderful network of family and friends. Thank you all for everything.

Joyous Greetings

Introduction

~

During the 1970s, when I was working on a narrative history of women in Europe, I came across an 1851 letter sent by two jailed French feminists to two groups of their "sisters" abroad, asking for support in organizing women to fight for their own "civil and political equality, and the social right for all." One copy of the letter went to the Americans who had assembled for the first national women's rights convention in Massachusetts the year before; the other was directed to the Englishwomen who had just formed the first female political rights association in Britain after petitioning Parliament for the suffrage.

I had never heard of the women who wrote this letter or those who received it, but the document fascinated me. The feminism it expressed seemed amazingly modern. These Frenchwomen demanded not only the right to vote and to hold political office but also the restructuring of society so that all workers made a satisfactory living, all children got a good education, and all the old, sick, and infirm received decent care. They also voiced the "inexpressible joy" that the "courageous declarations" of the other women had brought them, the sense of solidarity they felt on being "united" with American and English women fighting for the same cause. I wondered how two Frenchwomen in a Parisian prison cell in the middle of the nineteenth century had known where to send these letters. Was there contact between early feminists in different nations and, if so, how had it come about and what were its effects?[1]

This book answers those questions. The more I investigated, the more international connections I discovered. This astonished me because I assumed internationalism to be a twentieth-century development, facilitated by phones and faxes, e-mail and air travel. Yet these women not only exchanged letters, they also visited each other, read a common body of published writings, and shared and transmitted tactics and ideas. These two 1851 letters were not singular occurrences, but rather composed one exchange in a complicated series of transactions that stretched throughout the Western community, reaching from Worcester, Massachusetts, to Leipzig in German Saxony, from Sheffield, England, to Paris and other French cities.

Between 1830 and 1860 early feminists relied upon each other's support, took comfort from each other's struggles, and helped those in France and the German states who were forced into exile after the 1848 revolutions failed. I discovered that events historians had previously viewed as phenomena located within individual societies—from the growth of Saint-Simonian socialism in France to the women's rights conventions in the United States, from the British petition for women's vote to the contents of a German feminist newspaper—really occurred within the matrix of a feminism that transcended national boundaries. Isolated among their compatriots, early feminists reached out to their counterparts in other lands. In the middle decades of the nineteenth century, hundreds of people in the United States, Britain, France, and the German states formed an international community dedicated to changing women's status in society. I realized that what I was studying was actually an early, loosely knit, international women's movement, the first ever created. Participants considered themselves to be joined in working for a universal cause. "This great movement is intended to meet the wants, not of America only, but of the whole world," Paulina Wright Davis told an audience of 3,000 at a New York City women's rights convention in 1853.[2]

Part of what makes this movement seem so modern is its internationalism. But an equal if not larger share of its timeliness comes from the range and content of these feminists' demands. They discussed prostitution and rape, child raising and divorce, education and jobs. Far from being modest in their expectations, they rejected everything their society told them about women and created ways of being and doing that still seem progressive. In the middle of the nineteenth century, they not only claimed women's political, social, economic, and moral equality with men but also attempted to solve problems that continue to trouble us today. They often created names of their own, refusing to use a husband's surname if they married, discarding "Mrs." and "Miss," calling their children after feminist heroines and heroes. They argued that God must be female as well as male, interpreted and rewrote the Bible to transform sections disparaging women, and sometimes ended prayers with "A-woman" instead of "Amen." They taught their sons as well as their daughters to sew and to cook, certain that housework was not a specifically female function.

They reasoned that, given centuries of female subordination, any remedy which ignored both women's similarities to men and their differences from them could not succeed. So they advocated what I have called a "both/and" strategy, insisting that women needed the benefits of each position until true equality had been achieved. "People often speak of freedom for all, but they are accustomed to mean only men by the word 'all,'" German feminist Louise Dittmar wrote in 1849. "The state must recognize the woman as woman, supporting her human rights," like the suffrage or freedom of speech, "and also her womanly rights," which included legal protection from marital rape and wife beating, as well as state support for female higher education and job training to foster women's economic independence.[3] As we watch our courts rule that pregnancy leave discriminates against men, the "both/and" strategy seems increasingly necessary and valuable.

These early feminists did not just seek to transform women's lives but reached out to workers, slaves, Jews, and oppressed groups everywhere because they saw each cause as one—an international struggle for *human* rights. They defied the racial segregation and slavery of their day, they advocated democratic socialism because it promised to end both poverty and privilege, and they sought a common ground on which both religious and nonbeliever could stand. Although most of them came from the middle class, they often argued that this privilege enabled them to speak on behalf of their poorer sisters, who had no hope of engaging public attention. They also were fully aware of the fragility of class lines in this volatile era of boom and bust—how easily families could fall into poverty if the male breadwinner died. Challenging the limits on their own situation, their approach was inclusive: all would be free or none could be.

It is the extent of this radical feminism that makes these activists seem so up-to-date. Although women can now vote and run for office, much of feminism remains an unfinished project. What connects feminists today to those who lived 150 years ago is the fundamental belief that the entire system of female subordination and inferiority preached from pulpits and taught in schools, given force in law codes and in the lower wages women earn, has been constructed by men in their own interest. The only reason "why each woman should be a mere appendage of a man" is "that men like it," as Harriet Taylor Mill wrote in 1851.[4] Rejecting age-old teachings that male dominance is natural, God-given, and universal, feminists believe that it can and must be ended, for the benefit of all, men and women alike. This conviction is the heart of feminism, now as well as then.

Historians debate whether it is appropriate to use a word like "feminism" before it actually existed in the language. Although it came into use only in the late nineteenth century, no other term adequately describes the wide range of these people's convictions and beliefs. In addition to naming them feminists, I have also called them radicals, since they sought to address root causes of social problems—the origin of that word—as well as "departing considerably from the usual or traditional," one of its common meanings.

Working for goals most of their contemporaries considered impossible and wrongheaded, these mid-nineteenth-century feminists were dismissed in their own day and later as crackpots and utopians. Their story has never been noticed, much less told. Historians who wrote about international movements usually ignored or diminished women's contributions; historians who wrote about women almost always did so within the context of a single nation. The result has been separate histories of various national women's movements, but no account, until this volume, that sees the entire work of these pioneers from an international perspective.

Table 1.1 *Twenty Core Women*

NAME	BIRTH	DEATH
Mathilde Franziska Anneke	1817, Westphalia, Ger.	1884, Milwaukee, Wisc.
Louise Aston	1814, Magdeburg, Ger.	1871, Wangen, Ger.
Barbara Leigh Smith Bodichon	1827, Watlington, Eng.	1891, Hastings, Eng.
Fredrika Bremer	1801, Åbo, Fin.	1865, Årsta, Swed.
Paulina Wright Davis	1813, Bloomfield, N.Y.	1876, Providence, R.I.
Jeanne Deroin	1805, Paris, Fr.	1894, London, Eng.
Louise Dittmar	1807, Darmstadt, Ger.	1884, Darmstadt, Ger.
Désirée Véret Gay	1810, Paris, Fr.	1891, Brussels, Belg.
Jenny d'Héricourt	1809, Besançon, Fr.	1875, Paris, Fr.
Anne Knight	1786, Chelmsford, Eng.	1862, Waldersbach, Fr.
Harriet Martineau	1802, Norwich, Eng.	1876, Tynemouth, Eng.
Malwida von Meysenbug	1816, Darmstadt, Ger.	1903, Rome, Italy
Harriet Taylor Mill	1807, London, Eng.	1858, Avignon, Fr.
Lucretia Mott	1793, Nantucket, Mass.	1880, Philadelphia, Pa.
Louise Otto-Peters	1819, Meissen, Ger.	1895, Leipzig, Ger.
Bessie Rayner Parkes	1829, London, Eng.	1925, London, Eng.
Pauline Roland	1805, Falaise, Fr.	1852, Lyon, Fr.
Ernestine Rose	1810, Piotrkow, Pol.	1892, Brighton, Eng.
Elizabeth Cady Stanton	1810, Johnstown, N.Y.	1902, New York, N.Y.
Suzanne Voilquin	1801, Paris, Fr.	1877? Paris, Fr.

Others on the Periphery of the Core Group

NAME	NATIONALITY	DATES
Susan B. Anthony	American	1820–1906
Elizabeth Blackwell	Anglo-American	1826–1910
Maria Weston Chapman	American	1806–1885
Caroline Healey Dall	American	1822–1912
Julie Daubié	French	1824–1874
Margaret Fuller	American	1810–1850
Sarah Grimké	American	1792–1873
Mary Howitt	English	1799–1888
Harriot K. Hunt	American	1805–1875
Anna Jameson	English	1794–1860
Fanny Lewald	German	1811–1889
Eugénie Niboyet	French	1797–1889
Elizabeth Pease Nichol	English	1807–1897
Theresa Pulszky	Hungarian	1819–1866
Elizabeth Sturch Jesser Reid	English	1789–1866
Sarah Parker Remond	American	1824–1894
Bertha Meyer Traun Ronge	German	1818–1863
Amalie Struve	German	1824–1862
Flora Tristan	French	1803–1844
Anna Wheeler	Anglo-Irish	1785–1848
Frances Wright	Scottish	1795–1852

Who belonged to this movement? I began my research by charting their international connections—the travels, correspondence networks, and literature that linked them. I looked at important feminist actions that received transatlantic publicity—from a Frenchwoman running for the legislature to the American women's rights conventions. I studied the movements that first questioned the female role—anti-slavery, early socialism, and the German free religion movement. I then eliminated the "loners" (women like George Sand, Flora Tristan, and Margaret Fuller) who voiced feminist ideas and had important influence on other feminists but did not join with other women in organized movements. A core group of twenty women emerged from the original larger set of about fifty activists.

This cohort of international feminists, their actions and ideas, constitute the subject of this book. Because most of these women are unknown today, table 1.1 supplies the basic facts about their lives. One reason for their obscurity is the scarcity of historical work done on women. There are no biographies for most of them. Although men of equal importance have been the subject of a great deal of scholarship, especially in American history, women remain neglected. For instance, the speeches and writings of Lucretia Mott, a key figure in abolitionism, pacifism, and free religion, as well as women's rights, remain inaccessible. Her talks and sermons were printed in 1980 in typescript by a small press; her letters were published only in a severely edited 1884 publication produced by her granddaughter. The chief sources for her life are in the manuscript collections of specialized libraries not open to the general public.

But Mott is easier to work on than most of the other women in this study, since her papers have at least been gathered in archives. Most of these women were neither so well-known nor so fortunate, and key documents about their lives have been irretrievably lost. The historian Adrien Ranvier possessed a collection of the letters and writings of French feminist Jeanne Deroin when he studied her in 1907; all have since disappeared. Louise Otto, the most important feminist in German history, did not obtain an archive until the University of Leipzig established one in the 1990s. By then, no copy of her 1849 poetry anthology about German emigration to America, *Westward*, could be found. The lives of the less famous in this group—Louise Dittmar, Jenny d'Héricourt, Anne Knight, Ernestine Rose, and others—have been painstakingly pieced together by scholars working with nineteenth-century newspapers, pamphlets, and government documents. I could not have done my work without their labor and I gratefully cite their writings in my footnotes and bibliography.

It has been a tremendous pleasure to help restore these figures to the historical record. Laboring on this book and continuing the struggle for feminist principles today, I have taken heart from Lucretia Mott's words to the 1853 Woman's Rights Convention: "Any great change must expect opposition, because it shakes the very foundation of privilege."[5] I hope these pages you are about to read further that great and necessary change.

One

Panorama

In May 1851, two forty-five-year-old Frenchwomen, Jeanne Deroin and Pauline Roland, sat in a stone cell in Saint Lazare, the medieval prison for women in Paris. Wearing the convicted prisoner's uniform, a blue-checked neckerchief and a plain wool dress, they passed their time by writing. Leaders of the French women's movement, these close friends had already spent a year in jail for attending an unauthorized political meeting of the socialist Union of Workers' Associations, which they had organized.

As activists, journalists, and schoolteachers, Deroin and Roland had been pressing hard for women's complete political and social equality before they were arrested. In the revolutionary spring of 1848, Roland attempted to vote; Deroin wrote for and helped edit the *Voice of Women* (La Voix des femmes), a daily feminist newspaper whose offices became an organizing center. Believing in the power of group action, Deroin and Roland continually worked to bring women together: through newspapers and labor unions, in clubs and by petitions.

Almost from the beginning they had to fight their male associates for women's rights. Deroin wrote for a second newspaper in 1848, a monthly called *La Politique des femmes*; after a few issues appeared, the revolutionary government ruled that women could no longer participate in politics and the journal had to be renamed *L'Opinion des femmes*. Deroin then ran as a candidate for the legislative assembly in the spring of 1849. Criticized by French socialist P.-J. Proudhon on the grounds that just as men could not be wet nurses so women could not be legislators, Deroin retorted in print that "now we know what organ is needed to be a legislator."[1] During their trial in November 1850, Deroin reported that her male socialist colleagues had "begged" her to hide her leadership role in the union. Although she could not deny being on the Central Committee, she played down her part for the sake of solidarity.[2]

And now, in May 1851, Deroin and Roland composed a passionate letter, which they send not to the "brothers" who have limited their achievements, but to their "sisters" abroad—two groups of women fighting for the same cause. A short draft of the letter goes to the Female Political Association in the industrial city of Sheffield, England; the other, a longer version, to "the Convention of the Women of America," which met in New England in October 1850. News of the English and American women's actions, declare Deroin and Roland, "has resounded even to our prison, and has filled our souls with inexpressible joy."[3]

The Sheffield Female Political Association, the first in Great Britain, had been organized by Quaker feminist Anne Knight. A veteran English antislavery lecturer and organizer, Knight worked closely with Deroin in Paris during the 1848 revolution, publishing joint letters to prominent legislators asserting women's claims to equal rights. Knight supported Deroin's candidacy (she kept one of the pale blue election banners until her death); when she returned to England early in 1851, she contacted the Sheffield women who had fought for the People's Charter, a six-point plan to make English politics more democratic. That February, Knight and the Sheffield women convinced the radical Earl of Carlisle to present a petition to the House of Lords for the vote by "adult Females." These actions created the solidarity Deroin and Roland felt for their "Sisters of Sheffield."[4]

The bond with their "Sisters of America" came from the meeting of the first National Women's Rights Convention in the United States the year before. The American feminists at the convention represented nine states, but their view extended much further: "We are not contending here for the rights of the women of New England, or of old England, but of the world," declared Polish-born Ernestine Rose, who had lived in Berlin, Paris, and London before immigrating to New York.[5] The convention endorsed "equality before the law without distinction of sex or color," and the opening address proclaimed that

> the reformation which we propose, in its utmost scope, is radical and universal. It is not the mere perfecting of a progress already in motion, a detail of some established plan, but it is an epochal movement—the emancipation of a class, the redemption of half the world, and a conforming re-organization of all social, political, and industrial interests and institutions.[6]

In response, Deroin and Roland wrote that "your socialist sisters of France are united with you in the vindication of the right of Woman to civil and political equality." Explaining that they were convinced that these rights could be gained only "by the union of the working classes of both sexes to organize labor," the Frenchwomen entreated the Americans to carry on the struggle. "It is in this confidence that, from the depths of the jail which still imprisons our bodies without reaching our hearts, we cry to you—Faith, Love, Hope; and send to you our sisterly salutations," they concluded.

News of the women's rights convention was widely reported in the American press and its proceedings made their way to Europe in the few weeks it took a fast steamer to cross the Atlantic. Deroin and Roland were not the only Europeans to consider the news significant. The English philosopher and reformer John Stuart Mill wrote a long letter to his future wife, Harriet Taylor, describing the convention: "it is almost like ourselves speaking—outspoken like America, not frightened & servile like England—not the least iota of compromise—asserting the whole of the principle and claiming the whole of the consequences."[7] Mill, a reader of Deroin's *Voix des femmes*, had been urging Taylor to finish a "pamphlet" she was composing on women's rights; the U.S. convention furnished its opening. In July 1851 the newly married Harriet Taylor Mill published her thirty-page essay, "Enfranchisement of Women," in the prestigious *Westminster Review*. She began with an account of the Women's Rights Convention in Worcester and ended with the House of Lords petition. The bulk of the essay questioned "why each woman should be a mere appendage to a man" and concluded that "what is wanted for women is equal rights, equal admission to all social privileges; not a position apart, a sort of sentimental priesthood."[8]

Harriet Taylor Mill's son, who was in America on a business trip, delivered copies of the essay to Lucretia Mott in Philadelphia in June 1851. Mott saw that the essay found wide distribution in the United States. A well-known Quaker minister and abolitionist, Mott had met a number of British feminists, among them Anne Knight, on an earlier trip to England. The second National Women's Rights Convention, which met in Worcester in October 1851, featured both this essay—which "vindicates every position which we assumed, and reaffirms and establishes the highest ground taken in principle and policy by our movement" as the opening address explained—and Deroin and Roland's letter, which was the centerpiece of the evening session of the first day. Three months after the convention, early in 1852, Deroin published an *Almanach des femmes* in Paris. The first article was a ten-page French précis of Harriet Taylor Mill's essay, entitled "Convention des Femmes en Amérique."

This web of feminist connections extended into Germany. From 1849 to 1852, German activist Louise Otto published a feminist weekly called the *Women's Newspaper* (Frauen-Zeitung). She covered some early American conventions, and in August and December 1851 printed two articles on "Johanna" Deroin. Otto praised Deroin for editing feminist journals, for insisting that male socialists renounce "all privileges of [their] *sex*," and for running as a candidate.⁹ Otto's countrywoman, Mathilde Franziska Anneke, who had gone into exile in the United States, reprinted Deroin and Roland's letter to the American women in the German-language feminist paper she published from New York in July 1852; October's issue featured an article on Ernestine Rose.

These women and their coworkers created the world's first international women's movement. They knew and learned from each other, they wrote and paid visits, they read the same books. They connected through conventions, periodicals, and correspondence. Reaching out to their counterparts in other nations, they sent "joyous greetings to the distant lands," as Emma Goldman wrote of Mary Wollstonecraft. In the middle of the nineteenth century, they demanded full equality in the economy, religion, and culture, as well as in law and government. In politics, they claimed not only the vote but the right to hold office, to govern, to serve on juries, to conduct the same public lives as men. They not only published but often did so in feminist journals they founded and edited, printed by women they recruited and trained. They fought in revolutions, voted illegally, and refused to pay taxes. They consistently spoke in public for "a cause which is still in its rotten-egg stage (I mean its advocates are apt to have rotten eggs and dirtier words thrown at them)," as English feminist Barbara Leigh Smith Bodichon wrote in her diary after visiting Lucretia Mott.[10]

At the height of the Victorian era, these women dared to speak out in public about prostitution, forced marriage, the right to have sex or refuse it. They demanded that child custody be awarded to mothers instead of automatically going to fathers. They defined a new kind of marriage based on companionship and claimed the right to divorce if it failed. They saw prostitution not as a moral fault but as the direct result of an unjust economic system that forced women into only a handful of degraded and poorly paid jobs. They worried about all the victims produced by the undervaluing of women's labor: the housewives who toiled all day but did not "work," the women paid wages too low to live on, the prostitutes who worked the "fifth quarter of the day" to survive, the children who always suffered when their mothers were impoverished.

Holding prostitutes relatively blameless, they considered many "respectable" marriages to be legal prostitution, arrangements in which a woman with no other options sold herself to a single man. To remedy that situation, they worked to open new, better paid jobs for women, so that the average woman could secure the independence that feminists believed came only with the ability to support oneself. These early feminists insisted that women could do almost any job men did, and they founded the labor organizations and training centers, the colleges and medical schools necessary to realize their dreams. Inspired by the great scientific breakthroughs of their day—the telegraph, the railroad, industrial production—they believed they could create a peaceful, harmonious world without poverty for women and men of all races and classes.

Deroin and Roland sent out their letters in 1851, the heyday of this international women's movement. It had arisen two decades earlier, in the 1830s. During those years, key women in the United States, France, England, and, a few years later, in the German lands, developed a radical feminist outlook: they utterly rejected the traditional view that women's subordination was natural, God-given, and universal. They then insisted that women could and must redefine themselves, shaping new lives and claiming their own territory.

The demand for women's rights arose primarily from women who had been active in movements seeking to reform and improve society. Women who linked up with each other—on both national and international levels—often moved from supporting an initial radical cause, such as socialism, anti-slavery, or free religion into feminism because their ability to act was limited by men or other women in that cause. Like Deroin and Roland in French socialism, many women in radical movements became feminists both because those groups first allowed them room to grow and because the majority in these movements then sought to halt that growth. Women not previously active in such causes describe similar tensions, either within their own family or between a family that supported women's autonomy and a society that restricted it. Paradoxically, feminism required both nurture and opposition for its growth.

In France the cause that gave rise to feminism was socialism. The social problems created by the first phase of industrialization prompted many to question the equity of a system that rewarded factory owners with immense profits while pauperizing workers. On her fourth trip to England, in 1839, French socialist Flora Tristan criticized the "advances" of British industry:

> Unless you have visited the manufacturing towns and seen the workers . . . you cannot appreciate the physical suffering and moral degradation of this class of the population. . . . they are all wizened, sickly and emaciated; their bodies are thin and frail, their limbs feeble, their complexions pale, their eyes dead.[11]

Socialists differed from earlier protesters—the machine breakers known as Luddites—in that they believed industry could be made beneficial. "If at first I felt humiliated to see Man brought so low, his functions reduced to those of a machine," argued Tristan,

> I was quick to realize the immense advances which all these scientific discoveries would bring; brute force banished, less time expended on physical labor, more leisure for Man to cultivate his intelligence. But if these great benefits are to be realized, there must be a social revolution; and that revolution will come, for God has not revealed such admirable inventions to men

only to have them remain the slaves of a handful of manufacturers and landed proprietors.[12]

Tristan and other French feminists were inspired by the radical early
socialism of the Saint-Simonian and Fourierist movements, which
preached the equality of the sexes as essential to the creation of a peaceful
future society in which workers would no longer be exploited. In 1831,
male Saint-Simonians had called for "la femme libre," the "free woman"
who would lead humankind to social and sexual liberation. Within a few
months women in the movement formed their own group, published their
own newspaper, and tried to redefine their own emancipation, since the
movement's male leader excluded them from governing and emphasized
the sexual side of liberation. "At bottom," one of them complained, "male
Saint-Simonians are more male than they are Saint-Simonian."[13] Most of
the women who created a French feminist movement and linked up with
international feminism—Jeanne Deroin, Pauline Roland, Suzanne
Voilquin, Jenny d'Héricourt—had originally been followers of early male
socialists.

The linkage of women's social emancipation with sexual license in the
popular mind forced many socialist women, including Frenchwomen, to
repudiate "the shameless picture of the 'femme libre' of the Saint-
Simonians," as Louise Otto called it in 1843.[14] Although Otto was known
as "the red democrat," she, like many early feminists, found religion as
important as socialism in leading her to feminism. Otto and many other
women joined the radical new "free congregations" that arose in the
German states during the 1840s. These congregations, which were free in
that they belonged to no established church, either Protestant or Catholic,
ranged from advocating a liberally defined Christianity to anticlerical sec-
ular humanism. "Our church is the world, our religion is reason, our
Christianity is humanity, our creed is freedom, our worship, the truth,"
Louise Dittmar stated in 1845.[15]

As feminists in other radical movements discovered, men in these free
congregations both supported and limited women's rights. The creation of
the first college "for the female sex" in Germany, for instance, can be
traced in part to some women's outrage at being told in a public meeting of
congregational delegates that females should not be allowed to teach in
their kindergartens.[16] A number of radical German feminists, like Dittmar,
Louise Aston, and Mathilde Franziska Anneke, eventually rejected organized religion completely and questioned the double standard that judged
women more harshly than men for rejecting religious faith. In 1847,
Anneke wrote a long essay in support of Aston, exiled from Berlin the previous year, in part because she refused to say she believed in God. "Why do
opinions which men have been able to hold for centuries seem so dangerous to the government when held *by women*?" asked Anneke, who titled her
essay "Woman in Conflict with Social Conditions."[17]

English feminist Elizabeth Pease questioned the same double standard in 1841: "It is thought most unaccountable for a *gentleman* to say he sees nothing wrong in [the democratic movement of] Chartism—but for a lady to do so is almost outrageous."[18] The Chartist movement awoke women's hopes by demanding "universal suffrage" but frustrated them by being "too purblind or too poltron to proclaim that half the race are excluded," Harriet Taylor complained.[19] Although Chartism provided some women with connections both in Britain and abroad (Tristan attended Chartist meetings while in England; Knight used Chartist networks to create her Female Political Association), it generally relegated women to a subordinate role.

So too did the antislavery movement. As with socialism and the free congregations, the contradictions faced by females in the antislavery movement led some English and American women to radical feminism. Abolitionism on both sides of the Atlantic enlisted women's help "in the labour of collecting and going from house to house for signatures to petitions" but excluded them from "the muster roll for the counsel-board," as Anne Knight complained.[20] The turning point for many women came during the 1840 World Anti-Slavery Convention in London, when seven female American delegates, chief among them Lucretia Mott, were not allowed to take their seats.[21] Elizabeth Cady Stanton, there on her honeymoon since her husband was a delegate, dated the beginning of the U.S. women's rights movement from this rebuff. The strong connections forged during that visit between American and British women developed into a vital link in the early international feminist movement.

The movements in which feminism began were themselves internationalist. Socialism, antislavery, and even the free congregation movement looked abroad for support in their struggles and for confirmation of their beliefs. "Our country is the world, our countrymen are all mankind," went the abolitionist motto and this expansive universalism carried over when women created their own movements.[22]

Isolated in their own countries, feminists reached out to like-minded women in other lands. Lucretia Mott and Elizabeth Cady Stanton remained in correspondence for decades with the English radicals they met in 1840. When the American intellectual Margaret Fuller went to Europe in 1846, she naturally visited the English reformer Harriet Martineau and the French novelist George Sand. Feminists sent books as well as letters across the Atlantic. Mott mailed Sarah Grimké's *Letters on the Equality of the Sexes* to English friends; Margaret Fuller found Europeans familiar with her *Woman in the Nineteenth Century* when she traveled through Europe the year after it was published. "Pray let me have a few of your good books on this subject," wrote Anne Knight to the American abolitionists after recommending Scotswoman Marion Reid's 1843 *A Plea for Woman* to them. "These things ought to be sent darting off like lightning to all the world if possible."[23]

Feminists constantly cited each other's achievements to prove their points. In the first article she signed with her own name, Louise Otto argued that women's participation in the state "was not just a right but a duty." She built her case by arguing that British and American women had used the laws and constitutions of their nations to participate more fully in political life than Germans. She also referred to the dictum first stated by the French socialist Charles Fourier: "From the position women occupy in a country you can see whether the air of the state is thick with dirty fog or clear and free: women serve as the barometers of states."[24]

Early feminists drew on the same set of authorities, like Fourier or the eighteenth-century feminist Mary Wollstonecraft, to support their cause. French socialist Flora Tristan extolled Wollstonecraft's writings, and Mathilde Franziska Anneke translated parts of her *Vindication of the Rights of Woman* to make it accessible to German women.[25] They drew examples of female achievement from the Bible, from history, from all eras and nations. Sarah Grimké praised French author and salonière Germaine de Staël in her letter on the "Intellect of Woman," as did Scotswoman Marion Reid in her *Plea for Woman*.

By 1847, hundreds of women in the United States, Great Britain, France, and the German states had become feminists: they believed that women were not innately inferior nor ideally subordinate to men, but oppressed by them. "I long for the time when my sisters will rise, and occupy the sphere to which they are called by their high nature and destiny," declared Lucretia Mott in a sermon the year after she returned from London.[26] Throughout the 1840s Mott and others became convinced that they must work to change women's situation. "I came to the consciousness and to the knowledge that the position of women was absurd," recalled Anneke of this period. "So I soon began to do as much as I could, in words and print, for the . . . betterment of women."[27]

The impending revolutions of the late 1840s strengthened feminists' ability to work for radical changes in women's situation. In German history, this period is called the Vormärz (before March), a time defined by the revolution of March 1848. People all over Europe expected a revolution. "While [the French king] Louis Philippe lives, the gases, compressed by his strong grasp, may not burst up to light," wrote Margaret Fuller in 1847, "but the need of some radical measures of reform is not less strongly felt in France than elsewhere, and the time will come before long when such will be imperatively demanded."[28] In Germany especially, feminism added to the ferment of the period. "There is a vitality and a striving in our time which there has never been before," wrote Otto in 1847, "which women also are becoming aware of." In that year alone, four radical feminist texts appeared: Anneke's *Woman in Conflict with Social Conditions*, Dittmar's *Four Timely Questions*, Aston's novel, *From a Woman's Life*, and Otto's *Songs of a German Maiden*. Otto's poems ranged from ringing denunciations of the economic exploitation of poor women ("they die of hunger, / Thanking God, that the torment is over!") to hopes for a feminist future ("All Humankind will struggle upwards / To found a renewed empire of love / To give woman her right like man's").[29]

Revolution was in the air, especially in the continental capitals—Paris, Berlin, Vienna, and Rome. Radical movements, for democracy, for socialism, for uniting Germany or Italy as nations, awaited the death of the French king as the signal to arise. As it happened, French democrats began the revolution on February 22. Within a few days, with hardly any bloodshed, the king had abdicated and the republic been proclaimed. The speed and ease of the overthrow seemed almost miraculous. "I heard the shout of the *people-king*, and the din of martial music and guns up the Champs Elysée from my window, and a man said, 'Louis-Philippe is no longer king,'" remembered Anne Knight.

> Advancing to the scene of conquest, [the royal palace of] the Tuileries were found to be a triumphal arch, through which the shouting people were passing; and in the square of the Louvre, I saw the lightening of heaven flash against the regal walls! I heard heaven's own thunder in majestic unison with the people's music, and the rainbow with gorgeous splendour formed . . . a good omen.[30]

Revolutions quickly followed in the German and Italian states. "The electric current spread in all directions," remembered German feminist Malwida von Meysenbug, "Germany . . . now shuddered as from an underground fire. The news of [armed uprisings in] Vienna and Berlin followed swiftly. The prince of political darkness, Metternich, had fled!" The architect of international repression, Austrian foreign minister Prince Metternich, had masterminded the system of censorship, espionage, and armed intervention that supported the conservative monarchies of Europe between 1815 and 1848. "The news that a German Constituent Assembly would meet in Frankfurt filled me with nameless joy," continued Meysenbug. "The city was in boundless excitement. . . . Nature itself celebrated this festival of rebirth. Spring was unusually early and beautiful. . . . The railroads, the steamships incessantly brought crowds of joyful pilgrims, hastening to take part in the jubilee of freedom."[31]

These revolutions released an explosion of feminist activism. In France and Germany, feminists seized the moment, using the new atmosphere of liberation to claim rights for themselves and their sisters. At the end of May 1848, Jeanne Deroin had helped to organize the Club for the Emancipation of Women, the Fraternal Association of Democrats of Both Sexes, and the Mutual Society for the Education of Women. She also wrote regularly for the *Voice of Women*, the feminist daily whose office became the center of another club for women. Louise Otto attended workers congresses and wrote numerous articles for the *Leipzig Workers Newspaper*, including a May address to the Saxon minister of the interior in

which she insisted that women be included in any "reorganization of
labor."[32] One French group called themselves the Vésuviennes, the
women of Vesuvius, after the only live volcano on the European mainland.
Claiming the equal rights and duties of citizens, they explained that their
name "marvelously portrays our position and more than any other
expresses our thought." Images of lava, volcanoes, and underground fire
appear in women's writings of this era, signifying the sense of pent-up
energy released in an immense, satisfying explosion: "regenerative, not
incendiary," the Vésuviennes promised.[33] Nor was this explosive sense of
liberation confined to places that actually experienced upheavals.
Although economic prosperity and political reforms kept Great Britain
safe from revolution, a number of English feminists applauded the uprisings across the Channel. "What wonderful times we live in," wrote Julia
Smith, Barbara Leigh Smith Bodichon's aunt and Harriet Martineau's
friend, to a correspondent in Germany that spring. "These last four weeks
have had a century of history crowded into them....The old routine is broken up & mankind *must* think & feel & search out new ways."[34] Both supporters and opponents of the revolution marveled at its speed. "What
remains standing in Europe?" Czar Nicholas wrote Queen Victoria in
April. "Great Britain and Russia!"[35]

1848 reverberated loudly in the United States, the first nation to recognize the new French Republic. Celebrations of reformers and immigrants
erupted from New York to New Orleans. Abolitionists were especially
buoyed by France's speedy decision to end slavery in all its colonies.
Addressing the American Anti-Slavery Association in May, Mott argued
that even though black bondage was still growing in America, "yet, when
we look abroad and see what is now being done in other lands, when we
see human freedom engaging the attention of the nations of the earth, we
may take courage." Mott, like other radical feminists, believed freedom
was universal: all must be free or none could be. We cannot separate our
own freedom from that of the slave, continued Mott. They are "insepara-
bly connected . . . in France" and are "beginning to be so in other countries."[36]

"Can man be free, if woman be a slave?" poet Percy Shelley had asked
in 1818.[37] Mott and other antislavery activists on both sides of the Atlantic
had long connected abolitionism and feminism. Now, in the revolutionary
summer of 1848, the "great events" in Europe seemed to "make possible
the social reconstruction of reality, the reordering of things-as-they-are so
they are no longer experienced as given, but rather as willed, in accordance
with convictions about how things ought to be," as the historian Robert
Darnton wrote about the first French Revolution.[38]

In July 1848, Lucretia Mott traveled to upstate New York in part to
investigate conditions among the Seneca Indians for her church; she later
wrote that the Senecas were learning "from the political agitations abroad
. . . imitating the movements of France and all Europe in seeking a larger

liberty—more independence."[39] This expansive climate and her visit sparked the first women's rights convention in the United States, when over three hundred people, two-thirds of them women, met at Seneca Falls, New York, on July 19 and 20. Mott, Elizabeth Cady Stanton, and three other female organizers appropriated the most revolutionary document in American history—the Declaration of Independence—as their text. Holding that "all men and women are created equal," they claimed a wide range of rights for women: better education, jobs, pay, and access to the professions (including religious leadership), moral authority, and self-determination, as well as complete political equality. By placing themselves in the position of the American colonists, feminists seized the revolutionary high ground. This forced men into the unenviable position of the tyrant king George III and the other tyrant kings so recently overthrown in Europe. Stanton made the connection explicit in her speech to the meeting. Men like to deny women "rights...the maintenance of which is even now rocking to their foundations the kingdoms of the Old World."[40] Hostile newspapers, like the New York *Herald*, connected and condemned the actions of women in both societies:

> This is the age of revolutions. . . . [but] the work of revolution is no longer confined to the Old World, nor to the masculine gender. . . . Though we have the most perfect confidence in the courage and daring . . . of our lady acquaintances, we confess it would go to our hearts to see them putting on the panoply of war, and mixing in scenes like those at which, it is said, the fair sex in Paris lately took a prominent part.[41]

Parisian women had played an active role in the so-called June Days, when the republican government closed the National Workshops established to solve unemployment, and then turned its weapons on the socialist working class when they protested. This violence signaled the end of the most radical phase of the revolution. Thereafter, conservative sentiments began to reassert themselves in France and elsewhere in Europe. In England and the United States, many sympathizers drew back once the revolution seemed to turn to violent class warfare.

Feminism, however, remained energized by the revolutionary spirit well into the 1850s. The years from 1848 to 1856 are the heyday of the international women's movement, as radical feminists, like Deroin and Roland from their prison cell, reached out to others like themselves. Just as national feminisms arose from the tensions between support and opposition, so international feminism came into full flower in a climate in which revolutionary ardor was being chilled, but not yet frozen, by conservative repression. Making the effort of their lives, feminists created an amazing array of radical institutions in these years.

In 1849, for instance, four feminist newspapers were founded: Louise Dittmar's *Social Reform* and Amelia Bloomer's the *Lily*, an American journal far more radical than its name, in addition to Jeanne Deroin's *Women's*

Opinion and Louise Otto's *Women's Newspaper*. All emphasized solidarity with feminists in other nations, and in so doing often broadened their own claims for women. The *Lily*, begun as a temperance journal, evolved rapidly into a wide-ranging supporter of universal women's rights. It championed the reform of female clothing, frequently by citing instances of women wearing trousers in other societies. The *Lily's* cause gained wide publicity in Europe and became the subject of international feminist debate. Although she had doubts about dress reform herself, Louise Otto felt that international solidarity compelled her to join the discussion: "*New York—London—Paris*—the issue, which was only comical at the start, has now become serious and it is now time that we in Germany also have our say."[42]

News of Elizabeth Blackwell's being awarded an M.D. degree from New York's Geneva Medical College in 1849 spread rapidly and emboldened feminists to extend their demands. In France, for instance, *Women's Opinion* argued that "the example of Miss Blackwell gives us the opportunity to return to the question of women doctors in France," which had arisen the previous year. Then Suzanne Voilquin had led the United Midwives to demand state funding, a radical action even in the revolutionary spring of 1848. A year later, Blackwell's achievement made Voilquin's seem tame—the French midwives demanded too little. They should have pushed for full medical training, argued Deroin's paper. "We salute in [Blackwell] the emancipator, who opens the breach through which others may follow . . . [in] this noble cause which is at the same time the cause of all women and of humanity."[43] Bessie Rayner Parkes, then only twenty, met Blackwell in England that year and for the first time questioned "why should such a lucrative profession as medical attention of their own sex be denied women?"[44] Parkes and her friend Barbara Leigh Smith (later Bodichon), founders of the English women's movement, became staunch supporters of Blackwell and raised money for her New York clinic from English feminists for years.

Excluded from most established institutions, feminists began to found the colleges and schools needed to actualize their dreams. "Thanks to the woman's movement some half-dozen medical colleges are now open to women and two schools of design are established," wrote Marianne Finch in her *Englishwoman's Experience in America* of 1853.[45] English feminists created Bedford College for Women in 1849, the first English college to educate women to be more than governesses; Julia Smith and her niece Barbara Leigh Smith enrolled the first term. German feminists founded its equivalent in Hamburg in part to train women to teach in the radical kindergartens being established by the free congregations.

Feminists began to create larger groups and associations. A federation of German women, linking activists from the free congregations, was proposed in Otto's *Women's Newspaper*. In France, Deroin and Roland helped establish the Union of Workers Associations, an umbrella organization of

108 unions, a number of them all-female or combining both female and male workers. In the United States women's rights conventions, both local and national, began to meet on a regular basis, providing a nexus for the increasing numbers who attended, as well as the other American and European women who read about them and wrote letters of encouragement. Paulina Wright Davis, who had presided over the first two national conventions in Worcester in 1850 and 1851, proposed to the third national convention that "we should have a literature of our own, a printing press and publishing house, and tract writers, and tract distributors, as well as Lectures and Conventions. We must show the world that we are in earnest."[46] The convention, now attended by 2,000 instead of the 263 who assembled the first year, did not fund a journal, but Davis was able to publish her internationally oriented *Una* from 1853 to 1855. "We shall not confine ourselves to any locality, set, sect, class, or caste," declared her opening editorial, "for we hold to the solidarity of the [human] race, and believe that if one member suffers, all suffer."[47] The *Una* advertised Jeanne Deroin's *Women's Almanack*, published in both French and English in 1853, and a proposed English monthly, the *Woman's Advocate*.[48] Articles about women in Europe appeared regularly, as did letters from England by both Marianne Finch and another woman who identified herself only as "a Friend of the Cause."

Finch had met and admired Paulina Wright Davis and other American feminists when she came to the United States in 1851.[49] Travel often fostered a woman's feminism. Stepping out of her own society, being able to see it from a distance and to compare how women lived in other lands, enabled a woman to view the condition of women as mutable, not fixed and eternal. Harriet Martineau's chapter "The Political Non-Existence of Women" in her *Society in America* (1837), in which she used the Declaration of Independence and the U.S. Constitution to criticize the condition of women, was the most radically feminist of all her writings; Margaret Fuller's travel in Europe committed her more firmly to feminism and socialism.[50]

Swedish novelist Fredrika Bremer's trip to the United States from 1848 to 1851 transformed her into an active international feminist. "Her religious and social views had, in America, been materially influenced," remembered Mary Howitt, Bremer's English translator and a friend of the Leigh Smiths. "An intense desire animated her to aid in the liberation of every oppressed soul; above all, to rescue her country-women from the dark and narrow sphere allotted them."[51] Energized by her trip, Bremer rapidly published her two-volume *Homes of the New World*, in which she presented American feminists as the model for Europeans, particularly Swedes, to emulate:

> They resemble the most beloved women of our hemisphere; their grace of person is not less than their steadfastness in principle. But they have

something more than the women of Europe. Their glance seems to me to embrace a larger world; their intelligence a larger activity; and their heart seems to me large enough to embrace and elevate the human community in all its spheres.[52]

In 1854, Bremer published an international appeal in the London *Times* for women to form a peace alliance and began writing her explicitly feminist novel, *Hertha*. *Hertha* inspired legislation aiding women in Sweden and was widely admired in feminist circles abroad: Anneke named her third daughter Hertha, and a protégée of Barbara Leigh Smith Bodichon later renamed herself Hertha. Travel facilitated feminism for Bremer, for the American and British women who met in London in 1840, for Barbara Leigh Smith and Bessie Rayner Parkes, allowed to journey unchaperoned through Europe in 1850, and for countless others.

Some women particularly embodied these international connections. Anne Knight in England and France, Lucretia Mott in Philadelphia, and Jenny d'Héricourt in Paris and then Chicago—all functioned as important nodes in the radical feminist network, traveling, corresponding, and seeking out like-minded visitors from other nations. In the mid-1850s, for instance, d'Héricourt wrote articles rebutting Proudhon that French censorship forced her to publish in an Italian journal. Parkes translated d'Héricourt's articles and arranged for their English publication. D'Héricourt was visited in 1856 by Ernestine Rose, who wrote and spoke about her in the United States, and also by M. L. Mikhailov, a Russian whom she steered toward women's rights. Mikhailov wrote early feminist articles and translated Harriet Taylor Mill's "Enfranchisement of Women" into Russian.[53] D'Héricourt's 1860 feminist text, *La Femme Affranchie* (translated as *The Freed Woman* in an abridged American version four years later), called on the international feminist movement for support and ratification:

> To you all, my friends, both French women and foreigners, I dedicate this work. May it be useful *everywhere* in the triumph of the liberty of women, and of the equality of all before the law; this is the sole wish that a Frenchwoman can make who believes in the unity of the human family.[54]

Ernestine Rose personified, and saw herself as personifying, the international women's movement. Introduced at the Third National Woman's Rights Convention in Syracuse (1852) as "a Polish lady and educated in the Jewish faith," Rose, who had lived in Germany, France, and England before coming to the United States, repudiated those labels. "It is of very little importance in what geographical position a person is born," she began. "Yes, I am an example of the universality of our claims; for not American women only, but a daughter of poor, crushed Poland, and the down-trodden and persecuted people called the Jews, 'a child of Israel,' pleads for the rights of her sex."[55] Rose, known as the "Queen of the

Platform" for her skill in public speaking, lectured widely in the United States, not only at conventions but also on tours that ranged as far west as Michigan and southward to Virginia. She also served as the American movement's chief translator, able to communicate with Deroin and d'Héricourt in French and to render Anneke's German speech into English at the 1853 National Women's Rights Convention in New York.

Technological progress made all these connections increasingly easier, and the new inventions of the period facilitated the development of this international women's movement. When Harriet Martineau sailed to America in 1834, the shortest trip took a month; hers lasted forty-two days. Fifteen years later, Fredrika Bremer traveled from London to New York "on one of the great steaming Leviathans which cross the vast ocean in 12 or 14 days." "I hope to have it in my power to visit America next year," wrote a young German woman to the Worcester Convention in 1850. "Thanks to the invention of steam a voyage across the ocean is now a mere bagatelle!"[56]

Steam also seemed to herald a new era on land: "To *be* free is nothing— to *become* free is heaven," wrote Louise Otto about the first German railroad, which opened near her town in 1839. "I consider myself to be Fortune's favorite because I experienced this at first hand. . . . The first locomotive was the path breaker of a new era for all." The railways emboldened Otto to journey alone throughout Germany at a time when few women traveled by themselves. Bremer declared that the railway police and "all the arrangements, at the stations, for the convenience of travelers" made England and the United States places where "a lady may travel alone in comfort."[57] Increasing numbers of women began to journey and found they could do so in comfort without the previously requisite male escort to protect them. The United States set the tone here: Bremer and other female European travelers praised "that blending of brotherly cordiality and chivalric politeness," which made "the man of the New World . . . most agreeable" to encounter on a trip.[58]

The new trains and steamships carried newspapers and novels, letters and periodicals as well as passengers. In 1848, the *New York Herald* sent *La Presse* in Paris a list of steamer departures so that news of the revolution could arrive as quickly as possible; people waited at the docks in New York City for the latest installment of Dickens's novels. By the 1840s the reading public mushroomed as increasing numbers of women and men gained in literacy, leisure, and income. Europe and the United States formed a single reading community that increasingly demanded new fare. With financial rewards to be reaped, the most sought-after books were rapidly translated and published abroad, often in pirated editions. Lengthy novels flourished, frequently printed in monthly installments. Monthly periodicals ran to about fifty pages of closely packed type a month. Shorter magazines and newspapers proliferated as nations lifted prohibitive stamp taxes and newspapers crammed long columns of tiny print into a four- or eight-page format. Even though few feminist journals existed before 1848, women managed to publish in left-wing periodicals and newspapers, although they usually did so anonymously or under male pseudonyms.

Most women's only writing beyond schoolwork was correspondence. Letters provided one of the few ways in which a woman could learn to write as an adult, to present herself in prose as a full human being and so assume at least some of the authority of an "author." A number of feminists' first venture into print was either to publish letters originally written to friends or to write a letter intended for print to a newspaper or public figure. Anne Knight's lengthy dispatch of 1840 to the American abolitionist Maria Weston Chapman was reprinted on both sides of the Atlantic.[59] Letters, both private and public, also sustained important connections among women in different nations; some correspondence networks among feminists lasted for forty years.

Before 1839, letters were expensive (the price rose with distance) and were usually paid for by the recipient. Harriet Martineau had to pay for the hate mail that followed her across the Atlantic after her American trip. But postal reform—the invention of a uniform, inexpensive stamp purchased by the mailer—made a tremendous difference. "Our greatest achievement, of late, has been the obtaining of the penny postage," wrote Martineau, "It will do more for the circulation of ideas, for the fostering of domestic affections, for the humanizing of the mass generally, than any other single measure our national wit can devise."[60] The black one-penny stamp, with its profile of the young Queen Victoria, paid for a letter to cross the Atlantic. Senders could be more casual then. "I have no idea of thy husband's address—but, New York is, I suppose, sufficient," wrote one of Elizabeth Cady Stanton's English correspondents, and the letter arrived despite its lack of street or number.

By the mid-1840s, Knight had invented feminist labels printed in bright yellow, green, and pink, which she pasted to the envelopes of her domestic and overseas letters. These miniature broadsides crammed lines of tiny type into a two- by three-inch rectangle and ensured that a single missive could proselytize many. "Never will the nations of the earth be well governed," began one, "until both sexes . . . are fairly represented, and have an influence, a voice, and a hand in the enactment and administration of the laws."[61]

Although feminists used the post to the fullest, it was the recent invention of the telegraph that excited their imaginations. The steam that powered trains, ships, and machinery could be seen and understood; electric telegraphy worked as if by magic. Invisible, almost instantaneous pulses connected humankind in a new network: if a cable could be run from Frankfurt to Berlin, from London to Glasgow, from New York to Philadelphia, then surely cables could connect the capitals to each other around the world. Developed in part to provide a signal fast enough to be useful in running the railroads, the electric telegraph spread in the 1840s at the speed of the lightning to which it was often compared. "In the electric Telegraph, we behold a system of nerves weaving itself over the surface of the earth," Fredrika Bremer wrote in 1851, the year after submarine telegraphic cable had linked England and France. "By these airy wires, nation is bound to nation."[62]

In speeding communication, the telegraph, like railroads and steamships, quickened the pace of life. Especially in the big new cities, people moved and lived faster, to an *allegro* modern tempo. When Malwida von Meysenbug first came to London in 1852 from the women's college in Hamburg, she was struck by "the throngs of pedestrians crowding the sidewalks in feverish haste, as though life depended upon their overtaking one another. . . . Time is everything in London."[63] News traveled much more rapidly with the new technology. Until the telegraph it took days to send a message by stagecoach and packet from Paris to London, although in cases of extreme urgency a carrier pigeon could fly the distance in twenty-three hours if the weather was fair. Telegraphy shrank this to minutes. The Atlantic cable, briefly successful in 1858, seemed to complete the telegraph's "annihilation of space and time."[64]

To many, these amazing technological triumphs signified a new moral era as well, a time in which people of good will could solve the world's age-old problems of injustice, poverty, and war. "The very first message transmitted to us across the Atlantic, by means of the mightiest instrument of man," declared Lucretia Mott in a sermon, "was a prophetic view of greater peace on earth" (Queen Victoria's greetings to President Buchanan).[65] The blessings brought by the wonderful inventions, reinforced in many cases by the staunch confidence that God sanctioned innovation, heralded a new stage in human history—an era of progress. In "an age of changes like the present," Harriet Taylor Mill declared in her 1851 essay,

> it is the boast of modern Europeans, and of their American kindred, that they know and do many things which their forefathers neither knew nor did; and it is perhaps the most unquestionable point of superiority in the present above former ages, that habit is not now the tyrant it formerly was over opinions and modes of action, and that the worship of custom is a declining idolatry.[66]

Her defiant tone came from the consciousness of challenging age-old beliefs and systems. Many in the mid-nineteenth century felt confident that the future could and would be better than the present. People who were adults when the inventions were new had been born into a world without much so-called progress—a world in which most believed that the future would reproduce the past and that change, if it came, would probably be for the worse. In Europe, the restoration of ancient dynasties to absolute or barely restrained powers in 1815, maintained for decades by armed international alliances, seemed to negate the changes promised by the French Revolution of 1789. Writing in the mid-1850s, George Sand remembered her feelings at seventeen in 1821, when society's evils

> revolted me so deeply that my soul was prompted to protest against the work of centuries. I hadn't the notion of 'progress,' it wasn't popular then, and it hadn't reached me through my reading—so I saw no way out of my anguish, and the idea of working, even in my obscure and closely bounded social environment, to redeem the promises of the future could scarcely occur to me.[67]

But mid-nineteenth century visions of progress often excluded or ignored the female sex. "Our time is the time of progress," wrote Louise Otto in 1843, "as for the vaunted progress of women in the nineteenth century! Their situation has stayed almost completely the same."[68] Arguing that women's position had stagnated or even deteriorated in recent times, feminists insisted that progress must include women. "So was it *once*, *now* it has become otherwise," wrote a German woman to an 1847 meeting of the radical free congregations in the small city of Nordhausen. "Even here the spirit of the age cannot remain still; it comes to slay ancient prejudice, and to elevate Woman to human dignity!"[69]

In the United States, which increasingly prided itself on being the home of progress, feminists appropriated the concept for themselves. "A new era dawns upon us," concluded the final speaker at the Worcester woman's rights convention in 1851.

> Its approach is heralded by a thousand harbingers. The lightning coursing the telegraphic wires; the smoke-girt steeds rushing along our iron-rimmed ruts, are but embassies of a power whose will will yet place freedom on something more than a theoretical basis, and give equality of privileges a being as well as a name.

To "great cheers" the speaker made the consequences clear: "We must agitate. Give woman knowledge—give mankind knowledge and their rights must follow. . . . The world is emerging into day. It is putting on shining robes of light!"[70]

By the early 1850s, however, the repression that followed the European revolutions forced thousands of French and German radicals into exile. Anneke and her family came to the United States; Deroin and others moved to Britain. Just as the outbreak of revolution released an eruption of feminist activity, so reaction ended public feminism in France, Germany, and Austria. Laws were passed forbidding women (and children) from attending any political meetings; in 1851, the Prussian government outlawed kindergartens, which were seen as centers of radical indoctrination. Not only women's movements but also movements that had nourished feminism—socialism and the free congregations—went under. "Forbidding meetings of the 'Women's Circle for Needy Families' is no longer a novelty," went a Dresden woman's letter to Otto's *Women's Newspaper*. "But now they go so far as to keep individuals—not just groups—under surveillance and to hold them responsible for all they say and do which is not completely ultramontanist, reactionary, or 'gold-black.'" (The colors of the new German flag, minus the red.)[71] By the end of that year, Otto had been forced to move her newspaper to a German state that had not passed the "Lex Otto" (a law forbidding women to edit newspapers, aimed specifically at her). The three other German feminist papers had already ceased publication.

Otto and other feminists managed to maintain their institutions—women's groups, journals, schools, and unions—longer than most other radicals within their beleaguered societies. But executions, arrests, harsh prison sentences, and censorship finally silenced the left. "The city is full of soldiers," reported Rose from Paris in 1856, "nor is this the worst; for at any rate you see them, you know who is near you. But there is a much more formidable army, an *espionage*, against which you cannot guard except by a dead silence on all subjects connected with political freedom."[72]

The silence had been enforced by terror; from the summary execution of Robert Blum, the German hero of the revolution who had first published Louise Otto, to the sentencing of French socialists like Deroin and Roland to jail and transportation. Released from her first prison sentence at Saint Lazare in July 1851, Pauline Roland was rearrested six months later. Sentenced to prison in Algeria, she died from the harsh conditions in December 1852.

Those who were not silenced or dead, however, emigrated to freer societies, and some were able to contribute to women's movements in their new homes. Roland's death became known because Deroin published an account of it in her *Women's Almanack* of 1853, published both in London and on the isle of Jersey, home of the French exile community whose best-known member was Victor Hugo.

Paradoxically, while feminism within the European continental nations ended abruptly, international feminism briefly benefited from the new connections and cross-fertilization forced by emigration. Exiles like Deroin carried on by insisting that the women's movement was international. "Since 1848," she wrote in 1853, "societies of Women have been organized in France, in America, and in England—composed of females claiming their political rights. . . . We challenge all women to walk with us."[73] In America, Mathilde Franziska Anneke demonstrated that feminists connected across national boundaries.[74] Active in the German revolution, Anneke had published a radical, feminist newspaper and fought in the Baden uprising, before fleeing with her family to the United States. In April 1850, five months pregnant with her third child, she gave her first public lecture in Milwaukee. "The efforts of many American women became known to me," she remembered of that time, when she translated writings by Stanton and others into German, "I studied the worthy efforts

of Fanny Wright d'Arusmont, Lucretia Mott, Ernestine L. Rose, Pauline
Davis, and other highly esteemed women and strengthened myself thereby." In 1852, Anneke began to publish a *German Women's Newspaper* (in
German, with some English translations) and embarked on an "agitation"
tour for seven months, trying to recruit German immigrant women to
feminism.[75] The following year a group of American feminists invited her
to be a delegate to the New York City Woman's Rights Convention in
September 1853. Lucretia Mott introduced her at the meeting. With Rose
translating her words into English, Anneke declared that she rejoiced
when she learned that

> the women of America have met in convention, to claim their rights. I
> rejoiced when I saw that they recognized their equality; and I rejoiced when
> I saw that they have not forgotten their sisters in Germany. . . . The women
> of my country look to this [one] for encouragement and sympathy; and they,
> also, sympathize with this cause. We hope it will go on and prosper; and
> many hearts across the ocean in Germany are beating in unison with those
> here.[76]

The severity of the European repression radicalized some American
and English feminists. "I did not know before [her European trip with
Bessie Parkes] how intense, how completely a part of my soul, were feelings about freedom and justice in politics and government," Barbara Leigh
Smith wrote her Aunt Julia in 1850. "I did not think, when I was so glad to
go to Austria, how the sight of people ruled by the sword in place of law
would stir up my heart and make me feel as miserable as those who live
under it."[77] Leigh Smith and Parkes soon published their first and most
radical feminist writings: *Remarks on the Education of Girls* and *A Brief
Summary, in Plain Language, of the Most Important Laws Concerning Women*.
Both stressed international examples of women's success and insisted that
despite the temporary success of repression, "The genius of this age tears
away one restriction after another which has hitherto crippled society. . . .
It is for us to aid this work."[78] American feminists especially continued to
reach out to their embattled sisters in Europe. In 1853 and again in 1856,
the Women's Rights Conventions established committees and passed resolutions of support for "the supporters of the cause of women . . . the worthy successors of Pauline Roland and Jeanne Deroin, who, in the face of
imperial despotism, dare to tell the truth."[79]

But what could they do? Brave words failed to prevent the triumph of
"tyranny, by which every outcry of the human heart is stifled," as Anneke
later declared.[80] After 1856, radical feminism began to lose ground in the
United States as well as Europe. Women's movements, as well as all left-
wing activity, had been extinguished on the continent. "Whole nations are
manacled and gagged; not allowed even to utter the cry of anguish," wrote
an English socialist paper. "Behold . . . the fires of Liberty's altars
quenched, the dial of Time reversed, the middle-age tyranny of priest and

brigand reestablished."[81] In the United States, the revolutionary momentum of the women's movement ebbed, overwhelmed by the crises impelling the nation to Civil War. When Barbara Leigh Smith Bodichon visited the United States on her honeymoon in 1858, she found that

> instead of any tendency to ameliorate the condition of the slave I see nothing but increasing barbarity in the laws and firmer barriers raised against the certain encroachment of the universal spirit of freedom. Here, as in Europe, laws to stifle this spirit increase in severity. Despotism seems dominant.[82]

Bodichon and Parkes deliberately muted the radical feminism of their early years when they helped create the English women's movement in the late 1850s, reasoning that they could attract more supporters by not pressing for the vote or divorce.[83] International connections weakened as radical feminists withdrew from public life or turned to other causes. While some Europeans, like Jenny d'Héricourt, continued to champion the U.S. women's movement as an example, the Americans transformed themselves into the "National Women's Loyal League" for the duration of the Civil War. Lack of support from abroad eroded radicalism at home. In both the United States and Europe the 1860s witnessed a return to purely national concerns and early international feminists felt the times to be against them. Three months before her death in 1862, the seventy-five-year-old Anne Knight had a friend transcribe an 1848 letter she had written with Jeanne Deroin into her diary. The letter demanded the emancipation of women for the good of humanity. Below it, Knight added her final entry: "It is 14 years ago & where are we now? Still heaving our agonized chests under the couchemar of a military despotism. . . . how long? Lord, how long?"[84]

When national women's movements revived, as they did in the 1860s and 1870s, they were much less internationalist and far more conservative. International feminist organizations of the late nineteenth century focused more on suffrage, rather than the wide range of issues raised by the earlier movement. But the success of the first international women's movement should not be underestimated. It challenged the male dominance of Western culture and society in a way that would not be repeated until the late 1960s. It enabled some women to transcend national and class differences for feminist purposes in a period in which those differences intensified and increased. It created a coherent and convincing ideology that made wide-ranging claims for women's rights and equality, without surrendering a keen sense of women's difference from men. To advocate new roles for women required impressive courage and fortitude, "a heroism that the world has never yet recognized, that the battlefield cannot supply, but which woman possesses," as Ernestine Rose declared in 1856.[85] The achievements of early feminists become all the more astonishing when we realize how unusual these women were in their own day.

Two

⤳

Angels over Amazons

Early in 1849, Anne Knight sent one of her feminist packets to Anne Taylor Gilbert, a minister's wife in the north of England. Like Knight, Gilbert was in her sixties, from the middle class, a long-term antislavery advocate, and a published author. She might reasonably have been expected to welcome a call for women's rights. Instead, Gilbert wrote Knight at length about why the relations between women and men functioned best when women stayed at home and men represented them in political and economic life—a new ideal attainable for increasing numbers of households in the nineteenth century because of the era's prosperity. "Nature seems to have settled the question 'a priori,'" Gilbert argued,

> We have not lungs, we have not courage, we have not time for it (to say nothing of interruptions which might happen inconveniently during the sittings of Parliament) and modern science says further that *the division of labour* is the great secret of order and progress. As long as houses have insides as well as outsides, I think that the female head has enough on her hands, even, I might almost say, irrespective of the numerous demands now made upon her by benevolent and religious societies.

Scripture also supported women's domesticity and the Bible, nature, and science convinced Gilbert that Knight's views were "untenable." "I think yours a false movement," she concluded, "and . . . I put my protest against it."[1]

In both her life and her writings, Gilbert championed a domestic view of womanhood idealizing the life of a wife and mother within the home. Far more representative of educated women than a feminist like Knight, Anne Taylor Gilbert chose domesticity for herself, even though she had a successful writing career.[2] A widely published poet by her twenties, she succeeded with "Twinkle, Twinkle Little Star," which she wrote with her sister, and "My Mother," an emotional tribute to her own mother's care. "Who ran to help me when I fell / And would some pretty story tell / Or kiss the place to make it well? / My Mother," reads one of its twelve verses. At thirty-one, Anne Taylor agreed to marry a man she had never met, who asked her parents for her hand because he liked her religious poems. As Anne Taylor Gilbert, she gave birth to eight children in eleven years and virtually abandoned her writing. A son remembered her saying a "dear little child is worth volumes of fame." She lived her life by the values she glorified in her early poetry and championed in her letter to Knight. Women were different from men and should lead a life different from men's: "The rougher path was *his* to tread; / The mild domestic, *hers*. . . . Man's proudest glory is his head, / A Woman's, is her heart."[3]

By insisting on domesticity for women, Gilbert joined a growing number of writers and artists, moralists and reformers. From the early eighteenth century on, women were increasingly urged to restrict themselves to the domestic sphere. A woman's most important function became raising her children to healthy, virtuous adulthood, which a host of advisers argued could best be done by devoting almost all her time and attention to them and her husband. "A woman is born to dignify retreat, /In shade to flourish, and unseen be great," wrote the English poet Alexander Pope. "Fearful of fame, unwilling to be known, /Should seek but Heaven's applauses and her own." In 1865, when she wrote a memoir of her sister Fredrika Bremer, Charlotte Bremer Quiding quoted Pope's verses to justify her own choice of domesticity over her sister's choice of fame. "I could not see that the management of the business of the state was the province of women," Quiding argued.

> The sense of Pope's lines I considered to express in general woman's quiet, noble mission, although naturally there are exceptions. But one ought not to regard the exceptions, but only the general rule. . . . how dangerous it would be to encourage young girls [to live as Fredrika Bremer recommended]. Educated with this aim in view, they would become neither men nor women, and, when older, unfit for domestic life.[4]

Bremer and Knight were the exceptions; Quiding and Gilbert represented the views of the vast majority. Although they seemed to hold firm to traditional values, writers like Gilbert and Quiding actually were recommending a new role for women. Living solely as a wife and mother within the home, not needing to earn income or contribute actively to the family economy, was a modern way of life made possible only by fundamental economic transformations of the eighteenth and nineteenth centuries. The growth of commerce and industry made it possible for more families to live in this middle-class fashion, with their female members devoted to domesticity. The increase of the middle class and the spread of its values to much of the rest of society transformed both the home itself and the lives possible for women within it. As in the Bremer family, some women resisted this model. But like Charlotte Bremer Quiding, most women chose domesticity if they could afford it and advocated it for other women at the very moment when the nature of domestic life was changing dramatically.

Prior to the nineteenth century, the home was the chief economic unit of production throughout Western society. Families worked together to raise their own food and make their own clothing, to earn income at a family trade or by contracting out as a group. Adults and children, men and women, masters and servants or slaves—all played roles in this domestic economy. Women were definitely junior partners in the enterprise and were supposed to be subordinate to their husbands, but their visible contributions to the family's work gave them some authority and respect. Looking back on her childhood in Meissen in the 1820s, Louise Otto connected the prestige good housewives earned to their endless labor within the home. Soap, candles, clothing, bread, and all preserved foods were made by the women of the household. Woman's work made a real difference to a man's income and so "it was fitting to have respect for such a good wife. . . . In reality, the woman was one of the most necessary members of society, in the political economy."[5] In the American colonies, women's work made settlements flourish and they were honored for their contributions. A 1714 history of the Carolina frontier declared:

> The Women are the most industrious sex in that Place and by their good Housewifery, make a great deal of Cloath of their own Cotton, Wool and Flax;...The Girls are not bred up to the Wheel and Sewing only, but the Dairy, and affairs of the House they are very well acquainted withal; so that you shall see them, whilst very young, manage their Business with a great deal of Conduct and Alacrity.[6]

But from the early eighteenth century on, the family economy began to disappear.[7] Clothing and food production moved out of homes and into factories. As the household changed, so did the function of the housewife. Economic development lightened woman's labor by freeing her from production. Thus she could devote more time to child care and housekeeping. But freed from production, she also was seen as not really working in a society that prized work. The perception of the housewife's role changed drastically, from that of "busy" producer to "idle" consumer.

Because the rate of change paralleled industrial development, housewives in rural areas remained productive well into the twentieth century. But apart from the countryside, even extreme cultural pressure could not prevent the rise of a consumer society. The German housewife held on the longest. In 1840 the English author Mary Howitt wrote her sister that Heidelberg reminded her of "the times of our girlhood" in the early nineteenth century, "when we used to sit with our work forever in our hands and the practice of wearing gloves in the house and doing nothing was unknown. Everybody knits as mother does, and it looks quite familiar when the spinning wheel is brought out in winter."[8] German novelist Fanny Lewald remembered "the fanatical cleanliness of my fellow Prussians" during the same era when she was a young woman in Königsberg. "But if any housewife of that period . . . would have dared to lighten her burden, bought her bread from the baker, her dried fruit from a grocer, her processed meats from a butcher, she would have been considered a heretic, a criminal, who was shirking her domestic duties."[9]

Despite such pressures, the status of the housewife declined, even in Germany. By the time Lewald and Otto wrote their reminiscences, in the 1860s and 1870s, such "brave housewifery" was becoming a thing of the past and respect for the housewife eroded.[10] Increasing numbers of women became housewives just as the traditional role of the housewife was losing value and status. Even so, women chose domesticity if they possibly could because the other choices available to them were so much worse.

For women who had to earn income, the ending of home production was disastrous. Industrialization and the increased demand for piecework done at home degraded their skilled trades. Within two generations, for instance, the manufacture of clothing changed from a traditional household enterprise by which a women could earn a decent living, into piecework, by which hard labor brought starvation wages. Faced with such conditions in their own trades, men moved into industry. But when women worked in the new factories, they did so in the least prestigious jobs and were paid half the wages of men. All shared the abysmal environment of early industrialization: long hours, dangerous conditions, incessant toil geared to the pace of the machinery. Still, women preferred factory work if they could get it to the other job opening up for them—domestic service.[11]

By the nineteenth century, most women who had to earn income worked in homes in which they were the only servant. The demand for female servants kept increasing as men left domestic service for other jobs. The maid-of-all-work performed the heaviest and most distasteful chores and had the lowest status within the household. Faced with the choices of domestic service, factory work, or piecework at home, women avoided these labors if they could. Lower-middle and working-class women aspired to domesticity and embraced it as a modern improvement in their lives.

A family signaled its prosperity by freeing a wife from having to labor for income inside or outside the home, allowing her to stay at home, doing only housework and child care. First in England, later in the United States, France, and the German lands, women withdrew from work in family businesses and hired servants to help with the heaviest household tasks. Released from doing piecework or farming, from boiling laundry or hauling slops and coal, increasing numbers of women devoted their extra time to their children, husbands, and households and were praised for doing so.[12] "In general, it is for the benefit of a family that a married woman should devote her time and attention almost exclusively to the ways of her household: her place is the centre of domestic cares," advised the *English Family Monitor, or a Help to Domestic Happiness*, which went into many editions after its first appearance in 1828.

> What is gained to her in the shop is oftentimes lost in the house, for want of the judicious superintendence of a mother and a mistress. . . . The children always want a mother's eye and hand, and should always have them. Let the husband, then, have the care of providing for the necessities of the family, and the wife that of personally superintending it.[13]

As women ceased to work in family businesses, the home, previously the site of so much domestic industry, became increasingly idealized as a refuge away from work.

This modern opposition of work and home was accelerated by the growth of jobs for men outside the domestic economy. New positions in government bureaucracies, in the professions, and in business and industry enabled more men to enter the middle class, in addition to removing them from the home. As increasing numbers of men left the home to work and came home to relax, so women's function became to provide a restful haven for them. "The time is not distant when every American mother shall duly appreciate her domestic responsibilities; and when our homes shall be made attractive," predicted a guidebook for women in 1841.

> Then, when our husbands and our sons go forth into the busy and turbulent world, we may feel secure that they will walk unhurt amid its snares and temptations. Their hearts will be at home, where their treasure is; and they will rejoice to return to its sanctuary of rest, there to refresh their wearied spirits, and renew their strength for the toils and conflicts of life.[14]

Men insisted they could not function without this refuge. Women within the home make "present day life bearable," wrote the German liberal Georg Gervinus in 1853, "because the woman of today . . . is removed from the common bustle of life, because . . . she does not suffer the degradation of lowly occupations, the turmoil and heartlessness of work."[15]

Increasingly women at home were not believed to be working. Most nineteenth-century housewives in fact did a great deal of labor, raising their large families and maintaining their households. The typical middle-class family could only afford one servant, so the housewife usually worked alongside her. But since this labor was no longer seen by men, who worked outside the home, it became "invisible" and unacknowledged. And since it remained unpaid, in an economy increasingly based on money, it further lost value. By the middle of the nineteenth century, work had become

redefined as paid employment and was done either by men and or by
women too poor not to labor. Working for income became problematic
for a middle-class woman. Taking a job meant that she needed the money,
and she lost status as she sank into the "working" class. Thus a woman
remained domestic if at all possible: her family's prestige and status were
predicated on her staying at home and "not working." As the standard of
living continued to rise, more and more women became able to live in this
fashion. For women, the growth of the middle class meant the triumph of
domesticity.

Pressure toward domesticity was further compounded by political and
cultural changes that reduced other options for elite women. In this era,
wealthy, aristocratic, and even royal women began to adopt the domestic
style of life previously associated with the middle class. Traditionally
prized for their charm, beauty, wealth, and social connections, most elite
European and American woman in the early eighteenth century spent little time caring for their children or their homes. Many hired wet nurses to
suckle their babies.[16] Upper-class women employed other women as
maids, laundresses, nannies, housekeepers, and cooks to do housework
and child care for them. In many elite families, a remote style of parenting
prevailed, in which children lived separately, cared for by servants until
they were able to sustain the formal rituals of polite society. Charlotte
Bremer Quiding recalled how she and Fredrika, children in the early nineteenth century, saw their parents "rarely except at stated times of the day."
At eight A.M., fully dressed, the children greeted their mother. "She looked
at us with a scrutinizing glance during our walk from the door up to her
chair," Quiding remembered. "If we had walked badly, we had to go back
again to the door to renew our promenade, curtsey, and kiss her hand."[17]
An upper-class mother was expected to busy herself with social life, not to
devote herself to domestic concerns.

From the early eighteenth century, however, this aristocratic style of
life came under attack. Criticism of women who put social and political life
before the domestic sphere mounted. In books and periodicals, letters and
poems, men and women of a reforming cast of mind championed domesticity for all women, including queens and aristocrats. In 1788, for
instance, Thomas Jefferson complained from Paris that French women of
all ranks participated too much in politics. "But our good Ladies," he
wrote approvingly to an American woman friend,

> have been too wise to wrinkle their foreheads with politics. They are con-
> tented to soothe and calm the minds of their husbands returning ruffled
> from political debate. They have the good sense to value domestic happiness
> above all others, and the art to cultivate it above all others. . . . Recollect the
> women of this capital . . . hunting pleasure in the streets, in routs and assem-
> blies, and forgetting that they have left it behind them in their nurseries;
> compare our own countrywomen occupied in the tender and tranquil

amusements of domestic life, and confess that it is a comparison of Amazons and Angels.[18]

The new domestic female ideal was continually contrasted favorably to an older model of public female power. In Jefferson's comparison, the Amazons stood for the influential female rulers and salonières of eighteenth-century Europe, who had invaded the traditionally male territory of government and warfare. At the top of the social pyramid were the powerful queens and empresses: Maria Theresa, from 1740 to 1780 the first woman to rule Austria; her daughter, Marie Antoinette, queen of France from 1774 to 1793; Catherine the Great, who governed Russia from 1762 to 1796. Women rulers functioned like the male absolute monarchs of their day: ruthlessly protecting their family's claim to the throne, coolly making war and peace to best advance their nation's interests, tightly controlling and supervising domestic policy. Queens and royal mistresses, great ladies and courtiers, influential salonières and hostesses rivaled men in power and influence. Maria Theresa of Austria lived as a respectable wife and mother, but Catherine of Russia took and discarded lovers at will, using her sexuality to further her interests and please herself. An equal to the most powerful male rulers of the day, she became the embodiment of both women's achievements and men's fears. "Her forehead is lofty, and, if I am not mistaken, a long and terrifying future is written upon it," a secret agent wrote the French king early in her reign. "She is prepossessing and affable, but when she comes close to me I instinctively recoil, for she frightens me."[19]

Arriving in Russia at fourteen, Catherine parlayed a youthful marriage with the future tsar into an opportunity to seize the throne for herself. A medal struck to commemorate her accession shows her full-breasted and long-haired, wearing a helmet and armor, a true descendent of the Amazons. Voltaire's patron (he called her "the Semiramis of the North," after the queen of ancient Assyria), Catherine actively supported the arts and education, joining the many elite women who shaped European political and cultural life in the eighteenth century. Many also used their sexuality to advance their careers and interests by their liaisons, as Catherine did. "Under absolute monarchies women used their charms to extend their influence until they helped to decide the fate of empires," wrote Henriette Campan, lady-in-waiting to Marie Antoinette. "Too often the boudoir of the favorite became the king's privy council."[20]

The new Amazon used her sexual powers against men, to weaken and defeat them. Most late eighteenth-century reformers believed that women's participation in political life, always assumed to be at least partially sexual, was a chief cause of the corruption and decadence associated with absolute monarchy and aristocracy. "Female influence," women's supposed ability to control men's behavior by manipulating their sexual desires, was considered responsible for the ills of the old regime. The eighteenth century soon was called the "age of women" or the "century of women," a bygone era in which powerful females personified all the evils of aristocracy and absolute monarchy.[21]

This identification of women's power and public influence with the corruption of the old regime led to reform's coming to mean excluding all women from political life. "Nature . . . has given women so much power," declared English author Samuel Johnson, "that the law has very wisely given them little."[22] From Johnson and Pope to Rousseau and Goethe, most Enlightenment authorities agreed with the sentiments of Nicholas Restif de la Bretonne, that in "all of Europe Women [should] be returned to their proper place, and that by this means a reformation of moral values be effected."[23] Enlightened morality called for women to be excluded from political life and restricted to domestic life. This new "division of labor" seemed progressive and modern.

By the early nineteenth century, male reformers had achieved much of this goal. The new republics in France and the United States, the radical political reforms debated in England, and liberal political thought throughout the West, assumed an all-male body politic freed from alleged female influence. "The Fair Sex—Excluded by necessity from participation in our labours," went an American politician's toast in 1825 to the French general Lafayette, "[since] the presence of woman would make us slaves, and convert the temple of wisdom to that of love."[24] The great democratic gains of the revolutionary era—the weakening of royal and aristocratic power and the establishment of equality before the law—were gains for men only. Laws that eradicated class barriers between male aristocrats and male commoners restricted all women to a new group excluded from political activity. The Code Napoleon of 1804, later adopted in much of Europe, institutionalized this exclusion and classified women with other "incapacitated" groups: children, the insane, and convicted criminals. English common law, applied in much of the United States in this period, treated women similarly. By law, the husband became the head of the household and by law, his wife owed him obedience. He alone could decide where they lived, if she could inherit, work, acquire property, give money away, be a witness in a criminal case, or receive official papers. He could read her correspondence and have access to her bank accounts. He could "confine" her and "chastize" her, even punishing her with a beating if he saw fit. He had sole authority over their children and could make decisions about their lives alone; in a divorce case, he would automatically receive custody. The new law codes institutionalized the double standard of sexual morality, condoning adultery by husbands but punishing adulterous wives severely. The Napoleonic Code gave men (but not women) the right to kill an adulterous spouse caught in the act. Looking back over the immense changes of the era, Elizabeth Vigée-Lebrun, court artist to

Marie Antoinette, declared that "Women ruled then [in the eighteenth century]; the revolution dethroned them."[25]

In a very short period of time, between 1789 and 1815, the aristocratic, sexually threatening model of the Amazon gave way to the middle-class, domesticated ideal that Jefferson extolled as an Angel. The year after Catherine the Great's death, Russian law changed the succession to the throne and gave precedence to men. Few women ruled in the nineteenth century; royal power itself was on the wane. The most powerful female European monarch of the nineteenth century was Queen Victoria of England. In her long reign, from 1837 to 1901, she championed the new domestic model of womanhood and in so doing set a style for female monarchs that has lasted until today.

Victoria symbolized the new angelic ideal as clearly as Catherine stood for the reprehensible past.[26] Becoming queen at eighteen, after three elderly and unpopular kings, she embodied her nation's sense of a fresh start. Banishing mistresses, extramarital liaisons, and sexual innuendo from court, Victoria insisted on a "superlative chastity" in her circles, as one of her contemporaries put it. Consistently presenting herself as the epitome of domestic virtue—a chaste maiden, a devoted wife and widow, a loving mother—Victoria based modern royalty upon middle-class respectability and was extolled for doing so. "Her court was pure; her life serene," the poet Tennyson declared in an ode written for the Great Exhibition of 1851,

> God gave her peace; her land reposed;
> A thousand claims to reverence closed
> In her as Mother, Wife, and Queen.[27]

Praised for her virtuous womanhood and domesticity, Victoria featured it at royal occasions. At her Golden Jubilee in 1887, celebrating fifty years in power, she insisted that she and her ladies-in-waiting wear womanly bonnets (albeit of white lace and diamonds) rather than the traditional crowns and coronets.[28]

The sexual propriety associated with Victoria was intrinsic to the new model of domestic womanhood. Women had always been exhorted to be chaste and faithful, but in the aftermath of the French Revolution, standards tightened dramatically. Acceptable female behavior changed within a single generation. In 1826, for instance, novelist Walter Scott's great-aunt asked him to send her the works of the seventeenth-century writer Aphra Behn, which she wanted to reread. Scott complied reluctantly, since Behn's racy reputation and licentious subject matter made her unsuitable reading for a nineteenth-century lady. His aunt quickly returned the books. "I found it impossible to get through the very first of the novels," she explained, "but is it not odd that I, an old woman of eighty and upwards, sitting alone, feel myself ashamed to read a book which sixty years ago I have heard read aloud for large circles consisting of the first and most creditable society in London?"[29]

Sexual propriety, previously associated chiefly with strict religious groups, now became interwoven with middle- and upper-class female identity. The double standard, which condoned sexual knowledge and activity in men while condemning it in women, widened in this era. Walter Scott was not shocked by Aphra Behn, but he attempted to protect his aunt from reading now considered improper for respectable women. Men restricted their actions and their vocabularies when in polite female society.

By midcentury, female sexual respectability had become an important marker of class status. Women of the lower classes continued to be fair game: men of all ranks were still expected to "sow their wild oats." But women of the upper and middle classes were supposed to be treated with extreme sexual propriety and deference.

Although a few elite women resisted these new restrictions, most opted for sexual respectability, retreating from public life and any possible appearance of impropriety.[30] Barred from becoming Amazons, they turned to the virtuous behavior of Angels. In France, the power of the salonières was broken; in England, women who continued to take lovers were socially ostracized, especially by other women. In both Europe and the United States, this new domestic model of womanly behavior functioned importantly in the creation of national identities. Thomas Jefferson's Angel was an American Angel, and her behavior confirmed the moral validity of the newly created republic. In the United States, reformers praised American women for not being "French," for rejecting the ancien régime values of female sophistication, libertinism, and political involvement. English, German, and Russian reformers followed suit. A virtuous, domestic English, German, or Russian woman—maiden or matron—embodied her nation's triumph over French universalism. The male soldiers of these nations had defeated the imposition of French rule through warfare that lasted from 1792 to 1815. During the same time, female domestic virtue became touted as confirmation of national superiority and women were continually told that they could best support their country by rejecting so-called French values.[31] Inside France, aristocratic women distanced themselves from prerevolutionary mores by championing "the sacred duties of a wife and mother," as Mme. Necker de Saussure put it in a guide popular in both France and the United States.[32] Connecting the reform of women's behavior to national regeneration, they reinforced the belief that domestic womanhood contributed to a new national vision.

The French reformer Jean-Jacques Rousseau had pioneered these views in his novels, which continued to be popular well into the nineteenth century. Insisting that women had a crucial role to play in shaping their nation's future for good or ill, Rousseau made domesticity seem glorious and modern. His influential novel *Emile*, published in 1762, opened daringly with a paean to breastfeeding, proclaiming it the first step to national rebirth. By linking female domestic virtue to national honor and well-being, Rousseau anticipated the successful new social contract achieved in both postrevolutionary Europe and the United States. Ousted completely from the political sphere by the curtailment of royal and aristocratic power and the denial of democratic and civil rights, women would be glorified and honored if they remained contentedly within the home. "A virtuous woman is little lower than the angels," Rousseau declared in *Emile*,

> I would a thousand times rather have a homely girl, simply brought up, than a learned lady and a wit who would make a literary circle of my house and install herself as its president. A female wit is a scourge to her husband, her children, her friends, her servants, to everybody. From the lofty height of her genius, she scorns every womanly duty, and she is always trying to make a man of herself.[33]

Rousseau's opposition of a "women's world" of the home to a "man's world" encompassing the rest of existence became increasingly common in the late eighteenth and early nineteenth centuries. "To man—the sword and the quill. /To woman—the needle and spindle," went a typical example by late eighteenth-century French author Sylvain Maréchal,

> To man—Hercules' mace.
> To woman—Omphale's distaff.
> To man—the productions of genius.
> To woman—the sentiments of the heart.[34]

Men were the head, women the heart. Men were active, women passive. Men were aggressive, women gentle. And since the sexes had such different aptitudes, they were seen as ideally segregated into separate spheres. "A woman outside of her home loses her greatest luster," asserted Rousseau, in sentiments echoed by Anne Taylor Gilbert and a host of other writers. Such pronouncements had become clichés by the mid-nineteenth century. When Tennyson used one in his popular 1847 poem *The Princess* ("man for the field and woman for the hearth. . . . All else confusion"), he assigned it to the most elderly, conservative character, the prince's father.[35]

Such comparisons were as old as Western culture itself and drew on ancient symbols, like the distaff, which stood for woman's traditional association with spinning and clothes making. But as with so much else about modern domesticity, ancient symbols cloaked new conditions. In this period the territories allotted each sex became increasingly unequal as production moved out of the home. But the very structure of the comparison between man and woman implied equality. By balancing men's and women's functions and spaces evenly, these homilies masked the growing inequality between the sexes' respective spheres.

They also heightened the importance of "sexual character," as German writings of the period put it. Earlier comparisons of this sort turned not on gender but on class rank, charting the differences between aristocratic, bourgeois, and peasant behavior.[36] Differences between the classes had far outweighed differences between men and women. Now women of all social groups were newly defined as domestic beings. Separate and unequal, the sexes ideally lived in different spaces and performed different functions.

Clothing mirrored this shift. Prior to the nineteenth century, clothes differed far more by rank than by gender. Female and male aristocrats alike wore costumes so tight fitting they needed servants to help dress them. Both sexes wore delicate fabrics and light colors, used wigs, corsets, high heels and makeup, carried fans, snuff boxes, and lace handkerchiefs. Somber colors and simpler cuts denoted the middle class; smocks and kerchiefs, the peasantry.

By the middle of the nineteenth century, however, men of all ranks were adopting the utilitarian clothing of the male bourgeois. A dark jacket and trousers over a white shirt made for a relatively comfortable outfit, and elite men discarded their knee breeches, silk stockings, corsets, high heels, makeup, and accessories. Women's clothing, in contrast, remained modeled on the constricting and cumbersome dress of the eighteenth-century lady, with its corseted waist, full ankle-length skirt, and tightly fitting bodice and sleeves. Throughout most of the nineteenth century, long hair, unnaturally small waists, and ankle-length skirts strikingly differentiated women from men. Men's clothes demonstrated their new identification with work; women's clothes emphasized their femininity and domesticity.

Already a powerful marker of class, domesticity now also denoted femininity. Women who dressed differently or wanted a life outside the home were automatically seen—by themselves as well as by others—as wanting to be men. On both sides of the Atlantic, reformers extolled the "true womanhood" of domestic wives and mothers.[37] An entire literature of guidebooks about womanhood, in which proper domestic roles were described in minute detail for the growing middle-class female audience, flourished in this period. Sarah Stickney Ellis's series of lengthy volumes, the *Women of England*, *Daughters of England*, *Wives of England*, and *Mothers of England*, published in the 1830s and 1840s, achieved immense popularity. Combining femininity, domesticity, and national pride, Ellis interwove practical household hints with guidelines to female domestic virtue. "There are . . . a few simple rules" she wrote in a typical passage about the duties of sisters,

> No woman in the enjoyment of health should allow her brother to prepare his own meals at any time of the day, if it were possible for her to do it for him. No woman should allow her brother to put on linen in a state of

dilapidation, to wear gloves or stockings in want of mending, or to return home without finding a neat parlor, a place to sit down without asking for it, and a cheerful invitation to partake of necessary refreshment.[38]

Lauded for being virtuous sisters and daughters, wives and mothers, some women and their advisers exalted their new role and status as domestic angels. Rousseau told women they could command a domestic "empire," and this kind of hyperbole became commonplace in the nineteenth century. The American Sarah Josepha Hale, for instance, called her popular 1845 poem in which she glorified women's familial roles "Empire of Woman." If women leave to men "the outward world, for rugged toil designed," they will gain a "wondrous power, how little understood!" Hale promised. The daughter's "loving eye" lightens her father's "iron cares." The sister's "winning smile" tames her brother's "wild" nature. The wife, "angel-like," sustains her husband's "sinking soul," but it is as mother that women's greatest influence is felt. "The Mother's heart was hallowed from above," and she alone has the power "To fashion genius, form the soul for good, /Inspire a West [the artist Benjamin West] or train a Washington!"[39]

Glorifying women's virtue if they remained chastely domestic easily merged into glorifying women as innately virtuous. French reformer Louis Aimé-Martin championed "woman's mission" in his popular 1834 guide, *The Education of Mothers: or the Civilization of Mankind by Women*, published in multiple editions in England, France, and the United States. Arguing that the "Christian virtues" were easier for women to practice, since "women have fewer worldly interests, and are by nature less selfish than men," Aimé-Martin urged women to become "the regenerators of society" in their capacity as "the guardian angels of men's infancy."[40] Fitting easily into the bipolar scheme that assigned different capacities to the opposite sexes, such ideas rapidly caught on. Virtuous woman would reform immoral man. The home, removed from the world of work, would become a haven for virtue, which women would now embody.

Traditionally, however, women were supposed to defer to men's superior moral judgment. God's curse to Eve in Genesis for her disobedience, "thy desire shall be to thy husband, and he shall rule over thee," was cited repeatedly as a justification for women's inferior status. But by the nineteenth century, the locus of moral authority had begun to shift. Throughout the Western community, men withdrew from church going while women continued to attend.[41] Increasingly identified with religion and virtue, some domestic women claimed a new moral authority, at least within their territory of the home and family.

For the Anglo-American reading public, Coventry Patmore's immensely popular, two-volume love poem, *The Angel in the House*, best articulated women's new role in the 1850s.[42] Patmore extolled "the new chivalry" in which men "honored" women (the heroine's name is Honoria) by assuming that they are morally superior.

> Marr'd less than man by mortal fall,
> Her disposition is devout,
> Her countenance angelical.
>
> .   .   .   .
>
> Wrong dares not in her presence speak,
> Nor spotted thought its taint disclose
> Under the protest of a cheek
> Outbragging Nature's boast the rose.[43]

By the mid-nineteenth century, such views had become part of the new domestic model of womanhood adopted in many middle-class households. Men elevated their tone and conduct when in the presence of their female relatives and other women of equal or superior status. In practice, this meant excluding all references involving or suggesting sexuality. Female virtue, always identified with women's sexual chastity and fidelity, narrowed into Victorian prudishness. Sexual propriety now demanded that respectable women act as if illicit sexuality did not exist. White women in the plantation South were supposed to ignore the children their menfolk had sired on slave women. English women wanting to help prostitutes found themselves criticized for even raising the subject. "Silence was thought to be the great duty of all on such subjects," remembered Josephine Butler, an English reformer, of the 1850s.[44]

As angels in the house, upholding and embodying the strictest standards of sexual rectitude, middle-class women would automatically receive male deference and courtesy, as upper-class ladies traditionally had. Increasingly the growing middle class raised its daughters to be ladies—to be angels—to embody the female innocence and purity that had become such an important marker of class status. "What was not shocking then," recalled Fanny Lewald about her girlhood in Prussia,

> what was not unseemly for a woman and especially for a girl! A girl could not look at a statue in which people were naked and must turn her eyes away from a painting with naked figures and, if possible, shudder and blush. A girl could not undertake the smallest journey alone. . . . To have an independent opinion, or even an interest in the matters of the day was completely unmaidenly, and even unwomanly.[45]

Sexual innocence ended with marriage. "We raise them as saints, only to dispose of them as fillies," wrote George Sand about her niece's betrothal in 1843, but womanly dependence lasted for life. Supposed to defer to male authority unless it threatened their sexual virtue, women were repeatedly told they would only be respected if they put their husbands and children first. "I will meet the family with a consciousness that, being the least engaged of any member of it, I am consequently the most at liberty to devote myself to the general good of the whole," recommended Mrs. Ellis, "by cultivating cheerful conversation, adapting myself to the prevailing tone of feeling and leading those who are less happy to think and speak of what will make them more so."[46] Patmore paid tribute to "the gentle wife . . . Whose wishes wait upon her Lord / Who finds her own in his delight."[47] This new domestic model of womanhood rested upon a paradox, expressed by Mme. Celnart in her 1834 French guide to good manners. No matter how great a woman's "superiority of mind and the force of her will," she advised, "she must present herself as that creature made to please, to love, to seek support, that being who is inferior to man and who approaches the angels."[48] By deferring to men, women proved their superiority to men. This self-contradictory and self-defeating premise lay at the heart of the new model of domestic womanhood.

The female self must cultivate selflessness. The angel had to remain within the house, confining herself to domesticity, clipping her own wings and those of her daughters. In return, she would be supported financially and treated politely. The "new chivalry" was better than no chivalry at all, but it did not regain women the self-earned status they had lost when production moved out of the home. Although each family worked out its own balance of power, according to individual personalities and temperaments, the overwhelming testimony is that men still dominated, within the home as well as outside it. "My father was passionately fond of chess, but he did not like to lose the game," remembered Charlotte Bremer Quiding. "I determined to manage so that I won one or two games every night, in order that my father should not consider himself too clever; but by some wrong moves I always let him win the last game, for otherwise he lost his temper, and that he should be in a good temper was, after all, the main point."[49]

Quiding prided herself on her ability to "calmly submit" and, given the economic realities of the period, hers was the most sensible path. The bottom line was that women were becoming increasingly financially dependent on men. Deferring to them and making them happy was by far the safest course, and it was the one that most women followed and taught to their daughters, who in turn perpetuated it. "Obviously in [my mother's] scheme of things men were the important people," wrote English author Molly Hughes (1866–1956) about the nineteenth century, "Well, they are. And I shall never cease to be grateful to her for training me from childhood to appreciate this point."[50]

Of less importance than men, many women came to think of themselves as less competent, less responsible, and less adult than men. "It is too much, too much and few can stand under it," twenty-year-old Annie Wilson wrote her father, then prospecting in the California Gold Rush, in 1851 about his daughters' financial hardship back at home. "*Girls*, I mean. If we were boys it would be a different thing but for women who can do nothing but sit still and suffer alone and all within, it is a pretty severe trial." Wilson made it clear to her father that it was his responsibility to support his daughters and provide them with the "respectability of our Father's *roof*."[51] She, like other middle-class women threatened with financial hardship by a male relative's death or lack of income, did not consider herself capable of earning her own living. Middle-class men were supposed to take care of women, to be the stronger sex, to provide a bulwark between women and the harshness of the world. As long as men performed this function, many domestic women enjoyed the pleasures of dependency, of being financially and emotionally supported. Psychologically, the new domestic role allowed women to remain childlike, to rely upon a husband as they had previously relied upon a father. "Lofty pine and clinging vine," became a common metaphor for the ideal relationship between man and woman in this period.[52]

Dependence, however, inevitably meant weakness. Much of the new advice literature for middle-class women detailed the strategies of weakness: manipulation, duplicity, flattery, and pleasing. Excluded almost completely from the public sphere, women were told to use their "female influence" within the home. Women's "mild, dependent, softening influence" is "the source of mighty power," declared the Congregational ministers of Massachusetts in 1837. "The power of woman is in her dependence, flowing from the consciousness of that weakness which God has given her for her protection and which keeps her in those departments of life that form the character of individuals and of the nation."[53]

Power through weakness was a debilitating concept. Taught they had power only if they curbed their power, women found themselves in a double bind. If they asserted their energy and talents, they lost their femininity and threatened their sexual identity. But if they were properly "womanly," they had to accept a model of womanhood that stressed female weakness and incapacity. Science reinforced this model. Medical writings of the era exaggerated women's difference from men and connected the "medical axiom, that women are more sensitive, weak . . . and more liable to diseases than the other sex" to "the mysterious process of reproduction," as a popular English midwifery manual put it.[54] French historian Jules Michelet's two influential books—*Love* (1859) and *Woman* (1860)—argued persuasively that woman "ceaselessly suffers from love's eternal wound," menstruation. "Wherever woman does not blot out her sex by excessive labor (like our hardy peasant women, who, at an early age, make men of themselves), wherever she remains a woman, she is generally ailing at least one week out of four."[55]

Connecting female physical weakness to class status, like Michelet, doctors joined other cultural authorities in recommending that all women embrace domesticity if they possibly could. "Man was created independent because destined to govern the family, society, and nature," stated popular English obstetrician E. J. Tilt, "while woman was made dependent, tied to hearth and home by a long chain of never-ending infirmities, as if to point out the destined sphere where her activity could find more happiness, although a paler glory."[56]

By the middle of the nineteenth century, the new model of domestic womanhood was well established. Strongly connected to modernity, to middle-class status, and to female gender identity, supported by all existing social institutions, it proved remarkably long-lived. In 1931, English writer Virginia Woolf described its influence in her life. Asked to review a book, Woolf felt herself to be confronted with a phantom. "And the phantom was a woman, and . . . I called her after the heroine of a famous poem, The Angel in the House," Woolf declared in a speech on women's professions:

> She was intensely sympathetic. She was immensely charming. She was utterly unselfish. . . . She sacrificed herself daily. . . . [When]I took my pen in hand to review that novel by a famous man, she slipped behind me and whispered: "My dear, you are a young woman. You are writing about a book that has been written by a man. Be sympathetic; be tender; flatter; deceive; use all the arts and wiles of our sex. Never let anybody guess that you have a mind of your own."

Woolf ended by killing the angel in the house. "Had I not killed her, she would have killed me."[57]

The struggle to break free of domestic womanhood was far more difficult for women who grew up when the model was in full force, a century before Woolf wrote. But even then, some women contested this ideal. The 1837 Pastoral Letter of the Congregational ministers of Massachusetts, which advocated that women use their influence quietly within the home, was written to condemn an extremely successful antislavery lecture tour by Sarah and Angelina Grimké. Daughters of a South Carolina slave holder, the sisters spoke to over 40,000 New Englanders, often in "promiscuous" audiences that combined women and men. The ministers condemned the Grimkés' loss of "that modesty and delicacy which is the charm of domestic life" and thundered against their "unnatural" strength and appropriation of men's roles: "If the vine, whose strength and beauty is to lean upon the trellis-work and half conceal its clusters, thinks to assume the independence and the overshadowing nature of the elm, it will not only cease to bear fruit, but fall in shame and dishonor into the dust."[58] But the Grimkés continued to lecture. Early American feminists enjoyed quoting abolitionist Maria Weston Chapman's satiric verse rebuttal to the ministers

> Confusion has seized us, and all things go wrong,
> The women have leaped from "their spheres,"
> And, instead of fixed stars, shoot as comets along,
> And are setting the world by the ears!

. . . .
They've taken a notion to speak for themselves,
And are wielding the tongue and the pen;
They've mounted the rostrum; the termagent elves,
And—oh, horrid!—are talking to men!

. . . .
Our grandmothers' learning consisted of yore
In spreading their generous boards;
In twisting the distaff, or mopping the floor,
And *obeying the will of their lords.*
Now, misses may reason, and think, and debate,
Till unquestioned submission is quite out of date.[59]

By finding the strength to rebel against the conventional standards of domestic womanhood, radical feminists in the mid-nineteenth century resisted conservative male authority and refused the role of domestic angel and clinging vine. In so doing, they charted a new course for women in both Europe and the United States.

Three

Becoming Rebels

"I was a rebel at the age of five," the radical feminist Ernestine Rose liked to assert in the lecture tours that earned her the title "Queen of the Platform" in the United States before the Civil War.[1] The chief orator and linguist of the international women's movement, Rose excelled as a public speaker. "Her eloquence is irrestible," declared a reformer who heard her speak in England. "It shakes, it awes, it thrills, it melts—it fills you with horror and it drowns you in tears. I know not which predominates, intelligence or tenderness, knowledge or love; she excells in both."[2] In her numerous speeches Rose never detailed how she managed to rebel against a world that prized female deference and subordination, concentrating instead on the present and future of women's rights. But on a trip to Paris at the height of her career, she made contact with French feminist Jenny d'Héricourt and talked with her at length. The fullest description of Rose's early years, of how she recounted her passage away from conventional womanhood, comes from d'Héricourt's memoir of her, written shortly after their meeting in September 1856.[3]

At the time of their meeting, the two women were in their mid-forties, veterans of early socialist movements, and well-known in both international free thought and feminist circles. They got on well and published articles praising one another. Rose called d'Héricourt "a physician, a woman of noble character, great energy and talents; she is a thorough reformer, particularly for woman's rights and against priests and churches." D'Héricourt told her readers that "never was there a life more completely devoted to the triumph of progress than that of this admirable woman," Ernestine Rose, "so justly famous in the United States." D'Héricourt found Rose completely credible and without affectations. "She doesn't pretend because she has no desire to please, she has nothing to hide," the Frenchwoman wrote. "Her appearance conveys her personality: she neither conceals nor dyes her hair, which is beginning to grey."[4] When she confided in d'Héricourt, Rose presented her life as a series of difficult but successful rebellions against established authority.

Beginning at age five, when she first rebelled by refusing to return to a school that had punished her arbitrarily, Rose focused her account on her challenges to her father, the chief rabbi in a small Polish town. Never mentioning her mother, she portrayed a father both indulgent and harsh, a man who taught her Hebrew and allowed her to study the Bible (and did not make her return to the school she hated) but insisted that his only child "believe and obey." Although she admired her father's piety and learning, she continually questioned his practices and beliefs. He responded by telling her "little girls must not ask questions." In later life, Ernestine Rose dated her consciousness of women's oppression from these years, when she realized that unlike girls, little boys had more freedom to ask questions and study.

At twelve, she tested God's intentions. Convinced that a rational deity could not desire the rigorous enforcement of the Sabbath law that prevailed in her home and her community, she seized upon a saying that forbade any work, even to "breaking a piece of straw." Taking a stalk in her hands, she told God that she did not want to disobey him ("I would rather die") and asked that if the extreme interpretation of the Sabbath was indeed God's will, he would stop her from snapping the straw in two. When nothing happened, she broke the straw. In that moment, she broke with traditional religion and the God of her father, never even revealing the Hebrew names her parents gave her at birth. By age fourteen, she had ceased to believe in Judaism and refused to say the Jewish morning prayer, which calls for a woman to thank God "for having made me according to thy will," whereas a man thanks God "for not having made me a woman."[5]

Rose told d'Héricourt that her religious defiance led her father to betrothe her against her will when she was fifteen, in order to bind her "to the bosom of the synagogue by marriage." She begged her fiancé to release her, throwing herself weeping at his feet. Because she possessed a substantial inheritance from her recently deceased mother, her fiancé went to a Polish court to sue for possession of the dowry. In January 1826, when she was barely sixteen, she traveled alone by sleigh to the legal hearing. The night before she had to appear in court, the sleigh broke down and the driver went off to get help. "Wrapped in furs, the courageous child stayed alone from 11:30 at night until 4 in the morning in the midst of an immense plain of snow, listening to the howling of packs of famished wolves," recounted d'Héricourt. "The next morning she pleaded her case herself, winning by proving to the judges that it would do her no good to honor an engagement made against her will."[6]

The victory empowered her. On returning home, she discovered that her father had remarried a woman her own age—a situation she found intolerable. Using her mother's inheritance to finance her emancipation, she left her family, Poland, and the practice of Judaism forever. At seventeen she went to live in Berlin, and from then on she supported herself, making her way in the world alone.

Rose remained immensely proud of this success. At women's rights conventions, she told the story (modestly speaking of herself in the third person) to demonstrate that women could and should be lawyers, members of juries, and judges. Like d'Héricourt and other feminists, she continually insisted that her individual achievements proved the capacities of all women. As d'Héricourt wrote shortly after meeting Rose, "If I acquire any honor, I thus pay honor to women. I reveal their aptitudes."[7]

In Berlin, the young woman probably chose her new first names, Ernestine Louise; for her surname, she used both her parents' last names: Sigismund Potowski. Discovering that Polish Jews were an outcast group and could live in the city only if they had royal permission or found a Prussian citizen willing to post a bond for them, she obtained an audience with the king of Prussia, Frederick William III. The monarch suggested that she convert to Christianity, but Rose told d'Héricourt that she refused to abandon her principles. "If my reason prevents me from being Jewish, it cannot permit me to be Christian," she declared, and the king granted her permission to stay in Berlin. There for two years, she read widely ("not dead books, but living ones"), supporting herself with her inheritance and her invention of perfumed paper to deodorize rooms.[8]

She then traveled in Western Europe, reaching Paris shortly after the July revolution of 1830 that overthrew Charles X; she told d'Héricourt she had gone there because she believed "something could be done in France for the emancipation of women." Distracted later that summer by an uprising in Poland, Rose traveled eastward to take part in it. But afraid of being arrested by Austrian troops, she then retreated to London, where she lived for the next six years.

When the twenty-year-old Miss Sigismund Potowski arrived in London late in 1830, she became part of a constant flow of new inhabitants to the largest and most modern city in the world. Twice the size of Paris, five times as large as New York or Berlin, London was the swollen center of the world's first industrial society. Curious visitors came to see the probable future in the crowded, soot-grimed, gaslit streets of this "monster city," as Rose's contemporary, French socialist Flora Tristan, called it in 1840. Tristan, like many others, commented on the contrast between rich and poor, between "unbridled luxury" and "the hordes of pale, thin workers and the pitiful faces of their dirty, ragged children," present "in all great capital cities, but . . . more striking in London than anywhere else in the world."[9] In London, both Tristan and Rose rapidly made contact with groups attempting to reform such conditions.

As the center of the contradictions posed by industry and scientific progress, London attracted theorists and reformers, who saw modern change as the key to improving and transforming society. Overwhelming in its size and its complexity, London displayed the new age in all its splendor and squalor. Tristan described one of its sights as "the monumental chimneys belching their black smoke to the heavens to proclaim the existence of a host of mighty industries" and paid tribute to the metropolis's modernity:

> But it is especially at night that London should be seen; then, in the magic light of millions of gas-lamps, London is superb! Its broad streets stretch to infinity; its shops are resplendent with every masterpiece that human ingenuity can devise; its multitudes of men and women pass ceaselessly to and fro.[10]

Although Rose and Tristan narrowly missed meeting each other, they moved in the same London reform circles. Radical aristocrats and Quaker philanthropists, socialist artisans and working-class democrats, Unitarian ministers and utilitarian philosophers met to explore ways to improve society. There reformers discussed the expansion of democracy, the possibilities of socialism, the abolition of slavery, the need for education, and the eradication of poverty, crime, and warfare. For both Ernestine Rose and Flora Tristan, the most significant connection in this period was with the group that gathered to support the ideas of Robert Owen, a visionary manufacturer turned socialist.

By 1832, when Ernestine Rose met him, Owen was famous for his industrial success and notorious for his radical opinions. Rising from modest circumstances to riches, he built a model factory village at New Lanark, Scotland. Visitors thronged to his mill-town community, where Owen succeeded in increasing his profits while providing his workers with decent food and housing and educating all their children at his own expense. Convinced that if living and working conditions improved, "crimes would terminate, the miseries of humanity would cease, wealth and wisdom would be universal," Owen worked for legislation to regulate the factories.[11] When these efforts failed in the 1820s, he traveled throughout the United States, attempting to found model communities based on cooperation and equality. By then he had also become scandalous for his frequent denunciations of religion, which he considered "a mass of iniquitous error." Lucretia and James Mott were nearly expelled from their Philadelphia Quaker congregation simply for supporting the right to listen to the "Infidel Owenites."[12]

Rose participated in Owenite socialism during the years of its greatest extent and most radical actions. In the 1830s, the Owenites published a host of newspapers and books urging the transformation of society into egalitarian, cooperative communities, a system they named "communism" or "socialism."[13] They organized thousands of working-class men and women into the Grand National Consolidated Trades Union. When this umbrella labor organization collapsed under government repression, they opened numerous cooperative stores and labor exchanges. More than any other English reform group of their day, the Owenite socialites advocated female equality, welcomed women to their ranks, and encouraged them to write and speak for the cause. Ernestine Rose credited Owenism with providing her a platform in both its senses: the stage from which she made her first public speeches and a coherent set of beliefs she could support. "I stood on the women's rights platform before that name was known," she declared in 1854, "and twenty years ago I presided over an association for the protection of human rights which embraced all colors, and nations, and sects [the Owenite Association of All Classes of All Nations], and I stand on the same platform still."[14]

In the Owenite dedication to cooperation and equality, in its disavowal of traditional religion, and its insistence upon social utility and the greatest happiness of the greatest number, Rose found a spiritual home. Owenite socialism's "new moral world," with its absence of bigotry and superstition, its "friendship, and kindness, and charity for the Jew and Gentile," gave Rose a lifelong vision of a society in which "worship will consist in the practice of useful industry; in the acquisition of knowledge; in uniformly speaking the truth; and in the expression of joyous feelings which a life in accordance with nature and truth will be sure to produce."[15]

Owenite socialism also provided Rose and other women with a congenial milieu in which feminist ideas were seriously debated. At its most expansive, it included women as equals in its optimistic visions of the future. It supplied some women, like Rose, with platforms to speak from, meetings to attend, and newspapers to write in. But women's rights did not come first for either the paternalist Robert Owen or many of his followers, who preferred to see women continue to perform their traditional duties even within the movement's innovative socialist communes.[16] Rose told d'Héricourt that Owen had sometimes let her speak with him at his Sunday lectures, but she also explained that her speech came after "she had washed and put away with her own hands all the dishes used to prepare and serve tea" to the audience of 1,500.[17] In 1836, she and her new husband, William E. Rose, a twenty-three-year-old jeweller and fellow Owenite, decided to leave. The young couple sailed from England with a small Owenite colony bound for the United States but abandoned the group when they landed in New York City and began living on their own.

By the time she arrived in New York as a twenty-six-year-old bride, Ernestine Rose told d'Héricourt, "her existence had been defined: her mission was to emancipate thought, woman, and the slave."[18] Her first political act in the United States demonstrated that for her women now took precedence: she went door-to-door through lower Manhattan trying

to get signatures on a petition allowing wives to own property after marriage. A few months later, she was speaking throughout New York State
and within a few years, helped to create women's movements both in the
United States and internationally. In a speech given in 1856, shortly after
she had talked with d'Héricourt, Rose used the new perspective she had
gained through these movements to analyze and dramatize the struggles of
her early years. "We hear a great deal about the heroism of the battlefield,"
she declared. "What is it? Compare it with the heroism of woman who
stands up for the right and it sinks into utter insignificance." Praising her
audience for supporting the women's movement and so enabling it to
grow, Rose re-created her younger self as heroic, redefining traditional
heroism in the process.

> Who can tell the amount of moral courage and true heroism it required in
> her who first dared publicly to proclaim herself the co-equal of the lords of
> creation, and demand back her birthright they have so long unjustly
> usurped. . . . You cannot realize what it was 25 and 20 years ago to call public
> attention to these wrongs, and prepare the way . . . and yet woman had the
> moral courage to do it, and do it as fearlessly as now, for though she had
> nothing else to support her, she had the consciousness of possessing the
> *might of right* to sustain her.[19]

A confident, respected public figure when she recounted her past,
Ernestine Rose may well have projected qualities and views she developed
as an adult backward upon her early years, making herself appear more
eloquent, more rational, more independent than she actually was. And yet
her account of her development rings true, in tune with both the era and
the testimonies of other key women in the international women's movement. Rose's passage to feminism mirrors that of many of her coworkers.
Although her life differed in some respects from theirs—her Polish Jewish
background and the extent of her early travels—the similarities far outweighed the differences. In her social class and position within the family,
her marriage and motherhood, the importance of religion in her development, and her involvement in a radical organization, Rose's life provides
the overall pattern of how women became able to rebel against their traditional roles.

Most of these female rebels came from the same historical cohort as
Ernestine Rose, born between 1801 and 1819.[20] Rose and the others constituted a postrevolutionary generation, overshadowed by the great democratic struggles of the immediate past. The American and French
Revolutions, the titanic rise and fall of Napoleon Bonaparte, and the new
Romantic visions of art and life provided a mixed legacy for younger
women. The public struggles had been waged by men and their outcomes
created a public realm that was almost exclusively masculine. Women fig-
ured chiefly as symbols of the modern nation, like Britannia, Columbia,
Germania, or Marianne. A few achieved the status of minor heroines on

the revolutionary periphery, like Charlotte Corday or Molly Pitcher. But the revolutionary era in the Western world also provided heroic female examples for nineteenth-century girls to emulate. "The history of our first great revolution [of 1789] is ringed by a dazzling halo of the memory of the great number of women who honored their sex and their fatherland," Jeanne Deroin asserted in an argument for women's equal rights in 1848.[21]

The great majority of women who became rebels against conventional womanhood were daughters of conventional mothers who sought to make them into angels in the home. Unwilling to be limited to this role, these women's first rebellion was against their mothers' conventional values. As an example of how she "spontaneously" developed a "love of independence and feminine dignity" when she was "about fifteen," Suzanne Voilquin described how she rejected the values of her "silent and submissive mother . . . the Christian wife of the Middle Ages." When her mother urged acquiescence to her father's rudeness, explaining "where the nanny goat is tied, there she will have to graze," Voilquin reported that she replied,

> "No, no the goat can break her rope and go graze elsewhere." Although I could not sense the whole import of my act, my mother was terrified by this repartee in a child of fifteen. . . . After that altercation, our roles changed; my mother depended on me to gain respect for her sweet, weak nature.[22]

Only three of the women in this cohort—Jenny d'Héricourt, Pauline Roland, and Lucretia Mott—praised their mothers for their strength and enterprise. Mott's mother, an independent Nantucket whaler's wife, managed her family, home, and shop alone while her husband was at sea. D'Héricourt's mother moved her children to Paris after her husband's death to send them to better schools; Roland's mother assumed her deceased husband's position as head of the local post office. Most of the women who wrote about their childhood edited their mothers out of their lives and, like Ernestine Rose, wrote only about their fathers.

Unwilling to follow their own mothers and rejected as equals by their fathers, women like Rose searched—both in their mother's generation and in earlier eras—for unconventional foremothers. Their writings abound with strong female figures drawn from literature and history, cited to justify their own rebellion. Significant women from the Bible, like Deborah and Priscilla, influential medieval figures like Joan of Arc and Margrethe of Denmark, and powerful queens from earlier centuries, like Elizabeth of England and Isabella of Castile, inspired them throughout their lives. In their speeches and writings, they attempted to make their audiences aware of strong women forgotten by history. In an 1850 oration, for instance, Ernestine Rose exhorted her listeners not to forget the "Pilgrim Mothers. Did they not endure as many perils, encounter as many hardships, and do as much to form and fashion the institutions of New England as the Pilgrim Fathers?" In her Seneca Falls speech of July 1848, Elizabeth Cady

Stanton paid tribute to "the brave, intelligent and proudhearted Tinga, the negro Queen of Angola," as well as the more familiar European heroines, to demonstrate women's capacity for government.[23]

Of all the women this cohort admired, whose example excited their youthful imaginations, two stand out. When they needed examples of successful, unconventional women to emulate, early international feminists turned to two authors from the revolutionary generation preceding theirs: French intellectual and salonière Germaine de Staël (1766-1817) and English radical Mary Wollstonecraft (1759-1797).

"The shining names of famous women have cast light upon the path of our sex," American intellectual Margaret Fuller wrote in 1845, declaring that in de Staël's case, her "beams make the obscurest school-house in New England warmer and lighter to the little rugged girls who are gathered together on its wooden bench."[24] Throughout the Western community in this era, women who resisted domesticity invoked de Staël. As the leader of the moral and intellectual opposition to Napoleon Bonaparte, de Staël claimed the authority of the Romantic artist ("the unacknowledged legislators of the world" as the poet Shelley called them) for women. The daughter of Louis XVI's reformist finance minister and an eminent salonière, de Staël remained politically and sexually active during the very period when public pressure forced many women of her rank and status to retreat to the home. Her clashes with Napoleon became legendary. From the moment he declared himself consul for life, she attacked him as a tyrant in her writings and in the opposition salon she led. Refusing to kowtow, she saw herself and portrayed the heroines of her novels, *Corinne* and *Delphine*, as having the artistic genius to inspire social change.

In 1803, Napoleon confirmed de Staël's importance by singling her out for exile. She retaliated by continuing to oppose his regime, by meeting with his opponents, and by publishing pieces denouncing him. In 1811, he ordered the entire printing of her book on German Romanticism destroyed, seeing it as the source of powerful opposition to his empire. Forced to flee before Napoleon's armies in 1812, de Staël achieved her greatest triumph when she returned to Paris after his final defeat at Waterloo three years later. "Madame de Staël has reached the fulfillment of her dreams," a friend wrote in 1817, "her house is the most brilliant of all Paris and is as influential as she wishes to make it. . . . But her health is very poor." De Staël died at fifty of a stroke a few days later.[25]

"What a magnificent creature that mortal was!" Elizabeth Cady Stanton wrote her cousin in 1853. "How I do love that woman!"[26] Rebellious girls of the postrevolutionary generation "read for hope," as Elizabeth Barrett Browning put it in her 1856 feminist poem, *Aurora Leigh*.[27] They loved and identified with the male Romantic poets—Byron, Shelley, Goethe, and Schiller—but only Germaine de Staël provided them with a passionate and formidable female model of artistic opposition to the dominant culture of womanly domesticity. This was ironic, since De Staël never championed the rights of women in general; she saw herself as a great exception to the rules that bound other women.

After de Staël, the woman of the previous generation most admired by female rebels was English radical Mary Wollstonecraft. Her feminist treatise of 1792, *A Vindication of the Rights of Woman*, expanded the French Revolution's claims for the rights of man to include woman and argued that with decent education, women's equality to men would be undeniable. Lucretia Mott, Elizabeth Cady Stanton, Mathilde Franziska Anneke, Flora Tristan, and others championed Wollstonecraft and her book; Stanton placed her at the head of the list of women "whose earnest lives and fearless words, in demanding political rights for women," had inspired the 1881 *History of Woman Suffrage*.[28]

But Wollstonecraft left a difficult legacy. Associated with the most radical phase of the French Revolution, besmirched by her illegitimate daughter and her out-of-wedlock liaisons with men, Wollstonecraft's name was frequently "cast out as evil," as Mott complained. De Staël's aristocracy, her marriage, and her prestige somewhat protected her from similar criticism. But Wollstonecraft remained a pariah throughout the nineteenth century. "The reputation of this book [the *Vindication*] inspires such fear that if you so much as mention its name, even to so-called 'progressive' women, they will recoil in horror and exclaim, 'Oh, but that is an *evil* book!'" Flora Tristan complained when she had difficulty finding a copy of it in London of the late 1830s.[29] Wollstonecraft and de Staël provided heroic but controversial models for women of the postrevolutionary generation.

The twenty core women of the early international feminist movement came not only from the same generation but also from the same social stratum—the middle class, where the new model of womanhood held greatest sway. Only two Frenchwomen in the group, Suzanne Voilquin and Jeanne Deroin, were from the working class. Deroin wrote that "when she was too young to appreciate her social position" she dreamed of a brilliant future. But by her early teens "the necessity of labor" led her to understand "without money, I had to give up."[30] All the others, like Rose, came from homes in which women did not have to earn income—the dividing line between working- and middle-class lives for women in this period. Five grew up in wealthy circumstances, in large homes that employed many servants. The rest came from the growing middle class: the social milieu in which girls' and boys' lives differed the most from each other.

When they looked back on their childhood, many future women's rights advocates, like Ernestine Rose, relived their rage at being denied an education. Especially when they learned alongside boys in the primary grades, girls who excelled deeply resented not being able to continue their studies. "*We accomplished the same as boys and more*," Louise Otto asserted in a memoir. Educated equally with boys until the age of religious confirmation at

fourteen, Otto persuaded her parents to give her an extra year of schooling, but that was all they allowed her. "The wish was granted, but in 1834
[when she was fifteen], I still felt very bad about leaving school," she
remembered almost fifty-five years later.

> I was always angered when boys elevated themselves above us and looked
> down on us disdainfully because we were not allowed to learn many things
> which for them were deemed indispensible, or when they jeered at us that
> now after confirmation we no longer needed to think or to do anything
> except busy ourselves haphazardly with housework and needlework, go for
> walks and play the great lady![31]

Otto was the youngest of four girls, and Rose was an only child. The
disparity in education was even more galling for girls who saw their brothers provided with the schooling denied them. In this era, very few girls
could obtain even a high school education comparable to their brothers'.
No college in the Western world admitted women until the late 1830s,
and opportunities remained extremely limited into the twentieth century.
In a number of cases, early international feminists went on to found institutions to provide the next generation of young women with the education
they felt cheated of. Barbara Leigh Smith Bodichon, for instance, had
been educated equally along with her brothers by a teacher her father
imported from Owen's New Lanark school. But at eighteen, her younger
brother Ben went off to college at Cambridge, an impossibility for her.
She later wrote that this exclusion convinced her to fight for higher education for women—a promise fulfilled when she helped to establish Girton
College for women at Cambridge in 1869.[32]

The American feminist Elizabeth Cady Stanton recalled trying to take
her only brother's place when he died just after graduating from college.
Then eleven years old, she resolved "to study and strive to be at the head
of all my classes and thus delight my father's heart." Learning Latin,
Greek, and mathematics, while also becoming an expert horsewoman, she
found herself in the double bind that confronted female talent in that era.
The more girls achieved, the less "feminine" they became. Public achievement was considered appropriate only for men; women who succeeded in
this way were seen as masculine. In Stanton's case, the day she won second
prize in Greek at her school she ran to her father's legal office to bring it to
him. "Then, while I stood looking and waiting for him to say something
which would show that he recognized the equality of the daughter with the
son," she recalled, "he kissed me on the forehead and exclaimed, with a
sigh, 'Ah, you should have been a boy!'"[33] Many early feminists recalled
similar experiences.[34]

Pursuing the achievements and skills associated with boyhood could
provide the girls who became feminists with the independence and
strength of character necessary to avoid a completely domestic life. Ten
of the eighteen core women whose birth order is known were oldest

daughters or only children. Like Ernestine Rose and Elizabeth Cady Stanton, some functioned as their father's surrogate son during part of their childhood, learning subjects normally not taught to girls. Before her father's death when she was eight, for instance, Jenny d'Héricourt boasted that she "had progressed in arithmetic as far as fractions, could speak of the Greek and Roman great characters [which she would not have been taught at school and probably learned at home from her father], and knew by heart the fables of Lafontaine and several chapters of the New Testament."[35]

Paradoxically, the early death of an encouraging father could strengthen a girl's will and determination to succeed. Like d'Héricourt, the American feminist Paulina Wright Davis paid tribute to her father in later life for his love, truthfulness, and confidence in her abilities. Although he died after being thrown from a horse when she was eleven, he promised her he would be her "guardian spirit" and for decades she "had only to close my eyes to the outward and he was with me."[36] Some of the eight future feminists whose fathers died young were inspired by the growing independence of their mothers: Davis remembered her widowed mother taking up bookkeeping to support the family. Others, like Ernestine Rose or Louise Otto, were left a legacy by a parent's death, which they used to finance their independence. The early death of a father could plunge his family into poverty, exposing the precariousness of middle-class status and leading women to further question their prescribed domestic role.

"Who are these women? what do they want? what are the motives that impell them to this course of action?" asked the *New York Herald* in 1852 after the Third National Woman's Rights Convention in Syracuse. The *Herald* answered its own questions by calling the womanhood of feminists into doubt:

> The *dramatis personae* of the farce enacted at Syracuse present a curious conglomeration of both sexes. Some of them are old maids, whose personal charms were never very attractive, and who have been sadly slighted by the masculine gender in general; some of them women who have been badly mated . . . and they are therefore down upon the whole of the opposite sex; some, having so much of the virago in their disposition, that nature seems to have made a mistake in their gender—mannish women, like hens that crow; some of boundless vanity and egoism, who believe that they are superior in intellectual ability.[37]

The lives of the twenty core women shatter these stereotypes. They married in rates comparable to others in their class and age-group: 70 percent once and 20 percent for a second time. Many made extremely happy marriages to men who shared and supported their advocacy of women's rights.[38] Ernestine Rose "has a husband whom she loves tenderly and by whom she is tenderly loved," reported d'Héricourt in 1856, when the Roses had been married twenty years. The couple both worked at their Manhattan jewelry store, traveled together in the United States and abroad, and sang duets before radical gatherings. William Rose financed his wife's lecture tours, freeing her to speak for the causes they both supported. When he died in 1882, after forty-five years of marriage, a friend found her "very brave but very heartbroken at the loss of her faithful partner."[39]

At least eight other radical feminists also formed happy, egalitarian unions with men who shared their convictions. Lucretia Mott, like Ernestine Rose, remained in love with her husband of fifty-six years, lamenting each night they had to spend apart. "In the true marriage relationship, the independence of the husband and wife is equal," she wrote frequently on wedding cards and in marriage books, "their dependence mutual, and their obligations reciprocal."[40] Louise Otto and Bessie Rayner Parkes each made passionate love matches in their late thirties, which were then cut short by their husbands' untimely deaths. Parkes's close friend, Barbara Leigh Smith, created an unconventional but contented marriage with French Algerian doctor Eugene Bodichon. The couple spent winters in North Africa and summers in England. Paulina Wright Davis chose happily twice. At twenty she married a Utica merchant, Francis Wright, and at thirty-six, four years after her first husband's death, she wed Providence congressman Thomas Davis.

Harriet Taylor Mill, Louise Aston, and Matilde Franziska Anneke found happiness in their second marriage, but their unhappy first marriages certainly contributed to their passage toward feminism. "After the conclusion of an unhappy divorce trial of my first marriage, in which I was the victim of Prussian justice, I came into the consciousness and to the knowledge that the position of women was absurd," Anneke wrote in an autobiographical letter when she was sixty. "I soon began to do as much as I could, in words and print, for the spiritual and moral betterment of women."[41] Suzanne Voilquin took a similar path—her unhappy marriage contributed substantially to her consciousness of women's general oppression.

Of the six core women in the international movement who never married, at least three did so by choice. Swedish author Fredrika Bremer turned down three marriage proposals in order to pursue her career as a writer. In Germany, Malwida von Meysenbug considered marrying Julius Froebel, a radical who invited her to become his wife in exile in the United States, but she decided to attend the women's college in Hamburg instead. Pauline Roland, the French feminist, refused to marry on socialist principle but bore four children to two different fathers when she was in her early thirties.[42] Victorian reticence surrounds the lives of the three other unmarried feminists. Virtually nothing is known of the German Louise Dittmar's private life, and Englishwomen Anne Knight and Harriet Martineau left few clues about why they never married.

The only demographic difference between these feminists and other women was that they raised fewer children. It is not known if any had access to contraceptive devices or information. Half of the cohort of twenty had no children. In some cases this was not by choice. Ernestine Rose bore and nursed two babies who died very young. Anneke gave birth to seven children, one in her first marriage and six between 1848 and 1855 in her second; the two youngest were twin girls. But only three survived. Two died in infancy and two, including one twin, died in childhood of smallpox because their father refused to have them vaccinated. Only Stanton, with seven, and Mott, with five, matched the large families of the era, when the average woman bore eight children, five of whom survived. No other woman active in international feminism had more than three living children. Having fewer children made it easier for early feminists to leave home and travel, but it was not a factor in forming their beliefs.

Did women rebel against their conventional roles because "their personal charms were never very attractive," as the *Herald* put it? Although feminists certainly resented a culture that judged women solely on appearance, photographs of them do not portray an ill-favored group. Harriet Taylor Mill was considered a great beauty, but such judgments inevitably reflected the viewer's prejudices. Carl Schurz, Fritz Anneke's commander in the Baden uprising, remembered Mathilde Franziska Anneke on horseback by her husband's side in 1848 as "a still young woman [she was thirty-one] of remarkable beauty, much spirit, great kindheartedness, poetic fiery patriotism." A hostile observer found the identical scene grotesque and comical, describing Anneke as "an apparition . . . in a black riding habit, wearing dark glasses like a blind person, pistols in her belt" and pitying the Baden soldiers for having to march behind this mannish "Amazon."[43] Women who crossed gender lines by performing actions associated with men or by wearing male clothing were almost automatically perceived as ugly. But mannishness, like beauty, is usually in the eye of the beholder. "I received many fancy sketches of those monstrous women who met at Worcester to talk about their rights and wrongs," Englishwoman Marianne Finch wrote about her visit to the United States in 1851.

> In spite of myself I found their president (Mrs. Paulina Davis) fixed in my mind, as a coarse, masculine, overbearing, disagreeable person; with a dirty house, a neglected family, and a hen-pecked husband. Being unexpectedly introduced to her, *I was prepared* for anything monstrous, but to find Mrs. Davis, a fair, delicate-looking woman, with gentle manners, and a low voice, which she uses sparingly, completely set at nought all my pre-conceived notions.[44]

For her part, Davis consciously dressed and acted to counter the stereotype. "I am determined to do my utmost to remove the idea that all women's rights women are horrid old frights with beards and mustaches," she wrote Elizabeth Cady Stanton the year after Finch's visit.[45]

Calling a woman "mannish" or "masculine" in the mid-nineteenth century often meant only that she performed actions designated appropriate for men, like achieving literary success or demanding the vote. Thus French writer George Sand was seen both as notorious for her romances with men and as "masculine" for conducting her sexual life freely, as men did. Her literary achievements conveyed masculinity to even the most sympathetic contemporaries. "Thou large-brained woman and large-hearted man, /Self-called George Sand!" began one of Elizabeth Barrett's two sonnets about the French author. The English poet resolved the contradictions Sand posed to appropriate womanly behavior by portraying her as a bodiless angel, "unsexed" by God "on the heavenly shore, /Where unincarnate spirits purely aspire."[46] Although every mid-nineteenth century feminist had to deal with society's view that she became "unwomanly" by demanding rights associated with men, none had to face the twentieth-century assumption that most feminists are lesbians, defined as women motivated primarily by their desire to have sex with other women.

For much of the nineteenth century, romantic female friendships formed an important part of many women's lives. Women sent each other passionate love letters, hugged and kissed, walked hand in hand, spent weeks in each other's company, often sleeping in the same bed, and remained lifelong confidants, all while staying well within the bounds of appropriate womanly behavior. The accepted range of physical affection between female friends was far wider than in later eras.[47] Mathilde Franziska Anneke, for instance, estranged from her husband after their children died from smallpox, formed a passionate attachment to a Milwaukee friend, Mary Booth. The two women and their children lived together from 1860 to 1865 in Zurich, relishing each other's company and exchanging passionate love notes. You are "the morning-star of my soul, the beautiful, auroral glow of my heart; the saintly lily of my dream, the deep dark rosebud unfolding in my bosom day by day, sweetening my life with your ethereal fragrance," went one that Anneke kept all her life and left to her children.[48] Fritz Anneke corresponded amicably with both women throughout their time together, not because he was a complacent husband but because the relationship was seen by all as unexceptional and respectable. When Mary Booth died in 1865, Mathilde Anneke returned to her husband and her feminist activities in Milwaukee.

Anneke's romantic friendship with Booth did not play a part in her initial rebellion against a conventional woman's life; that came as a result of her unhappy first marriage and divorce. Ernestine Rose never spoke of female friends before her time in the women's movement. In general, women made friends after they joined movements instead of being led by friendships into movements. But there was one important exception. The two younger English feminists, Bessie Rayner Parkes and Barbara Leigh Smith Bodichon, met in their late teens, in the mid-1840s. Their close friendship certainly contributed to their ability to reject the view that "women, in the ordinary cant of the day, are supposed to have a mission," that women are "angels by nature," as Parkes wrote sarcastically at nineteen in 1848.[49]

Parkes and Bodichon came from wealthy, radical families who for generations had challenged the political and religious status quo. Bodichon's father, Benjamin Leigh Smith, sat in parliament as a radical from 1838 to 1847, supported a variety of liberal causes, admired Robert Owen, and never married his children's mother, making Bodichon and her siblings a "taboo'd family" in Victorian England.[50] Bodichon's first cousin, reknowned nurse Florence Nightingale, acknowledged their connection only after both had became public personages in the 1850s.

Parkes's grandfather was the radical scientist and theologian Joseph Priestley, who had emigrated to Pennsylvania in 1794 after an English mob destroyed his house and laboratory because of his support for the French Revolution. Parkes's father, a progressive attorney and political organizer in England, provided his daughter with a good education. Both parents kept a watchful eye over her, which led Parkes to admire "those free wild spirits the Smiths always seem to have, how glorious to feel them rush in one's own heart" and to credit Barbara with having "*stirred*" her up.[51] Spurring on each other's rebellious spirits and confirming each other's discontent, the two friends began to widen their circles. "I like to herd with the cracked," Bodichon declared to an aunt in 1859, "such as A.M.H. [Anna Mary Howitt, artist daughter of reformers William and Mary Howitt] and B.R.P. [Bessie Rayner Parkes]—queer Americans, democrats, socialists, artists, poor devils or angels; and am never happy in an English genteel family life."[52]

Abetting each other's rejection of conventional womanhood, Parkes and Bodichon expanded their friendship networks in the mid-1850s, as they created a woman's movement in England and linked up with their counterparts abroad. An early connection with the Anglo-American doctor Elizabeth Blackwell led them first to consider medical education for women and later to financially support Blackwell's New York clinic for women. Blackwell, the first women to earn an M.D. degree in the nineteenth century, cherished the "lifelong friendship" that began when Parkes and Bodichon called on her "one dull afternoon, in my bare lodging-house drawing room" shortly after her arrival in London in 1850. "My young friends hung my dull rooms with their charming paintings [Bodichon was an artist], made them gay with flowers and welcomed me to their family circles with the heartiest hospitality." When Blackwell returned to New York, Parkes wrote a poem about their friendship ("Fond memory of that first hour I have kept"), and the Englishwomen shared her letters and longed for "news of her *life*," as Parkes wrote Bodichon in 1852. "Such a noble letter [from Blackwell]," Parkes continued, "is it not beautiful for you and I to have this streak of sunshine in our misty American landscape. Are not all good friendships and intimate knowledges, streaks of bright sunshine in a misty, doubtful world!"[53]

Unusual for finding a kindred feminist spirit in each other while still in their teens, Parkes and Bodichon were also unusual in their religious upbringing. Both of them, like Harriet Martineau and Harriet Taylor Mill, were raised as Unitarians, the most rationalist denomination in Christendom. Unitarians, who "look upon this world as a place of education," as the influential Boston minister William Ellery Channing put it, had no general creed, confident that reason and conscience would lead to religious truth.[54] Distinguished by their refusal to worship the Christian Trinity of Father, Son, and Holy Ghost, Unitarians were considered radical and unorthodox, at the outer margin of acceptable religious belief. Their expansive views enabled women like Martineau and Mill, Parkes and Bodichon to speculate about what women's role in "this God's world" should be. "I do think so *totally* differently from all about me, and so must you except your Father and the Howitts that I sometimes feel quite mystified." In 1849 Parkes wrote Bodichon that "I go farther and farther every year, you know I began in many ways much more conservative than you; year by year conventual scales seem to fall from my eyes. I wonder what they will come to; I pray God they may become *quite* free."[55]

Unitarianism was the only existing religion in the early nineteenth century that supported and encouraged nontraditional roles for women. In both old and New England, a few male Unitarian ministers voiced doctrines and sponsored activities that enabled some rebellious women to move away from domesticity. Radical English clergyman W. J. Fox, for instance, published both Harriet Martineau's and Harriet Taylor's first writings in his *Monthly Repository* and introduced the dissatisfied Taylor to her future second husband, Utilitarian philosopher John Stuart Mill. Lucretia Mott, a Quaker minister in an increasingly conservative church, took lifelong inspiration from Channing's "liberal creed" that "our duty is not limited to our own particular sphere," that the moral individual must take action in an unjust world.[56] Barbara Bodichon declared that the sermon she heard Unitarian minister Theodore Parker give in Boston in 1858, in which "he prayed to the Creator, the infinite Mother of us all (always using Mother instead of Father in this prayer) . . . was the prayer of all I ever heard in my life which was truest to my individual soul."[57]

Such beliefs set Unitarians apart. Of the key women in international feminism, only a few raised as Unitarians were able to remain comfortably within their original religion. All the others abandoned the faith in which they had been raised. Whether Roman Catholic like Voilquin, Deroin, and Anneke, Lutheran like Aston, Otto, and Bremer, Presbyterian like Stanton and Davis, or Calvinist like d'Héricourt, to a woman they rejected traditional creeds. Even Quakers Anne Knight and Lucretia Mott found themselves considered heretical at times for their radical politics and social activism. However, the dissident Hicksite branch of Quakerism Mott adhered to did advocate women's rights and produced many feminists in the northeastern United States. Ernestine Rose was the only Jew among this cohort, but her passionate struggle against religious orthodoxy mirrored those of many others. "Above all else, God and religion seized my attention," remembered Jeanne Deroin of her Catholic childhood in Napoleon's Paris. But by her twenties, she had come to see "all religions as a tissue of absurdities invented to enslave the human race, which the laws make a weapon in the hands of the powerful of the earth to oppress the weak and which only serves to legitimize the injustices of the strong."[58]

Such views ran directly counter to the spirit of an age in which religion remained crucially important, especially for women. The two decades from 1810 to 1830, when these future activists received their religious training, witnessed a resurgence of belief throughout the Western community. In France and the German states, piety focused on the traditional Catholic and Protestant churches. In Great Britain and the United States, charismatic preachers and huge revival meetings brought tens of thousands to a heightened sense of their own lives as Christians, whom Jesus would personally save. "It almost seemed to me as if all Hell was let loose for my destruction and all Heaven for my conversion," a sixteen-year-old New Jersey girl wrote in her 1828 diary after six weeks of intense church-going. Women became the majority of churchgoers in this period throughout the United States and Europe. "The female breast is the natural soil of Christianity," Dr. Benjamin Rush concluded, expressing a popular view of the day.[59]

This shift had important political implications, especially in Europe. In the United States, the Christian revivalism known as the Second Great Awakening was connected to the upsurge of populist democracy affirmed by the success of the American Revolution. Being religious did not necessarily imply any particular political or class outlook, and a wide variety of denominations flourished in this period as the state churches of the colonial period lost their privileges in the new American republic.[60] But throughout Europe and the British Isles, religions remained established, supported by laws and taxes. "You know that in England the Sovereign is the head of the Church, and that the Church looks upon the Protestant religion as it is established as the State religion," King Leopold of Belgium wrote his niece, the future Queen Victoria.[61] Those not members of the official church suffered legal penalties ranging from special fees to denial of the vote and access to education and the professions. Penalties against non-Anglican Protestants—the Dissenters—and Roman Catholics stayed in place until the late 1820s in England. In Ireland, the Anglican Church remained established until 1869; penalties against Jews in Britain held until 1858.

Established religions everywhere continued to provide the only source of schooling and charity, the only agency that married people and buried them. Children were classified at birth by denomination, and denominational records remain the chief source of census information in both Europe and the United States into the late nineteenth century. When Mathilde and Fritz Anneke declared on their son's Cologne birth certificate in July 1848 that the father was Protestant, the mother Catholic, but the child was "without religion," they committed a revolutionary act of defiance against a society that still considered state, church, and personal identity to be intrinsically connected.

In France, the Roman Catholic Church was outlawed during the most revolutionary years of the 1790s. Its restoration confirmed the triumph of conservatism both in France and throughout Europe. But the same era that saw the resurgence and reestablishment of traditional religions in Europe was also the period in which women became "the sole consolation of the church," as a French bishop put it in the late 1820s.[62] The result was that women in general became identified both with traditional values and the counterrevolutionary status quo. Many families, especially in Catholic societies, divided politically and religiously along gender lines. Typically, men had revolutionary, radical, and anticlerical convictions; women often remained traditionalists and churchgoers. Suzanne Voilquin, for instance, remembered her "extremely revolutionary" father "smiling" at her mother's and sisters' "extreme devotion." "My mother . . . never argued with anything the church had proscribed; she believed in it and I imitated her. Nothing appeared more beautiful in my eyes than the ceremonies of the Catholic worship."[63]

Rejecting all this proved immensely difficult. Mid-nineteenth-century society still penalized men who voiced their religious disbelief. George Jacob Holyoake, the radical English editor who published Rose, d'Héricourt, and Parkes, served six months in prison for blasphemy in 1842. Even cultures that did not prosecute freethinkers excluded them from community life. Some delegates to the first convention of the Infidel Society for the Promotion of Mental Liberty in New York City in 1845 insisted on keeping their names secret because "their wives and their children depend [on them] for bread."[64]

In addition, many equated lack of belief in traditional religion with immorality. "An atheist can have no sense of duty," Italian revolutionary Guiseppe Mazzini asserted in midcentury.[65] Such prejudices fell especially heavily on women, who were supposed to incarnate religious devotion. Ernestine Rose told Jenny d'Héricourt that "because she did not accept the creeds of the churches...she was called an Atheist, a dangerous woman, a hellish spirit, and a paper of Bangor, Maine, stated that it would be shameful to listen to this woman, '*a thousand time below a prostitute*.'"[66] Even those sympathetic to women's rights had difficulty with a woman who rejected traditional religion. "You can have no idea what excitement Harriet Martineau's book [professing atheism] is making," English reformer Mary Howitt wrote her sister in 1851. "It is, to my mind, the most awful book that was ever written by a woman." Martineau lost a number of her female friends because of her defense of atheism; a male neighbor wrote that if he "were a bachelor or had no daughters" he could continue to "enjoy her society, but I should not like my daughters subjected to the censures that would be sure to follow them if we kept up intimacy after her announcement of such opinions as that book contains."[67] Those hostile to female emancipation reacted more harshly. Berlin magistrates exiled Louise Aston in 1846 in part because of her religious disbelief. Why does the state insist that women, but not men, continue to uphold religion? Anneke wrote the next year. "Because the truth frees us from the deceptive delusion that up above we will be rewarded for our love and pain, our enduring and serving; because it brings us to the recognition that we have equal rights to life's pleasures as our oppressors."[68]

Rejecting traditional religion caused these girls and women especial pain because it also meant rejecting their mothers' way of life. Not worshiping with one's family, refusing to join a congregation, pray, or take Communion were public acts that isolated female rebels. The most severe and difficult disapproval they faced came from their own families, not society at large. Malwida von Meysenbug, for instance, found that when she declared her lack of belief in God in her twenties, "The other members of the family shunned me and looked on me as a lost soul. . . . I was intentionally allowed to hear remarks like the following, which was made of a young girl, '*What a loveable creature! She does not pretend to have opinions of her own.*' They wanted to let me know how far I had strayed from the proper path."[69] The tensions caused by rejecting religion often led first to despair. "From earliest youth, existence seemed only a torment to me," remembered the German Louise Dittmar in the first publication to which she dared sign her name. "Life revolted me and only death seemed to provide deliverance from everything. And I admit that the same anger I felt against religion, which I considered the chief cause of all darkness, I also nourished against the male sex, which I saw only as the oppressor of the female."[70]

Like Ernestine Rose, the women who went on to create the international movement usually broke with their religion because of its limited views of women's role. Fredrika Bremer wrote a bitter dialogue after hearing a bishop's sermon on "Woman's Noble and Humble Mission," which asserted that even when women were correct, they must defer to men:

Man, with head erect, striking his breast proudly with his
    hand: "*I!*"
Woman: "Thou!"
Man: "*I will!*"
Woman: "Oh, very well!"
Man: "*Go.*"
Woman goes.
Man: "*Come back.*"

She comes back.
Man: "*Be merry*."
Woman dies.[71]

The solution Bremer and her coworkers found was to abandon traditional religion. Claiming more for women and worshiping in conventional
churches proved completely incompatible for them. Every key woman in
the international women's movement left religious orthodoxy behind. Six
became atheists like Rose, but most ended up in what they called free religion. "My free church, the one I believe in and am searching for and in
which I already live and worship in the depth of my soul," wrote Bremer
near the end of her life,

> is one in which disagreement concerning certain dogma and liturgical forms
> do not separate those who are united in the same exultant love. In the chan-
> cel of my church Fénélon and Channing, François de Sales and Hermann
> Francke, Hildebrand and Luther, Washington and Vinet, St. Birgetta and
> Florence Nightingale will pray and praise together; yes, from its wide aisles
> nobody is left out, who has seriously searched for and loved the highest
> good, that person may be called either Laotsee, Zarathustra, Buddha,
> Socrates or Spinoza![72]

As free religionists and freethinkers, Unitarians and atheists, these
rebels found that the fortitude gained by leaving traditional worship
enabled them to go on to reject other conventional roles for women. "Far
from returning to the proper path," remembered von Meysenbug of the
years when her family censured her, "I occupied myself more and more
with the idea of the emancipation of woman; emancipation from the prejudices which had hitherto bound her, to the untrammelled development
of her capacities and to the free exercise of reason, as had long been granted to man."[73]

The experience of rebellion gave these women the courage of their own
convictions. The next step was to join with others, to find a compatible
group that supported unorthodox beliefs, as Rose had found in the
Owenites. First in radical socialist, religious, and antislavery groups, later
in movements of their own, feminists made the connections and forged
the links necessary to create an international women's movement.

Four

First Connections

The June 15, 1833, issue of Robert Owen's socialist journal, the *Crisis*, featured a powerful feminist appeal. Insisting that demands for political equality and economic justice had to include women, the anonymous author forcefully sketched female oppression to argue her case:

> Is our condition as women so happy that there is nothing left for us to *desire* or *demand*? Up to the present hour, have not women through all past ages been degraded, oppressed, and made the *property* of men? *This property in women*, and the consequent tyranny it engenders, ought now to cease. Without . . . the most blind and barbarous injustice, one half the human race cannot be made *the servants of the other*.

Urging women not to marry unless their husbands agreed to share their rights, the author demanded "*equal marriage laws*—preferring infinitely a state of celibacy to *one of slavery*." The piece entreated women to organize in "*one solid union*. Let us no longer form two camps—that of the women of the people, and that of the women of the privileged class. Let our *common interest* unite us to obtain this great end," defined as "*liberty* and *equality* . . . the free and equal chance of developing *all our faculties*."[1]

This French "Call to Women" had first appeared fourteen months earlier in the Paris newspaper produced by female socialists who identified themselves as the "New Women" ("*femmes nouvelles*").[2] The *Crisis* printed an augmented English version of it because an associate of Robert Owen's, the Irish feminist Anna Wheeler, considered it significant enough to translate, to add her own passages to it, and to arrange for its publication. Read in London by John Stuart Mill, Harriet Martineau, and Ernestine Rose, the paper circulated to radicals in North America and Europe as well as throughout the British Isles. By publishing the New Women's feminist declaration in the *Crisis*, Wheeler ensured that it reached English-speaking progressives on both sides of the Atlantic.

The "Call" of these French socialist feminists affirmed solidarity with all women, attempted to enlist them in a worldwide struggle for justice, and portrayed the women's movement as a single, global cause. "At a time when all peoples rise up in the name of Liberty, when the proletarian demands his freedom, shall we women remain passive?" it asked, answering its own question with the assertion that women must unite to work for their own "social emancipation." By broadcasting this resounding appeal, Wheeler and the French feminists helped create an international women's movement. "The age of universal association is beginning. . . . and the moment has come for woman to have her place within it," the "Call" proclaimed.[3]

This international women's movement did not arise because aggrieved feminists in different nations independently decided to band together. Rather, it emerged from the matrix of international socialism, the only movement in the 1820s that explicitly sought to transform the current situation of women. In the circles that formed in London and Paris to support the theories of Charles Fourier, Robert Owen, and Claude Henri de Rouvroy, Count Saint-Simon, in the experimental communities founded on the American frontier and throughout Britain and France, unconventional women initially found a radical, international movement that challenged all aspects of the contemporary status quo. Arguing that society could not be effectively "reorganized" without the active support of "the female half of humanity," socialists sought to enlist women to their cause. First within the socialist community, later in opposition to their "brothers'" dominance, early feminists produced an international body of writings that ranged from short pieces like the "Call" to novels explicitly questioning the limitations on women's lives.[4] In addition, they wove a web of personal connections that provided them with important confirmation and support. Anna Wheeler not only published the New Women's writings but also befriended French socialists when they traveled to England. "I recover myself . . . with Mme Weeller [sic]," Désirée Véret, coeditor of the paper that published the "Call to Women," wrote about her 1833 stay in London.[5]

Organizing movements for women signalled a new era in the history of feminism. From the early fifteenth century on, some Europeans had recorded their convictions that women were as fully human as men, as capable of reason, judgment and action if not subordinated and mistreated. These "first feminists," like Christine de Pizan and Mary Astell, rejected religious and social traditions that preached female inferiority and advocated better education and marriage reform to improve women's situation.[6] Living in cultures that subordinated women and in nations governed by monarchs and aristocrats, they wrote before modern political movements existed. In these centuries, isolated female feminists conceived of themselves as intellectuals and authors rather than activists. Like the men of their day, they wrote as philosophers who sought to further their cause by reasoned arguments, logically refuting the standard justifications for female subordination.

The late-eighteenth-century revolutions in Europe and America, which overthrew traditional regimes and replaced them with more democratic institutions, gave rise to a wide array of new political groups. These were almost exclusively male, as men organized in clubs and associations, unions and parties. In America, activist women supported all the sides in the War for Independence of 1776-1783 but never publicly pressed for any of the political rights enacted by the new republic for themselves. In France, women went further. The French Revolution of 1789-1795, which challenged and overthrew the absolutist Bourbon monarchy, hereditary aristocracy, and the Roman Catholic Church, raised feminists' hopes throughout the Western community. In the early 1790s, treatises advocating women's rights appeared from Boston to Berlin.[7] Linking women's cause to that of the revolution, feminists pressed French politicians to include women in the new constitution they were debating. "Consider, I address you as a legislator," Mary Wollstonecraft wrote to Talleyrand in the dedication of her *Vindication of the Rights of Woman* of 1792, "whether, when men contend for their freedom, and to be allowed to judge for themselves respecting their own happiness, it be not inconsistent and unjust to subjugate women?" Accusing the French revolutionaries of acting like the "tyrants" they had just overthrown if they denied women "civil and political" equity, Wollstonecraft demanded "the Rights of Woman" on the grounds of "JUSTICE for one half of the human race."[8] Rapidly translated into French and German and reprinted in England and the United States, the *Vindication* became a talisman to the women who went on to create the international women's movement forty years later. Lucretia Mott kept it on the central table of her house for decades; Mathilde Franziska Anneke devoted three issues of her women's newspaper to her German translation of it.[9]

In France the *Vindication* was but one of a number of demands made for women's rights. It was during the revolution of 1789, Jeanne Deroin later wrote, that women finally "awoke" from the "long sleep" of "the dark ages of society."[10] Deroin paid special tribute to Olympe de Gouges, who rewrote the central document of the revolution, the *Declaration of the Rights of Man* of 1790, into a *Declaration of the Rights of Woman* in 1791. Claiming for women all the rights men established for themselves, Gouges added a "Social Contract between Man and Woman" to provide for egalitarian marriage. Other Frenchwomen sent proposals to the government, attended parliamentary sessions, went to political meetings, and rallied in the streets. Early in 1793, some middle- and working-class activists formed the Society for Revolutionary Republican Women to press for women's right to participate in politics and defend the nation. The nucleus of a woman's movement seemed to be forming.

But all such possibilities ended abruptly in October 1793, when the revolutionary French government outlawed all female political participation. Reasoning that "a woman should not leave her family to meddle in affairs of government," male revolutionaries excluded women from sessions of parliament and forbade them to form any "clubs or popular societies." Olympe de Gouges, who dedicated her work to Queen Marie Antoinette, was guillotined as a royalist. Ironically, in her *Declaration* she had argued that "if woman has the right to mount the scaffold [to be executed], she also has the right to mount the rostrum [to make political speeches and vote]."[11] By denying women any political rights except the dubious privilege of equality in execution, the revolutionary French government dashed feminists' hopes. "Was not the world a vast prison, and women born slaves?" Wollstonecraft concluded in her last work, the despairing novel *Maria, or the Wrongs of Woman* of 1797.[12] Throughout the Western world, cultural and economic pressures combined to bar women anew from political life.

The feminist voice fell silent both in Europe and the United States from the 1790s to 1825. The exclusion of the female sex from modern political life retarded the development of women's movements and also stifled women's demands for more rights for over a generation. Opposed not just by the traditionalists and conservatives they had always battled, but now also by the progressive and revolutionary men they considered their natural political allies, individual women who had developed feminist convictions lost heart. "Sad and discouraged . . . I sought in vain to break the ties which attached me to the world," Jeanne Deroin recalled of this period in her life, when she was in her early twenties. Her rage over reading the section of the Code Napoleon mandating that a wife owed obedience to her husband had led her to reject conventional politics, religion, and views of womanhood. But she found no one else who shared her views and so "happiness, freedom, equality became words empty of sense . . . and life seemed only a painful nightmare."[13]

Female rebels like Deroin remained isolated in these years of political repression in Europe. After the final defeat of Napoleon in 1815, the restored French Bourbon monarchy joined with Russia, Prussia, and Austria in using armed international intervention to crush uprisings and block change throughout the continent. Harsh laws punished political organizing and union movements; severe censorship and heavy taxes on printed matter controlled communication and the spread of ideas. In the late 1820s, though political life remained frozen in Central and Eastern Europe, ultraconservatism began to thaw in the West. Britain, France, and some German states in the Rhineland hesitantly allowed more civil liberties, a free press, and the formation of political organizations. But women did not benefit directly from these gains, since both liberals and conservatives agreed that the political realm should remain exclusively male. Even radical British philosophers who judged the value of existing institutions by applying Jeremy Bentham's utilitarian precept of "the greatest happiness of the greatest number" excluded women from their proposed democratic reforms. "One thing is pretty clear, that all those individuals whose interests are indisputably included in those of other individuals, may be struck off [from political rights] without inconvenience," wrote James Mill, Bentham's associate and John Stuart Mill's father, in an 1824 article on government for the *Encyclopaedia Britannica.* "In this light may be viewed all children up to a certain age, whose interests are involved in those of their parents. In this light, also, women may be regarded, the interest of almost all of whom is involved either in that of their fathers or in that of their husbands."[14]

The more democratic politics in the United States excluded women on the same grounds. In 1790, the state of New Jersey gave the vote to male and female property holders. But in 1807, women's suffrage was repealed, in part because "female reserve and delicacy are incompatible with the duties of a free elector," who had to cast a ballot publicly and risk being pelted with garbage. "Timid and pliant, unskilled in politics . . . [women] will of course be directed or persuaded by [their male relatives]. And the man who brings his two daughters, his mother and his aunt to the elections, really gives five votes instead of one," reasoned an article reflecting the majority view.[15] Pioneering in so many other ways during these years of the early republic, the United States no less than Europe embraced the doctrine of separate spheres for women and men.

Only a few radical male visionaries challenged female subordination during the first quarter of the nineteenth century. The English poet Percy Bysshe Shelley, married to Mary Wollstonecraft's daughter, questioned the situation of women in a number of lengthy poems, especially the fiery "Revolt of Islam" of 1818. Calling women's condition "slavery," the poet asked, "Can man be free if woman be a slave?" a phrase later feminists often cited.[16] The French social philosopher Charles Fourier declared in an 1808 treatise that "as a general thesis: *social progress and changes of historical period take place in proportion to the advance of women toward liberty. The extension of the privileges of women is the fundamental cause of all social progress.*"[17] Such assertions, although cherished by the female rebels who came across them, were rare and ineffectual. Shelley died young; Fourier remained obscure, his ideas ignored for decades.

Under these circumstances, unconventional women might reject domesticity individually, but they remained isolated from like-minded women, as Anna Doyle Wheeler was in her early life. Twenty years older than the French New Women she later befriended, thirty years younger than her heroine, Mary Wollstonecraft, she grew up in an Irish gentry family when the model of domestic womanhood gained sway. Initially embracing the role of wife and mother, she married against her parents' wishes at fifteen, in 1800. By twenty-seven she had borne her alcoholic husband six children, only two of whom survived. Taking refuge in reading, she arranged for packets of books to be mailed to her home in rural Ballywire. Her daughter remembered her "deep in the perusal of some French or German philosophical work" or Wollstonecraft's *Vindication of the Rights of Woman*, "stretched out on a sofa."[18] In 1812, Wheeler left her home and husband and took her children to live with her uncle, the governor of the island of Guernsey in the English Channel. Wheeler's social position protected her from the ostracism directed at middle-class women who fled similar marriages. "During these six years of isolation, I learned everything that a woman is condemned to suffer when she is separated from her husband," Flora Tristan wrote of the 1820s, when she lived apart from the man she married at seventeen. "Except for a small number of friends, no one believes what she says, and, placed by malevolence outside of everything, she is . . . nothing but a miserable *Pariah*, to whom people believe they are showing kindness when they are not actually insulting her."[19]

Individual rebellions of this nature led women to contrive individual solutions. Tristan left her children with her mother and worked as a governess in England; Wheeler moved in with her uncle; Deroin, still single, supported herself as a seamstress. Seeing themselves as isolated individuals, female rebels in these years suffered alone, unable to make contact with others like themselves.

Conditions began to change in the late 1820s. More liberal political conditions in Western Europe and the proliferation of reform associations in Jacksonian America allowed the rise of a new social philosophy that condemned all established religions and governments, argued for the abolition of private property, and predicted a new era of human development based on communal ownership of the means of production like land and factories. For Anna Wheeler and the French New Women, for Ernestine Rose and Jeanne Deroin, Harriet Taylor and Mathilde Anneke, for the scores of female "co-operators" and "associationists" whose names have been forgotten, early socialism provided crucial support and confirmation for rebellion against conventional womanhood. "The slavery of woman, of all the abuses the most hateful the most immoral is that which I have always protested with the greatest force," Deroin wrote in 1832. "Consequently of all the principles of the doctrine the emancipation of woman is the one which contributed the most powerfully to the determination which seized me to adopt Saint-Simonianism."[20]

Challenging the basic institutions of contemporary Western society, early socialism offered an optimistic alternative model in which cooperation replaced competition and scientific progress, communal ownership, and equal distribution provided bountifully for all. "You look forward, as I do, to a state of society very different from that which now exists, in which the effort of all is to out wit, supplant, and snatch from each other . . . and where the whole motley fabric is kept together by fear and blood," Irish socialist William Thompson wrote Anna Wheeler in 1825.

> You look forward to a better aspect of society, where the principle of benevolence shall supersede that of fear; where restless and anxious individual competition shall give place to mutual co-operation and joint possession; where individuals in large numbers, male and female, forming voluntary associations, shall become a mutual guarantee to each other for the supply of all useful wants . . . where perfect freedom of opinion and perfect equality will reign amongst the co-operators; and where the children of all will be equally educated and provided for by the whole, even these children no longer the slaves of individual caprice.[21]

Socialism envisioned a marvelous global civilization made possible by the Industrial Revolution, developments in the traditional sciences, and "a new science, the *social science*, or the science of promoting human happiness," Thompson wrote.[22] People would embrace a socialist way of life once they became aware of its superiority and "the old immoral world" of private property, established religion, monarchy and aristocracy, poverty and war would fade away and disappear, Robert Owen believed. "There will be nothing between nations but industrial, scientific, and moral relations; the future will be peaceful," asserted the New Women's "Call" that Wheeler translated. "No more war, no more national antagonism, love for all. The reign of harmony and peace is establishing itself on earth."[23]

First in Owenite socialism, then in Saint-Simonianism, feminists found supportive, internationalist allies whose connections stretched throughout the Western world. The Saint-Simonian "missionaries were abroad from Constantinople to the Mississippi," English author Harriet Martineau wrote about the 1820s. Socialist newspapers and manifestoes circulated to a wide range of radical enclaves across Europe and America. The Saint-Simonian movement was the most influential. French novelist Victor Hugo, German poet Heinrich Heine and Russian revolutionary Alexander Herzen were among the many leading intellectuals of the 1830s and 1840s influenced by its doctrines. Karl Marx, who encountered Saint-Simonian ideas as a young man in the Rhineland, later credited them with "genius" in foreshadowing "all the ideas of later socialists which are not strictly economic." John Stuart Mill, who welcomed Saint-Simonian proselytizers to England, paid tribute to the group's "boldness and freedom from prejudice" and extolled "the European importance of that movement."[24] Vital to the history of feminism, the Saint-Simonians created the conditions that gave rise to the self-defined "New Women," the first female group to form an independent movement dedicated to women's interests and rights.

The extravagance of these early socialists' hopes and their failure to materialize, even within their own newly created communities, led to these movements being labeled as "utopian" by the middle of the nine-teenth century. For Karl Marx and Friedrich Engels especially, at pains in the 1840s to distinguish their own "scientific" socialism from that of oth-ers, the "utopian socialism" of Saint-Simon, Owen, and Fourier inspired the passionate hatred reserved for close relatives. "They still dream of experimental realization of their social utopias," Marx and Engels wrote in their 1848 *Manifesto of the Communist Party*,

> and to realize all these castles in the air they are compelled to appeal to the feelings and purses of the bourgeois. By degrees they sink into the category of the reactionary conservative socialists . . . differing from these only by more systematic pedantry, and by their fanatical and superstitious belief in the miraculous effects of their social science.[25]

Condemning early socialists for ignoring class struggle, Marxism shaped the way they have been remembered. But 170 years ago, decades before Marx and Engels wrote, early socialism's optimistic dreams provided cru-cial hope and energy to the female rebels who encountered them. "From the midst of debris, from the realm of shadows a ray of Light escapes; Saint-Simonianism appeared," began Deroin's 1832 essay linking her belief in socialism to its support for women's emancipation. "It promises to reorganize, to regenerate society, it provides us with a magical picture where the future is painted in the most brilliant colors."[26]

In addition to its hopeful visions and its critical view of existing institu-tions, early socialism introduced unconventional women like Deroin and Wheeler to a congenial community of like-minded people, providing sec-ond families to replace the original ones whose values they had rejected. Jeanne Deroin, Désirée Véret, Ernestine Rose, Mathilde Anneke, and Louise Otto made happy marriages with men they met in the socialist movement. Others like Anna Wheeler found support for independent lives and feminist convictions within its circles. In 1818, the thirty-three-year-old Wheeler broke completely with conventional family life by join-ing a Saint-Simonian socialist community in Normandy. A few years later, she began moving among a series of European capitals where she sought out and associated with the leading radical philosophers of the day: Fourier in Paris, Thompson in Dublin, Bentham and Owen in London. Becoming convinced that Fourier's and Owen's theories were essentially the same, she tried unsuccessfully to convince them to work together.

By 1824, when William Thompson met her, Anna Wheeler had become able to voice "those bolder and more comprehensive views which perhaps can only be elicited by concentration of the mind on one darling though terrific theme . . . the condition of women, of one half the human race, in what is called civilised society," as he put it. Convinced that social-ism and the cause of women were inextricably linked, Wheeler inspired Thompson to write down what she had "so often and so well stated in con-versation, and under feigned names in such of the periodical publications of the day as would tolerate such a theme."[27] The resulting *APPEAL of One Half the Human Race, WOMEN, Against the Pretensions of the Other Half, MEN, To Retain Them in Political, and Thence in Civil and Domestic Slavery* was the first feminist treatise in thirty years. Begun as a passionate rebuttal of James Mill's exclusion of women from political rights, the *Appeal* fused democracy, socialism, and feminism into a single cause. Claiming democratic rights and civil liberties for women, the *Appeal* argued that if the greatest happiness of the greatest number was truly the principle on which a society should be based, then limiting the vote to adult men violated that doctrine. (At one point it discussed restricting the vote to adult women, since women "could not rule by force" and so would be more inclined to promote the well-being of "the whole race.")[28] Consistently asserting that since women were adult human beings they were entitled to all that men were, the treatise presented women's condition in contemporary society as a slavery produced by the denial of rights. Focusing on the situation of wives, the *Appeal* argued that marriage made men into tyrants, thus reinforcing despotism in society, and made women into slaves:

> Woman is then compelled, in marriage, by the possession of superior strength on the part of men, by the want of knowledge, skill and wealth, by the positive, cruel, partial and cowardly enactments of law, by the terrors of superstition, by the mockery of a pretended vow of obedience, and to crown all, and as the result of all, by the force of an unrelenting, unreasoning, unfeeling, public opinion, to be the literal unequivocal *slave* of the man who may be styled her husband.

Invoking the situation of female slaves "in the West Indies and every other slave-polluted soil" to illumine the condition of nominally free women in Britain, the authors insisted that "white slaves" had it worse, since in addition to being owned outright, they were forced to feign love for their masters. (The themes of slavery and emancipation, central to the development of this international feminist movement, are examined in detail in the next chapter.)

Daring to discuss sexual issues, the *Appeal* argued that female slaves, prostitutes, and legal wives were united in their forced submission to men's "voluptuousness" and "caprice of command" in sex. The *Appeal* further declared that *"woman is more the slave of man for the gratification of her desires, than man is of woman,"* since "to man . . . by the permission of law and of public opinion, the gratification of every sexual desire is permitted," whereas woman "is not permitted to appear to feel, or desire. . . . she must always yield, must submit as a matter of duty, not repose upon her equal for the sake of happiness."[29]

Using women's sexual oppression in marriage and prostitution to criticize contemporary society and its system of individual competition, the *Appeal* argued that only socialism would truly liberate women, since it was the sole economic system that could free women from male domination.

"If women cease to be dependent on individual men for their daily support, if the children of all the pairs of the community are educated and maintained out of the common stock of wealth and talents, if every possible aid of medical skill and kindness is afforded impartially to all," the condition of women would be transformed. As an adult "co-operator," with an income of her own and the community behind her in times of trouble, no woman need sell herself to a man to survive, either by marriage or prostitution. Since "women's love must under such circumstances be earned, be merited, not, as now, *bought* or *commanded*," the double standard of sexual morality would disappear.

Expansive and internationalist like the socialism it championed, the *Appeal* addressed women throughout the world: "Women of England! Women, in whatever country ye breathe—wherever ye breathe, degraded—awake!" began its concluding section. Like the New Women's "Call" seven years later, the *Appeal* benefited from socialism's international network of newspapers and publications. It was translated into French and the radical press in France and the United States reprinted portions of it.[30] Thereafter, Wheeler wrote and spoke "always on one subject, the present condition of women and their rights as members of society and equals with men," a friend recalled.[31] In an 1829 speech on the "Rights of Women," she urged "enlightened advocates" to form groups "to obtain . . . the removal of the disabilities of women and the introduction of a national system of *equal education* for the Infants of both sexes," so as "not to leave our daughters the bitter inheritance of ignorance and slavery."[32]

To conclude her speech calling for a feminist movement, Wheeler paid tribute to the best-known woman in international socialism of the 1820s, her Owenite associate Fanny (Frances) Wright: "May she find an echo in every instructed woman, and an active ally in every man! Grateful posterity will no doubt associate her name with the *illustrious men of the present age*, who, having discovered the principles of real *social science*, gave them to the world under the name of CO-OPERATION."[33]

At the time of Wheeler's "Rights of Women" speech, Fanny Wright was well-known on both sides of the Atlantic. A Scottish heiress orphaned at three, she and her sister Camilla had traveled from England to the United States in 1818. Three years later, when she was twenty-six, Fanny Wright published her *Views of Society and Manners in America . . . by an Englishwoman*, a collection of letters that established her as an author and appeared in French and German translation.[34] On a visit to France, Wright became entranced by General Lafayette, then sixty-seven and almost forty years her senior. Whether she saw him as a potential father, lover, or combination of the two is unclear, but she followed him to the United States in 1824. There, she became a convert to socialism after hearing Robert Owen address President John Quincy Adams and the assembled Houses of Congress in Washington, D.C., early the next year.

Between 1825 and 1829, ten Owenite communities formed in the United States to demonstrate the success of the "New System" of socialism. Owen and Wright each created an experimental society: Owen at New Harmony in Indiana; Wright at Nashoba in the wilderness of Tennessee. Crossing the Atlantic frequently, they shuttled between these communes and the European capitals where they publicized their achievements and recruited new settlers. Before an international audience, they challenged most of the established conventions of contemporary Western society.

Owen had come to America with a fund of goodwill based on the undeniable success of his Scottish industrial community of New Lanark, where providing decent homes and good schools for workers had produced a superior labor force and impressive profits. Initially welcomed by sympathetic audiences of leading American intellectuals, businessmen, and politicians, Owen rapidly lost support when he denounced religion and marriage along with private property. Issuing a "Declaration of Mental Independence" on July 4, 1826, the fiftieth anniversary of the U.S. Declaration of Independence, Owen called for an end to "a TRINITY of the most monstrous evils that could be combined . . . PRIVATE, OR INDIVIDUAL PROPERTY—absurd and irrational SYSTEMS OF RELIGION—and MARRIAGE, founded on individual property combined with some one of these irrational systems of religion."[35] Within a few months, the Owenite communities were being denounced not for their participants' actual behavior but for their sponsor's abhorrent beliefs. "If we are allowed to judge of the moral character of the New Harmony society, by the licentious principles of their founder and leader," fulminated a local newspaper, "it would be no breach of charity, to class them all with whores and whoremongers, nor to say that the whole group will constitute one great brothel."[36]

Wright met even harsher condemnation, since she shared Owen's unorthodox opinions but not his status as a successful, married, middle-aged man of industry. "That a lady of fortune, family, and education, whose youth had been passed in the most refined circles of private life, should present herself to the people in this capacity [as lecturer] would naturally excite surprise anywhere," wrote English novelist Frances Trollope about Wright in 1831. "But in America where women are guarded by a seven-fold shield of habitual insignificance it has caused an effect which can scarcely be described."[37] Wright compounded the effect by daring to speak and write explicitly about sexual and racial matters. To Owen's advocacy of socialism, free thought, and "new moral marriage," Wright added her own radical solution to "the crying sin" of American slavery: the "amalgamation of the races" through freely chosen sexual unions between blacks and whites. Arguing that racial intermingling was well under way in the slave South through rape and coercion, Wright envisioned Nashoba as a community in which such matings could occur "in good taste and good feeling," eventually "peopling" the United States "with a race more suited to its southern climate, than the pure European."[38]

Such views made her "universally obnoxious," former president James Madison wrote Lafayette, to a rigidly segregated United States where white racial prejudice enforced by socially sanctioned violence seemed to many foreign visitors to be a national characteristic. Harriet Martineau wrote that after she advocated the abolition of slavery on her American trip in 1835, she "was subjected to insult and injury, and was even for some weeks in danger of her life while travelling where the tar-barrel, the cowhide, and the pistol were the regimen."[39] In this era even the most radical American abolitionists shunned Wright's solution of racial interbreeding. When a white schoolteacher, Prudence Crandall, sought to open a Connecticut school for black girls in 1833, she promised in a public letter to work for education but not amalgamation—a tactic that did not prevent a campaign of violence that closed the school.[40]

But Europe was different. American abolitionists, black and white, who traveled there agreed with James Mott that although Europeans shared Americans' views on women, "they have not the unholy prejudice against color" that characterized most whites in the United States. "I should like to be in my native land again," African-American Josephine Brown wrote after living in France and England but explained that she could not return, since "the treatment I receive from the people here is so different" from the segregation and prejudice she experienced in Massachusetts.[41] Wright retained the approval of radical European socialists like Anna Wheeler for her interracial community and publicized Nashoba widely to gain support for her experiment. In a letter to Mary Shelley, one of a number of famous people she solicited for help, Wright promised the author of *Frankenstein* that Nashoba would "undermine the slavery of colour existing in the North American republic," as well as providing "an establishment where affection shall form the only marriage, kind feeling and kind action the only religion, respect for the feelings and liberties of others the only restraint, and union of interest the bond of peace and security."[42]

These ideals foundered in the swamps of Tennessee, but their failure took place before an international audience of socialists, antislavery advocates, and reformers attracted by hopeful publicity generated by Wright and Owen. Like all Owenite communities, Nashoba failed to create a viable socialist economy and relied instead on its sponsor's subsidies. In addition, Wright's settlement reproduced some of the worst features of plantation life. A handful of whites ruled over about thirty purchased and donated black ex-slaves whom they forced to labor—by public whippings on occasion—to pay back their purchase price. When some black women asked for a lock to keep men out of their bedroom, they were rebuked by the white board of directors for not trusting in the force of the community's doctrine that "the proper basis of the sexual intercourse" was "the unconstrained and unrestrained choice of *both* parties." Believing that blacks were at least a generation away from equality, Wright hoped to raise the children "distinct from their parents" to effect "the advancement of the negro race." Later she applied this solution to American life in general with a call for "national boarding schools" for all children over two.[43]

After the failure of Nashoba, Wright arranged for its African-American members to be transported to the independent black republic of Haiti, where their freedom was assured. She then moved to New York City and continued to scandalize public opinion. Wright and Owen's son, Robert Dale Owen, converted a former church into a Hall of Science, where they lectured on free thought, education, women's rights, and contraception, as well as publishing a radical newspaper. Robert Dale Owen wrote *Moral Physiology: Or a Brief and Plain Treatise of the Population Question* in 1829, the first birth control text published in America.[44] The next year Wright returned to France and gave birth to a daughter, marrying the father, a French Owenite teacher, a few months later. The last twenty years of Fanny Wright's life were consumed by property and custody battles with her husband that left her "a heart-broken, harassed woman," Ernestine Rose said in 1857.[45]

Wright's career highlighted the contradictions of an era that viewed women, especially younger women, almost exclusively through the lens of sexuality. Although collectively known as "the sex" and routinely complimented on their physical charms, women lost their precarious claim to moral authority if they referred at all to sexual matters. When Elizabeth Barrett Browning made an oblique reference to prostitution in her 1856 epic poem *Aurora Leigh* ("all the towns / make offal of their daughters for its [man's body's] use"), she wrote a friend that it had been the most offensive part of the work, far more than her subplot about an unwed mother, because prostitution was something that "a woman oughtn't to refer to, by any manner of means, says conventional tradition."[46] Public opinion tried to find a sexual meaning wherever possible. When the Saint-Simonian New Women named their newspaper the *Free Woman* (La femme libre) in 1832, the title was read as meaning a woman who freely engaged in sex. Fearing ridicule, the editors changed the paper's name after the first issue.

In Wright's case, her attempt to create an interracial community without formal marriage gave weight to conservative fears that once a woman left the domestic sphere, she would violate every taboo by advocating sex between the races, renouncing all religion, and bearing a child out of wedlock. Wright's reputation as "that Jezebel beast of a woman," as a U.S. critic called her in 1836, loomed over nineteenth-century women and was routinely invoked when they spoke in public or demanded rights.[47]

To the feminists who attempted to found women's movements, Fanny Wright provided a heroic but problematic model. Her name led a list Mathilde Anneke made of the women whose "worthy efforts" had "strengthened" her in 1849 when she was forced to emigrate from Germany to America. Elizabeth Cady Stanton, Susan B. Anthony, and

Matilda Joslyn Gage used her portrait for the frontispiece of their 1881 *History of Woman Suffrage*.[48] Wright embodied feminism in the popular imagination for much of the nineteenth century, linking women's rights to scandalous sexual behavior. But she never formed important connections to other women and never sought to create a women's movement. Although she was in Paris when the Saint-Simonian New Women organized, and then in the United States during the first women's rights conventions, she ignored both these events, as she had Wheeler's attempt to create a women's movement in England. Like many unconventional, activist women in male-dominant societies, Wright connected primarily to men. Seeing herself as an individual female exception to the ignorance and dependence that made other women fit only to be "kept mistresses," she followed her own idiosyncratic path, remaining isolated from the other women of the period whose ideals most closely resembled her own.[49] A lone star, she inspired others to form women's movements while remaining aloof from them herself.

This lack of connection among women of achievement like Wright and other feminist women made the formation of early women's movements difficult. Feminists naturally searched for women whose actions demonstrated the capabilities of their sex, who challenged the confinement of privileged women's lives. They assumed that such models would ally themselves with women's movements but often were proved wrong. For instance, by the early 1830s the French novelist writing under the male pseudonym George Sand (Aurore Dupin Dudevant), who dressed like a man and smoked cigars, had sexual liaisons and wrote passionately in favor of divorce, had eclipsed Fanny Wright in the public eye as the incarnation of emancipated womanhood. From the beginning of her lengthy and successful career as a novelist who passionately defended woman's right to follow her heart, even if that necessitated love affairs or divorce, Sand inspired her generation of women in Europe and America to challenge conventional feminine behavior. "*You* sanctify my feelings and my costume / *You* give me courage in my lonely, bitter pain," the German feminist Louise Aston wrote in an 1846 hymn to George Sand, while the Englishwoman Eliza Ashurst called her the "Mary Wol[l]stonecraft of the age."[50] "All the aspiring and discontented women known to me in America . . . were the offspring of George Sand," declared a Unitarian minister, and the pejorative noun "George-Sandism" appeared in English, French, German, and Russian to denounce the sexual freedom Sand claimed for women.[51]

Although Sand, like Wright, represented female emancipation to the world at large, she remained hostile to feminists' attempts at organizing women's movements. When the feminist editors of the *Voice of Women* (La Voix des femmes) nominated her for the French legislature in 1848, she angrily repudiated them and proclaimed in a public letter that she did not share their principles. When she was proposed for membership in the prestigious, all-male *Académie Française* in 1863, she wrote a pamphlet denouncing the idea of female academicians, arguing that the time when women could participate in public life lay far in the future.[52] The antifeminism of Sand and other women of achievement undercut attempts to form organizations to work for women's interests. Early feminists had to confront and overcome the painful reality that their beliefs estranged them from most other women, even the talented women they admired or those who belonged to groups whose interests they shared. "I am . . . but too well aware, that my remarks . . . will draw upon me the hate of most men, together with that of the greater portion of the very *sex*, whose rights . . . I attempt to advocate," Wheeler told the audience of socialists and Unitarians assembled to hear her 1829 speech encouraging women to organize on their own behalf.[53] But what distinguished feminists from nonfeminist activists was their willingness to keep trying to form connections to other women like themselves.

For Anna Wheeler, as for so many others in this period, such connections had to be made with women in other nations. From 1829, when Wheeler first called for a women's movement, to 1832, when she made contact with the French New Women, conditions in England worsened for advocates of women's rights. The centerpiece of nineteenth-century liberalism, the Great Reform Act of 1832, widened the property suffrage to include one out of five men but deliberately excluded women by adding the word "male" to a voting bill for the first time in English history. The admired Liberal government of the 1830s, which weakened royal and aristocratic privileges, granted the broadest civil rights in Europe, and freed the slaves in British territories overseas, assumed that political life was for men only. Wheeler's rage at James Mill's exclusion of women from political rights sparked the writing of the *Appeal* in 1825; her bitterness at the Reform Act of 1832, which "had not a word about justice to women" in it, led her to search for allies across the channel in France, where the July revolution of 1830 raised radicals' hopes for change.[54]

Although France remained a monarchy, three days of violent uprisings in Paris forced the replacement of the conservative Bourbon king by his more liberal cousin, Louis Philippe. The twenty-year-old Ernestine Rose saw Lafayette present the new ruler to the people at the Hôtel de Ville in Paris that summer.[55] After order was restored, socialist and workers associations expanded in France, in part because expectations had been raised without being fulfilled. The most influential and important of these groups were the Saint-Simonians, who organized to implement the visions of the comte de Saint-Simon in the years following his death in 1825.

Born in 1760, Saint-Simon fought in the American War of Independence, supported the French Revolution, dreamed of constructing a canal through Panama, and subsidized a salon of scientists in Paris before coming to believe that industrial production heralded a new era of human history. Convinced that society could be "reorganized" to value

productive labor and end the ancient privileges given monarchs, aristocrats, and the Roman Catholic Church, he predicted that an elite cadre of
scientists and industrialists would lead the world to a global civilization in
which technology produced immense wealth for all. The principle of
"association" would replace competition and a "New Christianity" based
on economic justice would inspire harmony among different classes and
societies.

From the late 1820s, Saint-Simon's followers, many of them engineers,
doctors, and men of science, created a political and religious movement
bearing his name. Fusing their faith in scientific progress to a radical rein-
terpretation of Christianity, the Saint-Simonians attracted thousands of
people, about a third of them women, to their weekly lectures and meetings. Jeanne Deroin, Pauline Roland, Désirée Veret, and Suzanne
Voilquin, all later active in international feminism, were among the
Frenchwomen drawn to the movement at this time. Their experiences
with Saint-Simonianism shaped the women's movements they created,
both in France and internationally.

Male Saint-Simonians sought to appeal to women by advocating female
emancipation. Believing that social progress demanded women's participation in all aspects of public life, they built upon their founder's dying assertion that "the man and the woman—there is the social individual."[56]
Accepting the prevailing view that women were men's opposites, the
Saint-Simonians reasoned that society's problems stemmed in large part
from the oppression of the female sex by male egoism and "brute force."
This unnatural state had led to the atrophy of virtues they identified as
female, like peace and cooperation. The solution was to believe "in the
coming regeneration of the human race by the Equality of *man* and of
woman," and to preach this gospel "to Germany, to America, to Siberia."
"Throughout all of Europe and in America, *civil war, mean and hideous war*
is augured," reads a typical Saint-Simonian broadside. "Women alone can
stop it, and they alone can later make the nations let fall the swords with
which they . . . fight."[57]

The women who went on to form an independent feminist movement
initially found these beliefs empowering. "A great, a good, a just man has
proclaimed us the equal of man, and many have followed his wise example," asserted the New Women's "Call," which Wheeler translated.
"Honour to those generous men—a halo of glory awaits them in the new
world!"[58] Deroin, Voilquin, and others recorded the hope and optimism
Saint-Simonianism awakened in them. "When I learned about the notion
of indefinite progress, eternal like God, and came to appreciate the fundamental idea of our liberty and the religious future in these words of Father
Enfantin's 'God, Father and Mother of all men and women,' I experienced
a sort of bedazzlement," remembered Suzanne Voilquin. "I felt an
immense joy at rediscovering my mind, heart, and action free by virtue of
those holy formulas."[59]

By the time these women joined Saint-Simonianism, it had evolved into a spiritual family that merged political action, religion, and close personal relationships. Rereading the New Testament to justify social revolution, Saint-Simonians saw themselves as a modern band of holy apostles, dedicated to realizing Jesus' mission to create a heaven on earth. Declaring that churches and governments had corrupted his original teachings, they preached their new social gospel with missionary zeal. By basing their movement on Christianity, instead of repudiating all religions as the Owenites and the Marxists did, the Saint-Simonians adopted the same successful strategy used by many other activist groups in this era of religious revival. Even among radical feminists, only a minority like Rose or Anneke moved into militant atheism, and their antireligious stance distanced them from most others in the movement. From the abolitionist circles of New England to the free congregations of Germany, most nineteenth-century radicals justified the massive social changes they sought by seeing their cause as a modern revival of Christianity and themselves as early Christians, if not Jesus himself. "All honor to Mary Wollstonecraft," Lucretia Mott declared to the National Woman's Rights Convention in 1866. "Her name was cast out as evil, even as that of Jesus was cast out as evil; but her name shall yet go forth and stand as the pioneer of this movement. I want to note the progress of this cause, and know now that Woman's redemption is at hand, yea, even at the doors."[60]

Radical Christianity, which could embrace freethinkers like Wollstonecraft or Rose, also cut across class and racial barriers in the 1830s and 1840s. It provided activists in different cultures with a common language and frame of reference from which to work for social change. "We come to tell men what they have been told by everyone who has taken a step along the road of progress," French Saint-Simonian Gustave d'Eichthal wrote English radical John Stuart Mill in 1830, that "what they have been told by pagan legislators, but above all by the legislators of Providence, Moses and Jesus Christ; we say to them, LOVE ONE ANOTHER, because that alone is the law of the prophets. And these words...mean *love humanity as a whole and make your love practical*, accomplish what Moses has promised and Jesus Christ has prepared."[61]

The Saint-Simonians organized as a spiritual family focused on the parent–child bond. "My fathers my mothers . . . number me among your children," Désirée Véret wrote in a typical letter published in *Le Globe*, the Saint-Simonian newspaper. "I am with respect and devotion your daughter."[62] Although it advocated female equality, the movement remained dominated by men: only 20 percent of its hierarchy were women. In 1831 the charismatic Prosper Enfantin became "Supreme Father," and the movement split over his leadership and controversial views on sexuality and women's role. Enfantin proclaimed that Saint-Simonianism had entered a stage of "waiting" for a woman messiah who would redeem the world by promulgating a "new morality." At the same time, he paradoxically dismissed women from the Saint-Simonian hierarchy, arguing that women could not redeem themselves but must be "set free" by men. Insisting that female emancipation could best be achieved by the "rehabilitation of the flesh," he sought to institute social arrangements that allowed for sexual infidelity, arguing that this would benefit women, who were innately more "inconstant, fickle, and volatile" than men. Drawing on Fourier, who had sought to classify the variety of human passions and construct a community that could balance and satisfy them all, Enfantin proposed three different moral codes: one for the "constants," one for the "mobiles," and the third for a "couple-pope" at the head of the movement. He called on "every woman to reveal her every need, her every suffering, to formulate for herself her law of the future." Women within the movement responded by debating "the host of weighty questions" about "the freedom of women."[63]

By limiting women's role within Saint-Simonianism while simultaneously calling upon them to develop their own ideas, Enfantin created conditions that fostered the growth of an independent women's movement. When he withdrew to an all-male rural retreat "with forty of *his Sons*," a group of young female members organized in Paris to "work for the freedom and association of women." In April 1832, they published the first issue of their own newspaper, the *Free Woman*, with the "Call to Women" that Wheeler later translated on the front page. The lead editorial stated that the journal would "publish articles only by women"

> because we have deeply felt the slavery and nullity that weighs upon our sex, we are raising up our voices to call upon women to come with us and demand the place we should hold in the temple, the state, and the family.
>
> Our goal is association. Until now women have had no organization that allows them to give themselves to something great, they have only been able to concern themselves with petty individual matters that have left them in isolation. . . . we have faith that many women will rally to us, and that others will imitate us by forming their own groups.[64]

From 1832 to 1834 these seamstresses and schoolteachers, housewives and pieceworkers managed to produce thirty-one issues of a journal distributed by Saint-Simonianism's far-ranging network of bookstores and reading rooms in the United States and Britain as well as throughout France. Although they benefited from their Saint-Simonian connections, they soon developed a critical perspective about the movement and its male leaders. "Women alone will say what freedom they want," began an 1832 article.

> Whoever else may desire our freedom, I want it, and that is the essential point. I wanted it before encountering the Saint-Simonians or Monsieur Fourier. . . . Men have advised, directed, and dominated us long enough. It is now up to us to work for our liberty by ourselves; it is up to us to work for it without the help of our masters.[65]

Complaining that male Saint-Simonians "act toward women the way governments act toward the people. . . . They think they see a tendency toward usurpation on our part when we dare to demonstrate our *will*," the group began to call themselves "the New Women."[66]

They soon asserted that "the cause of women is universal and not exclusively Saint-Simonian." So they dropped Saint-Simonian terms from their newspaper's title and changed its name to the *Women's Tribune* to reflect a "new format" that included all "women capable of understanding their century." The journal fostered debate and soon arrived at a feminist perspective that creatively challenged basic social conventions, such as women's names. Arguing that all surnames signified male dominance, either by a father or a husband, the New Women published under first names that identified them as women: Suzanne, Jeanne-Désirée, Jeanne Victoire, Joséphine-Félicité. "This custom which obliges the wife to take her husband's name is nothing but a branding iron which prints on the slave's forehead the initals of the master's name, so that he can be known by all as his property," wrote Jeanne Deroin, who never used her husband's surname, Desroches. "Men give birth to doctrines and systems and baptize them in their name, but we, on the other hand give birth to men," reasoned Jeanne-Désirée (Désirée Véret). "We should give them our names, and take our own only from our mothers and God. This is the law that nature dictates to us. If we continue to take the names of men and doctrines, we will be slaves without knowing it. . . . we will never be the equals and mothers of men."[67]

By discarding their surnames but keeping their own first names, the New Women arrived at a radical solution to a problem that has continued to plague feminists until the present day: what should a woman call herself, especially after marriage, in a culture in which surnames signify her connection to a male relative? Early advocates for women's rights usually published either as "a lady" or under false female first names, like Judith Sargent Murray's "Constantia" or Anna Wheeler's "Vlasta." By the 1840s, the male pseudonym used by George Sand became more common among women authors in Europe: Marian Evans wrote as George Eliot, Charlotte Brontë as Currer Bell, Jenny d'Héricourt as Félix Lamb, and Louise Otto as Otto Stern. Coming out from behind the male pseudonym became a rite of passage for a number of feminists. "Surely you will excuse the womanly fear which counseled me to hide behind the visor of a male name," Otto wrote in 1845. Explaining that she had not wanted her work to be judged "just because I was a woman," she first established herself as a "male figure" in journalism so that she could "participate as a sister of equal birth."[68]

In Britain and the United States, Quaker women pioneered discarding honorifics like "Miss" or "Mrs.," a practice adopted by other female activists in the late 1830s. At the 1837 Anti-Slavery Convention of American Women in New York City, the organizers noted that "a large proportion of the members who decline the appellation of Mrs. or Miss, were *not* members of the Society of Friends."[69] "I have very serious objections, dear Rebecca, to being called Henry [the name of her husband, Henry B. Stanton]," Elizabeth Cady Stanton wrote a friend ten years later in reasoning that echoed Deroin's.

> There is a great deal in a name. . . . Why are the slaves nameless unless they take that of their master? Simply because they have no independent existence. . . . Our colored friends in this country who have education and family ties take to themselves names. Even so with women. The custom of calling women Mrs. John This and Mrs. Tom That, and colored men Sambo and Zip Coon, is founded on the principle that white men are lords of all. I cannot acknowledge this principle as just, therefore, I cannot bear the name of another.[70]

Writing under their self-created names, the New Women applied their feminist perspective to socialism itself. Early articles reversed the standard socialist formula that the emancipation of the worker would lead to the emancipation of women and declared that "only by emancipating woman will we emancipate the worker," a slogan Anna Wheeler used as the headline for her translation of the "Call to Women."[71] But more thoughtful analyses in later issues broke down the false opposition of "women" and "workers." The New Women insisted that since most women *were* workers, the concept of emancipation itself must be expanded to include both groups:

> If we respond to women who plead for a remedy to their sufferings and those of children . . . by saying to them: "demand your moral freedom," do we not resemble those who tell the people when they are hungry: "demand your political rights," as if those rights could satisfy them and reorganize their work? I am certainly far from believing that *material emancipation* is *everything* that *the people and women need*. I know that they also need *social emancipation*, but, I repeat, one cannot be established without the other, for they are essentially connected and cannot be separated.[72]

This expansive "both/and" approach characterized early feminism. Convinced that the true emancipation of women necessitated both the economic reforms that only socialism could provide and the end of male domination in domestic as well as public life, the New Women resisted a forced choice between them. "If you preserve this old belief that woman's sole purpose is to bear children, clean man's house, and give him pleasure," while creating a socialist society, "you will always fail," they warned. Arguing like Thompson and Wheeler that capitalism had intensified men's domination of women by giving them sole political and economic power, the New Women maintained that the only effective remedy was "a complete change in our position," the true emancipation of women possible only in "a new social order in which *association* would replace isolation" and women could find jobs to support themselves:

> As long as a man provides us our material needs, he can also demand that in exchange we submit to what ever he desires, and it is very difficult to speak out freely when a woman does not have the means to live independently.
>
> This brings us to the complete reform of society. A new educational system for children . . . there will be a *social provision for them*. A new organization of housework . . . [which] will employ no more than a small minority of women, only those with a taste for it.[73]

Just as the New Women enlarged the socialist vision of what "female emancipation" necessitated, so too did they transform Saint-Simonian views on love, marriage, and the family. Unlike male Saint-Simonians and Owenites, who emphasized the need for freedom from marriage to facilitate the formation of new sexual relationships, the women stressed their need for decent jobs and education in order to avoid sexual oppression. In an argument that would become standard in international feminism by the 1840s, the New Women maintained that under present conditions, most marriages resembled prostitution, in which women sold themselves in order to survive:

> It [prostitution] exists in sumptuous palaces and elegant hotels, as well as in the dirty hovels of alleyways. . . . It is with that unhappy young woman who fights against misery by obstinately holding down a job that does not, however, pay enough to relieve her from the hunger which devours her. . . . Prostitution exists with you, young girl of the privileged class. . . . you too will be sold. Your father will give you away as a wife, not to the one most worthy of you, but to the one who will bring the most money. . . . Thus, prostitution is everywhere.[74]

Early feminists distinguished themselves by insisting that all women were united by their economic oppression in an unjust society and that only radical change could eliminate prostitution in its widest meaning. "Few are Mary Wollstonecrafts, few can write like George Sand," English socialist Catherine Barmby asserted in an 1848 article, "Woman's Industrial Independence." "Man, moreover has monopolised the labour market; or such departments as may be distasteful to her only are open. What then is often her end? Prostitution or suicide!" In her widely reprinted *Address* urging the revolutionary government of Saxony to transform women's labor conditions in 1848, Louise Otto made the same point: "This lack of earnings, and especially of work, of a secure position in life, throws women into the arms of prostitution. One woman exposes herself to public shame and contempt, the other suffers her secret disgrace in a marriage contracted for calculation, without love."[75]

In the last issues of the *Women's Tribune* and in Claire Démar's pamphlet, *My Law of the Future*, the New Women began to explore what life might be like "once woman is delivered and emancipated from the yoke" of male domination. From London, Véret called upon women to expand the concepts of "wife" and "mother" to become a truly "FREE *woman.*" In Paris, Voilquin published an essay advocating divorce "in this time of transition."[76] Démar's piece, popular enough to be reprinted, went furthest. Stating that in the liberated future, "woman's existence and social position will derive only from her own ability and her own works," Démar reasoned that this was impossible if she were also "condemned to spend a more or less long period of her life attending to the upbringing of one or more children." Arguing that the emancipation of women depended on their liberation from motherhood, Démar concluded that children should be raised by "social mothers" who had "the ability to raise, develop, understand childhood" rather than the "blood mother" who would then "be able to classify herself according to her *ability* and receive compensation for her works."[77]

In 1833, Démar committed suicide in despair, causing a number of New Women to wonder whether radical social change was possible. By the end of 1834, the Saint-Simonian movement disbanded, further splintered by Enfantin's decision to go to Egypt in search of the female messiah. Some of the New Women, like Voilquin, joined the small group that accompanied him. Véret moved to England; Deroin and others remained in Paris, raising their families and finding work as teachers and writers. But their ideas continued to influence those who went on to form women's movements, both internationally and within their own societies. Anne Knight, the English Quaker antislavery worker, copied almost a hundred pages of feminist passages in French from the *Women's Tribune* and *My Law of the Future* into a diary she kept all her life. In the early 1840s, Knight, who wrote often to British and American abolitionists, had some of the New Women's ideas printed on hundreds of brightly colored labels that she pasted to letters she mailed to her far-flung correspondents. "If woman be the complement of man," went one she often sent, "all our social transactions will be incomplete, or otherwise imperfect, until they have been guided alike by the wisdom of each sex."[78] The expansive visions of the New Women reappear in the writings of feminists in Great Britain, Germany, and the United States as well as France. Although a direct connection cannot always be traced, the influence is unmistakable. "In reading various writings of the Saint Simonians," Theodore Stanton later wrote about his mother, "you are continually encountering ideas and even phrases that you find in almost exactly the same words in the publications of Elizabeth Cady Stanton."[79] The connections formed between the New Women and other feminists expanded in the 1830s and 1840s as increasing numbers of women began to organize movements on their own behalf.

1. German feminist Mathilde Franziska von Tabouillet (later Anneke) in 1840, a few years before the bitter divorce which convinced her to work for women's issues.
(Columbia University Library)

2. Swedish novelist Fredrika Bremer at the time of her 1849 voyage to America.
(American Swedish Historical Foundation)

3. American feminist Paulina Wright Davis in the 1850s, when she presided over U. S. Women's Rights Conventions and edited the *Una*. (*Library of Congress #914080 LC-US262-37939*)

4. French Feminist Jeanne Deroin during her later years in London, when Elizabeth Cady Stanton visited her. This is the sole surviving portrait of Deroin. (*Bibliothèque nationale de France 74B 64911*)

5. French feminist Jenny d'Héricourt when Ernestine Rose talked with her in Paris in 1856.
(Bibliothèque nationale de France 78A 40464)

6. Quaker feminist Anne Knight used to give out this visiting card, which was photographed in Paris, 1855. The text she's pointing to reads: "By tortured Millions / By the Divine Redeemer / Enfranchise Humanity / Bid the outraged World / BE FREE."
(Library of the Religious Society of Friends in Britain)

7. English writer Harriet Martineau at the time of her 1834 journey to America, cupping her ear to compensate for her partial deafness. *(Columbia University Library)*

8. Englishwoman Harriet Taylor (later Mill) in the early 1830s, when she began to write on women's issues. *(The British Library of Political and Economic Science, London School of Economics)*

9. American Quaker feminist Lucretia Mott at the height of her fame in 1858.
(Friends Historical Library, Swarthmore College)

10. German feminist Louise Otto during the 1848/49 Revolution, when she began publishing her *Women's Newspaper*.
(Columbia University Library)

11. International feminist Ernestine Rose in New York City, 1858, a few years after the European trip where she spoke with Jenny d'Héricourt in Paris.
(Library of Congress #914080 LC-US262-52045)

12. American feminist Elizabeth Cady Stanton at the time of the 1848 Seneca Falls Convention, flanked by her sons, Henry and Daniel.
(Coline Jenkins-Sahlin)

13. Frenchwomen and girls selling the feminist daily, *Voix des Femmes* (The Voice of Women) on the streets of Paris in March, 1848.
(Illustrated London News)

14. Frenchwomen on the barricades in 1848, drawn for an English newspaper. The banner reads "Bread or Death" and the surrounding text reports that both women "were shot whilst in the attitudes indicated in the Illustration."
(Illustrated London News)

15. Jeanne Deroin's pale blue 1849 election banner with Anne Knight's translation pasted to it. The text asserts that "a legislative assembly composed entirely of men is . . . incompetent to make the laws which regulate a society composed of both men and women." *(Library of the Religious Society of Friends in Britain)*

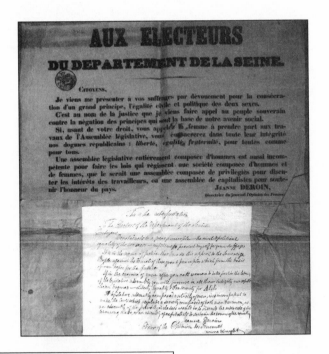

16. Mastheads of four feminist newspapers: Louise Otto's 1849 *Frauen-Zeitung* (Women's Newspaper), Paulina Wright Davis's 1853 *Una*, the Saint-Simonian New Women's 1831 *Tribune des femmes* (Women's Tribune), and Amelia Bloomer's 1849 *Lily*.

96

No. 1. THE AMERICAN COSTUME.   No. 2. THE FRENCH COSTUME.

17. On the left, American feminist Amelia Bloomer wears the "reformed" dress soon known as the "Bloomer costume." On the right, a woman in the latest French fashion of 1851. Reprinted abroad, this U. S. article also illustrated the unnatural compression of the ribs and internal organs caused by the fashionable corset. *(National Library of Medicine, Bethesda, Maryland A 12220)*

18. An 1848 French cartoon of a Women's Club. The women are demanding "First, that the petticoat be replaced by the breeches. Second, that husbands stay at home at least three times a week. Third, that no other distinctions finally exist between man and woman than those which it has pleased nature to grant them." *(Bibliothèque nationale de France 84B 96887)*

CLUB FÉMININ.

Nous demandons 1° Que le jupon soit remplacé par la culotte.
2° Que les maris s'occupent de l'intérieur au moins trois fois par semaine.
3° Enfin qu'il n'existe entre l'homme et la femme aucune autre distinction que celle qu'il a plû à la nature de leur accorder

19. A Daumier cartoon from his 1849 series "Socialist Women." The woman is saying, "So, you're my husband, you're the master. . . . But I've got the right to throw you out of your house. . . . Jeanne Deroin proved it to me yesterday evening! . . . Go have it out with her!"
(Print Collection, New York Public Library)

20. German caricatures of "Emancipated Women" in 1847. Clockwise from the upper left, the drawings depict "The Female Don Juan," "The Female Painter," "The Female Protector," and "The Female Professor."
(The Research Libraries, New York Public Library)

Five

⸺

Emancipating Themselves

At the height of the German revolution of 1848–1849, Louise Otto began organizing an independent women's movement. In the lead editorial of the first issue of her *Women's Newspaper* (Frauen-Zeitung), she called for women of all social classes, from the wealthy to impoverished workers, to band together for their common good: "My Sisters, unite with me, so that we do not remain behind, when everything and everyone about us near and far presses forward and struggles. We too want to demand our participation and gain from the great World Liberation, in which all humankind, of which we are half, finally must share." She then criticized male revolutionaries for ignoring women and excluding them from the reforms they demanded for themselves: "But freedom is indivisible! Free men cannot bear enslaved men around them—nor enslaved women. We must question the upright intentions and mental power of all male freedom fighters if they champion only the rights of men, and not those of women at the same time.

At the end of her editorial, Otto printed a "*Call* to German Women and Girls for the Establishment of a True Female Emancipation," entreating all "like-minded" women to contact her.[1] Building on earlier networks formed among German women, she created a feminist movement centered about her weekly news journal.

Otto was writing this editorial seventeen years after the Saint-Simonian New Women printed their 1832 *Call to Women* and in far different circumstances from the earlier group, but the similarities between their two appeals are clear. Both attempted to unite women of all ranks into a separate organization to work for their own interests. Both insisted that the participation of the female half of humanity was essential to any political and economic progress. Both dared to criticize male allies who had initially encouraged women's development but later refused to acknowledge their rights. Both applied the concepts of slavery and emancipation to women's situation. What connected these early feminists in the years between the July revolution of 1830 in France and the European upheavals of 1848 was a common body of international literature providing both news and confirmation of a shared outlook and sensibility. Support from "like-minded" foreigners lay behind Louise Otto's ability to organize a women's movement in Germany. In later life, looking back on how she had first become able to articulate feminist demands, Otto paid tribute to this international influence. "It is generally well known how during the 1830s a fresh breeze blew through the world, progressive movements and new perspectives everywhere struggled for acceptance," she wrote. "The position of women likewise came under discussion, and became one of the issues of the day because many would have liked to do more than was permitted them. I myself, even living in a small town and only twenty-four, took up my pen to lay claim to and defend the right of my sex to independence."[2]

Corroboration from abroad was essential to women like Louise Otto, who lived far from Paris or London and lacked the personal contacts that supported the Saint-Simonian New Women in the early 1830s. Growing up in Meissen, Saxony, Otto came of age in a culture that both Germans and others considered to be exceptionally traditional, particularly with regard to women. Everywhere, but "especially in Germany, women's destiny in common has always been: wife, mother, household," the conservative J. Hillebrand declared approvingly in his influential 1818 essay, "On Germany's National Development." Progressives deplored the German view "that a woman needs no more for her happiness than a looking glass and sweets, and that her worth lies only in the kitchen with a child at her breast," Otto wrote in an 1843 article. But they agreed with traditionalists that in the German lands, woman's status did not equal that of other Western nations.[3] "They only think of her as a *hausfrau*, not a rational being and intellectual companion," English reformer William Howitt complained after living in Heidelberg with his wife Mary for three years. "A German never talks on any subject superior to common chit-chat, to a woman. . . . a Mrs. Somerville or Martineau writing on astronomy or political economy would set all the wigs of the old philosophers and professors on fire."[4] The image of "the German who complacently smokes his meerschaum, while his wife, yoked with the ox, draws the plough through its furrow," as Elizabeth Cady Stanton put it in her speech to the Seneca Falls Women's Rights Convention in 1848, was used by feminists throughout the Western community to personify the exceptional subordination of German women in this period.[5]

In these circumstances, support from outside was crucial for women who wanted more than a purely domestic life. Otto considered herself one of a tiny group of German women who had "developed despite all restricting circumstances," but added, "how unhappy these few must be in their isolated position!"[6] Education and literature assuaged her loneliness. Otto's happiest childhood memories were of school, especially "the general enthusiasm" of "the memorable years" following the 1830 revolution in France, when her teachers "gave us commentaries on things that children otherwise could not have understood," and she and her fellow students "eagerly devoured the newspapers." Although her formal education ended at fifteen, she found "quiet hours to read challenging works," a habit acquired in childhood when one of her three older sisters read aloud "from English or German novelists" while the others did housework. After the death of her parents and her eldest sister when Louise Otto was sixteen, she continued to study while living in the household of a "narrow-minded" aunt, astonishing a male visitor with her ability to knit while reading Hegel.[7] In her early twenties, Otto started writing in private, justifying the act in her diary as "a duty to follow this vocation which God has given us." She began publishing late in 1842, at age twenty-three; her first feminist pieces appeared early the following year.

Breaking the public silence considered appropriate for their sex in this period was the crucial first step toward the creation of women's movements. Today, we tend to draw a line between writing and action, but in the 1830s and 1840s writing was the single most important and influential feminist activity women undertook. "I view my appearance today in this arena [a Mannheim newspaper] . . . as a *deed*," the German Louise Dittmar asserted in an 1847 article in which she reiterated Otto's argument that any real progress in society demanded female participation:

> For the first time a woman speaks out openly about what she understands as freedom of her conscience; she sees *self-determination* as a second creation, the creation of her self-liberating spirit. She herself provides an example which will incur the hostility of narrow-minded and hypocritical natures.[8]

The confirmation gained from reading helped women like Otto and Dittmar find courage to risk the censure and disapproval that they knew awaited them when they published. By appearing in print at all, women challenged the contemporary ideal of female domesticity. To Otto's generation, born in the first decades of the nineteenth century, writing for a public audience "was still considered a bold venture, a daring stepping out from the circle of womanliness when one risked publishing one's name in the press," she recalled.[9] The phrase "public woman" or "fille publique" meant "prostitute," and conservative opinion equated women's writing with prostitution. For women, publishing "deprives them of all delicacy" and "has pretty much the same effect on them as it would to walk abroad through the streets, physically stark naked," American author Nathaniel Hawthorne asserted in 1842.[10] There was no tradition of great women writers. "I look everywhere for grandmothers and see none," English poet Elizabeth Barrett complained three years later.[11] In these circumstances, even writings celebrating marriage, home, and children—provided they were written by female authors—were sought out by women eager to prove female capacity for a life beyond domesticity. "When I was in Edinburgh [in 1840 on her honeymoon] I bought one day a little volume because of its title, *Records of Woman* . . . by Mrs. Hemans," Elizabeth Cady Stanton wrote a few years later about the English poet whose first volume was *The Domestic Affections*. "How proud I am when I see one of my sex doing anything well."[12]

Early feminists scoured publications for confirmation of their beliefs in print, whether in poetry, novels, newspaper articles, or political pamphlets. In a section of her 1845 *Woman in the Nineteenth Century* in which she opposed the view that men should be the "heads" and women the "hearts," American intellectual Margaret Fuller cited a wide range of reading to strengthen her argument:

> This morning, I open the Boston "Daily Mail," and find in its "poet's corner," a translation of Schiller's "Dignity of Woman." In the advertisement of a book on America, I see in the table of contents this sequence, "Republican Institutions. American Slavery. American Ladies."
>
> I open the "*Deutsche Schnellpost*," published in New York, and find at the head of a column, *Juden und Frauen-emancipation in Ungarn*" —"Emancipation of Jews and Women in Hungary."[13]

Reading often encouraged writing. By the time she produced her *Women's Newspaper* in 1849, Louise Otto had penned numerous newspaper articles and published five novels as well as an anthology of her poems.[14] Most of her writing, whether fiction or nonfiction, poetry or prose, dealt with current social and political issues: German national unification, the plight of poor workers, religious freedom, and women's rights. In her use of fiction and poetry to call attention to the world's ills, Otto joined an important trend in Western literature of this period. Novelists such as Charles Dickens and Victor Hugo focused on social and economic problems like poverty and conditions in the new factories and cities, often highlighting the disadvantaged situation of women and children. "The novel has become an essay on morals, on political economy, on the condition of women, on the vices and defects of social life," the U.S. *North American Review* noted in 1844.[15]

Throughout the Western world, early feminists drew support from this growing international body of publications that rejected conventional limits on women's lives. The authority of the printed word gave weight to their own opinions, imparting "the advantage novels give to a cause," as a radical English journal put it in 1846.[16] Unlike socialist literature, which primarily reached those committed to its ideals, fiction circulated widely, especially among women and girls of the growing middle class. By the end of the eighteenth century, novel reading was so associated with the female sex that a series of works, from Mary Wollstonecraft's *Vindication of the Rights of Woman* of 1792 to Jane Austen's *Northanger Abbey* of 1817 disparaged and ridiculed the practice.[17] Although "any kind of reading I think better than leaving a blank still a blank," wrote Wollstonecraft, "when . . . I advise my sex not to read such flimsy works, it is to induce them to read something superior."[18] Thirty years later, novelists were weaving serious topics, including feminism, into their fiction.

This dissident literature, which easily crossed national borders, could reach previously isolated individuals, like the young Louise Otto in Meissen. Emboldened by the confirmation of their views in print, some, like Otto herself, produced feminist writings of their own, further expanding the body of works available to women readers. "Only after the [French] July revolution [of 1830] and the political progress of the year 1840, did light begin to illumine the wilderness of women's literature," Otto later wrote, "and the question of emancipation, which until then stayed very much in the background, came to the fore and soon became the banner around which" we rallied.[19]

By the time Louise Otto published her first article on women's emancipation in 1843, she had already encountered feminist ideas in her wide-ranging reading of foreign authors, some of whom became her heroes. During these years, Romantic artists challenged both aesthetic conventions and the political status quo. In Europe especially, where expressions of political discontent were severely controlled, the arts became the vehicle of social criticism. "Romanticism is liberalism in literature," French writer Victor Hugo declared in the preface to his tragedy *Hernani*, whose performance triggered riots in Paris in 1830. The death of the English poet George Gordon, Lord Byron, fighting for Greek independence from the Turks in 1824, embodied the heroic artist's dedication to social change.

Louise Otto hung portraits of Byron, Nikolaus Lenau, a dissident Hungarian poet, and French novelist George Sand in her study during these years.[20] Sand's influence was especially significant. Romantic artists were men—Byron, Keats, Shelley, Schiller, Goethe, Beethoven, Chateaubriand, Hugo—but in the 1830s George Sand appropriated the model for women. Although Sand considered herself a lone exception to the rules that bound other women and later repudiated attempts to form women's movements, her life and writings inspired many early feminists. Leaving her husband in 1831, she moved to Paris, where she defied middle-class conventions by dressing like a man, taking famous lovers, and publishing a series of successful novels featuring independent heroines, which were read throughout Europe and America. Her influence, especially on women, was immense. "There is no woman of spirit who is not a bit of a George Sand," a Viennese critic wrote in 1848. Elizabeth Barrett and Louise Otto were among the many female writers who produced pieces lauding her accomplishments in the 1840s.[21]

Sand's early works challenged "the barbaric injustice of the laws that still control a woman's existence within marriage, family, and society," as she wrote when her first triumph, the novel *Indiana*, was reprinted in 1842. Originally published in 1832, *Indiana* featured a heroine who leaves a loveless marriage, much as Sand herself had done. "You can make me keep quiet, but you can't keep me from thinking," Indiana declares to her husband, presenting her situation as one demanding emancipation:

> I know that I am the slave, and you the master, the laws of this country have made you my master. You can tie me up, pin my hands behind my back, control my actions. You have all the rights of the one who is stronger, and society confirms those rights—but you have no right over my will, monsieur, and you cannot command it. Only God can change or rule it.[22]

Sand was by no means the only female author read internationally in these years who pointed out the oppression in the lives of supposedly privileged women. Swedish novelist Fredrika Bremer became immensely popular abroad as well as in Scandinavia. When she arrived in New York City in 1849, she was besieged by fans at her hotel.[23] Bremer's novels were rapidly translated into German; Quaker reformer Mary Howitt then produced the English translations from the German volumes she read during her stay in Heidelberg. "Female human beings should be depicted in *the novel* as those who through their own willpower want to conquer all outer resistance and validate their talents so that they make themselves independent and happy and become a blessing for others (or for society)," Bremer wrote a woman friend in 1845.[24] Portraying family life, she wove support for independent womanhood into her homey narratives, as in this scene from her 1848 novel, *Brothers and Sisters*:

> Lagertha Knutson trembled and turned pale with the eyes of so many riveted upon her. . . . But when the General said pleasantly, "And you have ventured alone, and so late in the year, to take so long a journey—and quite alone?—look you, I call that brave and unusual in a young lady!"
> Lagertha replied, in a gentle but determined voice, "People may do anything that they will."
> "Bravo! I like to hear that!" exclaimed the old soldier.[25]

Early feminists especially prized English novelist Charlotte Brontë's *Jane Eyre*, both Fredrika Bremer and Susan B. Anthony numbering it among their favorite books.[26] Today the plot of *Jane Eyre* has become a cliché, recycled in thousands of romantic stories in which the governess wins marriage with a wealthy, mysterious hero. But when the novel first appeared in 1847, it exhilarated radicals and shocked traditionalists. "We do not hesitate to say that the tone of mind and thought which has over-thrown authority and violated every code human and divine abroad and fostered Chartism and rebellion at home [in Britain], is the same which has also written *Jane Eyre*," Lady Eastlake declared in the prestigious *Quarterly Review*.[27] By adhering to her own independent convictions, Brontë's poor, plain, orphaned protagonist triumphs over a society that tries to keep her in the lowly position allotted to single women without money. As she struggles to survive while maintaining her integrity, Jane Eyre voices sub-versive opinions about both her own situation and that of the female sex in general. "Women feel just as men feel; they need exercise for their facul-ties, and a field for their efforts as much as their brothers do; they suffer from too rigid a restraint, too absolute a stagnation, precisely as men would suffer," she affirms shortly after beginning work as a governess.[28] "Women of the broad earth—whether English or American, French or German, it was for you that Charlotte Brontë wrote, for no conventional puppets, no dolls of fashion!" asserted American author Caroline Healey Dall in her 1855 obituary of Brontë. "*Jane Eyre* was a fearfully honest book. That was why it startled the echoes of all the corners of the earth and gathered them into one hoarse cry of opprobrium."[29]

To sympathetic readers, both the writings and the lives of these female authors demonstrated the need for concerted action to improve women's situation. Louise Otto made that point in her poem "To George Sand" and in an article she published on *Jane Eyre*, as Dall did in a report aimed at reforming the laws of New England states concerning women:

> A George Sand, breaking loose from the ties which bound her to society. . . .
> A Fredrika Bremer, a Charlotte Brontë, full of restless longings, of unsatis-fied aspirations, show you the path before you. Why is it that a low wail runs through all the literature that women have given to the world? . . . It is because women feel a helplessness that they think without remedy. Show them that it is not so.[30]

Presenting scenes of women's oppression that contradicted the reigning ideal of female domesticity was the first task of early feminists who wished to remedy the situation of their sex. "Women whose lives have been tor-mented by great misfortunes should make their troubles speak," wrote French socialist Flora Tristan in 1838. "They should expose the hardships they have endured as a result of the position laws have imposed on them and prejudices they are imprisoned by. . . . Because reform can not take place, and there will be no probity and freedom in social relationships, without the effect of such revelations."[31]

Public speaking remained rare and difficult for women in this era, but increasing numbers became able to voice demands for the improvement of the female condition in print. Unlike lecturing, or most other ways of earning income, writing could be done privately in the home, hidden from disapproving relatives and neighbors if necessary. English author Harriet

Martineau remembered that she first wrote secretly, "before breakfast or in some private way." Fredrika Bremer never let her tyrannical father know she had published.[32] Anonymity and pseudonyms also protected women authors, especially at the beginning of their career. Louise Otto wrote her first article on female emancipation under her "half pseudonym" of Otto Stern. Like her, a number of early feminists protected themselves by using pseudonyms, initials, or publishing anonymously at first, later gaining the confidence to appear in print under their own names. Louise Otto discarded her pen name after a few years. Elizabeth Cady Stanton abandoned "Sunflower," as Mathilde Franziska Anneke did "Freimund Geissel," and Jenny d'Héricourt "Félix Lamb." "And now, having written about ultraists, I have become somewhat emboldened myself," concluded an 1849 article in the *Lily*, an American women's rights journal. "Sufficiently to subjoin in place of my previous signature— Annj—my whole name. Lydia Ann Jenkins." Female authors who retained their pseudonyms, like the Europeans George Sand and George Eliot, or the Americans Fanny Fern and Grace Greenwood, did so because of their success: the pen name sold books long after their true identities became known.[33]

Writing under a male identity freed women from the cultural constraints limiting what respectable females were supposed to say. Louise Otto published two articles about women's situation in 1843, the first as Otto Stern, the second under her own name. "Louise Otto" began her piece on women's rights "with diffidence," presenting herself as "a young woman who modestly requests only a word on behalf of an entire sex, which she belongs to with love and joyfulness." Acknowledging that men "could express themselves better, deeper, more thoroughly than I," she built her case for women's political participation by paying homage to her era's conception of womanhood, which designated the emotions as female and the intellect as male. Women's feelings, particularly their love of home, justified their love of the fatherland and their involvement in its struggles. The intensity of their feelings came "precisely because we are directed to rule in a limited arena and in quiet, because we are not made for the more hurriedly paced life of men, whom we may follow with our eyes, but not with our steps!" Reassuring her readers that her views about women would not "suppress our best part: *femininity* through innoculation with alien, masculine strivings," Louise Otto modestly concluded that she would only write again "if encouraged to do so."[34]

As "Otto Stern," however, the young author could be far bolder. Entitling her first published article "On Women's Emancipation," she wholeheartedly endorsed the need for massive improvement in women's condition and made fun of those who took the other side, all in the confident, jocular style of a male journalist of the day: "Our time is the time of progress. Do we, the stronger sex, wish to advance from rung to rung up the high ladder of intelligence, of individual and universal freedom and not permit our other half to take a single step forward?"[35]

Comparing the situation of Germans to the relative freedom enjoyed by women in England, France, and the United States, the piece concluded with a ringing denunciation of German stodginess and conservatism. Ostensibly quoting an unnamed woman "he" had met at the Dresden lecture series that had inspired this article, "Otto Stern" ended with this woman's words, probably uttered by Louise Otto herself. "I don't care about the academic establishment!" she had declared, repudiating the authority of the prestigious German university system, with its all-male professoriate and student body. "It will always remain a triumph for us women that a man [Carl Eduard Vehse, the lecturer on women's emancipation] put our need into words. Once such a real, deep need to speak is brought forth, it cannot go back to its earlier muteness, its progress *must* sooner or later be felt, no matter 'how?' or 'where?' Life provides the proof."[36]

Louise Otto's delicate balancing act between the male and female stereotypes of her day was characteristic of other early feminists. Since "the world" was male territory, women who wanted a life outside their province of "the home" had to counter the charge that they wanted to become men. Repudiating domesticity without putting one's sexual identity in question proved difficult, even for those older and far more established than Louise Otto. In 1849, for instance, Quaker minister Lucretia Mott made a speech replying to Richard Henry Dana, a prominent U.S. literary critic who had recently argued that women's involvement in public life violated their "womanly nature" and meant they were acting in roles reserved for men. Even from the security of her position as a happily married wife, mother, and grandmother, a veteran antislavery activist, and one of the best-known women in America, Mott also wrestled with the conundrum presented by sexual stereotypes. "So far from her 'ambition leading her to attempt to act the man,'" Mott asserted,

> she needs all the encouragement she can receive, by the removal of obstacles from her path in order that she may become a "true woman." As it is desirable that man should act a manly and generous part, not "mannish," so let woman be urged to exercise a dignified and womanly bearing, not "womanish." Let her cultivate all the graces and proper accomplishments of her sex, but let not these degenerate into a kind of effeminacy, in which she is satisfied to be the mere plaything or toy of society, content with her outward adorning, and with the tone of flattery and fulsome adulation too often addressed to her.[37]

These early feminists usually acknowledged that genuine differences existed between the sexes but argued that they were relatively minor, had been exaggerated by contemporary society, and should not prevent

women from participating in public life. "With regard to the rights of
women, I am persuaded . . . that our rights are the same as men's,
altho' circumstances may render our status different," American abolitionist Sarah Grimké wrote the English activist Elizabeth Pease in
1842.

> It is plainly the right of all human beings to cultivate the powers which God
> has given us; it is plainly the duty of woman to nurse her offspring; it can-
> not be the duty of man because God has not furnished him with the nour-
> ishment necessary for the infant. . . . When [men] better understand the
> rights of women as human beings, they will see that they are co-equal with
> their own.[38]

Reconciling women's differences from men with their equality to men
had been a major concern of the Saint-Simonian New Women in the early
1830s. The expansive vision they achieved—that women were both equal
to and different from men—runs through the feminism of this period. If
women are equal to men, then they deserve to vote because men vote,
Ernestine Rose often argued, and if they are different, then they deserve to
vote because men cannot represent them. "It is because woman is equal to
man and because she is not the same as man that she must take part in the
work of social reform," Jeanne Deroin asserted when she campaigned to
be a member of the French legislature in 1849.[39] Louise Otto consistently
upheld the Saint-Simonian principle that both male and female participation were essential for society's well-being. "Man and woman are formed
by the hand of God or Creation—whatever you wish to call it—as two
creatures fully equal at birth," she wrote in her *Women's Newspaper*. "Only
when both are united do they form a whole. . . . It is a sin, not only against
woman but against *humankind* and against the principle of Creation, to
force women into perpetual servitude, to limit her to the narrow circle of
domesticity and thus to exclude her from those other aims of humanity
that are not related to the family."[40]

The wide diffusion of Saint-Simonian arguments and their usefulness
to early feminists should not blind us to the difficulties women encountered in employing them after Saint-Simonianism's collapse in the mid-
1830s. Throughout the Western community, the linkage of women and
any word meaning greater independence—emancipation, freedom, liberation or liberty—was invariably interpreted sexually. Reinforced by the
spread of "George-Sandism," which endorsed women's "freedom of the
heart" to pursue romantic liaisons, public opinion construed female claims
for rights and improvement as meaning only the desire for greater sexual
activity. Under these circumstances, feminists sought to uncouple claims
for female emancipation from those for sexual liberation. In her first Otto
Stern piece, as well as in many subsequent writings, Louise Otto attempted to distinguish between "the emancipation of women," desired by "all
who prize progress," both in Germany and abroad, and "the emancipation

of the flesh" of the French Saint-Simonians, the source of "the shameless picture of the *femme libre*" before which "every German woman lowers her eyes."[41] Former Saint-Simonian New Women encountered the same problem. When some of them created the Society for the Emancipation of Women in Paris in 1848, they added a footnote on the front page of their *Manifesto* to define their use of this controversial term:

> The word emancipation, in its positive and legitimate meaning, signifies, above all, intellectual and moral liberation. This first and superior condition being, for both sexes, the normal basis of all social progress. . . . The word emancipation is still so often abused that this explanatory note seemed necessary to us.[42]

Such precision signified a diminution of feminist claims. In early Owenism and Saint-Simonianism, as well as in the teachings of Charles Fourier, female sexuality was considered a legitimate natural desire deserving of full satisfaction. But in the aftermath of Saint-Simonianism's collapse, many questioned the wisdom of women pursuing sexual freedom when theory outstripped practice. Sexual unions without traditional guarantees of male responsibility "are much more unequal than legal marriages," a male Owenite editor concluded, since if the man deserted, the woman "is loaded with reproach . . . and left with the burden of a family. . . . [It is] not so much an emancipation of woman as an emancipation of man."[43] A number of women who had been active in the socialist circles that questioned traditional sexual behavior in the 1820s and early 1830s later repudiated a freedom that seemed to benefit only men. "The [Saint-Simonian] family group that I was a part of was not powerful enough, nor was it organized strongly enough, to replace paternal protection," former New Woman Suzanne Voilquin wrote in her 1866 memoirs.[44] Pauline Roland, who bore four children out of wedlock to two Saint-Simonians, denounced "this false theory that the mother alone is the family," after the fathers failed to help support their children. Ernestine Rose, who lived with her husband in an Owenite community at Skaneateles, New York in the 1840s, opposed a resolution condemning marriage at a later Free Convention and substituted one stating "that the only true and natural marriage is an exclusive conjugal love based on perfect equality between one man and one woman; the only true home is the isolated home based on this exclusive love."[45]

Given these difficulties, one might expect early feminists to abandon words like "emancipation" or "liberation." Instead, they provided elaborate explanations for using such terms. "The heading of our page is not of our choosing," American Paulina Wright Davis asserted about an English article entitled "Emancipated Women" that she reprinted in her feminist journal, the *Una*. As editor, Davis could have chosen any title she wished. Instead, she blamed Swedish novelist Fredrika Bremer (who had nothing to do with the piece in question):

The term as applied has no meaning, for there is no class of women who can claim, in the present age of the movement, that they are "set free of bondage, slavery, servitude, subjection, or dependence," which is the definition given by Webster of the word emancipated. It was, we believe, first applied to a class [of women] by Fredrika Bremer, whose limited knowledge of English may be an apology for her use of words and phrases, which are not only inexpressive, but in exceeding bad taste.[46]

Writing in an anthology about European women's movements compiled by Theodore Stanton in 1884, two German feminists articulated the dilemma such words presented. "The women's movement . . . was brought into disrepute as the 'Emancipation of Women,'" they wrote, echoing Louise Otto's early writings. "The greatest stumbling-block in our way has been the signification given to this term, and we tacitly agreed to avoid its use, although it was impossible to find one which could exactly replace it."[47]

This was precisely the problem. Demanding women's emancipation while not offending contemporary sensibilities proved impossible, since female independence and rights, even when stripped of any claims to sexual liberation, contravened the domestic model of womanhood. "There is, indeed, something unfeminine in independence," wrote the Englishwoman Mrs. Sandford in her 1831 guidebook for women. "It is contrary to nature and therefore it offends."[48] In this difficult situation, early feminists continued to employ the radical concept of emancipation to signify women's need to be liberated from bondage, but they tended to blame foreigners—whether the French nation as a whole or the irreproachably moral Fredrika Bremer—for the word's unsavory connotations when applied to women.

Encouraging these tendencies to division and fragmentation was the growing power of the nation-state, which linked female domesticity and chastity to national identity. The period when early feminists attempted to make international connections to each other was the age of nationalism in the West, when the United States and European nations sought to carve out independent identities and territories, to distinguish themselves as individual cultural and political entities. "Every people has its special mission, which will co-operate towards the fulfillment of the general mission of humanity," declared the "Act of Brotherhood" issued by the revolutionary organization Young Europe in 1834. "That mission constitutes its *nationality*. Nationality is sacred."[49] Despite women's automatic exclusion from all-male nationalist organizations, they were not immune to their era's growing prejudices and stereotypes, even when they worked for international causes. "National vanity makes us want the country where Providence ordained our birth to reign supreme. This malevolent disposition toward other nations, the bitter fruit of past conflicts, constitutes the greatest obstacle to progress and often prevents us from acknowledging the causes of the evils which the foreign visitor calls to our attention," French socialist Flora Tristan wrote in her book on England, the product of four extended stays there in the 1820s and 1830s. But in the same work Tristan, who labored for years to create international connections, also reproduced standard French clichés about England: that the people were cold and silent, the weather dreadful, and the horses ugly. Such animosities even overrode her customary criticism of her own nation for its injustice to women. "In France, and any country which prides itself on being civilized, the most honored of living creatures is woman," she wrote, merging Fourier's principle with conventional nineteenth-century chivalry. "In England, it is the horse."[50]

The growing British economy and empire, its reformed government and relative freedom, led even English feminists critical of women's situation to sing their country's praises. "We see that no other spot of earth ever before contained such an amount of infallible resources as our own country at this day," Harriet Martineau wrote in 1843, "so much knowledge, so much sense, so much vigour, foresight, and benevolence, or such an amount of external means. We see the progress of amelioration, silent but sure."[51] Such feelings intensified as Britain avoided revolution in 1848 and celebrated its unrivaled prosperity and domestic peace at the Great Exhibition of 1851, the first world's fair. Held in the newly erected Crystal Palace of Industry, an immense modern shell of iron and glass, the exhibition dazzled all who saw it. "It was the spirit of spring," wrote Fredrika Bremer, traveling in England that year.

> Free trade had borne its fruits; beneath its flag Commerce and Industry had blossomed with fresh life; the price of corn had fallen, bread was cheap. With strong and powerful growth the Tree of Liberty . . . had penetrated into the very heart of English life. The Crystal Palace was its great and magnificent blossom, and multitudes of men, like swarms of bees, flew on the wings of steam to this universe flower, by which all the nations of the earth had promised to meet, and to which, all manufactures, all industry, all soils, had sent their fruits to be the pleasure, and the admiration of all.[52]

By midcentury, British achievements had produced a smug sense of superiority and an imperviousness to criticism whether from home or abroad. "Why is it that an Irishman or Frenchman's hatred of England does not excite in me an answering hatred?" English historian Thomas Babington Macaulay wrote in his diary in 1849. "I imagine that my national pride prevents it. England is so great that an Englishman cares not what others think of her, or how they talk of her." Two years earlier on a visit to England, American author Ralph Waldo Emerson concluded that such bombast had become a national trait: "The habit of brag runs through all classes from *The Times* newspaper through politicians and poets . . . down to the boys at Eton. In the gravest treatise in political economy, in a philo-sophical essay, in books of science, one is surprised by the most innocent exhibition of unflinching nationality.[53]

Americans tended to be critical of the English in this period, prizing their own nation's democracy and equality over the snobbery and self-sat-isfaction of the "mother country." "The adulation of an English audience for rank and title is disgusting to an American republican," James Mott wrote after he and his wife Lucretia traveled through the British isles in 1840. "During our stay we . . . contrasted the residences of the lords and nobles . . . with the wretched abodes of thousands. . . . The difference in condition is very striking to any observant American, and should be a warning to us to adhere to such institutions in our country, as will secure and perpetuate a truly democratic form of government, in which the greatest good of the greatest number is the first object, instead of the good of the few at the expense of the many."[54]

The United States gave hope to progressives on both sides of the Atlantic in these years. "Slavery out of the question, our country is a century in advance of England on the score of reform, and of general intelligence and morality," radical abolitionist William Lloyd Garrison wrote to his wife in 1840.[55] Many foreign visitors, however, wanted to tour the slave states to see America's "peculiar institution" firsthand. The paradox of slavery and racial prejudice coexisting with genuine political freedom and equality for white men—accompanied by a touchy pride in the superiority of all things American—characterized the United States to many Europeans in these years. Asked by a friend to bring something "exclusively American" back from her 1834–1836 visit, Harriet Martineau decided that a New York judge she encountered epit-omized the young nation:

> He was the first article I met with that could not by any possibility have been picked up anywhere out of the United States. He was about six feet high, lank as a flail, and seeming to be held together only by the long-tailed drab greatcoat into which he was put. He had a quid in his cheek whenever I saw him, and squirted tobacco juice into the fireplace or elsewhere at inter-vals of about twenty seconds. . . . He was a dogged republican, with an uncompromising hatred of the blacks, and with an indifferent sort of pity for all foreigners.[56]

National stereotypes and prejudices shaped views about France and the Germanies as well as the United States and Britain in these years. Despite political conservatism and peaceful conditions in the 1830s and 1840s, France remained associated with the revolutionary bellicosity of 1789 and the Napoleonic era, reinforced by the short-lived revolution of 1830. France also denoted both romance and style, the claims of the heart as well as of the arts and fashion. These seemingly contradictory qualities were depicted in a French cartoon of 1848, which drew France as the heart of

Europe, a heart composed of artists and soldiers.[57] "If you are in Paris how you must be enjoying yourself . . . the beautiful city, the pictures and the historical associations; the *human*," the young English feminist Bessie Rayner Parkes wrote her friend Barbara Leigh Smith in 1847. "With me the spirit of the revolution in the beginning almost overpowers the crime, so that in spite of Robespierre I think of the whole with pleasure." To those more radical, Paris remained the center of revolutionary hopes. "It is not true that in Paris there is only external beauty; that it is only the city for the thoughtless and the frivolous," Ernestine Rose wrote in the *Boston Investigator*. "No! to me it speaks the language of universal brotherhood; it seems the capital of the world, the representative of mankind; its inmost heart vibrates for all times, nations, and grades."[58] Many within France also considered that "la grande nation" led the world in both civilized living and social reform. "It is pre-eminently for France to study keenly to resolve a problem" (the persistence of poverty) "manifested in this day and age in all the industrial nations of Europe," the revolutionary government confidently declared early in 1848.[59]

French assurance, based on its national history, its military triumphs, its sense of being the center of the civilized world, contrasted with German doubts in this period. "Russia and France possess the land / Great Britain rules the sea, / Ours is the cloudy realm of dreams / Where there's no rivalry," poet in exile Heinrich Heine wrote in his 1844 satire, *Germany: A Winter's Tale*.[60] Divided into thirty-nine independent states, governed by absolute monarchs who restored aristocratic privileges and feudal obligations after 1815, controlled by rigorous press censorship as well as police surveillance, the German lands struggled to win both the national existence and the political liberties already achieved in France, England, and the United States. Associating both unification and constitutionalism with the hated French, whose revolutionary armies had conquered and occupied their lands, a number of German rulers managed to block all change, including any public discussion of railroads, within their territories. "Many excellent reforms have encountered a long and obstinate resistance on this side of the Rhine simply because they were said to be a product of the upheaval of 1789," two German feminists later wrote, concluding that "the women's movement" had suffered especially from this "unfortunate origin."[61]

Forbidden almost all forms of political expression before the 1840s, German men who wanted change met in all-male "brotherhoods" ostensibly centered about activities designated as exclusively masculine, like sharpshooting and gymnastics. Resenting their image as impractical philosophers who debated but could not act, radical Germans made poetry their vehicle of political criticism. The revolutionary Ferdinand Freiligrath's 1844 "Deutschland Ist Hamlet!" received wide acclaim, and in one of her first articles Louise Otto wrote that "political poetry has awakened the German woman."[62]

As in other societies of this period, idealized female domesticity came to incarnate a new national identity that repudiated the politically active women of the French ancien régime. Gretchen at her spinning wheel in Goethe's *Faust* and Lotte slicing bread and butter in his novel *Werther*, as well as the chaste, industrious mothers and daughters who "weave heavenly roses into earthly life" in Schiller's poem "Dignity of Women," provided appealing German models of feminine virtue in the first decades of the nineteenth century.

To counter these powerful and linked forces of nationalism and female domesticity, early feminists turned to universal concepts, which, they argued, transcended both geographic boundaries and gendered divisions. "Humanity," "equality," "rights," and "freedom" appear in feminist writings throughout the West in these decades. Of all these internationalist ideas that they applied to women's situation, "'emancipation'...the catchword of our day," as Louise Otto called it in her first article, proved the most significant and widely used. Despite the sexual connotations of "female emancipation," the phrase was too potent and liberating to be discarded. Identifying privileged women's condition as slavery immediately stripped away the poetry and metaphor shrouding this group's supposed propensity to be angels within the home. "It is easy to call women angels because it makes them easier to render slaves," radical English editor Douglas Jerrold asserted in an 1847 article. "Sugar-plum phrases for the sex, as many as you will—but no equalising statutes."[63] By appropriating the empowering concept of emancipation to express their view that women's situation was an oppressed condition that demanded transformation, early feminists like Louise Otto and Désirée Véret, Harriet Martineau and Lucretia Mott drew on a universal idea especially influential in the 1830s and 1840s.

Derived from a Latin verb that meant freeing a wife or child from the power and control of the father of the family, the word's history crossed temporal and political borders. As the European slave trade expanded in the seventeenth and eighteenth centuries, the word came to specify freeing the enslaved Africans shipped to the Americas. From the French Revolution of 1789 on, emancipation was increasingly used to signify the hoped-for liberation of other oppressed groups. The Third Estate, composed of the disenfranchised French peasantry and bourgeoisie, won emancipation through the revolution from traditional laws favoring the aristocracy and clergy. In societies that continued to support established state churches, emancipation came to mean the removal of legal penalties for religious dissidents. The "emancipation of the Jews" was debated throughout Europe in this period; the issue of "Catholic emancipation" dominated English politics in the late 1820s. "Peasant emancipation" emerged as an issue in eastern Europe, where serfdom still prevailed. In the United States and most European colonies in the New World, emancipation came to mean the abolition of the institution of slavery itself, and emancipation societies formed to accomplish that goal.

Feminists began to apply the concept of emancipation to women's situation during the French Revolution. The major feminist writers of the revolutionary era, from Wollstonecraft to de Gouges, compared women's status to that of slaves and called for their liberation from men. The German Theodor von Hippel, in his 1792 *On Improving the Civic Status of Women*, forcefully argued that men had reduced women to slavery and accused the revolutionary French government of perpetuating that injustice by denying women equal rights.[64] William Thompson and Anna Wheeler's 1825 *Appeal of One Half the Human Race, Women, Against the Pretensions of the Other Half, Men, To Retain Them in Political, and Thence in Civil and Domestic Slavery* was organized around the linked themes of slavery and emancipation. The Saint-Simonian New Women's writings of the early 1830s repeatedly called women's condition slavery, asserted that men were their masters, and demanded emancipation for the female sex.

Emancipation inspired the next organized movement of women. The feminism pioneered by the Saint-Simonian New Women in France was paralleled by that developed by some activist antislavery women in Britain and the United States in the 1830s. Radically challenging female domesticity, these abolitionists had impact both on their own societies and on other nations within the Western community. Their organizations were short-lived, but like that of the New Women, they made lasting contributions to international feminism. And like the New Women, these antislavery activists simultaneously helped weave the connections that became the loosely knit international women's movement. This network, in turn, sustained them when their original campaigns failed.

Like early socialism, abolitionism was an international cause that initially welcomed female participation. Enlisted as subscribers and supporters but not allowed to be actual members of the antislavery societies that formed in Britain in the late eighteenth century, women committed to this work began to assert radical ideas of their own by the 1820s. While white male leaders worked for the "gradual" abolition of slavery in the British West Indies, arguing that slaves were not yet ready for freedom, and for "colonization" societies in the United States, which would return blacks to Africa, English Quaker Elizabeth Heyrick shifted the terms of the debate by publishing her radical pamphlet *Immediate, Not Gradual Abolition* in 1824. Male antislavery advocates divided over the timing of emancipation, but female antislavery societies, created in Britain in the 1820s and in the United States in the 1830s, almost uniformly supported Heyrick's more radical position. "We ought to obey God rather than man," the Sheffield [England] Female Anti-Slavery Society declared in 1827, explaining their decision to advocate immediate emancipation: "Confidence here is not at variance with humility. On principles like these, the simple need not fear to confront the sage; nor a *female* society to take their stand against the united wisdom of this world."[65]

In Britain, where slavery had been outlawed since the late eighteenth century, female emancipation societies focused on ending the system in the sugar islands of the British West Indies. Invoking the medieval right to petition the government, traditionally available to even the lowliest of subjects, British female abolitionists collected immense numbers of signatures for their cause. They amassed 187,000 in ten days in 1833 to end West Indian slavery, and 662,000 more in 1838 to reject the oppressive West Indian apprenticeship system for former slaves.[66] Opposed by male politicians, who laughed when their petitions were delivered to the House of Commons, as well as by traditionalist men within abolitionist ranks, British antislavery women inspired their American counterparts. "We have been told repeatedly that the ladies of Great Britain (by petitioning Parliament) did much towards hastening the cause of Emancipation, in the British West Indies," the 1836 report of a Rhode Island female antislavery society asserted. "And shall we, the republican daughters of Columbia, be less zealous in the cause of Freedom than they?" Thousands of American women joined the campaign to gather signatures for antislavery petitions in these years, contributing to an increase of such magnitude that the House of Representatives enacted the Gag Act, under which such petitions were tabled unread from 1836 to 1844.[67]

Female petitioning spread in this period to France, where it had not previously been part of the political culture. Between 1836 and 1838 the feminist magazine *Gazette des femmes* printed news of female antislavery petitions from abroad as well as numerous petitions for Frenchwomen's rights to equality in law, political life, education, and marriage. Flora Tristan petitioned the French Chamber of Deputies to reestablish divorce and to abolish capital punishment in 1837.[68] Two years later, Harriet Martineau noted in her diary that

> A Frenchwoman has lately petitioned the Chambers for participation by women in the rights of citizenship. Women are not excluded, and must be therefore supposed to be included. Mr. Child [David Child, husband of U.S. antislavery activist Lydia Maria Child] says her positions are unanswerable, her logic the closest. Accordingly, there was much "hilarity on the *côte gauche* [left side]." They could only laugh, for she left them without a plea.[69]

Mutual support flowed back and forth across the Atlantic in these years, as female abolitionists increasingly communicated with each other. "Having recently been appointed Secretary to our Emancipation Society, I have felt extremely desirous of reopening the correspondence with yours," Mary Wigham in Edinburgh wrote Maria Weston Chapman in Boston in 1839, "knowing as I do, what a stimulus it is to the zeal of the friends of the great cause here, to receive from time to time accounts of your unwearied and indefatigable labours on behalf of the oppressed; and being informed

. . . that it is equally grateful to your feelings to be assured of the continued sympathy felt with you by your fellow labourers on this side of the wide Atlantic."[70]

Although abolitionism remained an international enterprise, antislavery women in the United States began to extend their activities in the 1830s. For British women who did not travel to America, abolitionism remained a distant cause with little local impact on their lives. In the United States, however, slavery, segregation, and racism were woven into the national fabric. Institutionalized in the South, which tightened its slave codes and antiabolitionist laws after Nat Turner's rebellion in 1831, slavery became increasingly justified and defended there in the decades before the Civil War. In the North, where slavery had ended or was being phased out, schools, jobs, and churches became increasingly segregated. Free blacks encountered prejudice founded on the assumption of their racial inferiority in all aspects of life. "Tell us no more of southern slavery; for with few exceptions . . . I consider our condition but little better than that," declared free black Bostonian Maria W. Stewart in an 1832 lecture. "Such is the powerful force of prejudice. Let our girls possess whatever amiable qualities of soul they may. . . . it is impossible for scarce an individual of them to rise above the condition of servants."[71] Blacks and whites constituted two separate nations, divided by the white bigotry that permeated even the antislavery movement. Until 1830, most white opponents of slavery worked for the most extreme segregation of all—removing all blacks from American life by shipping them "back" to "colonize" an Africa they left generations earlier. Only a few white Quakers joined free blacks in calling for emancipation within the United States.

Any attempt to integrate American life encountered violent hostility, like that met by white Quaker schoolteacher Prudence Crandall in Connecticut in the early 1830s. Admitting a single black female pupil to her school caused white parents to remove their daughters. When Crandall attempted to open an all-black school for girls the following year in the same location, her white neighbors refused to sell her food, threw dead animals and manure onto her property and down her well, broke the school's windows, tried to burn the building down, petitioned the state legislature against her, and had her arrested. Free black communities and abolitionists opposed to colonization faced even greater violence. White mobs periodically rampaged through black neighborhoods in northern cities in the 1830s and 1840s, destroying property and beating people up with impunity. Abolitionists both white and black were routinely pelted with eggs and garbage and were often tarred and feathered; others had buildings burned down around them, some were murdered. In these circumstances, advocating abolitionism and integration required heroic dedication and considerable moral strength.[72]

Radical Christianity provided the spiritual energy that enabled most black and white abolitionists to challenge racism and slavery. In the early

1830s, a new fervor for immediate emancipation transformed antislavery into a movement that defied accepted conventions. Like the Saint-Simonians, American antislavery activists saw themselves as a modern band of embattled apostles, carrying on Jesus' work to transform the world. "If persecution is the means which God has ordained for the accomplishment of this great end, EMANCIPATION," abolitionist Angelina Grimké wrote radical antislavery editor William Lloyd Garrison in 1835, after he had been dragged by a mob through the streets of Boston, "then, in dependence *upon Him* for strength to bear it, I feel as if I could say, LET IT COME; for it is my deep, solemn, deliberate conviction, that *this is a cause worth dying for.*"[73] For whites, such convictions had to be forged in opposition to their churches (most of which segregated blacks into a "Negro pew"), since in this period all white U.S. denominations, including the Quakers and the Unitarians, either accepted slavery or urged disengagement from "worldly" issues and refused to denounce the racial status quo. In contrast, free black churches often became strongholds of abolitionism, but women within these congregations faced a double bind. Initially allowed more latitude in behavior than middle-class white women because of their outcast race (which exempted them from white male "chivalry") and their lower economic status, many free black women aspired to the domesticity and patriarchalism that signaled middle-class respectability. Urged "to encourage and support the manhood of our men," as a black state convention phrased it, free black women often found that embracing refinement placed the same constraints on their behavior as those experienced by their white counterparts.[74] In these circumstances, radical antislavery women, both black and white, who wanted to widen their activities for the cause relied on their inner convictions, on their own interpretations of the Bible, on "the light of truth in the soul," as Lucretia Mott later put it, to validate their unconventional behavior.[75]

Mott's own development provided an inspiring example of female strength and leadership both to women within the United States and to those abroad who learned about her through the wide-ranging antislavery network. Raised on Nantucket Island, she attributed her independence to having seen her mother and other women managing businesses and supporting their families while their men were off at sea.[76] Instructed at a coeducational Quaker boarding school, Lucretia Coffin became a teacher at fifteen and married her fellow student James Mott at eighteen. In 1818, when she was twenty-five and the mother of two, she made her first speech in a Quaker meeting; in 1821, she was appointed to the unpaid Quaker ministry and began to travel and speak at other meetings.

Although a disproportionate number of U.S. women active in both abolitionism and women's rights had Quaker backgrounds like Mott's, they did not come not from orthodox groups but from the dissident Hicksite branch considered heretical by the mainstream Society of Friends.[77] The Motts and their five children left their original

Philadelphia meeting in 1827 for a Hicksite congregation, in part to pursue antislavery work through the Free Produce movement. Dedicated to boycotting slave goods like cane sugar and cotton and providing substitutes harvested by free workers such as maple sugar and linen, Free Produce reached across the racial boundaries that so deeply divided American society. While James Mott divested his dry goods store of slave-made materials, Lucretia Mott began preaching against slavery and slavery's products. Strengthened by supportive letters from antislavery activists in England, the Motts became acquainted with black Philadelphia families also involved in this work.[78]

Crossing the racial divide in the United States could provide the same enlarged perspective that reaching across national boundaries gave women who made international connections. Lucretia Mott turned away from colonization after James Forten, a prosperous free black sailmaker and Revolutionary War veteran, spoke against it to her when she preached at his Philadelphia church in 1830. A few weeks later, Forten invited the Motts to hear the twenty-four-year-old William Lloyd Garrison deliver an address. Lucretia Mott counseled Garrison to speak out more boldly: "If thou expects to set forth thy cause by word of mouth, thou must learn to lay aside thy papers and speak from the heart. First emancipate thyself [from a prepared speech]. Think of thy message and the words will come."[79]

Outspokenness soon came to characterize radical abolitionism. In 1831, Garrison began publishing his fiery antislavery weekly, the *Liberator*, declaring in his lead editorial "I will not equivocate, I will not excuse, I will not retreat a single inch—and I WILL BE HEARD!" Bearing the motto "Our Country Is the World, Our Countrymen Are All Mankind," the *Liberator* soon became an interracial and international forum of antislavery activism. Initiating a "Ladies Department," Garrison urged women to challenge existing conventions, providing encouragement by publishing their writings and speeches and publicizing their activities. "I started up and with one mighty effort threw from me the lethargy which had covered me as a mantle for years," free black Sarah Mapps Douglass wrote the *Liberator* in 1832, "Has this not been your experience my sisters?"[80]

Women created emancipation societies favoring immediate abolition that often included both white and black members. Excluded from the all-male American Anti-Slavery Association, which formed in 1833, they extended their activities by writing, petitioning, and fund-raising for the movement. Many of the most radical antislavery treatises of these years were penned by women: Lydia Maria Child's *An Appeal in Favor of That Class of Americans Called Africans* (1833), which affirmed black inclusion in its title, and the public letters of Angelina and Sarah Grimké, daughters of a South Carolinian slaveholder who renounced their heritage and became abolitionists.

By publishing, antislavery women challenged the limits of acceptable female behavior. By speaking for their cause in public, they violated contemporary practice. There are no records of any German woman lecturing before the late 1840s. In 1847, Louise Dittmar published talks she had given before the small Mannheim Monday-Club, but when Louise Otto delivered her address to the Saxon governmental committee on workers in 1848, she did so only in print, not in speech.[81]

In France, Flora Tristan embarked on an ambitious one-woman lecture tour of major cities in 1844. Inspired by her conception of herself as a lone "woman guide" doing "apostolic work" in preaching socialism, she spoke to groups of male workers and left an anguished account of her difficulties:

> I have to climb to the sixth . . . floor in frightful houses having long, black, dirty passages and dilapidated, dirty, stinking stairways. . . . I enter the workshop, where . . . there is no space. . . . Then twenty or thirty men gather around me as best they can. . . . In order not to suffocate from the heat of this whole crowd thus confined in so small a space, they almost always leave the windows open—and I, bathed in perspiration, remain there one or two hours between two drafts, risking inflammation of the lungs. . . . One or two men always stay below, and one on the staircase, to be on the lookout to warn us of a police raid.[82]

The rigors of this tour led to her death later that year, when she was forty-one; no other Frenchwoman followed her example until the Revolution of 1848.

In Britain, a few female preachers and socialists lectured in these years, but the best-known woman to speak in public was Victoria, who became queen at eighteen in 1837. Her reign was frequently cited by American feminists as proof of women's capacity to govern. "If it is right for Victoria to sit on the throne of England it is right for any American Woman to occupy the Presidential Chair at Washington," Amelia Bloomer declared in numerous speeches during the 1850s.[83] But Queen Victoria, profoundly antifeminist and committed to domesticity, provided no model for women seeking a broader role. Consistently denouncing women's rights and women's movements throughout her long rule, which lasted until 1901, Victoria even argued that "*we women*, if we are to be *good* women, *feminine* and *amiable* and *domestic*, are not *fitted to reign*." Never believing that her achievements affirmed the capacities of other women, she wove domesticity into the life of a female monarch. "One often saw her sitting on a garden bench and—knitting stockings for her children," Louise Otto wrote about Victoria's German visit of 1845. "This seemed a very exaggerated kind of mother love for a queen!"[84]

In the United States, female public speaking was condemned as masculine "Fanny Wrightism." A few courageous women, like the free black Maria W. Stewart, defied this prejudice. But in the late 1830s, increasing numbers of activist female abolitionists escalated their efforts to end slavery and racism and began to lecture in public. Early in 1837, the Philadelphia Female Anti-Slavery Society proposed that women delegates be sent to the all-male Anti-Slavery Convention later that year: "When our brothers and sisters are crushed and bleeding under the arm of tyranny we must do with our might what our hands find to do for their deliverance, pausing only to inquire 'what is right,' not 'what is universally acceptable?'"[85] When Bostonian antislavery women voted for a separate national female convention, the Philadelphians acquiesced and helped organize the meeting in New York City that May.

Early feminists, in Europe as well as in America, debated the merits of all-female or mixed groups and usually adopted a pragmatic both/and approach. "I should be very glad if women generally and men too, could so lose sight of distinctions of sex as to act in public meetings on the enlightened and true ground of Christian equality," Lucretia Mott wrote Abby Kelley, who attended the first women's convention. Advising women to "mingle in discussion and take part with their brethren" whenever possible, Mott also argued that in "present circumstances," with male opposition likely to disrupt proceedings, women should also meet separately, which would be useful in "bringing our sex forward, exercising their talents, and preparing them for united action with men, as soon as we can convince them that this is both our right and our duty." The argument that women had not only a right but a duty to participate in public life runs through feminist discourse in this period: it furnished the opening to Louise Otto's first article published under her own name.[86]

The 1837 all-female Anti-Slavery Convention of American Women, the first public political meeting of women in the United States, brought together 174 delegates, about 10 percent of them black, from ten states to organize support for abolitionism and opposition to racial prejudice. With Lucretia Mott presiding, the convention began with a reading of Psalm 27 ("The Lord is my light and my salvation; whom shall I fear?"), and delegates followed her lead in interpreting Christianity to mean radical action against unjust conditions. They unanimously passed resolutions that abolition was "the cause of God, who created mankind free," that "kind usage" did not exonerate slavery, that "the combination of interests" between North and South maintained slavery, that fugitive slaves should not be returned, that petitioning should be continued "with the faith of an Esther," that slavery "desecrated" both white and black marriages, that education at all levels be sexually and racially integrated, and that the Free Produce movement be supported. Believing that "an unnatural prejudice against our colored population is one of the chief pillars of American slavery," they urged whites to "mingle" with blacks and "to act out the principles of Christian equality by associating with them as though the color of the skin was of no more consequence than that of the hair, or the eyes."[87]

Controversy arose over women's public speaking, even within this radical group. A resolution declaring "that as moral and responsible beings, the women of America are solemnly called upon by the spirit of the age and the signs of the times, fully to discuss the subject of slavery," passed without objection. But the next resolution, which urged "woman, to plead the cause of the oppressed in our land, and to do all that she can by her voice, and her pen, and her purse, and the influence of her example, to overthrow the horrible system of American slavery" occasioned "animated and interesting debate respecting the rights and duties of women" and passed, but not unanimously.[88] Woman's public use of her "voice," as distinguished from private "discussion," challenged conventional behavior and prevailing Christian teachings that the sexes be divided into separate spheres of activity. The convention moved that woman should disregard "the circumscribed limits with which corrupt custom and a perverted application of Scripture have encircled her" and repeated this argument in the six publications it authorized:

> Woman is now rising, in her womanhood, to throw from her, with one hand, the paltry privilege with which man has invested her, of conquering by fashionable charms and winning by personal attraction, whilst with the other, she grasps the right of women to unite in holy co-partnership with man in the renovation of a fallen world.[89]

Deliberately flouting male ministerial authority by claiming full moral and political autonomy for the female sex was revolutionary. "We Abolition women are turning the world upside-down," Angelina Grimké wrote Sarah Douglass after the convention, referring to the tune "The World Turned Upside Down," which was played at the British surrender in the American Revolution.[90] Encouraged by support from other women, the Grimkés began an extended New England lecture tour that summer. Speaking to "promiscuous" audiences of both men and women, the sisters received severe criticism from ministers, authors, and antislavery workers. Opposition initially strengthened their dedication. "If we surrender the right to *speak* to the public this year," Angelina Grimké wrote two male abolitionists, "we must surrender the right to petition the next year and the right to *write* the year after and so on. What *then* can *woman* do for the slave when she is herself under the feet of man and shamed into *silence*."[91]

Debate widened as the Grimkés continued to lecture and publish works supporting their position. Many activist women asserted that "in striving to strike [the slave's] irons off, we found most surely that we were manacled *ourselves*," as Abby Kelley wrote in 1838. From this realization, it was a short step to insist upon emancipation for all women as well as for the women and men trapped in slavery. "Are we FREE!" Maria Weston Chapman declared at the convention. "It is because we have burst our manacles in the effort to undo those that weigh so heavily" on slaves. To the Grimkés, the causes merged into a single struggle. "My idea is that whatever is morally right for a man to do is morally right for a woman to do," Angelina wrote a friend in 1837. "This is part of the great doctrine of Human Rights & can no more be separated from Emancipation than the light from the heat of the sun; the rights of the slave & woman blend like the colors of a rainbow."[92] This argument informs Sarah Grimké's 1838 *Letters on the Equality of the Sexes, and the Condition of Women*, distributed in Britain as well as the United States. Drawing on the Bible and ranging widely through world history, Grimké argued for full emancipation from "the bonds of womanhood"—the religious and political system of male dominance that reduced all women except a few female rulers to the status of "slaves" or "dolls." "I need hardly advert to the names of Elizabeth of England, Maria Theresa of Germany, Catherine of Russia, and Isabella of Spain, to prove that women are capable of swaying the sceptre of royalty," she wrote. "I mention these women only to prove that intellect is not sexed; that strength of mind is not sexed and that our views about the duties of men and the duties of women, the sphere of man and the sphere of woman, are mere arbitrary opinions, differing in different ages and countries, and dependent solely on the will of erring mortals.[93]

The Second Anti-Slavery Convention of American Women, which met in Philadelphia in 1838, intensified feminists' struggles to participate fully in public life. Unable to find a church or assembly room in which they could meet, abolitionists built Pennsylvania Hall, a large auditorium dedicated "to the rights of free discussion." Inviting male sympathizers to attend, the women convened despite a threatening mob that broke windows and rioted throughout the convention. Encouraged by their president, Lucretia Mott, who urged delegates to overcome their "false notions of delicacy and propriety" about addressing a mixed audience and their fears about "a little *appearance* of danger" from the rioters, the audience listened to William Lloyd Garrison, Maria Weston Chapman, Abby Kelley, Mott herself, and Angelina Grimké Weld (she had married abolitionist Theodore Weld in an egalitarian ceremony the previous week).[94]

The strains of public speaking, even before a sympathetic group, should not be underestimated. Chapman left the convention with "brain fever" and never spoke in public again. Sarah Grimké virtually ceased giving speeches after Boston abolitionists criticized her "peculiar and monotonous" delivery in 1837. Angelina Grimké Weld withdrew from public life after her marriage and lectured infrequently thereafter. Abby Kelley, who gave her maiden speech at the convention, became an antislavery agent the following year and lectured widely but testified to the arduousness of her work at the Worcester women's rights convention in 1851. "I did not rise to make a speech—my life has been my speech," she told the audience. "For fourteen years I have advocated this cause by my daily life. Bloody feet, Sisters, have worn smooth the path by which you have come up hither."[95]

Given these difficulties, Lucretia Mott's experience and expertise as a speaker proved crucial. Older than most of the other antislavery women and an accomplished lecturer accustomed to addressing audiences, Mott provided an impressive and consistent example of women's ability to function in a public forum. Harriet Martineau found her "noble," "firm," and

"philosophical" when she heard her preach in 1836; Henry David
Thoreau wrote that "her self possession was something to see, if all else
failed, it did not," after he attended an 1843 lecture.[96] One of the fullest
descriptions of Mott's impact on an audience comes from Marianne Finch,
an Englishwoman who heard Mott deliver a sermon against the Fugitive
Slave Act in 1851:

> A very plainly dressed little woman rose [Mott was thin and barely five feet
> tall, considered small in her own day] . . . Taking off her bonnet, [she]
> revealed a very ugly Quaker's cap, an expansive forehead, and a pair of beau-
> tiful soul-lit eyes.
>   As soon as she spoke, I felt myself her captive. Her voice was inexpress-
> ibly sweet, deep-toned, and earnest. Her manner easy and dignified; her
> Christianity broad and practical, without bigotry and mysticism; her words
> flowed freely, but not superfluously, and seemed the best she could have
> chosen to express her meaning. Above all, she seemed to take a deep interest
> in what she said, and to wish her hearers to do the same. . . . Lucretia Mott
> deserved her fame.[97]

Those present at the 1838 convention and at later meetings threatened by
violence confirmed her unshaken composure in the face of danger.[98]
   On the second day of the Philadelphia convention, the mob swelled to
thousands. Refusing to provide police protection, the mayor advised that
black women cease attending. His suggestion was rejected by the delegates, who walked arm in arm in linked black and white pairs to the convention. That evening, the mob set fire to the hall, which burned to the
ground as the fire department refused to act. In a meeting the following
morning, the antislavery women resolved to increase their interracial
socializing.[99] In the following year, a number of women joined previously
all-male emancipation societies and began to serve on committees as well
as continuing to speak in public.
   These events received wide publicity and support from English writer
Harriet Martineau, who had achieved a unique public status before her
1834–1836 travels in the United States. Her *Illustrations of Political
Economy*, published between 1832 and 1834, a series of colorfully written
pamphlets demonstrating laissez-faire principles, pleased both economists
and the reading public. This success made Martineau a widely respected
author on a topic considered quintessentially masculine, and feminists
touted her triumph for decades. "She *is* wonderful," Bessie Rayner Parkes
wrote Barbara Leigh Smith about Martineau in the early 1850s. "Now we
have other clever women more of her stamp, 20 years ago I think there was
not one. She was the first, she has helped on by her example all the others.
20 years ago its a bold thing of a woman to write on political economy."[100]
   Rewarding herself for the success of her pamphlet series with a voyage
to North America, Martineau was won over by the abolitionists' principles
and courage after she spoke at a mob-threatened meeting of the Boston

Female Anti-Slavery Society in 1835. Enthusiastically reporting on the radical antislavery activists for the English press, she rapidly produced three books about her journey: *Society in America, Retrospect of Western Travel*, and *The Martyr Age of the United States*. "It is a wide world that we live in, as wonderful in the diversity of its moral as of its natural features," this last work concluded. "A just survey of the whole can leave little doubt that the abolitionists of the United States are the greatest people now living and moving in it." Martineau emphasized women's achievements and called the first Anti-Slavery Convention of American Women "a great event in history—from the nature of the fact itself, and probably from the importance of its consequences."[101] Corresponding frequently with the women she met on her journey, Martineau remained in close contact with them for the rest of her life.

In addition to championing the antislavery activists, Martineau also provided women in the United States with a thoughtful and influential analysis of their situation. "Political Non-Existence of Women," a chapter in *Society in America*, began by asserting that the principles of the Declaration of Independence could not be reconciled with the exclusion of women from equality and political rights. Arguing that "children, idiots, and criminals, during the season of sequestration" were the only "fair exceptions" to democratic representation, Martineau declared that "Jefferson in America, and James Mill at home" (whose exclusion of women had inspired Thompson and Wheeler's 1825 *Appeal*) were "as disgraceful as any advocate of despotism." Countering the common argument that women did not want rights and acquiesced in their own subordination, Martineau stated, "I for one do not acquiesce. . . . I know that there are women in England who agree with me in this—I know that there are women in America who agree with me in this. The plea of acquiescence is invalidated by us." Democratic principles should prevail:

> The fearful and absurd images which are perpetually called up to perplex the question,—images of women on wool-sacks in England [presiding over parliament], and under canopies in America [being inaugurated as president], have nothing to do with the matter. The principle being once established, the methods will follow, easily, naturally, and under a remarkable transformation of the ludicrous into the sublime. The kings of Europe would have laughed mightily two centuries ago, at the idea of a commoner . . . stepping into the throne of a strong nation. Yet who dared laugh when Washington's super-royal voice greeted the New World from the presidential chair, and the old world stood still to catch the echo?[102]

Read by Mott and other American antislavery women, Martineau's writings provided important validation from abroad as women's widened activities began to divide the abolitionist movement.[103] Shortly after the third female antislavery convention, which met without incident in Philadelphia in 1839, a number of activist women attended the annual meeting of the American Anti-Slavery Society in New York. For two days, delegates debated whether the word "persons" should be substituted for "men" on the membership roll, which would allow women to participate. An affirmative vote led to further discussion of women's right to speak, to serve on committees, and to fill offices within the society. The women and their allies argued that "the whole human family is included in the generic term *man*," and carefully substituted "they" for "he" in their speeches.[104]

A second positive vote did not end the controversy. Wider roles for women were championed by Garrison, who was pushing for more radical antislavery tactics in these years. In 1838, he helped create the New England Non-Resistance Society, almost half of whose founding members were female. Nonresistance renounced all forms of violence, including any participation in a government that used force. Nonresisters refused to vote, believing moral suasion to be more powerful than political action, a position especially appealing to radical Quakers, who were pacifists, and to women, who could not vote anyway. "I am no preacher of the milk-and-water passive spirit of non-resistance to wrong," Mott later declared.

> I have no idea, because I am a Non-Resistant, of submitting tamely to injustice inflicted either on me or the slave. I will oppose it with all the moral powers with which I am endowed. I am no advocate of passivity. Quakerism, as I understand it, does not mean quietism. The early Friends were agitators; disturbers of the peace; and were more obnoxious in their days . . . than we are.[105]

By 1840, the issue of women's rights was inextricably connected to non-resistance, and antislavery societies began to divide over policy. The Garrisonians argued that racial prejudice, which made slavery possible, must be countered in all aspects of life and thus women's active participation was essential. More conservative abolitionists sought to end institutionalized slavery by political means, avoiding the controversial issues of both racial prejudice and feminism—"abolitionism made easy," as Abby Kelley called it. Matters came to a head at the May 1840 meeting of the American Anti-Slavery Society, when Kelley, along with four men, was nominated to the Business Committee. Although the vote was in her favor, 557 to 451, over three hundred men walked out and formed the American and Foreign Anti-Slavery Society, which excluded women and nonresisters from membership. "I am getting rather off from woman's rights," veteran abolitionist John Greenleaf Whittier wrote a friend shortly after the meeting. "This last exploit of my good friend Abby in blowing up the Amer. A. Slavery Society is too much for me. Abolition women. . . . Think of the conduct of Mrs. Adam—how Delilah shaved Samson—how Helen got up the Trojan War—and last but not least this affair of Abby's and the society."[106]

One month later, these events were reenacted in London at the World Anti-Slavery Convention that met there in June. Led by Lucretia Mott,

seven American women crossed the Atlantic as delegates, but their creden-
tials were rejected on the first day of the convention after an all-male
debate in which they were not allowed to speak. Forced to sit in a back
gallery and silently observe the proceedings, the American female delegates soon bonded with the British women who joined them as spectators:
the abolitionists Anne Knight, Elizabeth Pease, Hannah Webb, and her
sister Maria Waring, the reformers Mary Howitt, Elizabeth Reid,
Elizabeth Ashurst, and her sister Matilda Ashurst Biggs, the authors Anna
Jameson, Amelia Opie, and Marion Reid, and the philanthropist Lady
Byron.[107] Although the Americans complained about the failure of the
more conservative English antislavery and Quaker women to back them,
they welcomed the friendship and support they received from this like-
minded group. Mott filled her diary and letters home with news of these
allies, who provided a whirl of social events as well as corroboration of her
views on women. "Anne Knight is as indignant as we are," Mott wrote her
children two days after the vote on female delegates.

> She says [abolitionist women] do all the drudgery of the Anti-Slavery
> work—go through all the lanes & alleys to get signers of Petitions . . . &
> then are not allowed to hold meetings and mingle in a way to hear and fur-
> nish themselves with arguments wherewith to meet their opponents. She is a
> kind of independent who has made her way in France and other countries.[108]

Harriet Martineau, selected to represent Massachusetts but too ill to
attend, sent Mott "sympathy . . . amidst your present trials" and "love from
my heart" and introduced her to "two of my best friends"—Elizabeth
Reid, who would found a women's college in London nine years later, and
Julia Smith, Barbara Leigh Smith Bodichon's aunt.[109] Mott became especially close to Irish abolitionists Hannah and Richard Webb (who printed
Anne Knight's labels) and their extended family, whom she introduced to
her new friend, the twenty-five-old bride Elizabeth Cady Stanton. "I was
right glad you had an opp[ortunit]y to see & admire that bright, open,
lovely, Eliz. Stanton," Motts wrote the Webbs the following year. "We had
not seen her till we met in England & I love her now as one belonging to
us."[110] Mott kept the Webbs informed of Stanton's progress to feminism.
"She infused in her speech a homeopathic dose of women's rights," she
wrote them in 1842, "and does the same in many private conversations.
She wishes as many copies of S. Grimké's Letters on the Equality of the
Sexes as we can send her. . . . In a letter to me some time ago she says, 'The
more I think on the present condition of woman, the more I am oppressed
with the reality of her degradation. The laws of our country, how unjust
are they!—our customs how vicious!'"[111]

Elizabeth Cady Stanton considered the convention a turning point in
her development. "These were the first women I had ever met who
believed in the equality of the sexes and who did not believe in the popular
and orthodox religion," she wrote in her memoirs. "The acquaintance of

Lucretia Mott, who was a broad, liberal thinker on politics, religion, and all questions of reform, opened to me a new world of thought. As we walked about to see the sights of London, I embraced every opportunity to talk with her. It was intensely gratifying to hear all that, through years of doubt, I had dimly thought, so freely discussed by other women, some of them older than myself—women too, of rare intelligence, cultivation, and refinement."

Their caliber made the rejection by the convention all the more galling. "Judging from my own feelings," Stanton remembered, "the women on both sides of the Atlantic must have been humiliated and chagrined, except as these feelings were outweighed by contempt for the shallow reasoning of their opponents and their comical pose and gestures."[112]

At the time, however, the 1840 London Anti-Slavery Convention was a decisive defeat for supporters of women's rights. Both the Garrisonian wing of abolitionism and the claims of U.S. antislavery women to wider roles lost to the more conservative majority. The American Anti-Slavery Women never held a fourth convention and women remained excluded from the powerful American and Foreign Anti-Slavery Society. The formation of a U.S. women's movement out of the matrix of abolitionism was severely checked in 1840, just as the creation of a French women's movement had been stopped by the collapse of Saint-Simonianism in 1834. But like the New Women, who found continued support from international contacts, American and British antislavery feminists remained heartened by validation from abroad. "There are a few women in Limerick—a few in Cork—a few in Waterford—a few in Wexford, with you, heart and soul," Richard Webb wrote Maria Weston Chapman from Ireland in 1841. "They read the Liberator and the [Anti-Slavery] Standard & your names are household words among them."[113] Correspondence, publications, and visits continued to unite feminists throughout the 1840s.

While national women's movements ceased formation until the revolutionary year of 1848, the loosely knit international women's movement sustained individuals in different countries. The sudden appearance of women's movements in France, Germany, and the United States in 1848 seemed like volcanic eruptions both to contemporaries and historians, who write of the "spontaneous" appearance of these organizations. But as with volcanoes, these explosions were the end result of a slow accumulation of subterranean forces. In the 1840s, the international women's movement provided room for the lava to build.

Six

The Pressure Builds

Lucretia Mott's daughters wanted to meet the celebrated English novelist Charles Dickens, who arrived in Philadelphia on his American tour in the spring of 1842. Mott had not planned to call on the thirty-year-old author, already famous for *The Pickwick Papers*, *Oliver Twist*, and *The Old Curiosity Shop*, since she disapproved of "man-worship," read very little fiction, and considered him "not quite one of our sort." But she changed her mind after Dickens left his calling card at her house with a "kind and sweet letter" of introduction from English reformer Elizabeth Reid. Holding Reid in high esteem after the World Anti-Slavery Convention of 1840, Mott wrote her Irish friends Richard and Hannah Webb that "there is no woman in London, whose draft I would more gladly honor. So now I have a grand excuse to call . . . and our girls are in high glee."[1]

When the Motts visited Dickens, they warned him not "to be deceived by the outside appearance" of slavery when he traveled in the South "but to try and get a peep behind the scenes." To enlighten the writer, Lucretia Mott gave him a copy of *American Slavery As It Is: Testimony of a Thousand Witnesses*, an 1839 catalogue of slavery's horrors compiled by abolitionist Theodore Weld, Angelina Grimké Weld's husband. "If you see Mrs. Lucretia Mott tell her I have not forgotten the slave," the novelist told a young Philadelphian visitor in London later that summer. In the two books Dickens produced that year, his travel memoir *American Notes* and his novel *Martin Chuzzlewit*, he made extensive use of the text Mott had brought him. Citing bloodcurdling examples from its pages, Dickens roundly condemned all aspects of slavery and severely criticized any American who tolerated or justified the institution. He adopted Lucretia Mott's uncompromising abolitionism wholeheartedly, and her role in shaping his position on slavery is clear.[2]

But Mott had no success in altering the influential novelist's antifeminist views of women. This lack of headway typified the difficulties early feminists encountered in this period. Dickens was one of the new, young cultural authorities of the 1840s who helped solidify the belief that women must confine themselves to domesticity. Glorifying the angel in the home while stigmatizing all women who ventured into public life, Dickens contributed powerfully to the stereotype that "all these women reformers are either old maids, or divorced wives, and as homely as sin," as the American magazine *Yankee Notions* put it a few years later.[3] Although Dickens's most brutal caricature of a nondomestic woman— slovenly, self-involved Mrs. Jellyby who neglects her family to pursue her delusions of aiding far-off missions—did not appear until 1853, his earlier novels abound in ugly, ludicrous, "strong-minded" females who wrongly believe that women should participate in public life. "Literary ladies" are automatically satirized as vain, pretentious figures. One of Martin Chuzzlewit's first encounters in the United States is with "a wiry-faced old damsel, who held strong sentiments touching the rights of women and had diffused the same in lectures." The novel's redoubtable Mrs. Hominy, described as a "woman of masculine and towering intellect," "a philosopher and an authoress," is lampooned for her long-windedness, her self-importance, and her international pretensions. Mott's visit may even have contributed to this particular hostile Dickens portrait of an activist woman:

> Mrs. Hominy was a writer of reviews and analytical disquisitions. Mrs. Hominy had her letters from abroad . . . regularly printed in a public journal, with all the indignation in capitals and all the sarcasm in italics. Mrs. Hominy had looked on foreign countries with the eye of a perfect republican hot from the model oven and Mrs. Hominy could talk (or write) about them by the hour together.[4]

In the 1840s early feminists throughout the Western community faced the same formidable opposition from a wide array of cultural and political authorities that Mott encountered in Dickens. Older conservatives and reactionaries could be expected to oppose wider roles for women, but many of the most successful younger writers and artists of the day also adopted Dickens's confrontational, antifeminist stance. In 1844, for instance, popular French artist Honoré Daumier published forty cartoons caricaturing "bluestockings," a derogatory term for any woman who aspired to learning. "When we think *very* ill of a woman, and wish to *blacken* her character, we merely call her 'a *blue*-stocking,'" the American author and literary critic Edgar Allan Poe wrote face-tiously that same year.[5] Depicted as hideously lean or grotesquely fat, neglectful of their children and unfaithful to their husbands, Daumier's ugly female intellectuals are mercilessly ridiculed for their pretensions to scholarship, artistic production, public influence, and wider roles for women. "Look at men! How they abuse their rights," grouses one harridan. "Just because one day in a moment of weakness you tie the marriage knot with one of them, they expect you ever after to fix the knot in their cravats! But I have decided from now on to follow the principles propounded this very morning by Artémise Jabutot in his remarkable article in the *Free Women's Gazette: down with knots and trouser buttons!*"[6]

Contrasted with attractive women who do sew on buttons, these blue-stockings are automatically mocked, especially if they are middle-aged or older. Such satire was by no means confined to the old world. In the 1840s American periodicals began to ridicule "public women" as well. Responding to an 1847 call urging Philadelphia women to become active abolitionists, the new illustrated magazine *Judy* advised instead that women "had better embrace their husbands, be faithful in the cause of fireside comforts, and promulgate the principles of domestic happiness." Since domesticity was invariably equated with femininity, any woman who aspired to more was considered not really female. "There are men, women, and Margaret Fuller," Poe wrote of America's most famous female intellectual in these years.[7]

Such attitudes discouraged early feminists. "I belong . . . to the minors in the State, who, as the wise-acres say, ought, for the good of the State, always remain so," wrote Fredrika Bremer from Stockholm in an 1841 sketch she entitled "At Forty Years of Age."

> Two things I believe in, and the third I take to be certain:
> First. That the wise-acres are right.
> Second. That no compulsion, as now, but free choice, free conviction (which must be preceded by a complete emancipation), ought, and one day shall, decide woman's social position.
> Third. That I shall not live to see the day when such an emancipation takes place.[8]

This discouragement and the hostility that engendered it help explain the lag in the formation of national women's movements between 1840 and 1848. Although early feminists remained connected and sustained by the international movement, they ceased organizing on women's behalf in both the United States and France in these years. Lucretia Mott and Elizabeth Cady Stanton had discussed creating a women's movement in the United States when they met at the World Anti-Slavery Convention in

London. Why did they then wait eight years? "Were I to go back . . . to see what had roused women," Paulina Wright Davis wrote in her 1871 history of the American women's movement, "I should first be obliged to go into a long history of the despotism and repression which German jurists call soul-murder."[9] Both personal concerns and national politics contributed to this delay.

Individual feminists spent much of this period either ill or preoccupied with other matters. Lucretia Mott, Harriet Martineau, and Anna Wheeler suffered from serious medical conditions. Wheeler died in 1848. Martineau recovered but then became enthralled with mesmerism, which she believed had healed her, and later traveled to Egypt and Palestine. Mott also got well but fell into a depression after her mother's death in 1844 and spent much of the 1840s enmeshed in controversies within the Society of Friends, which alternated between treating her as a respected authority and a dangerous heretic. Paulina Wright (later Davis) began to lecture to women in the northeastern United States on anatomy and health, using a mannequin and books she had received from France, where Jenny d'Héricourt and Suzanne Voilquin trained as midwives. Voilquin then moved to Russia, where she practiced her new trade; d'Héricourt turned to writing novels, which also engrossed Fredrika Bremer and Louise Otto in these years. Mathilde Anneke went through an unpleasant divorce and had to support herself and her daughter by writing and translating. Ernestine Rose bore two children who died young and then went to live in an Owenite commune at Skaneateles, New York, from 1843 to 1846. Harriet Taylor raised her three children and remained torn between her duty to her husband, John Taylor, and her attraction to the young philosopher John Stuart Mill, with whom she frequently traveled. Louise Aston, married at twenty to a forty-four-year-old English industrialist, had a daughter in 1841 and left her unhappy marriage three years later.

Elizabeth Cady Stanton, Pauline Roland, and Jeanne Deroin each bore three children in these years. Deroin trained as a schoolteacher and finally obtained her diploma after failing the qualifying exam several times. Roland wrote history books and articles to support herself. Stanton lived as a traditional wife and mother. Anne Knight, who maintained her active correspondence with the antislavery network, met a great deal of discouragement in these years from those she tried to interest in feminism. "I do feel amused at your undismayed heat in the assertion of the rights of women," her friend and fellow Quaker, Helen Richardson, wrote from Switzerland. "I do think we have not fair play . . . but I mean to be a quiet witness, leaving posterity to engage in my labours."[10] Knight kept a number of these letters rejecting her views, and they may have contributed to her decision to move to France in 1846.

Discouragement about feminist causes came even from those sympathetic to the plight of women who wished for a life beyond the home.

"How exquisitely absurd, it just strikes me, would be any measure after Miss Martineau's own heart, which should introduce women to Parliament as we understand its functions at present—how essentially retrograde a measure!" poet Robert Browning wrote Elizabeth Barrett in 1846, a few months before they married. "Parliament seems no place for originating, creative minds—but for secondrate minds."[11] Whipsawed between being told they were too good for public life or not competent enough to pursue it sapped feminists' energy. "I suffered from mental hunger, which, like an empty stomach is very depressing," Stanton later wrote of this period in her life.

> The general discontent I felt with woman's portion as wife, mother, housekeeper, physician, and spiritual guide, the chaotic conditions into which everything fell without her constant supervision, and the wearied, anxious look of the majority of women impressed me with a strong feeling that some active measures should be taken to remedy the wrongs of society in general, and of women in particular.[12]

Writing near the end of her long and successful life, Stanton stressed her agency and activism in 1848. But before that year of revolution, delay was caused not only by personal concerns but also by political problems. Both in Britain and the United States, the issue of women's active participation continued to divide the two rival antislavery societies. The smaller group, led by William Lloyd Garrison, kept the allegiance of most feminists. The other attracted male politicians, including Elizabeth Stanton's husband, Henry B. Stanton, and was ultimately more successful in achieving popular support, but only by moderating its stance on African-American rights and continuing to exclude women. Becoming active in the new, abolitionist Liberty Party earned Stanton and others the contempt of the Garrisonians, who maintained their policy of nonresistance and refused to engage in political campaigns or vote. "How sure I am now that [Henry Stanton] has thus sold himself," Mott wrote the Webbs in 1842.[13]

Fervor for the immediate abolition of slavery and the solidarity it engendered among women who wished to play an active part in the struggle never reached much beyond the original small circle. "We find our ranks rapidly thinning," Paulina Wright wrote Maria Weston Chapman from Utica, New York, in 1843. "The colorphobia is raging here now. . . . we find many who claimed to be our friends now entirely thrown off."[14] A second World Anti-Slavery Convention, held in London in 1843, continued to exclude women and confirmed female abolitionists' sense of being in the doldrums. "Oh! what a lifeless meeting this Convention proved," Elizabeth Reid wrote from England, "how different from one that I remember—when shall I see the like again? I went to Freemason's Hall several times with Lady Byron, and the sisters, but felt flat and dull—I was so disappointed to find no friends there."[15]

Although many of the women in favor of immediate abolitionism remained deeply committed to the cause, they attracted few new recruits. Except for the German free religion movement in the second half of the 1840s, no other progressive cause of the period gave women the opportunity to participate in public life as actively as radical abolitionism had done. Early feminists worked for a variety of organizations but usually found themselves confined to female auxiliary groups designed to support male activists, denied the right to be full members or delegates to conventions. Nascent pacifist societies, for instance, attracted a number of feminists, among them Anne Knight, Lucretia Mott, Eugénie Niboyet, Pauline Roland, and Paulina Wright Davis. Mott began preaching against war, especially the wars against "this much-injured people," the American Indians, as she called them. She also helped organize a peace petition sent to Englishwomen in 1846, when frictions over the Oregon territory seemed to threaten war between Britain and the United States. Both Mott and Davis severely criticized contemporary Christianity for not living up to its own pacific ideals. "The murder of an innocent man must be a crime in the code of any enlightened religion," Wright declared in a speech she delivered to a number of women's groups in the 1840s. "But the incidental murder of thousands of innocent and even meritorious men, women, and children is allowed, approved, and even praised, by the Christianity that sanctifies our national wars simply because they are national."[16] In France, Eugénie Niboyet created a short-lived peace society in 1844 and edited its journal, *La Paix des deux mondes* (The peace of the two worlds) during the six months it ran, but she remained the sole woman in an all-male group. Anne Knight frequented the all-female Olive Branch societies that organized in England in these years and attended the 1849 Peace Congress in Paris. But she encountered as much resistance to equal rights for women among male pacifists as male abolitionists had demonstrated at the World Anti-Slavery Convention in 1840. "We harmonized in the conviction that Right was of no sex . . . [but] have been told *none but men* can buy their birthright," she wrote in a furious public letter to the English politician Richard Cobden after the Peace Congress:

> Let us not be urged to prick our fingers to the bone in "sewing circles" for vanity fair, peace bazaars, where health and mind equally suffer in the sedentary "stitch, stitch, stitch," ever toiling, never to see a Right! . . . while our poor brother is groping his way in darkness without the good sense and clear discernment of his sister at his side.[17]

A similar pattern prevailed in other reform movements of the 1840s. Sought for their fund-raising activities, petition drives, and moral support, women remained relegated to subordinate roles, barred from public speaking, from committee membership, and from leadership. The British Anti-Corn Law League, founded to overturn tariffs that kept bread prices high, depended on its Ladies Committee for the substantial revenues that sustained its campaigns: over £25,000 was raised in 1845 by thousands of women selling their needlework and fancy goods at charity bazaars. But even such subsidiary activity for a cause that directly concerned the home challenged the doctrine of separate spheres and was severely criticized. "Petticoat politicians" working for the league risked "political prostitution," thundered the London *Times* in 1842, arguing that to "make a woman a politician is to make her a monster."[18]

The working-class British Chartist movement, founded in 1838 to demand universal suffrage, equal representation, the secret ballot, and pay for members of Parliament, initially seemed to give women space to claim rights of their own. Female democratic associations formed to work for passage of the Charter, and in 1839 a London women's group issued a manifesto declaring that since Victoria was on the throne "in defiance of the universal rights of man and woman," they felt entitled to assert "our rights as free women (or women determined to be free) to rule ourselves."[19] But Chartism soon defined "universal" suffrage as applicable only to men and relegated women to subsidiary roles, which most of them seem to have accepted. "A married woman's occupation ought to be the management of her own house," a female Chartist declared in 1840 to the wide approval of her audience. "The man ought to be the bread-provider, and the woman the bread-distributor." Chartist women usually justified their entry into politics as proof that the times were out of joint, forcing them to leave the "domestic sphere" in which they preferred to remain. Most of the women who supported the Chartist movement did so because they were related to male Chartists, and they generally confined their activities to sewing banners, petitioning, and listening to male speakers, often sitting in segregated galleries.[20] When Flora Tristan attended the 1839 National Chartist Convention in London, she noticed just two other women in a group of about eighty. Only the most radical feminists opposed Chartism's exclusion of women from its democratic political goals. "The pledge of Universal Suffrage for man and woman must be absolute," communist Catherine Barmby declared in 1842. "We must have unsexual Chartism! How can the stream of freedom flow clearly when slavery is at its foundations? How can we allow the political subalternity of woman when we advocate her social equality? If woman is not free, man must ever be a slave."[21]

Gender divisions also permeated international socialism in these years, when Charles Fourier finally attracted followers both in France and the United States who clarified and promulgated his early writings. They emphasized his belief in "associationism" (the formation of socialist communities that would reorganize both households and labor) while downplaying his complicated and controversial doctrine of liberated sexual relations. This made it easier for early feminists to support the theories of the thinker, who insisted that women's situation was the truest measure of social progress. Désirée Véret Gay, Eugénie Niboyet, Flora Tristan, and

Anna Wheeler all corresponded with Fourier in these years and traces of
his thought appear in their work, as well as in Anne Knight's diary, Louise
Otto's articles on female emancipation, and early U.S. women's rights
journals.[22]

Fourier's greatest impact in these years came in the United States,
where his ideas were advocated by young reformer Albert Brisbane and
newspaper editor Horace Greeley. In the 1840s a second wave of socialist
colonies, or "phalanxes," formed in America, paralleling the creation of
Owenite communities in the 1820s. Twenty-five short-lived Fourierist
settlements sprang up before 1848, ranging from Brook Farm near Boston
westward to communes in Michigan, Wisconsin, and Iowa.[23] From its
inception, however, this new communitarian movement placed women on
the periphery. "Debarred" from attending the first large-scale celebration
of Fourier's birth in the United States, held in 1842, "a few Ladies, sincere
believers in the great principles discovered by Fourier" begged "to be
allowed to bid those engaged in the glorious Cause of Association, God
speed."[24] In the communes themselves, women were relegated to subordinate roles, responsible for food preparation, housework, and child care
under arduous conditions. Because they owned far fewer shares of community stock than men, Fourierist women rarely had equal voting rights
and earned much less than their male associates. Most phalanxes set
female wages at a little more than half of men's, even for identical work
like teaching.[25] Some female "associationists" later paid tribute to the phalanxes for introducing them to women's rights, but others left bitter
records of the unfairness they experienced there. "A woman may perform
the most disinterested duties. She may 'die daily' in the cause of truth and
righteousness," Abigail May Alcott, mother of author Louisa May Alcott,
wrote in 1843 during her year at Fruitlands, the community founded by
her husband, Bronson. "She lives neglected, dies forgotten. But a man who
never performed in his whole life one self denying act . . . is celebrated by
his contemporaries, while his name and his works live on from age to age.
A man passes a few years in self denial and simple life, and he says, 'Behold
a God.'"[26]

As the phalanxes collapsed in the late 1840s, some Fourierist women
attempted to raise funds and rally other females to the cause. "Act for
yourselves," French immigrant Angélique Martin wrote in the movement's journal, the *Harbinger*. "It is high time that the *Mother of Mankind*
should cease to play the *child*!"[27] Others lamented the lack of female leadership within the communes. "Where are the ladies? Where is the *one* . . .
around whom might be a rallying?" a female associationist wrote a friend
early in 1848.[28]

Part of the problem came from the American Fourierists' conservative
approach to domesticity and family life, which gave women little opportunity to come to the fore; part stemmed from the conflict between early
socialism and abolitionism in the United States. Socialists tended to view

chattel slavery as only one manifestation of the general economic oppression of all workers. "In my eyes slavery is no longer the greatest human misfortune since I have become acquainted with the English proletariat," Flora Tristan wrote in 1840, explaining that although she did not want "to commit the sacrilege of condoning any form of slavery," slaves were often treated better than factory workers.[29] Antislavery activists disagreed. "It may be asked whether all this poverty, filth, and degradation is not as bad as our slavery," James Mott wrote about Ireland in 1841. "I am fully prepared to say NO; for slavery is all this and more." The impoverished Irish were at least "free, and can go and come as they please, to some extent at least, as the crowded steerage of ships to America bear witness."[30] Like Mott, U.S. women active in immediate abolitionism found Fourierism's gradualist approach and analysis of slavery repugnant, and conflict between the two causes divided those who favored wider roles for women.[31]

With the failure of most reform movements of the 1840s to advocate equal rights for women, writing again became the chief way for feminists to express themselves and connect with each other. In 1840 English author Anna Jameson informed her German friend, Ottilie von Goethe, about the American female delegates to the first World Anti-Slavery Convention.[32] Printed works naturally had greater circulation and impact than private correspondence. Marion Reid, a Scotswoman who attended the convention, published a feminist treatise in 1843, asserting that "the scornful sneers" of those who "condescend to notice opinions such as mine" had prompted her to write. Her outspoken *Plea for Woman* went into three editions in Britain, five in the United States, and may have been translated into French and German.[33] Using Shelley's line, "Can man be free, if woman be a slave?" as her epigraph, Reid asserted that "the subjugation of the [female] sex is general and undoubted" and that "this state of things prevails in a greater or less degree in every country, and in every state of society." The only solution was to give women "equality of right or power."[34]

Defining equality broadly, Reid stressed the importance of economic independence, since "the incapacity of a married woman to hold property is the root from which all the evils complained of spring." With no right to their own earnings or income, wives remained subjected to their husbands, unable to protect themselves or their children from male violence and brutality. The all-male legal system invariably sided with men:

> Was there ever a woman tried by a jury of her peers? . . . In cases of the assault or murder of husbands by their wives...is it to be expected that a jury of men will pay the same attention to the palliations of the dreadful catastrophe—such as the misery produced by long-endured, but at last unendurable insult and cruelty—as if the case were reversed?[35]

Rejecting the argument that "female influence" gave women sufficient power to balance male legal rights, Reid asserted that "man exerts as much—or greater—personal influence as woman does, and has all the privileges of citizenship besides." To counter the insistence that women remain at home, she raised the specter of "thousands upon thousands of unprotected [i.e., without a man to support them] females, who actually prefer leaving their only proper sphere, and working for their own subsistence—to starvation. . . . Ought not such wicked creatures to be exterminated?"[36] Consistently applying antislavery arguments to the female condition, Reid asserted that the denial of liberty prevented "the human being from developing its powers" and had the effect "of crushing, cramping, and debasing the human mind; of implanting a slavish spirit, and of substituting cunning for true wisdom," having "a pernicious influence" on both men and women.[37]

Countering the common argument of her day that middle- and upper-class women's "delicacy" would be ruined by their participation in public life, Reid maintained that "however pleasant it may be for women themselves to intrench themselves in decorum and refinement" distant from "painful" subjects like prostitution, "such is not the manner in which those terrible disorders can be remedied. . . . there are no vices so desperate that they ought not to be unfolded to female eyes, of which females are themselves the partakers and most miserable victims." The only alternative was to embrace the doctrine of womanly weakness and dependency, "to believe, that for one half of the human race, the highest end of civilisation is to cling upon the other, like a weed upon a wall."[38]

The *Plea for Woman* was the last treatise championing women's rights produced by an antislavery activist in these years, but a number of other feminist writings appeared in 1843, among them Louise Otto's articles on women's emancipation. Both Reid and Otto argued for the improvement of the female situation within existing social structures and governments, adding women's rights to a series of reforms that included widening German liberty and abolishing American slavery. Later divisions between liberals and socialists, as well as between religious Christians and anticlerical communists have led historians to classify such works as "bourgeois" rather than "socialist," but this obscures how fluid reform movements were before the revolutions of 1848. Louise Otto was active in both the free religion movement and socialist circles, soon earning the sobriquet "the red democrat." In her sermons, Lucretia Mott often preached a heartfelt Christian socialism which argued that by "striving to take advantage of one another . . . we are oppressing, not only the slave, but the poor laborer." Seeking to hold Americans to their highest national ideals, she argued that "true Christian democracy and republicanism" would lead to "that equality which is our nation's boast" and prevent the development of "large classes, crushed by existing monopolies, laboring for their scanty pittance."[39]

Believing that Christianity forbade both exploitation and violence, Mott presented a radical vision that foresaw the elimination of poverty, slavery, and war, as well as the oppression of women. Her reliance on the "inner light," the individual's God-given ability to discern what was right, led to a remarkable open-mindedness in these years, when she adopted "truth for authority, not authority for truth" as her motto. During the 1840s, Mott denounced wars against Native Americans and attempts to "civilize" them by forcing them to adopt white ways; she supported strikes and campaigns to raise wages of the poorest laborers both in Philadelphia and abroad; she renounced all use of violence, including that of parents to punish their children; and she excoriated those who criticized foreign conditions while ignoring oppression in their own nation. "There is a great zeal for the relief of Hindoo woman," she declared in an 1846 sermon, "but let us look at home and behold worse than their funeral pile, the immolation of woman at the shrine of Priestcraft. . . . Ah! Have you Brethren unfettered yourselves from a prejudice that is tending to immolate one half the whole human family?"[40]

Mott's open-mindedness did not extend to embracing the views of Robert Owen, whom she and her husband met on their trip to Britain in 1840. "The most successful refutation of his visionary scheme is to suffer him to be his own expositor," she wrote to the Webbs, while James Mott declared in his book on England that he "did not see why anyone should deem it worthwhile to oppose [Owen], for he has not such powers of mind as will enable him to bring about any great change, or accomplish any mighty work."[41] Owenism, like immediatist abolitionism, ran out of steam in the 1840s—a fact admitted by almost everyone except Robert Owen himself, who maintained an unwarranted optimism as his movement collaped around him. "We are disjointed, cast down, and powerless," wrote the last secretary of the Owenite Congress in 1845. "A spirit of discord has been among us, and blown our strength and purpose to the winds."[42]

The hopes awakened by early socialism, however, continued to inspire some to embrace feminism even after Owenism and Saint-Simonianism disintegrated as political movements. In the late 1830s, Englishwoman Catherine Watkins (later Barmby) published articles in favor of women's right to decent jobs and education in Owenite journals under the pseudonym "Kate." Married in 1839, she helped her husband, socialist Goodwyn Barmby, found a communist church that created a number of branches and provided a center for radical lectures and publications until its demise in 1849. Heavily influenced by Saint-Simonianism, these British radicals attempted to meld socialism, religion, and women's rights into a new, transformative movement. Catherine Barmby published a feminist pamphlet in 1843 arguing that without "the total emancipation of the woman," society would remain in its present "unhappy condition." Her *Demand for the Emancipation of Woman, Politically and Socially* appeared in her husband's newspaper, *New Tracts for the Times,* and reached France and the United States as well as Great Britain.[43]

Like Marion Reid, Catherine Barmby began by quoting Shelley and asserting women's claim to complete political and legal equality "because she is subject to like wants, expected to pay the same taxes . . . and because all other laws act as severely, many more severely upon her than upon man." Reid relied on law reform and education to improve women's lot; Barmby advocated a "new order of societary destiny." Reid argued that the female sex deserved equal rights because women's domestic duties took as much skill and ability as men's business obligations, but she also believed that women were naturally domestic and would not choose to hold political office even if they were allowed to do so.[44] Barmby, in contrast, voiced one of the earliest denunciations of female "household drudgery" and sought to achieve the "domestic emancipation" of women by means of "the communization of society," which would assure woman's financial independence and so "her freedom at the hearth and the board . . . from the tyranny of her husband."[45]

The most passionate sections of Barmby's pamphlet demanded women's "ecclesiastical emancipation," their right to participate equally in all moral and religious organizations, from Freemasonry to the Roman Catholic Church. To achieve female emancipation, she recommended the establishment of a feminist "woman's magazine" and "the formation of a 'woman's society' in every city, town and village possible" where "women might converse, discuss, and speak upon their rights, their wrongs, and their destiny; they might consult upon their own welfare, and that of the great human family, and thus prepare each other."[46] Insisting that emancipation could not succeed until woman claimed "the primary right of the suffrage" Barmby concluded with a denunciation of custom and fashion, which "tyrannises over her throughout all countries":

> Custom forces the Japanese women to gild their teeth. . . . it plaisters the face of the Russian women with paint; it cramps the feet of the Chinese females; and it makes the Turkish women tinge their finger nails and dye their eye-brows. . . . and in the present civilized countries caprice and fashion habit our sex in robes as many as they are ridiculous. This must not be in the future. The free woman must be adorned with a new dress. . . . The emancipation of woman from the garb of her slavery will be the outward sign of her liberty.[47]

While Western feminists in the late nineteenth century often used examples like Chinese foot binding or Indian suttee to demonstrate their own culture's superiority, those in earlier decades usually pointed out the universal similarities of female oppression. William Thompson included a passage that compared foot binding to corset wearing in a book about establishing communes. Louise Otto emphasized a paragraph in her 1844 novel, *Kathinka*, which likened the "crippled feet" of Chinese girls to the "crippled character" of German ones, who remained so "undeveloped" that they lost the "free use of their mental abilities."[48]

Catherine Barmby's pamphlet reached radicals throughout the Western community, who circulated such works among themselves. American intellectual Margaret Fuller read *The Demand for the Emancipation of Woman, Politically and Socially,* as did the White Quakers of Dublin, a dissident group with which Anne Knight had contact. In 1840, Goodwyn Barmby met French socialist Flora Tristan in Paris, where she gave him a copy of her new book on England.[49]

The individualistic Tristan had become a writer and speaker for international socialism and feminism in the late 1830s. Although she never made important connections to other feminists, her vivid writings and colorful actions influenced a number of British and French activists. Born to an aristocratic Peruvian father and a French mother whose marriage was not recognized by French law, she grew up in poverty, went to work young, and married her employer at seventeen. Leaving him after bearing three children in four years, the twenty-one-year-old Tristan had to earn her living as a paid companion and governess to a series of English ladies while her mother raised her own children.

Her first public rebellion occurred in London in 1831, when Tristan visited the House of Commons dressed as a Turkish man. Women were forbidden to attend Parliament until 1835, when they were permitted to witness proceedings from a balcony guarded by a grilled screen. Finding a sympathetic accomplice in the representative of the Ottoman Empire, Tristan spent the evening there in an open disguise. Dismayed by the "extreme discourtesy, coarseness—brutality, even" of most members of the House of Commons, Tristan formed a lifelong admiration for Irish M.P. Daniel O'Connell, who spoke that evening with his customary eloquence. O'Connell, "the Great Liberator," had led the campaign for Catholic emancipation—the removal of laws discriminating against Roman Catholics—and in these years he continued to press for Irish independence and land reform as well as supporting international abolitionism. Initially opposed to female delegates participating in the World Anti-Slavery Convention of 1840, O'Connell wrote a public letter supporting them after Lucretia Mott chided him for offering "flattering compliments which we could not receive in place of rights denied." Elizabeth Cady Stanton long remembered his advice on that occasion that "it is always good policy to claim the uttermost and then you will be sure to get something."[50]

Two years after her visit to the British Parliament, Tristan traveled to Peru to obtain assistance from her father's family. This unusual voyage sensitized her to the universal discrimination against women and led to her first publication, the 1835 pamphlet *On the Necessity of Extending a Decent Welcome to Foreign Women.* Proposing the formation of a society with headquarters in major cities where women could safely congregate,

Tristan gave voice to the difficulties facing the lone female traveler, who was usually assumed to be a prostitute:

> [She] will . . . suffer a thousand mortifications, a thousand breaches of hospitality and even of politeness. . . . She will be received at the celebrated Hôtel de l'Angleterre [in Paris] with a certain air we cannot give a name to. You may be sure that they will start by saying to her: "Madame is *alone* (emphasizing the word *alone*); and after her affirmative reply they will tell the servant boy or maid to take her to the worst chamber in the house. . . . Nevertheless, she will be made to pay ten francs *more* for her poor room than *a man* would be charged.[51]

On her return from South America in 1834, Tristan made contact with radicals in both Paris and London—among them Charles Fourier, Eugénie Niboyet, Robert Owen, and Anna Wheeler—as well as attending weekly meetings of the editorial board of the feminist *Gazette des femmes*. In 1838, she achieved fame with her passionate Peruvian travel memoir, *Peregrinations of a Pariah*. Portraying herself as a romantic outcast, she movingly articulated both sympathy for women's lot in general and an even greater self-pity for her own travails.

Tristan's conviction that she was doomed to be a lone "pariah" presented potential allies with the same problem posed by her contemporaries Frances Wright, George Sand, and Margaret Fuller. All eloquently gave voice to feminist beliefs, but their most important personal connections were to men. Seeing themselves as isolated pioneers, they had contempt for most other women of their day and neither sought to create nor to join movements on behalf of the female sex.

This perennial problem—the woman of achievement in a male-dominant society who identifies with men and sees herself as a lone exception to the rules that limit other women—was exacerbated in the first half of the nineteenth century by the prevailing ethos of romantic individualism. A myriad of poems, plays, and novels stressed the solitude of the artist, the isolation of genius, the heroism of the outsider. Women who aspired to artistic equality with men often cast themselves in this Byronic role as "the one and only." In this, Tristan resembled George Sand, with whom she was occasionally confused. When Tristan's husband shot her on a Paris street in 1838 after a lengthy custody dispute, newspapers initially reported Sand as the victim. Sand and Tristan both lost their fathers as small children, married young and unhappily, and left their husbands to pursue independent lives. Sand's talent and money sheltered her from the ignominious jobs that Tristan was forced to take, but they shared a romantic style, an interest in socialism, and the conviction that the free right to divorce was what women chiefly needed to remedy their situation.[52]

In the last years of her brief life, Tristan produced two works that influenced women active in international feminism, among them Anne Knight,

Jeanne Deroin, and Pauline Roland.[53] Her 1840 *Promenades dans Londres*, retitled *La Ville monstre* for a cheap fourth edition aimed at workers, mounted a powerful socialist attack on industrial capitalism four years before Friedrich Engels's *The Condition of the Working Class of England*. Denouncing "the horrifying oppression" of "the labourers and workers who create all the wealth," Tristan predicted an "inevitable and terrible struggle between the proletariat and the aristocracy" and declared that "the people are no longer satisfied with partial emancipation; they understand at last that every man is a *citizen of the world*, all are part of the great human family, naturally dependent one upon the other."[54]

Ranging widely over English life, Tristan published two idiosyncratic chapters about women. The first, on prostitution, agreed with other early feminists that the growth of the practice in the nineteenth century was due to the unequal distribution of wealth and women's lack of basic rights. But it also denounced prostitutes in language as melodramatic as that used by the puritanical "female reform" societies of the day that sought to raise "fallen" women. "I cannot understand the prostitute," Tristan wrote, after explaining that she could understand brigands and mercenaries. "She is wedded to sorrow and doomed to degradation: physical torture endlessly repeated, moral death every moment, and—worst of all—*boundless self-disgust!*" Tristan's chapter on English women is equally contradictory, alternating between sympathy for their situation and contempt for the ways in which they differ from the French.[55]

Tristan's final published writing, *The Workers' Union* of 1843, combined the goals of early socialism with the fervor of early Christianity to envision an international "consolidation of the working class." Taking O'Connell's Catholic Association as her model, Tristan argued that if French workers each contributed two francs a year, a network of clean, modern, and convenient "workers' palaces" could be erected. Housing two to three thousand people and containing their own factories and farms, these socialist centers would provide education for all children, care for the sick, and refuge for the elderly.[56]

In her dealings with both workers and women, Tristan alternated between heartfelt sympathy and the grandiosity of seeing herself as their lone savior. Frequently identifying herself with Jesus, she articulated their need for emancipation while denigrating their abilities. Denouncing the prejudice that had led to "woman (one half of humanity)" having "counted for nothing in human society," Tristan simultaneously allotted five seats to men and only two to women on the Workers' Union committees, explaining that "today's working women are much less educated and intellectually less developed than male workers."[57] Although she justified such arrangements as "transitory," other passages, in which she stigmatized "women of the masses" as "brutal, mean, and sometimes hard" or declared that "there are few working-class couples who are happily married," led to severe criticism from those she sought to aid.[58]

Tristan spent the last two years of her life publicizing *The Workers'*
Union, which rapidly went into three editions. She enlisted subscribers to
defray printing costs, among them George Sand, Pauline Roland, Jeanne
Deroin's husband, Antoine Desroches, and Fanny Wright's husband,
Phiquepal d'Arusmont. She wrote numerous letters about the work to
famous figures in France and abroad: the abolitionist Victor Schoelcher,
the painter Eugène Delacroix, the actress Rachel, and the German socialist Arnold Ruge. Finally, she embarked on a strenuous six-month lecture
tour of France in 1844, speaking to workers and organizing groups until
she suffered an ultimately fatal stroke that autumn. Four years after her
death, over 7,000 Bordeaux workers dedicated a monument to her memory, bearing the slogan Liberty, Equality, Fraternity, Solidarity.[59] Passionate, individualistic, romantic, and often unhappy, Flora Tristan personified the struggles of an activist woman against the confinement of her era.

The American intellectual Margaret Fuller similarly exemplified a talented woman at odds with her society who wrote passionately about the
disadvantages of the female lot. From her unusual childhood in Massachusetts (her father taught her Latin at six and had her reading Shakespeare at
eight) to her untimely death at forty in a shipwreck that occurred as she
was returning home after three years in Italy, Fuller attracted public
notice. Attending an elite coed Cambridge day school with future jurist
Oliver Wendell Holmes, author Richard Henry Dana, Unitarian ministers
William Henry Channing and James Freeman Clarke, Fuller equaled or
supassed her male classmates. But they went on to become members of the
famous Harvard University class of 1829, an impossibility for the female
Fuller. Undaunted, she mastered German and continued her studies until
her father's early death forced her to teach in order to support her family
and herself.

Touring America in 1835, Harriet Martineau saved Fuller from intellectual isolation. Martineau befriended the younger American and invited
Fuller to return with her to England. "I sigh for an intellectual guide," the
twenty-five-year-old Fuller wrote in her diary. "I have had some hope that
Miss Martineau might be this friend, but cannot yet tell. She has what I
want,—vigorous reasoning powers, invention, clear views of her objects,—
and she has been trained to the best means of execution."[60] Fuller could
not abandon her family responsibilities to go abroad at that time, but
meanwhile Martineau introduced her to famed poet and essayist Ralph
Waldo Emerson and thus to transcendentalism, the most exciting American intellectual movement of the day.

Originating from a discussion group of liberal Unitarian clergy, among
them William Henry Channing and Theodore Parker, the Transcendental
Club enlarged in 1836 to include philosophers, writers, and four women,
among them Margaret Fuller. Valuing nature, intuition, and imagination
while rejecting both traditional religion and capitalist acquisitiveness, the

transcendentalists stressed individual self-development and the creation of a genuinely American literature, liberated from the outmoded traditions of Europe. In addition to Emerson, the group included reformers George and Sophia Ripley, who later founded the commune at Brook Farm, idealistic schoolmaster Bronson Alcott, writers Henry David Thoreau and Nathaniel Hawthorne, and Hawthorne's sister-in-law, Elizabeth Peabody, who ran an important bookstore in Boston. Fuller thrived intellectually in this closely knit circle, her ability to read and interpret German writers and philosophers giving her authority.

She struggled nonetheless to reconcile herself to "old-maid" status, which was accorded to a woman who had not married by her mid-twenties. "Perhaps the next generation, looking deeper into this matter, will find that contempt is put upon old maids . . . merely because they do not use the elixir which would keep them always young," she wrote at thirty-three. "No one thinks of Michael Angelo's Persican Sibyl, or St. Theresa, or Tasso's Leonore, or the Greek Electra, as an old maid."[61] Like other exceptional women of her day, Fuller wrestled with the seeming contradictions between the life of the mind and the domesticity expected of the female sex. I like having "an active mind" and "the friendships of such men as Mr. Emerson, Mr. Ripley or Mr. Alcott," she wrote a friend in 1837. But all this must not "interfere with domestic duties," which are integral to "women's estate."[62]

Fuller's early "intimate friendship" with Harriet Martineau foundered on the harsh criticism the American made of the Englishwoman's 1837 analysis of the United States, *Society in America*. Fuller wrote the author that she found in the book "a degree of presumptuousness, irreverence, inaccuracy, hasty generalization, and ultraism on many points," lamented "the haste in which you have written and the injustice which you have consequently done to so important a task," and never understood why Martineau resented her comments. In these years, Fuller distanced herself from the antislavery movement. "As far as I know you seem to me quite wrong as to what is to be done for woman," she wrote American abolitionist Maria Weston Chapman, Martineau's closest friend. "She needs new helps I think, but not such as you propose."[63] Instead, Fuller attempted to "elevate" women in America so they could meet educated men on equal terms by organizing an all-female discussion group in Boston—a series of "Conversations" conducted from 1839 to 1844.

At Fuller's Conversations, a group of about thirty women each paid the substantial sum of $20 to meet for ten weeks on Saturday mornings to discuss topics ranging from education to Greek mythology. "The rapidity with which she appropriates all knowledge . . . her passionate love of all beauty, her sympathy with all noble effort; then her energy of character and the regal manner in which she takes possession of society wherever she is, and creates her own circumstances; all these things keep me full of admiration," wrote one participant about the first series, adding that Fuller's abilities "inspire me with new life, new confidence in my own power, new desires to fulfill 'the possible' in myself." Some found her domineering, especially in her insistence that controversial social topics like abolitionism be avoided, but Elizabeth Cady Stanton and others later paid tribute to Fuller's "vindication of woman's right to think."[64]

During this period Fuller became the first editor of the *Dial*, a transcendentalist journal, and also published some of her translations from the German, including *Die Günderode*—the letters written by the contemporary author Bettine von Arnim to her friend Caroline von Günderode. In 1843, Fuller printed her first feminist work in the *Dial*, an article entitled "The Great Lawsuit: Man vs. Men; Woman vs. Women." This piece argued passionately for female equality and brought Fuller to the attention of radical editor Horace Greeley. He printed a large extract from it in his New York *Tribune*, which also featured a regular Fourierist column. The next year he invited Fuller to move to the city, expand her article into a book, and join his newspaper staff as a reporter. Fuller flourished during her time in New York City, where she wrote a wide-ranging column that appeared three times a week. She also pursued a passionate but ultimately unsuccessful romance with a German Jewish businessman, James Nathan.

In 1845, the book-length version of her feminist article appeared, now as *Woman in the Nineteenth Century*. Wishing "the conditions of life and freedom recognized as the same for the daughters and the sons," Fuller expanded her original essay by adding poetry and mythology, philosophic musings, and personifications of ideal women. "We only ask of men to remove arbitrary barriers. We would have every path laid open to Woman as freely as to Man," she wrote in words echoing Wollstonecraft's *Vindication of the Rights of Woman*:

> If you ask me what offices [women] may fill, I reply—any. I do not care what case you put; let them be sea-captains if you will. . . . In families that I know, some little girls like to saw wood, others to use carpenter's tools. Where these tastes are indulged, cheerfulness and good-humor are promoted. Where they are forbidden, because "such things are not proper for girls," they grow sullen and mischievous.[65]

Praising Fourier, Goethe, and eighteenth-century Swedish mystic Swedenborg for recognizing women's equality, Fuller criticized the double standard for catering to the male sexual drive. "It has been inculcated on women, for centuries" that "a man is so constituted that he must indulge his passions or die! . . . On this subject, let every woman . . . see whether she does not suppose virtue possible and necessary to Man."[66]

Rapidly reprinted in a second American edition, *Woman in the Nineteenth Century* was paid the dubious compliment of being pirated by an English publisher. In 1846, when Fuller traveled in Europe as the *Tribune's* foreign correspondent, she found her work known abroad. Crossing the Atlantic with wealthy radicals Marcus and Rebecca Spring, Fuller spent six months touring Britain and France. A semicelebrity herself, she met a host of famous figures: elderly poet William Wordsworth, author Thomas Carlyle and his wife, Jane, William and Mary Howitt, Unitarian minister W. J. Fox, French author and politician Felicité de Lamennais, socialists Clarisse Vigoureux, Pierre Leroux, and Pauline Roland. Fuller prized her encounter with George Sand, although a friendship between them did not develop. "Her whole appearance and attitude, in its simple and ladylike dignity, present an almost ludicrous contrast to the vulgar caricature idea of George Sand," she wrote a female friend in America. "Her way of talking is just like her writing,—lively, picturesque, with an undertone of deep feeling, and the same skill in striking the nail on the head every now and then with a blow . . . while talking, she *does* smoke all the time her little cigarette. . . . For the rest, she holds her place in the literary and social world of France like a man, and seems full of energy and courage in it. I suppose she has suffered much, but she has also enjoyed and done much, and her expression is one of calmness and happiness.[67]

Two male revolutionaries in exile made the greatest impression on Fuller and became her friends: Italian patriot Guiseppe Mazzini and Polish poet Adam Mickiewicz. "Your mission is to contribute to the deliverance of the Polish, French, and American woman," Mickiewicz wrote her after they met in Paris in 1847.[68] Instead, Fuller traveled on to Italy, where she found romance with an ardent republican, the Marchese de Ossoli. Instead of connecting with activist women, Fuller embraced Mazzini's cause of unifying the seven Italian states into an independent nation freed from the bonds of both local monarchies and the Austrian empire. An eyewitness to the Roman uprising of 1848, Fuller continued to write, producing both dispatches to the New York *Tribune* and a new book on socialism and revolution. Elizabeth Barret Browning saw Fuller and this manuscript in 1850, just before the American began her voyage home. Barrett Browning advised Fuller not to return, since as "one of the out and out Reds" with "those blood colours of Socialist views," she "would have drawn the wolves on her, with a still more howling enmity, both in England and America." The manuscript was lost when Fuller, her son, and his father drowned in July within sight of Fire Island, New York.[69]

Contemporary feminists speculated that if Fuller had lived she might have led the women's movement. I wonder what might have happened if she had gone to Germany and looked up Bettina von Arnim, whose writings she had translated. A women's movement emerged in the German states during this period, but not in Italy. By publishing subversive literature and by participating in the radical new religious and political societies that formed, von Arnim and increasing numbers of other German women began to venture along the feminist path already taken by their counterparts in France and the United States. First in groups organized by men, later in opposition to the prejudices of these "brothers" and the limits they placed on female behavior, German feminists contributed to the development of women's movements during the years just before the revolutions of 1848.

When Louise Otto published her articles on female emancipation in 1843, she joined the growing number of German writers just beginning to criticize conditions in their homeland. Until the mid-1840s most rulers of the thirty-nine separate German states maintained rigid social control by exiling all who sought change, including poets like Heinrich Heine and Georg Herwegh, professors like the seven at the University of Göttingen dismissed for supporting a constitution, or political theorists like Friedrich Engels and Karl Marx. Margaret Fuller was shown the house in which exiled radical poet Ferdinand Freiligrath lived in London; the exiled socialist Arnold Ruge attended workers meetings at Flora Tristan's in Paris.[70] One of the more daring protests against German autocracy was Bettina von Arnim's 1843 work of political and social criticism, *This Book Belongs to the King*. Connected by birth and marriage to the German literary elite, von Arnim exhorted the new king of Prussia, Friedrich Wilhelm IV, to alleviate the miserable poverty in his realm by adopting liberal policies and humanitarian values. Widely read in the rest of Europe (French feminists reprinted sections of it in their newspaper the *Voice of Women* in 1848), the work met only intransigence at home. Von Arnim concluded that "to help the poor now means preaching revolt" and began to associate with the radical circles that coalesced in Germany during these years.[71]

Forbidden virtually all political activity, many German progressives moved into religious reform. Creating "free congregations" independent of the conservative state Roman Catholic and Protestant churches, they used the German tradition of individual religious liberty to challenge government bans on political meetings and revolutionary discussions. Identified as German Catholic or Free Evangelical, these congregations often crossed the denominational divisions that so structured German life. Protestants met with Catholics: a few groups had Jewish members, and others included agnostics and free thinkers. Functioning as quasi-political bodies in a culture that linked religious affiliation to citizenship, these new assemblies saw themselves as the nuclei of social regeneration. At their weekly meetings, dissenting clergymen, along with male and female parishioners, discussed the radical transformation of society as well as the economy, politics, and family life. Calling for "a holy revolution" based on the Christian principle of love, as German Catholic leader Johannes Ronge phrased it, they shared an optimistic vision of Germany's peaceful future development. "Above all, it is the religious movement to which we owe the rapid progress of feminine participation in the questions of the age," Louise Otto wrote in 1847. "German Catholicism proclaimed a universal spiritual equality before God, of priests and laity, the learned and the simple, men and women."[72]

Breaking with the Roman Catholic Church in 1844 by criticizing the veneration of a robe supposedly worn by Jesus, then rapidly excommunicated, the former priest Ronge saw himself and was seen by many contemporaries as a latter-day Martin Luther, leading a second German reformation. Appealing to an international audience for support (his apologia was translated into English and called on "men of Europe and of America" to follow him), Ronge was also influenced by international feminist ideas. "In general it can be taken as an axiom," he wrote in a passage inspired by Fourier, "that the more a people respects its women, the higher the entire people stands and the freer it will be—past and present prove this."[73] Published by Robert Blum, the same editor who printed Louise Otto's first writings, Ronge and other dissident clergy believed that society could never be improved unless the individual truly changed. Changing the individual meant first making marriage more egalitarian, then transforming the family, child raising, and education, and, finally, recasting political life. The active participation of women was seen as essential to realizing these hopes.

Welcomed into the free congregations, women joined in great numbers, constituting 40 percent of the 100,000–150,000 Germans who entered these groups between 1841 and 1852—a far greater rate of participation than in any other mass movement of the day. Becoming part of a free congregation was seen as a radical political act, for women as well as men. "For me this step was extremely important," remembered Malwida von Meysenbug. "It separated me forever from my past; by it I publicly renounced the Protestant church and joined a truly democratic society."[74]

Appealing especially to young adults from the lower middle class, the free religion movement provided a unique space for both single and married women in German culture. Within the shelter of these supportive groups, women began to take part in meetings and discussions, to raise funds through charity bazaars and lotteries, and to manage the movement's growing social welfare programs. A number of congregations established coeducational kindergartens and elementary schools to pass their ideals on to their children, and women often became teachers in those schools—a radical act in Germany, since male clergy controlled primary education. Johannes Ronge gave women equal voting rights within the group he led and by 1845, the topic was under discussion in a number of congregations. "Women's right to vote [in the congregation] proves the adult status and the emancipation of women," declared the German Catholic Saxon Synod the next year.[75]

Active participation encouraged some female members to claim more, both for themselves and for other women. "For three years we vigorously sought to further the cause of religious reform," the freethinking Hamburg Women's Club of 1847 wrote in a report.

We cannot, however, struggle for freedom of conscience without becoming free ourselves. For it is the blessing of all true human striving that a human being wins his own spiritual power when he works for the general good. The more clearly and self-consciously we came to an appreciation of the signifi-cance of our own spiritual lives, the more we felt called upon to work with joy and commitment for the intellectual and material well-being of our sex.[76]

Including Jews as well as Protestants and Catholics, the Hamburg Women's Club defied the traditional religious divisions, which carried as much weight in the German lands as racial divisions did in the United States. Until the 1848 revolutions, only a few very liberal German states gave Jews equal rights; in most areas they suffered discrimination ranging from a denial of citizenship to special penalties and fees. Crossing reli-gious, racial, and national boundaries, and reaching out to women in dif-ferent groups made it easier to challenge the traditional subordination of the female sex. Both the Hamburg Women's Club, which founded the first female German college, and the Mannheim Monday Club, which gave radical feminist Louise Dittmar a sympathetic forum in which to present her ideas, included Jewish members.

In addition to making it possible for women to participate in groups that overturned tradition, free religion also provided the same mixture of encouragement and frustration that made feminists of women in other radical movements. Like abolitionism in the United States and Saint-Simonianism in France, German free religion wanted women's support but sought to control their behavior far more than men's. Ronge's mar-riage, as well as those of other former priests, was lauded for following Luther's example and teachings, and male clergy in the free congregations frequently argued that only marriages based on love were valid. But when female author Louise Aston expressed the same ideas in 1846, Berlin authorities banished her from the city.

The case generated debate about women's role, both inside and out-side the free religion movement. Aston divorced in 1844 and then moved with her three-year-old daughter to the Prussian capital, where she hoped to make a living as a freelance writer. In Berlin, Aston frequented literary cafés and taverns, "smoking cigars in the company of academically edu-cated men," she later wrote, adding that if fraternization were a crime then she had committed one. German opinion, even in left-wing circles, disparaged such behavior for women. "*Women's emancipation* marches onward in a remarkable way in Germany, especially in Berlin," liberal editor Ernst Keil, who published a number of Louise Otto's pieces, wrote in 1845,

It has the most astonishing results. In that city's brilliant circles, girls of 19 and 20 speak with near fantastic authority about Guizot, Thiers [French politicians], courts and the law of search and seizure, which borders on the fabulous. Many of these miniature George Sands no longer disdain cigars, recently an elegant lady even stopped a gentlemen smoking a cigar on the street in order to get a light for her own. What priceless prospects! How long will it be before they put on trousers, whip men back into the kitchen, and suckle their children on horseback! . . . In any case—the devil take them![77]

In 1846 Aston published *Wild Roses*, a passionate poetry collection containing hymns to George Sand and free love. Within a few days, the police, who had already received anonymous denunciations of her conduct, persuaded the government to exile her on the grounds that her way of life and ideals threatened civic peace and order. Publicizing her case in *My Emancipation, Proscription, and Justification* and her autobiographical novel, *From a Woman's Life*, both published in Brussels in 1847, Aston credited early French socialism, English Chartism, and the 1844 uprising of Silesian weavers for "writing a new page in history" and inspiring her defiance.[78]

Mathilde Franziska von Tabouillot (later Anneke), also a divorcée supporting herself and her daughter by writing, championed Aston in an 1847 essay, "Woman in Conflict with Social Circumstances." Ridiculing the double standard of morality, she asked why a divorced woman is always considered "guilty," argued that Aston had only expressed the same ideas admired when enunciated by Spinoza or Hegel, and urged support for the author and her writings:

> The voice of this little book [Aston's *Emancipation*] awakened from their slumbers many female sleepers, who have not yet nodded off too deeply over the bubbling of their cooking pots. . . . The frank consciousness of her beliefs and thoughts . . . will arouse a unique sympathy in women and men of our day.[79]

Marrying radical army officer Fritz Anneke later that year, Mathilde Franziska Anneke continued to support Aston in the "communist salon" she and her husband ran in Cologne. In Mannheim, Louise Dittmar gave talks before the Monday Club—an offshoot of the local free congregation—which questioned any double standard of morality and claimed "a sense of self-worth for *every person*, for each *sex* equally." Dittmar, who had previously published four books anonymously, printed these talks under her own name later in 1847.[80]

Other reformers believed that Aston had gone too far. Johannes Ronge contrasted "beautiful, sanctifying femininity" to the repulsive "emancipation mania" enacted by women like Aston, who "take over completely male spheres of activity and imitate . . . male manners." Louise Otto, who despised Aston and thought she brought women's cause into disrepute, continued to distinguish between acceptable and unacceptable female emancipation. But Otto also began to demand more for women in these years. One of the most widely reprinted poems in her 1847 collection, *Songs of a German Maiden*, was "Freedom for All," which argued that the French Revolution had failed because women were not included in supposedly universal rights. She urged Germans to remedy this injustice, "to found a renewed empire of love, / To bring woman her rights like man."[81]

Hundreds of German women who had some contact with the free congregations developed a feminist consciousness in the 1840s and began to demand improvements in the female condition. "Even here, the spirit of the age dare not stand still," wrote Helene Menzzer in a poem addressed to an 1847 conference of the free congregations. "It comes to slay ancient prejudice / And to elevate woman to human dignity!"[82] The free religion movement created a cohort of feminists in the German lands similar to those in other Western nations of the same period. Convinced that women's situation could and should be improved, it was these activists who seized the moment when revolutions exploded early in 1848.

Seven

∽

Volcano Time

Margaret Fuller filled her 1847 European dispatches to the New York *Tribune* with warnings of revolutions to come. "At this moment, all things bode and declare a new outbreak of the fire, to destroy old palaces of crime," she reported from Italy that October. "May it fertilize also many vineyards!" European observers recorded similar hopes and fears. "The propertied must no longer stop up their ears," Louise Aston wrote in her 1847 novel, *From a Woman's Life*. "Or they will call forth a revolution which brings down the entire structure of society, compared to which the French Revolution [of 1789] was only a political game of ninepins."[1] Fuller connected oppression in Europe to slavery in America: "I find the cause of tyranny and wrong everywhere the same," she wrote in her October column. "I listen to the same arguments against the emancipation of Italy [from the Austrian empire], that are used against the emancipation of our blacks; the same arguments for the spoliation of Poland [by the Russian empire] as for the conquest of Mexico [by the United States in the 1846 war]."[2]

Some American abolitionists thought the time ripe for change in the United States, Lucretia Mott, for example, often quoting Jesus: "Look on the fields; for they are white already to harvest." But conditions in the United States did not augur the dramatic explosions anticipated in Europe.[3] In the Old World, conservative governments had succeeded in blocking almost all movements for political and social reform since the final defeat of Napoleon Bonaparte in 1815. Especially in the large states of the east—the kingdom of Prussia, the Russian empire, and the Austrian empire, which then included northern Italy as well as Hungarian, Czech, and German territories—repression remained the order of the day. Kings and princes retained powers as absolute as any in France before the Revolution of 1789. Without any constitution, civil liberties and rights depended on the whims of reigning monarchs. State churches, local aristocracies, and feudal obligations further limited individual freedom. Under the unwearied direction of the "coachman of Europe," Prince Metternich, Austrian minister of foreign affairs for almost forty years, stringent censorship, police espionage, political exile, and international military intervention stifled dissent.

By the mid-1840s, however, rumblings of discontent began to be heard. The deadly potato blight worsened the already meager harvests of 1845 and 1846. By 1847, the British controlled famine-stricken Ireland by stationing 13,000 police there—far more than in any other European nation. In April of the same year, hungry working-class women and men stormed public markets and battled troops in Berlin, the Prussian center of conservatism. This "Potato Revolution," as the press soon nicknamed these food riots, lasted for three days before order was restored. If we do not improve the lot of the most miserable in our society, Louise Otto predicted in 1847, "then the time will inevitably come when the proletariat will rise up against the bourgeoisie, the way this group is now opposing the barons."[4]

Even the relatively liberal French monarchy of Louis Philippe came under threat as politicians and journalists increasingly denounced government by the very wealthy, only one out of thirty-six adult Frenchmen possessing the income necessary to vote. The widening gap between rich and poor, the glaring impoverishment of the new proletariat class of industrial workers, and the growing misery in the crowded cities prompted thoughtful observers to call for timely reforms to prevent upheavals. At the end of January 1848, respected political analyst Alexis de Tocqueville counseled his fellow members of the French Chamber of Deputies not to ignore working-class denunciations of the unequal division of property. "It is said that . . . because there is no visible disorder on the surface of society, we are far from revolution," he warned. "Gentleman, I think you are mistaken. . . . my profound conviction is that we are lulling ourselves to sleep on top of an active volcano."[5]

By comparing France to a volcano ready to explode, Tocqueville drew on a prevalent metaphor of the day. Periodic eruptions in these years of Europe's two live volcanoes—Etna in Sicily and Vesuvius near Naples—fascinated contemporaries, who considered such spectacles compelling and sublime. "It is really a grand and awful sight," Barbara Leigh Smith wrote about Vesuvius. "To see it as I have seen it . . . looking across the water to the dark mountain at night, and watching its crown of fiery vapour, and the long lines of lava running down its sides. . . . To think there is a hole right down into the red-hot centre of the earth, to the very place where the devil is!"[6]

In the 1840s Italian dissidents, fearful of Austrian censorship, ostensibly corresponded about volcanoes, using the phenomenon as a code word for political and social unrest. "In the hot summer of 1846," just before an eruption, "Vesuvius was very quiet—but people trembled before this quiet because all the springs . . . began to dry up," German novelist Fanny Lewald wrote about a sojourn in Italy. "Today Berlin seems to me as terrifyingly quiet as Vesuvius was then." Early in January 1848, the first revolution of that tumultuous year broke out in Sicily. A few weeks later, Karl Marx and Friedrich Engels sent their call for an uprising of the international proletariat, *The Communist Manifesto*, to a London publisher. The "social volcano," as Fredrika Bremer called it, was beginning to erupt.[7]

Events in Italy presaged the greater explosion in France at the end of February. The government's cancellation of an opposition party's political banquet on February 21 led to three days of violent street fighting followed by the king's sudden abdication. The creation of the second French Republic on February 24 transformed political life. Overnight, a democratic-socialist ethos replaced the outworn bourgeois monarchy. The new government declared its support for the Saint-Simonian principle of people's "right to work" and rapidly opened national ateliers to provide jobs and income for the very poor. It quickly abolished the death penalty for political crimes, limited hours of work, reduced taxes, denounced the practice of slavery (still legal in the French West Indies), and proclaimed universal suffrage.

This revolution soon spread to other lands. On March 11, Prague erupted and Vienna on March 13, as Metternich fled for his life to England. Budapest followed on the fifteenth, Milan and Berlin on the eighteenth, and Venice on the twenty-second. American consuls in Europe rapidly supported the revolutionaries by being the first nation to give diplomatic recognition to the new French government, by celebrating the people's victory in Prussia, and by providing passports for Italian rebels—gestures of solidarity from the world's largest existing republic to its new counterparts abroad.[8] Less than a month after the initial upheavals in Paris, revolution had transformed the European political and social landscape.

From the beginning, women actively participated in the 1848 revolutions. They demonstrated against governments, helped build barricades of paving stones, earth, lumber, and furniture to block soldiers' progress through the cities, and numbered among the first victims of the fighting. "Even the women quelled the troops," wrote Fuller about Sicily, "showering on them stones, furniture, boiling oil, such means of warfare as the household may easily furnish to the thoughtful matron."[9] The *Illustrated London News* printed a drawing of two women atop a Paris

barricade carrying a banner inscribed "Bread or Death." "The foremost
was well-known in the Quartier," the text explained. "She was a fine
woman, with black hair, and wore a light blue silk dress; her head and arms
bare. She and her companion were shot." Two lithographs of the spring
uprising in Prague portray an armed woman in skirts on a barricade along
with several men: in one she urges an attack, in the other, she fires a
flower-bedecked rifle. One of the earliest illustrations of the French
National Workshops centers on a sitting woman holding a child in her lap;
other sketches from Paris show female as well as male bodies loaded into
tumbrils collecting the dead from the streets at night.[10]

European women's participation in urban uprisings dates back to the
Middle Ages and traditionally signaled the breakdown of social order
under the pressure of extreme suffering and deprivation. The 1848 revolutions resembled the riots of the past in their use of street violence to over-
whelm existing governments, but they also pointed to the future by raising
new political possibilities, which had been blocked for more than a generation. Throughout Europe, hopes for democratic civil liberties and voting
rights, for socialist welfare reforms and limits to economic exploitation,
and for national independence or unification in states still controlled by
the large empires bloomed during this "springtime of peoples." "It seemed
in those days as if the new world awakened to a new morning, something
springlike and festive coursed through the air," remembered Marie von
Brunow, a radical German democrat, of the early months of 1848. "All the
old antiquated customs fell with one blow, for once there was no bureau-
cracy and no social prejudice, no more barriers to companionable dealings
between the sexes."[11]

Women continued to demonstrate their support for the revolutions
once the fighting subsided. They sewed the new national flags and dressed
in the national colors—red, gold, and black for Germany, red, white, and
green for Italy, red and white for Poland and Switzerland, red, white, and
blue for France and Hungary. Frequently used to symbolize revolutionary
ideals (both the "Republic" and "Liberty" were usually portrayed as
female), real women also participated in public ceremonies. They
attended the funerals of fallen revolutionaries, sometimes defying government bans to do so; they thronged streets and plazas for festivals celebrating the new nations and governments.[12] We "no longer wish to remain
alone in the quiet circle of the home," declared a newly formed Berlin
Women's Association, "but also to be able to help and further events outside as well."[13]

In these months of change and optimism, of experiment and possibility,
early feminists seized the revolutionary moment to demand that women
be included as equals in democratic and socialist reforms. Especially in
France, they pushed for "the complete, radical abolition of all the privileges of sex, of race, of birth, of rank, and of fortune," as Jeanne Deroin
and Anne Knight wrote in a public letter that June.[14] All spring they

sought to extend the revolution's gains to include women, to use popular symbols and slogans of the day to win support for their cause. Throughout the Western community, they appropriated the potent metaphor of the erupting volcano to express their own sense of the liberating release of demands long pent up. Lava, volcanoes, wind, and fire appear repeatedly in their writings. "Nothing but the fire of a great public enthusiasm" coupled with "the free winds of an ENTIRE franchise" will bring needed changes, Anne Knight declared in a public letter to radical English reformer Lord Brougham, himself invited to stand for the French legislature in 1848. "Germany, which had appeared to be so soundly asleep, quaked as from an underground fire," Malwida von Meysenbug remembered of that spring, adding that when her conventional mother asked what more she could wish for, she replied "self-government" for all, borrowing the word from English to express this foreign concept. "Volcanoes nearer here . . . Am I inclined to climb," wrote Emily Dickinson from Massachusetts. "A Crater I may contemplate / Vesuvius at home"[15]

One of the first French cartoons of feminists in 1848 shows armed women erupting from a volcano. On March 28, a few days after it appeared, the new feminist newspaper, the *Voice of Women*, carried an account of "a legion of young women workers, well-dressed with admirably modest outfits" who had gathered the previous day at the Place Vendôme under "a beautiful banner in the national colors on which gold letters spelled out this single word *Vésuviennes*" (the women of Vesuvius). The editors reported that these young women were "poor, disinherited workers who have joined in a community whose aim is to improve their condition" and speculated that they had chosen their name because "the general interest" of the day had demanded it.[16]

The creation of women's movements in 1848–1849 required the sense of possibility and energy produced by revolution. Revitalized by the explosive first revolutionary months and encouraged by the hopes arising from conservatism's rapid initial defeat, feminists plunged into action in the spring of 1848. First in France, then in the United States and Germany, they organized to claim rights on behalf of all women. Early in March, Pauline Roland tried to vote in the municipal elections at Boussac, where she had been living in a socialist commune. Although accompanied by Pierre Leroux, who was elected mayor, she was not permitted to cast a ballot, but her attempted act received publicity.[17] On March 2, Désirée Véret Gay petitioned the new government "to appoint female delegates to the commission on labor," to provide work for the female poor, and to open national restaurants, bathhouses, and laundries staffed by women.[18] On March 16, two new groups, the Society for the Emancipation of Women and the Committee for the Rights of Women, asked the government to implement female equality in politics, social life, work, the family, and education. "There cannot be two liberties, two equalities, two fraternities," they asserted. "Men's liberty and equality are clearly those of women as well." Insisting on women's inclusion in the new revolutionary political settlements, they demanded that "along with the 'people-as-king' must be proclaimed the 'people-as-queen,' or better still, they should both be included in the 'people-as-sovereignS'[sic]."[19]

On March 20, a women's club began to publish the *Voice of Women*, billed as a "Socialist and Political Journal, the Organ of the Interests of All Women." Edited by Eugénie Niboyet, it appeared six times a week, publishing a wide range of French feminists' demands and concerns. Arguments for political rights, for equal education, for a reorganization of female labor, and for an appreciation of women's history fill its closely printed pages, along with news of the many women's political clubs and organizations founded at the time. "Men are no longer permitted to say 'We are humanity,'" proclaimed the front page of the first issue. "Liberty for all men *is* liberty for all women."[20]

The *Voice of Women* and the other feminist journals that burst into print in 1848 and 1849—the French *Women's Politics* and *Women's Opinion*, the German *Women's Mirror*, *Freedom Fighter*, *Social Reform*, and two *Women's Newspapers*, the American *Lily*—represented an amazing outpouring of female energy. Producing even a single issue required the efforts of scores of people, most of them women, working as editors, reporters, writers, printers, publishers, saleswomen, and distributors. A four-page daily like the *Voice of Women* or a fifty-page monthly like the *Lily* demanded reams of material on a regular basis. To fill their pages, journals printed feminist writings from the 1830s and 1840s as well as contemporary reportage, drawing on a wide range of international as well as national sources. Most issues of *The Voice of Women* carried a review of recent events from foreign journals; the first contained reports from Switzerland, Germany, Belgium, England, Ireland, Poland, and Italy. The second number began publishing a French translation of Bettina von Arnim's 1843 treatise, *This Book Belongs to the King*, under the title *On Poverty in Germany*. The third reproduced an internationalist label Anne Knight had first printed in the early 1840s:

> *Young women of the Gauls* had the right to make the laws,
>   they were *legislators*.
> In some tribes, *African women* have the *right to vote*.
> *Anglo-Saxon women* participated in England *in the*
>   *legislature*.
> *The women of the Hurons*, one of the strongest tribes of
> North America, made up a *council, the elders followed*
>   *their advice*.
>
> .   .   .   .
> We struggle for liberty![21]

The longest running of these periodicals, Louise Otto's weekly *Women's Newspaper*, which lasted from 1849 to 1852, regularly carried a section called "A Look Around," which printed news from Europe and America, as well as from all over Germany. When Otto reported on the first appearance of Louise Dittmar's *Social Reform*, she heralded this feminist monthly as part of an international effort to question "the spiritual and material chains that bind the entire female sex" in the context of "the great all-encompassing World-Movement which has suddenly shaken the artificially preserved ruins based on privilege to their foundations."[22] Even Amelia Bloomer's upstate New York *Lily* regularly printed letters and articles from "abroad," relying on European news to round out its American offerings. "The interests of the whole human family are so linked together that whatever is done for the elevation of one class affects all," Elizabeth Cady Stanton wrote in December. "Every revolution of the moral world brings for woman a brighter and happier day."[23]

In addition to broadcasting feminist ideas to subscribers and others who might encounter an issue, these journals also functioned as nuclei around which women's movements coalesced. The writers and readers of the *Lily*, Otto's *Women's Newspaper*, the *Voice of Women*, and other periodicals were those who organized national movements on behalf of women in the late 1840s and early 1850s. Fueled by feminist ideas from the years before the revolutions, these movements united national and international concerns. Feminists drew on universal concepts and symbols, kept track of each other's triumphs and defeats, and used similar arguments and strategies to press for women's gains. In 1848, Jeanne Deroin, Anne Knight, Louise Otto, Lucretia Mott, and others shared an optimistic belief that democratic socialism, often augmented by a politically radical Christianity, could bring about swift and lasting change. While national differences shaped what individual women and movements were able to accomplish, international feminism supplied common themes and concerns.

The actions and writings of Jeanne Deroin demonstrate this interplay between national particularities and international themes. Living a private life after her involvement in the Saint-Simonian movement of the early 1830s, Deroin spent the 1840s bearing three children, studying for her teacher's license, and then directing and working in a coeducational school. In February 1848, she entrusted her children to the care of close female friends, left her job, and launched into an array of feminist projects. She helped found the Society for the Emancipation of Women and joined the Society for the Voice of Women, writing frequently for the newspaper it published. She sent letters to male editors of radical journals and attended men's political clubs to press for women's rights. "One evening . . . as M. Cabet [a leading French socialist] was presiding over a well attended club," remembered Jenny d'Héricourt, herself secretary of the Society for the Emancipation of Women, "he was requested by a woman to put the question: *Is woman the equal of man in social and political rights?* Almost every hand was raised in the affirmative. . . . This vote in the Cabet club was repeated in three others in my presence. The men in jackets [the garb of the middle and upper classes] laughed at the demands of the brave Jeanne

Deroin; the men in blouses [the tops worn by male workers] did not even smile at them."[24]

Deroin, along with Désirée Gay and Eugénie Niboyet, followed up these votes by writing a letter to Etienne Cabet congratulating him for backing women's emancipation. By March 26, the *Voice of Women* reported that Jeanne Deroin had already sent "four successive addresses to members of the provisional government" calling for women's equality. "Courage, woman," the editors wrote. "You are strong, you are patient; you counter the sarcasms of impotence with a pure life; the holy cause of our liberties is safe in your hands!"[25]

Deroin and her coworkers sought to convince the new revolutionary government that its democratic pronouncements rang hollow and would not succeed if they excluded women. "You say there are no more proletarians," argued the Committee for the Rights of Women on March 22. "But if women are not included in your decrees, France still contains more than 17 million proletarians."[26] French feminists repeatedly invoked the 1789 ideals of liberty, equality, and fraternity, maintaining that only full female participation could transform these words from empty slogans into a lasting and beneficial reordering of society. Using the Saint-Simonian argument that the Revolution of 1789 had failed *because* it excluded women, and, thereby, the supposedly female virtues of peace, reconciliation, and social harmony, Deroin and others passionately contended that the revolution of 1848 would also fail if women remained "the helots of the new Republic." Citing Olympe de Gouges's 1791 argument that if woman had the right to mount the scaffold to be executed, she also had the right to mount the rostrum to cast her ballot and give political speeches, Deroin insisted that only genuine female equality could prevent a resurgence of the militarism, despotism, and restoration of monarchy that followed the first French Revolution. Enabling the revolution of 1848 to succeed made claiming women's equality "more than a *right*, it is a *duty*."[27]

Frequently employed by early feminists, this phrase alluded to the current liberal axiom that the performance of duties should be balanced by the granting of rights. Making the argument that women's fulfillment of family and social obligations entitled them to civil and political liberties, feminists also asserted that duty itself impelled them to take unconventional actions on behalf of the female sex. In Germany, Louise Otto justified her unprecedented step of addressing a public letter about the situation of female workers to a governmental committee in the spring of 1848 as her "holiest *duty*," taken not "*despite* the fact that I am a weak woman, but *because* I am one."[28]

Presenting themselves and other women as moral beings who had performed the duties expected of them, feminists then moved easily to the argument that fulfilling these obligations entitled women to the political and legal rights accorded men. "How can you leave women with only duties to fulfill without giving them rights?" Deroin wrote in the *Voice of Women*. "Are women to be excused from paying taxes and obeying the laws of the state?"[29] Support for these views came from overseas. In April Emma Willard, director of the Female Seminary in Troy, New York (which educated Elizabeth Cady Stanton), sent a public letter to the French government urging that women be given power in the new political system, which let all adult men vote. Arguing that France should not subject the female sex to "that, for which America fought her independence, taxation without representation," Willard declared that enfranchising all Frenchmen while "forgetting" women violated fundamental principles of justice.[30] "None but a misanthropic wolf should now be found guilty of denying to his tax-paying sister her right to vote," Anne Knight charged in her public letter to Lord Brougham.[31]

"Among the many important questions which have been brought before the public, there is none that more vitally affects the whole human family than . . . Woman's Rights," declared Elizabeth Cady Stanton in a lengthy speech she delivered to a series of audiences in the summer and fall of 1848. Stanton and other early feminists contended that men could not morally justify denying their female relatives the privileges they considered vital for themselves. "All the members of the great human family have the same right to liberty," reasoned Deroin in a reply to a letter "from an unemancipated woman" printed in a radical newspaper. "Women no longer want to be loved as in the past, but to be honored as citizens, daughters, sisters, wives, and mothers of free citizens."[32]

Nineteenth-century proponents of the doctrine of separate spheres often exalted women's role as mothers in justifying their exclusion from public life. "Republican mothers" and "mother-educators" would redeem modern society from ancien régime corruption by concentrating their energies on their children's upbringing. "On the maternal bosom the mind of nations reposes," asserted the 1841 American edition of Louis Aimé-Martin's influential, oft reprinted French guidebook, *The Education of Mothers; or, the Civilization of Mankind by Women*.

> Their manners, prejudices, and virtues—in a word, the civilization of the human race—all depend upon maternal influence.
> The reality of the power is admitted, but the objection is stated, that it is only exercised in the family circle, as if the aggregate of families did not constitute a nation! Do we not perceive that the thoughts which occupy the woman at home, are carried into public assemblies by the man?[33]

Faced with such popular and widespread glorification of full-time motherhood, women who wished for more than a domestic role had difficulty in claiming equal political and social rights on behalf of mothers, whose physical labors of pregnancy, birthing, breastfeeding, and child care were seen as preventing their full participation in public life. Jeanne Deroin, who paradoxically had left the care of her children to others during the revolution, was one of the few radical feminists who made the argument in these years that motherhood, whether actual or potential, entitled all women to equal treatment. Her *Textbook on Social Right for Women*, which was both published and presented as a course of lectures in the hectic spring of 1848, argued that evil had entered the world when male "egoism" subordinated women and gave the rights and privileges of mothers over to patriarchal fathers. This sinful imbalance would only end when women reclaimed their equal status. "O woman! Mother of the human race, you who carry in your bosom all its sorrows, you who have submitted to all martyrdoms, you the holy model of the always suffering worker, always oppressed, always subordinated, raise yourself up and speak in the name of humanity," she concluded. "God himself commands you to do it; it is more than a right, it is a duty."[34] Fusing democratic socialism and radical Christianity, Deroin envisioned "a sublime humanitarian maternity" which would regenerate society by treating everyone with "the tender forethought and the fairness of a mother of a family who watches with equal care over all her children, giving to each of them according to their needs and rewarding them according to their merits." Humanity will only progress, she wrote the following year, "when women understand . . . that all men are brothers, that all women are sisters, and that all of them are the mothers not only of their own children, but of their sisters' children, and especially of those who hunger and thirst, those who suffer and weep, those who are orphans or abandoned."[35]

By basing women's claims to equality on their maternity, however radically that term was defined, Deroin anticipated arguments more often made at the end of the nineteenth century. By then, the concepts of women and motherhood were routinely merged; both bourgeois and socialist feminists argued that women's supposed propensity to mother society as a whole entitled them to equal rights. During the 1848 revolutions, however, feminists more often turned to women's roles as sisters to justify their activism. Sisterhood could easily be connected to both the political goal of fraternity and the socialist ideal of brotherhood. Insisting that these essentially masculine concepts had to encompass female relatives in order to succeed, European feminists attempted to include women in the new revolutionary settlements by advancing their claims as equal siblings in the same familial community. French feminists frequently wrote of "fraternity, equality, and liberty," changing the usual word order to reflect their view of the importance of this term for women. Generally avoiding the far less common word "sorority," they asserted that "fraternity" encompassed women and French feminists routinely signed their letters "Salut fraternel." "In the name of fraternity, I demand that your sisters will never be excluded by you from your banquets and meetings," Jeanne Deroin wrote in a public letter to the French government. Louise Otto's widely reprinted May address to the Saxon Committee on Workers invoked the concept of brotherly solidarity and charged its members not to "*forget women in the organization of labor.* . . . Are these not your wives, sisters, mothers and daughters, whose interests must be watched over as much as your own?"[36]

Sisterhood also signified the bonds linking women to each other. In the course of the nineteenth century "sisters" also came to designate women united in a common cause.[37] Many early feminists used the sister model to provide their first conceptions of what form a women's movement might take. In her 1847 novel about the German free religion movement, Louise Otto proposed that women striving for equality form a "secret sisterhood" of kindred spirits, identified by a "golden pin in the shape of a violet, encrusted with amethysts." Barbara Leigh Smith suggested that she and her close friends found a "united sisterhood" whose community would enable them to pursue "any profession, any pursuit." American women active in radical abolitionism consistently asserted that the bonds of sisterhood connected black and white women across the racial divide and routinely referred to other members of the movement as their brothers and sisters.[38] "For us, there are no longer the rich, nor the poor, distinctions of belief, of age, of rank, of profession," Jeanne Deroin wrote in April 1848. "We are all sisters and we should extend our hands to each other, to mutually help ourselves."[39]

The radical Christianity many early feminists developed in the 1830s and 1840s reinforced their belief in the egalitarian political concepts of sisterhood and solidarity. As "brothers and sisters in Christ," dedicated to drastically reorganizing society, early feminists throughout the Western community developed a new theology connecting the fulfillment of Jesus' vision of heaven on earth to ending all injustice and exploitation, whether of women, workers, or slaves. Fredrika Bremer, Jeanne Deroin, Sarah and Angelina Grimké, Anne Knight, Lucretia Mott, Louise Otto, and Pauline Roland all believed that a true reading of the Bible, stripped of "the perverted application of the Scriptures" that had developed under centuries of male dominance, supported radical democratic socialism, abolitionism, and feminism. The fall from the original state of grace resulted when "one half of the human race wanted to dominate the other, half of humanity was oppressed and the principles of love and devotion, of order and peace were subordinated," wrote Deroin in her *Textbook*. "Discord, disorder, and violence reign on earth and they will not cease from reigning until men have understood that all the laws which they have established alone are incomplete and in opposition to the law of God."[40] Relying on the first account of creation in Genesis 1:27 ("male and female created he them") rather than the more familiar story of Adam and Eve in Genesis 2, early feminists reasoned that male rule over women, which was God's punishment for Eve's disobedience, represented a fallen state of human nature rather than a model one. It then followed that both women and men must work to reform the world, to abolish inequality and injustice wherever they occurred. "There prevailed then a phrase, 'the Sisterhood of Reform,'" wrote American activist Thomas Wentworth Higginson about the 1840s, which referred to "a variety of social and physiological theories of which one was expected to accept all, if any."[41]

The optimism of reformers, augmented by the success of the first phase of the 1848 revolutions, led many early feminists to unite their beliefs in radical Christianity and democratic socialism. In these years, Fredrika Bremer began to call herself a "Christian socialist" and sought out communities that attempted to live by these ideals. In 1846, Bremer published a sketch extolling Kaiserswerth, an unconventional German nursing center that also impressed Florence Nightingale. In her 1848 novel, *Brothers and Sisters*, she presented a fictional American Fourierist community as a model for both Europe and the United States.[42] During the same period Lucretia Mott frequently preached about doing away with "monopolies which furnish facilities to the rich to become richer, and cause the poor to become poorer," consistently arguing that both Christianity and democracy forbade the economic exploitation of workers or slaves. In the summer of 1848 Anne Knight printed a public letter denouncing "all monopolies" as "anti-Christian," whether capitalists over workers, plantation owners over slaves, or men over women.[43]

Similar hopes appear in Fanny Wright's last book, *England the Civilizer*, published in January 1848 and read by Elizabeth Cady Stanton and Susan B. Anthony. Like Deroin, Wright presented an optimistic socialist vision that drew on Christian symbols and phraseology. The "three saviours of our race . . . science, industry, and women" would bring about "one universally comprehensive system of peace, and justice, order, and love." "Since woman will be party to the contract," Wright concluded, "and set on the religious bond of human confraternity, her seal of love and justice," humanity can look forward to "the opening of a new era":

> Maternal love is relieved of its burdens. . . . Age is saved from neglect and dependence. . . . Liberty becomes the portion of our race, by *the union of all for the independence of each*. The dove of peace descends upon earth, and love becomes the universal bond of the species, by our recognizing happiness for the unique end of our being, and by uniting as one family to fertilize one common earth; each secure in the aid and protection of all, without care for the day or anxiety for the future.[44]

These optimistic dreams gave way to political realities as feminists met severe opposition in France. Throughout the spring, left-wing newspapers and magazines satirized and attacked "the red Liberty bonnet worn by a blue stocking"—the efforts of emancipated women to enter political life *via* the revolution. *Charivari* published eighteen prints making fun of the Vésuviennes while Daumier continued to ridicule feminists who invoked Jeanne Deroin to justify their unconventional behavior. In March 1848 the prorevolution journal *La Liberté* praised "the woman dedicated to obedience, to silence, to trustful love, and to humble devotion" as "far more beautiful" than "the woman voter, the woman in the National Guard, the woman who lectures, the misunderstood and rebellious woman" and refused to print Deroin's rebuttal, saying she just wanted publicity.[45]

This hostility intensified in April, when campaigning for the general election of a Constituent Assembly began. Seeking to nominate a woman who was well-known enough to garner votes, the *Voice of Women* proposed George Sand as a candidate. Within a few days, the novelist published a furious letter repudiating the feminists:

> 1. I sincerely hope that not one elector will want to lose his vote in participating in the fantasy of writing my name on his ballot;
> 2. I do not have the honor of knowing a single one of the ladies who form clubs and edit newspapers;
> . . . I cannot permit being taken, without my consent, as the standard-bearer of a small coterie with whom I have never had the slightist connection, whether agreeable or annoying.[46]

Sand represented French public opinion far more than the editors of the *Voice of Women*. During the election campaigns, conservative sentiment reasserted itself. In one Breton district "the rumor was put about that our delegate was going to preach female emancipation, Saint-Simonianism and communism," reported a local club. "He was pelted with stones and garbage." The nine hundred male deputies elected on April 23 stood far to the right of the previous provisional government: over half supported monarchy and both moderate republicans and democratic socialists fared poorly. When the lone Fourierist delegate, Victor Considérant, proposed that the new constitution grant women's suffrage, the assembly voted 899 to 1 against his measure.[47]

Faced with such enmity, the editors of the *Voice of Women* retreated. On April 28, they printed a compromise petition calling for a complete recognition of all women's civil rights but demanding the vote only "for widows over twenty-one and single women," those who did not have a husband to "represent" them. Attacks mounted on women's political clubs as men invaded their meetings and disrupted proceedings. The club of the *Voice of Women* excluded men in May, charged them double admission in early June, and then was closed by the police, ostensibly to prevent disorder. Désirée Véret Gay, elected in March by women laborers of the second arrondissement to direct their workshop and represent them at the all-male Luxembourg Commission, was dismissed by the government in the middle of June. On June 18, Anne Knight, Jeanne Deroin, and and a third woman, A. François, sent a public letter from "your devoted and affectionate sisters" to the government, reproaching their "brothers" for "not being generous" to the female "half of humanity," which supported their "principles and ardently desires to take part in the sacred work of social regeneration."[48]

Within the week, the government moved against the socialists, closing the National Workshops and using the army when workers protested. These bloody "June Days" pitted the bourgeois republican government against the Parisian proletariat and signaled the breakdown of democratic-socialist unity. Left-wing leaders went into exile, political clubs came under police supervision, newspapers had to post bond in order to publish, and written denunciations of the government became illegal. As part of this reactionary legislation, the government ruled on June 28 that women could no longer be members of political clubs.

Knight and Deroin instantly protested this measure, writing public letters to Athanase Coquerel, the Protestant minister who sponsored the ban. "You say that woman is not made for public life. . . . Is it because of the disorder and violence that prevail in the tumultuous assemblies in which only men are admitted?" wrote Deroin, adding that women's presence could only improve such meetings. "I demand for all men and all women freedom of conscience, freedom of speech and writing, freedom of assembly, so that the poor as well as the rich can express their thoughts," she concluded. Knight invoked the situation of other nations in her plea:

> A [U.S.] brother minister of religion told me in Paris that if two-thirds of the members of Congress were changed for women, all would be better for America. An English Minister has written that if one-half of our [parliamentary] fox-hunters and steeplechase amateurs were changed for women, the country would soon be raised to the highest degree of prosperity. . . . Ally thyself with these two noble brothers and form a glorious trio. . . . Raise the only true tri-coloured flag destined to make the tour of the globe, with this inscription, "Liberty, Equality, Fraternity, Justice, Mercy, and Truth!"[49]

These efforts failed. On June 20, the *Voice of Women* ceased publication and its editor, Eugénie Niboyet, withdrew from public life. Deroin and Gay continued the struggle, publishing two issues of a new journal, *Women's Politics*, before the government ruled that women could not participate so directly in political life. Deroin managed to print a single issue of its successor, *Women's Opinion*, in August before funds ran out. Blocked at least temporarily in France, feminists looked abroad for support. "Paris is not the only city where women take an active part in politics," declared the June issue of *Women's Politics*.

> In Italy, they fight with men for the freedom of their country.
> In England and America, they have long lectured in public, and the number of their audience is always more than a thousand.
> In Leicester, a club of Chartist women, led by Mrs. Cully, organized a female society. More than 4000 attended their meetings.[50]

These hopeful claims signaled a shift in feminist activism during the summer of 1848 from Europe to the United States. "My friends write to urge me to return," Margaret Fuller wrote from Rome in a dispatch published in the June 15 *New-York Daily Tribune*. "They talk of our country as the land of the Future." Although Fuller decided to remain in Rome, in part because she thought "that Future . . . more alive here at present than in America," the revolutions of 1848 galvinized feminists in the United States.[51]

Americans applauded the news of the upheavals and rapidly celebrated the defeat of European monarchs and empires. On March 25, a revolution festival in New York City featured fourteen addresses in four different languages capped by a day-long parade down Broadway. Both at home and abroad the United States was seen as the natural ally of the new European republics. An 1848 French poster honoring the unity of peoples showed America, in the form of a frontiersman holding a musket, standing in the center of a group composed of the other revolutionary nations: Hungary, Germany, Italy, Switzerland, Poland, and France.[52] Because of their European emigrant roots, many Americans had close personal ties with the "old countries" and retained a keen interest in European happenings. "The importance that we attach to the great events which have taken place in France and Europe" and a desire "to receive the freshest news here" led the editor of the *New York Herald* to arrange in April for special shipments by steamer of copies of *La Presse* from Paris. By May, Lucretia Mott was telling the annual meeting of the American Anti-Slavery Association that recent happenings in Europe had given her great hope:

> This law of progress is most emphatically marked in our day, in the great reformatory movements. . . . Was there ever a period in history when nations were so prolific of events as at the present moment . . . calling into action the high moral sentiments of the people and tending to arrest the sword of the destroyer?[53]

The news that France had outlawed slavery on April 27, which reached New York just before Mott spoke on May 9, especially heartened American abolitionists. "When we look abroad and see what is now being done in other lands, when we see human freedom engaging the attention of the nations of the earth, we may take courage," she told the antislavery meeting. Stressing the inevitability of progress, even in the face of the expansion of slavery in the United States, she told her audience that "a large public meeting . . . called the other day to hail the events in France" demonstrated improvement, since "it was scarcely ten years since Pennsylvania Hall was burned by a mob" protesting the second Anti-Slavery Convention of American Women. Mott concluded by asserting that European developments had focused American abolitionists' attention on "other oppressive systems," leading them "to clearly behold what are the universal rights of man" and "to assist the oppressed laborer to obtain" those rights.[54]

The events of 1848 energized Mott, who had been silent on women's rights for much of the 1840s. Throughout the year, she repeatedly expressed the sense of progress, of movement and possibility created by the revolutions in Europe, which she voiced in New York City in May. "The spirit of freedom is arousing the world; and the press universal will echo the glad sound," she wrote that summer after visiting some rural settlements of escaped slaves in upstate New York. A member of the Indian Committee of the New York and Philadelphia Quaker Yearly Meetings, Mott also investigated conditions among the Senecas on this visit. "They too are learning somewhat from the political agitations abroad, and . . . are imitating the movements of France and all Europe in seeking a larger liberty—more independence," she wrote a friend in a letter Garrison published in the *Liberator*.[55]

Visiting her sister, Martha Wright, in Auburn, New York, Mott also wanted to see Elizabeth Cady Stanton, who had moved to the nearby village of Seneca Falls the previous year. Although they corresponded, Mott and Stanton had not met since their 1840 encounter in London and both were eager to renew the contact. "I found in this new friend a woman emancipated from all faith in man-made creeds, from all fear of his denunciations," Stanton recalled. "It seemed to me like meeting a being from some larger planet, to find a woman who dared to question the opinion of Popes, Kings, Synods, Parliaments, with the same freedom that she would criticize an editorial in the *London Times*, recognizing no higher authority than the judgment of a pure-minded, educated woman."[56]

In July 1848, the visit of the fifty-four-year-old Mott released the thirty-two-year-old Stanton from the depression and "general dissatisfaction" she suffered in managing her household and three small children, a malaise that gave "Fourier's phalansterie community life and co-operative household . . . a new significance for me," Stanton later wrote. On Thursday, July 13, Mott, Wright, Stanton, and two other Quaker women, Jane Hunt and Mary Ann McClintock, spent the day together at the Hunts, discussing their "discontent" and resolving "to do and dare anything" by scheduling a convention on women's rights for the following week. Newspaper announcements appeared the next day. Frederick Douglass's antislavery *North Star* printed the call amid lengthy coverage of a Rochester festival celebrating the end of slavery in the French West Indies. On Sunday the group met a second time "to concoct a declaration." Stanton had drawn one up, she wrote a friend, but feared "it is not as perfect a declaration as should go forth from the first woman's rights convention that has ever assembled."[57]

These feminists rewrote the 1776 American Declaration of Independence to champion the rights of women. "We hold these truths to be self-evident; that all men are created equal" became "that all men and women are created equal." Paralleling the familiar structure of the original document, the Seneca Falls Declaration seized the moral high ground for women by identifying them with the rebellious American colonists, relegating men to the unenviable position of tyrant-king George III. Transforming the eighteenth-century charges against the English monarch into a nineteenth-century compendium of feminist demands, the committee made a wide range of claims for women. Like men, women should have the right to vote, should be represented in government, should have legal standing in courts, and should be able to own property and initiate divorce. In addition, they deserved better access to higher education, the professions, and jobs that paid a decent wage. This group of dissident members of the Society of Friends (Stanton was the only non-Quaker of the five) also claimed moral authority for women: the right to serve as ministers, to decide their own "sphere of action," and to insist on a single standard of sexual morality for both women and men. Their final indictment accused man of belittling woman, of endeavoring "in every way that he could to destroy her confidence in her own powers, to lessen her self-respect, and to make her willing to lead a dependent and abject life." In the face of this oppression, the authors pledged to enter upon "the great work before us": "We shall employ agents, circulate tracts, petition the State and national Legislatures, and endeavor to enlist the pulpit and press in our behalf," as well as holding "a series of Conventions, embracing every part of the country."[58]

This small organizing committee did not originate the use of the Declaration of Independence as a model. A number of American activists, from radical abolitionists to the New York State women who petitioned their legislature for a married women's property act in March 1848, had previously rewritten the declaration to support their causes. But these five women creatively paraphrased the original text to survey a wide range of feminist grievances. Stanton and Mott may also have been inspired by Martineau's chapter, "The Political Non-Existence of Women," in her 1837 *Society in America*, which both of them had read. It severely criticized the original declaration for excluding the female half of humanity.

The resulting Woman's Rights Convention at Seneca Falls, held on July 19 and 20, 1848, attracted an audience of about three hundred people rapidly recruited from local religious and political reform networks.[59] Women outnumbered men about 2 to 1, and sixty-eight of them signed the declaration along with thirty-two men. Organizers, both at the time and later, stressed their nervousness. Even the experienced Lucretia Mott, accustomed to speaking in public and having chaired earlier conventions of antislavery women, was not allowed to preside. "The president of the meeting was not Mrs. Mott, but Mrs. Mott's husband," she explained to the 1853 National Woman's Rights Convention. "Our first meeting was not prepared—had not yet acquired sufficient moral courage to place a woman in the chair."[60]

The Seneca Falls convention concluded with a decision to reconvene two weeks later in the nearby but far larger city of Rochester, New York,

since "there were still many new points for discussion" and the participants believed "that the gift of tongues had been vouchsafed to them."[61] At
Rochester, women not only presided but reworked a number of the earlier
claims to make them more radical and inclusive. The Seneca Falls proposal for women's vote, the ninth of eleven resolutions, occasioned much
debate and barely passed. At Rochester, it led the list of demands and easily received assent. A Seneca Falls complaint that women "ought to be
enlightened in regard to the laws under which they live, that they may no
longer publish their degradation, by proclaiming themselves satisfied with
their present position" was transformed at Rochester into the assertive
demand "that we deplore the apathy and indifference of woman in regard
to her rights, thus restricting her to an inferior position in social, religious,
and political life, and we urge her to claim an equal right to act on all subjects that interest the human family."

Finally, the Rochester convention focused attention on economic injustice, adding female "industrial" rights to their agenda and appointing
women "to investigate the wrongs of the laboring classes, and to invite that
oppressed portion of the community to attend the Convention, and take
part in its deliberations." A number of women spoke about the exploitation caused by low rates of pay, some from first hand experience. In
response, the convention helped found a Working Women's Protective
Union in Rochester, and Stanton moved a resolution that "those who
believe the laboring classes of women are oppressed ought to do all in their
power to raise their wages, beginning with their own household
servants."[62]

One hundred people signed the Seneca Falls Declaration; 107 signed
the one at Rochester. Both conventions took place in the heated atmosphere caused by the international explosions of 1848. "This is the age of
revolutions," the *New York Herald* began its article on Seneca Falls, written
shortly after news of the June Days in Paris had reached America.

> To whatever part of the world the attention is directed, the political and
> social fabric of the world is crumbling to pieces. . . . The principal agent,
> however . . . has been the rougher sex...though it is asserted that no incon-
> siderable assistance was contributed by the gentler sex to the late sanguinary
> carnage at Paris. . . . By the intelligence, however, which we have lately
> received, the work of revolution is no longer confined to the Old World, nor
> to the masculine gender. The flag of independence has been hoisted, for the
> second time, on this side of the Atlantic.

Comparing American feminists to their French counterparts, the *Herald*
concluded with the pseudochivalric wish that "Miss" Lucretia Mott and
"several other of our lady acquaintances" not offend male "hearts" by
"putting on the panoply of war" or "mixing in scenes like those at which
. . . the fair sex in Paris lately took prominent part."[63]

Participants as well as critics emphasized the revolutionary atmosphere of that explosive year. Although Lucretia Mott spoke often at Seneca Falls and Rochester and was praised at the first convention as "the moving spirit of the occasion," none of her speeches from that summer survive. The text of Elizabeth Cady Stanton's "*great* speech," as Mott called it, delivered on the second day of the Seneca Falls convention, does exist. Stanton may have repeated this lengthy address at the Rochester convention, and she delivered it again in various upstate New York towns during September and October of 1848.[64]

The entire Seneca Falls speech is infused with a tone of revolutionary possibility, of the universality of the cause of women's rights, and of participation in an international crusade. Drawing on the expansive feelings produced by the European revolutions of that year, Stanton asserted a radical international feminism throughout what she later referred to as her "maiden speech."[65] She began with the Saint-Simonian axiom that women must work for their own liberation: "Man cannot speak for her, because he has been educated to believe that she differs from him so materially, that he cannot judge of her thoughts, feelings, and opinions by his own." Asserting that the cause of women's rights was the most important question before "the whole human family," Stanton declared that "every allusion to the degraded and inferior position occupied by women all over the world has been met by scorn and abuse. . . . In every country does [man] regard her as a being inferior to himself, and one whom he is to guide and control." To prove the universality of female oppression, Stanton then maintained that "the same feeling" is "manifested" in men from Arabia to Germany, from the Muslim mosques of the East to the "carpet-knights" and legislators of the West, "who consider her incapable of saying what laws shall govern her." Criticizing France, England, and the United States especially for subordinating women, since these "Christian countries" boasted of being in "a more advanced state of civilization and refinement," Stanton turned to world history to demonstrate women's achievements and claims to equal rights. To the familiar examples of Catherine the Great of Russia and Elizabeth of England, she added Zenobia and Semiramis, queens in the ancient world, Isabella of Spain, Margaret of Denmark, Maria Theresa of Austria, and "the brave, intelligent and proud-hearted Tinga, the negro Queen of Angola," as well as "that whole nation of famous women, the Amazons."[66]

Turning to the current arguments opposing equal rights for women, Stanton asserted that although "men, bless their innocence," liked to think of themselves as possessing reason "while women are mere creations of the affections," the Adam and Eve story proved the opposite, since "the Evil One . . . thought that man could be easily conquered through his affection for the woman, but the woman could be reached only through her intellectual nature. So he promised her the knowledge of good and evil."

Refuting "man's claim to physical superiority," she insisted that "we cannot say what the woman might be physically, if the girl were allowed all the freedom of the boy in romping, climbing, swimming, playing with hoop and ball" and referred to the strength and agility of Tartar and Native American women as well as Croats, Wallachians, and Germans to prove her point.

Stanton then argued that in any case, rights did not depend on equality: "We need not prove ourselves equal to Daniel Webster to enjoy this privilege [of voting], for the ignorant Irishman in the ditch has all the civil rights he has." The address climaxed in a threatening invocation of the European revolutions, made all the more inflammatory by reference to the June Days. Men call woman "an angel," "to make her believe . . . that she is not fitted to struggle with the tempests of public life, but needs their care and protection!" Stanton thundered.

> Care and protection—such as the wolf gives the lamb—such as the eagle the hare he carries to his eyrie!! Most cunningly he entraps her, and then takes from her all those rights which are dearer to him than life itself—rights which have been baptized in blood—and the maintenance of which is even now rocking to their foundations the kingdoms of the Old World.

Criticizing conditions in the United States, Stanton returned to European references and examples at the end of her oration, urging her audience to take Joan of Arc as their model: "The same religious enthusiasm that nerved Joan of Arc to her work nerves us to ours." Ending with the image of a storm of opposition "from those who have entrenched themselves behind the . . . bulwarks of custom and authority, and who have fortified their position by every means, holy and unholy," Stanton drove home the identification of a women's movement with the forces of revolution in 1848.[67]

News of these women's rights conventions reached Europe in 1848 only through private sources; it was not until the following year that journals abroad carried reports of the American meetings. In September, Mott wrote the Webbs in Ireland that "the cause of WOMAN" now occupied her time and sent them the proceedings of the two conventions as well as "an Indian little bag for one of your daughters."[68] International connections among feminists grew after 1848, when the failure of the revolutions forced Europeans to reach out to their counterparts in other lands. During 1848, however, organizing women's movements in their own societies consumed their time and energy.

The only nations in which women's movements developed in the late 1840s were those that supported revolution, either at home or abroad. The events of 1848 inspired prorevolutionary American feminists to expand their demands on behalf of women and proceed optimistically. "The progress that we see in every work of truth and reform ought to lead us to hail each step in the advance field of woman's duties and rights,"

Mott wrote Stanton in October. "Look back to the days of our own grand-mothers and be cheered."[69] In contrast, antirevolutionary sentiments in Great Britain retarded the development of a national women's movement there. Political reform and economic growth produced a unique sense of national superiority and self-satisfaction, shared even by English feminists critical of women's situation. "Often I think / Of how thrice glorious is the time we live in," Bessie Rayner Parkes wrote in an early poem:

> Thank God I was born now! I watch with love
> That is a passion all the dawning life
> Which England nourishes, and often dream
> Of those far-peopled realms beyond the sea
> Which owe all to her blood.[70]

In 1847, radical editor George Jacob Holyoake published a call for a women's movement in two dissenting newspapers, as well as correspond-ing with "several ladies of literary pursuits" to persuade them to found a "Woman's Journal." "Where are women's political unions—self-originat-ed and self-sustained?" he asked. "Let them take their own affairs into their own hands. . . . Let women do this, and the Rights of Woman ques-tion will be settled forthwith. Let them draw up a list of their legal disabil-ities, and take the usual constitutional modes of obtaining redress. Let them have societies and public meetings of their own." Holyoake met with no success. "Intelligent women," he wrote—who included Harriet Martineau, Bessie Rayner Parkes, and Barbara Leigh Smith—failed to rise to his challenge. One suggested that he contact Margaret Fuller, then trav-eling in England, but Holyoake believed "it was not good taste to press upon an American lady a task that ought to be undertaken by an English one."[71]

Many English radicals remained aloof from the European revolutions, taking pride in their nation's ability to avoid such upheavals by timely reforms. Although female novelist George Eliot complained in the 1850s that English conservatism made the nation "as slow to be set on fire as a *stomach*," in March 1848 she wrote a friend that "our little humbug of a queen is more endurable than the rest of her race because she calls forth a chivalrous feeling, and there is nothing in our constitution to obstruct the slow progress of political reform."[72] A "monster" Chartist demonstration, held in London on April 10, caused the liberal government to evacuate Victoria to the Isle of Wight, to enlist the Duke of Wellington to deploy the army, and to swear in 15,000 special constables to police the event—one of whom was the exiled Louis-Napoleon Bonaparte, elected president of France the following December. Asked by their leaders to avoid vio-lence, the 20,000 male Chartists who attended the gathering remained peaceable, which prompted a flurry of smug self-congratulation from the English establishment. "The 10th of April, 1848, will long be remembered as a great field day of the British Constitution," wrote the London *Times* the following day. "The spectacle will not be lost on those nations which are yet in the vortex of change. They will know where to look for the stability they long for. Happily they will find in one of the ancient European sisterhood of nations a safe method of constitutional freedom."[73]

The contrast in 1848 between stability at home and revolution across the Channel confirmed the English conviction that their nation's good fortune depended on their separation from Europe and its turbulence. "The gravest citizen [of France] seems to lose his head," wrote the new poet laureate, Alfred, Lord Tennyson, in 1850.

> A kingdom topples over with a shriek
> Like an old woman, and down rolls the world
> In mock heroics stranger than our own;
> Revolts, republics, revolutions.
>
> . . . .
>
> God bless the narrow seas!
> I wish they were a whole Atlantic broad![74]

The English often connected revolution in France to demands for women's rights. A John Leech cartoon published in *Punch* at the end of March, "Paris Fashions for 1848,"sketched a belligerent, middle-aged woman with a Liberty cap on her head, wearing a sword and brandishing a pen, sitting in front of a sheet inscribed "La vote des femmes." Pride in avoiding militant revolution strengthened many Britons' sense of national superiority.

This complacency affected even a social critic like Anna Jameson, who had published a series of essays deploring women's status. At the end of April, she wrote her friend Ottilie von Goethe, "What a state of excitement you have been in throughout Germany. England has escaped very well, wonderfully well—for the Chartist Convention turned out rather ridiculous than otherwise. . . . And thanks to that progressive principle which is the vital part of our constitutional government we can have changes and improvements without destruction and without disturbance."[75]

In June 1848, radical member of Parliament Joseph Hume moved that the vote be given to all householders, male and female alike. Although Benjamin Disraeli spoke in its favor, the motion failed, causing little stir among feminists; only Anne Knight responded to it and she was still living in France at the time. In the mid-1850s Jameson helped organize younger Englishwomen to lobby for their rights, but in 1848 the absence of the heat and explosion generated by revolution retarded the formation of a women's movement. The personal divisions and animosities that feminists overcame in France and other nations, in part because of the urgency of the revolutionary moment, persisted in Britain. Harriet Taylor and John Stuart Mill despised Harriet Martineau; Martineau herself feuded with most other reformers, including Mill, William and Mary Howitt, and

Anna Jameson. When Anne Knight reached out to Barbara Leigh Smith and Bessie Rayner Parkes in 1850, the younger feminists dismissed her as "cracked."[76] Revolutions created the energy and pressure that enabled feminists to overcome similar fissures in the United States, France, and Germany, but not in Britain. This is the chief reason why no women's movement developed there in these years but did develop in the relatively backward German lands, where early feminists both participated in a wide variety of revolutionary activities and managed to take the first steps toward creating a movement of their own.

News of the February Revolution in France sparked uprisings in Germany by March 1848. Within the month, Louise Otto began composing her public letter to the newly formed Saxon Commission on Workers, convened to investigate "the organization of labor." To justify her unprecedented act of addressing a governmental body in a letter published by the *Leipzig Workers Newspaper* in May, which attracted wide notice and was reprinted in numerous left-wing journals, Otto wrote that "the interest I have long taken in the fate of the working classes" compelled her to write. "The history of all times, and especially of today, has taught us that those who forget to think about their rights will also be forgotten," she explained. "This is why I will exhort you about my poor sisters, about poor working women." Almost a year later, in April 1849, Louise Otto published the first issue of her own *Women's Newspaper*. In the lead editorial, she repeated and expanded on her earlier words. Taking "I enlist women citizens in the realm of freedom" as her journal's motto, the thirty-year-old editor explained:

> The history of all times and especially of today teaches us *that those who forget about themselves will be forgotten!* I proclaimed this to the world in May of 1848, when I first directed my words to the men in Saxony who occupied themselves with the question of labor—in speaking for my sisters, I admonished them not to forget about the poor women workers. . . . this is why I am editing a *Women's Newspaper*. Amid the great upheavals in which we all find ourselves, women will see themselves forgotten if they do not think about themselves![77]

From the spring of 1848 on, early German feminists like Louise Otto, who had previously been active in dissident political and religious groups, used revolution in their own land to push for female rights and equality. The multiplicity of German states in this period influenced both the revolutions themselves and women's activism within them. Instead of a single national pattern like the one that prevailed in France, with the revolution in February and the beginnings of reaction in June, the Germanies exploded in a series of eruptions over the course of two years, 1848 and 1849. In a number of smaller, relatively progressive Western territories that rapidly granted constitutions, suffrage, and civil rights, powerful conservatives contested such liberalism by force of arms. In Baden, for instance, revolutionaries fought three military campaigns to uphold political change, the first in April 1848, the second in September 1848, and the third in the summer of 1849. Aside from individual developments within the thirty-seven smaller German states, overall policy was ultimately determined by the two giants, the kingdom of Prussia and the empire of Austria. Throughout the German territories, nationalism complicated the revolutions. In Austria, Hungarians, Czechs, and Italians fought for national independence; in Prussia and elsewhere Germans sought to unify their separate states into a single political entity.

After violent uprisings in March, both Prussia and Austria rapidly granted civil liberties, including freedom of the press, and promised egalitarian constitutions with democratically elected parliaments. Both states participated in the spring elections for a German Constitutional National Assembly, which met in Frankfurt on May 18, 1848. The relative ease and speed with which these dramatic changes occurred convinced many Germans that all progressive goals that had been thwarted for so long— from democratic socialism to national unification—could soon be realized. "The news that a German Constituent Parliament would meet in Frankfurt [where she lived] filled me with boundless joy," Malwida von Meysenbug wrote. "The city was in unrestrained excitement. At the meeting of the Free Congregation that I had attended all winter instead of the Protestant church, the speaker did not ascend to the pulpit to make some commonplace observation, but rather he spoke fiery words of inspiration from the altar, exhorting the congregation to be ready to fight a joyful battle for the most sacred rights of humanity.[78]

As in France, prorevolutionary women participated actively, fighting on the barricades and in the numerous military campaigns that marked the German struggles. In October 1848, as the Austrian army attacked revolutionary Vienna, left-wing Frankfurt deputy Julius Fröbel observed numerous armed women among the city's defenders. "I'm a Hungarian," one shouted, "I've shot wolves. I know how to use weapons. They will proceed through the city only over my dead body!" A second young woman told Fröbel to hold his fire until the enemy drew near and rejected his suggestion that she nurse the wounded, declaring, "No, we want to die together with the men." A number of wives joined their husbands on campaigns. Amalie Struve acompanied her spouse, revolutionary leader Gustav Struve, in the Baden uprisings, developing battle plans and arranging for munitions shipments until she was imprisoned for six months in late September 1848.[79] Mathilda Franziska Anneke rode by her husband's side during the 1849 Baden revolution, later explaining that she acted out of her "passionate hatred of tyrants and suppressors of sacred human rights."[80]

Other women made their presence felt by thronging streets for demonstrations and parades and by organizing memorials and funerals for fallen male heroes of the revolutions. Often dressing in the German national colors, they provided a symbolic but significant political presence. Restored governments later outlawed such tributes. Women sewed and displayed the red flags of socialism and the red-black-gold banners of the new German nation. In later years, many remembered the huge national standard that flew from St. Stephen's Church in Vienna throughout the summer of 1848. In August, a women's group in Mainz presented new national flags they had made to a local male political club in a public ceremony, offering their "most splendid sisterly greetings." In return, a male representative of the club made a qualified call for women's participation in public life.[81]

German conservatism about women made such entry extremely difficult, even within revolutionary institutions. The newly founded, all-male Mainz Democratic Association invited radical feminist Louise Dittmar to speak on female emancipation. They allowed women to attend but not to join discussions. When Malwida von Meysenbug wanted to view the opening of the Frankfurt parliament, she was told that the meeting place "was so small that it was only open to men." Squeezing into a balcony with the wives of some male deputies, Meysenbug observed the assembly's proceedings secretly. The subject of women's rights was not addressed. The only public role allotted the female sex by the Frankfurt parliament was the traditional function of symbolizing the nation: a painting of "Germania," portrayed as a woman in medieval dress with the imperial crown at her feet, hung in the chamber. The new Austrian parliament, which met from May to October 1848, discussed women's rights only once, when a census-based suffrage was proposed. The deputies expressed their fears that letting women vote might necessitate granting the same privilege to children and the insane and concluded that women were not entitled to vote, since their husbands and fathers already represented them.[82]

As in other nations, this combination of raised hopes and thwarted participation propelled feminists into action. Barred from the new German parliaments and male political associations, activist women responded by creating institutions of their own. Louise Otto founded her *Women's Newspaper* in part because left-wing male journals refused to publish the articles she sent them. The hostility shown by male revolutionaries to female kindergarten teachers at a public demonstration in August 1848 prompted the women present to found the first college for women in Germany, which opened in Hamburg in January 1850. Exclusion from male democratic associations led directly to the creation of at least ten parallel Democratic Women's Associations (Demokratischer Frauenvereinen), which sought to organize "freethinking" women to push for equality in law and public life. Over three hundred Viennese women joined one formed in August 1848. Electing a female president, Karoline Perin, the women pledged "to spread the principles of democracy to all women's circles," "to strive for equal rights for women" by founding schools and establishments of higher education, and "to proclaim the deep-felt gratitude of the women of Vienna for the blessings of freedom."[83]

The Viennese Democratic Women's Association disbanded in November 1848, as the Austrian army conquered the city and stifled all dissent. Karoline Perin was arrested and then threatened with a public flogging. Faced with such harsh repression, some German feminists began to think of leaving their homeland. In July 1848, Mathilde Anneke was about to give birth, and her husband was in jail. She wrote a friend that "the land on the other side of the ocean waves beckons to me."[84]

Anneke and other German feminists did eventually emigrate to America, but they did not do so immediately. Instead, they created some of the longest-lived institutions of the brief 1848–1849 revolutions in Germany. Their women's newspapers, democratic associations, and educational establishments, from kindergartens to the Hamburg College for the Female Sex, lasted into the 1850s. Taking heart from the international struggles that the revolutions inspired, feminists retained their optimism in the face of repression and made their greatest efforts in the years after 1848. "There is a young, democratic Germany," the revolutionary Emma Herwegh wrote from Paris in 1849. "A Germany that has separated from the old world and its sins, which will not lay down its arms until Poland, Bohemia, Italy, until all Europe is free, the last dungeon opened, the last chain broken." Sooner or later, she continued, we will all be able to proclaim, in the words of "the noble French republican condemned to the galleys here a few days ago: The future belongs to me! Long live the democratic and social republic!"[85] As revolutions in Europe went under, the hopes and energy fueled by 1848 enabled early feminists throughout the Western community to make the 1850s the heyday of the international women's movement.

Eight

∽

The Heyday

In 1853, when the international women's movement was most active, American feminists organized two women's rights conventions, one in New York City in September, the second a month later in Cleveland, Ohio. The Cleveland gathering was the fourth in a series of U.S. national conventions that took place annually until 1860 (except in 1857), tumultuous gatherings that attracted large and often hostile crowds. But throughout the hubbub caused by male protesters, women's rights advocates exulted in their recent achievements, both internationally and within the United States. Referring to Frenchwomen's 1848 attempts "to have equal representation with men" and to Harriet Taylor Mill's 1851 *Westminster Review* article advocating the enfranchisement of women, Lucretia Mott urged her Cleveland audience to take hope from French author Victor Hugo's recent pronouncement that "the eighteenth century proclaimed the rights of man; the nineteenth century will proclaim the rights of woman." "Now these steps are beginning to be followed out everywhere," Mott affirmed.[1]

Optimistic assertions about progress at home and abroad had been made even more strongly in New York the previous month. The New York City Convention, with its audience of 3,000 crammed into the rotunda of the Broadway Tabernacle in lower Manhattan, heard Lucy Stone, an eloquent antislavery and women's rights orator, declare that advocates of women's rights had "reason to congratulate ourselves on the progress of our cause" in the five years since the Seneca Falls and

Rochester conventions of 1848. A graduate of Oberlin College, dressed in the new bloomer costume of a black velvet coat and knee-length skirt worn over black silk trousers, her hair cut short and brushed back, Stone embodied the confidence that led American feminists to hold two major meetings in a single year.[2]

These American conventions linked feminists internationally, and supporters in both the United States and Europe acknowledged the importance of this connection, especially after conservative regimes hostile to feminism replaced the revolutionary French and German governments of 1848. The lead article in the first issue of Jeanne Deroin's yearly *Women's Almanack* for 1852, published in Paris just before she went into exile in London, extolled the 1851 "convention of women in America." Portraying the Worcester meeting as a triumph for international feminism, the piece gave a glowing review in French of Harriet Mill's article.[3] "Conventions are good," Fredrika Bremer affirmed in her 1853 account of her travels in America. "I rejoice at the nobility and prudence with which many female speakers stand forth . . . at the depth of woman's experience of life, her sufferings and yearnings, which through them come to light."[4] Bremer thought that women's rights conventions augured a new era for the female sex, "both in Europe and this country," a sentiment echoed by Ernestine Rose a few years later. "Our movement is cosmopolitan," Rose told the 1860 U.S. Woman's Rights Convention. "It claims the rights of woman wherever woman exists, and this claim makes itself felt wherever woman is wronged."[5]

The 1853 New York City convention especially demonstrated the international nature of feminism in this period, drawing a larger and far more varied group of women's rights workers than the Cleveland meeting the following month. Supporters from Illinois, Indiana, Ohio, and Wisconsin joined adherents from New England and the mid-Atlantic states. Two foreigners even served on the organizing committee for this convention, Englishwoman Mary Jackson and German exile Mathilde Franziska Anneke. Little is known of Jackson, but Anneke's life illustrates the internationalism of feminism in the 1850s.

A strikingly handsome woman of thirty-six, standing six feet tall with black hair and blue eyes, Anneke personified the vitality and resilience of early feminism. She ran a "communist salon" in Cologne with her second husband, radical military officer Fritz Anneke, and helped him edit and produce the left-wing *New Cologne Newspaper*—the journal Marx and Engels designated as the official successor to their *New Rhineland Newspaper* when they were forced into a second exile in 1849. While Fritz Anneke was imprisoned from July to December 1848, Mathilde Anneke, who gave birth in late July, ran the journal alone, calling three September issues the *Women's Newspaper* (Frauen-Zeitung) to avoid press censorship. The following June, the Annekes rode into battle together, fighting in the third Baden uprising. After conservative troops conquered the fortress at

Rastatt and the revolution went under, they fled first to Switzerland and then to the United States, arriving after a seven-week voyage in November 1849.

Mathilde Anneke, who gave her first public lecture in Milwaukee in April 1850, when she was five months pregnant with her second son, made contact with "many American women," among them Lucretia Mott, Ernestine Rose, and Paulina Wright Davis. By 1853, when she addressed the New York Convention, Anneke had completed an ambitious women's rights "agitation tour," lecturing to audiences in a number of midwestern and eastern cities "about the rise of women, demanded the social improvement of their position, the right to work, and most of all, the right to vote."[6] From February 1852, she produced a bilingual monthly feminist newspaper, the German-American *German Women's Newspaper* (Deutsche Frauen-Zeitung), working from her family's new home in Newark, New Jersey.

Anneke's appearance at the 1853 convention was the result of a deliberate program of outreach by American organizers to both "the Old and the New World." Paulina Wright Davis, who presided over the first two national meetings at Worcester, later wrote that she had "spent the summer" of 1851 "writing letters North South East and West to the truest and broadest minded of this country and of Europe, in order to bring them together to celebrate the anniversary of the first National Convention." Anneke herself assured Americans that German women looked to them "for encouragement and sympathy" and that "many hearts across the ocean in Germany are beating in unison with those here."[7]

Former slave turned preacher Sojourner Truth also addressed the unruly 1853 New York assembly. The self-named Truth was an exotic figure, representing the segregated community of black Americans. In the racist United States of the 1850s, women's rights conventions were the only venue besides antislavery meetings where blacks shared a platform with whites and lectured on equal terms. Truth herself had addressed conventions at Worcester in 1850 and Akron, Ohio, in 1852 before she spoke in New York. Six feet tall, Truth was a powerful and effective public speaker who drew on her own and her audience's familiarity with scripture to make her points. Setting off her dark brown skin with a white turban, collar, and shawl worn over a long black dress, she disparaged the men who hissed and booed women's rights speakers. "In the old times, the kings of the earth would hear a woman," she declared, referring to Queen Esther pleading for her people before Ahasuerus,

> I know it feels a kind o' hissin' and ticklin' like to see a colored woman get up and tell you about things, and Women's Rights. . . . Women don't get half as much rights as they ought to; we want more and we will have it. Jesus says, "What I say to one, I say to all—watch!" . . . I'm a sittin' among you to watch; and every once and a while I will come out and tell you what time of night it is.[8]

Despite hostile audiences, convention participants received tremendous confirmation from overseas letters of support, which were usually
solicited by the organizers, read out loud during the meetings, and then
published in the convention's proceedings. Deroin and Roland's prison
letter, along with greetings from Harriet Martineau and a report from
London by Rebecca Spring, who wrote describing new schools for women
and displays of women's work at the Great Exhibition, were featured in
1851. Letters to other early conventions came from France and Britain.[9]

Corroboration from abroad confirmed both Americans' and Europeans' sense of the validity of their embattled cause. Harriet Taylor Mill's
1851 "Enfranchisement of Women," which ended by predicting "that the
example of America will be followed on this side of the Atlantic," was
referred to at almost every subsequent U.S. women's rights meeting, as
well as being reprinted many times as a pamphlet and becoming one of the
best-selling tracts of the U.S. women's rights movement. As Harriet Martineau wrote the Americans, "This article will materially strengthen your
hands, and I am sure it cannot but cheer your hearts."[10]

Feminists in the United States frequently spoke about women's efforts
in France during 1848 and repeated the Frenchwomen's argument that the
1848 revolution, like that of 1789, failed to achieve its goals because "it
was represented by only one half of the intelligence of the [human] race,"
as Mott declared at Cleveland.[11] Speakers at U.S. women's rights conventions often contrasted their nation's liberty to the repression of Europe.
Referring to German laws forbidding women to attend political meetings
or edit journals, Paulina Wright Davis linked the condition of rights in
general to feminism's fortunes: "What wonder that with woman degraded,
the fire of freedom burns low on the German altar? Political liberty cannot
dwell with domestic bondage."[12]

The organizers of the 1853 New York Convention were especially concerned to strengthen international ties. After the assembly passed the standard resolutions calling for female equality in political rights, law, employment, public life, and morality, Paulina Wright Davis moved that a
committee be established "to prepare an address . . . to the women of
Great Britain and the continent of Europe, setting forth our objects and
inviting their co-operation in the same," since "this great movement is
intended to meet the wants, not of America only, but of the whole world."
In addition to Anneke, Davis, Mott, Rose, and Stone, this committee also
included two internationally renowned doctors—Harriot Hunt of Boston
and Anglo-American Elizabeth Blackwell.

Blackwell came from a large and well-connected feminist family. Her
brother Henry married Lucy Stone and her brother Samuel wed
Antoinette Brown, the first ordained woman minister in the United States.
Her sister Anna lived in Paris for many years, where she translated Sand
and Fourier and was a foreign correspondent for both Horace Greeley's
Tribune and the *English Woman's Journal*. Her sister Marian attended

women's rights conventions, and her sister Emily also became a doctor. News of Blackwell's obtaining an M.D. degree spread rapidly. Her feat received immense publicity in the United States. The satirical English magazine *Punch* produced a seven-stanza tribute to "Doctrix Blackwell," and Jeanne Deroin's *L'Opinion des femmes* printed a long article about her in June 1849.[13]

Harriot Hunt, less well-known today, was a nineteenth-century celebrity—one of the famous Americans foreigners sought out when they traveled in the United States. Fredrika Bremer, Marianne Finch, and Barbara Leigh Smith Bodichon all recorded their positive impressions of her; Bremer and Finch corresponded with her for years. A practicing physician since 1835, Hunt applied to Harvard for a medical degree after Blackwell had been accepted by Geneva. Dr. Oliver Wendell Holmes admitted her, but riots by students prevented her from attending. Hunt went to many national women's rights conventions, beginning with Worcester in 1850. "That call [to the convention] thrilled my entire being," she wrote in the memoirs she published in 1856.[14] The American women's rights conventions provided confirmation and support to feminists throughout the Western world in the first half of the 1850s.

Both emigration, as in Anneke's case, and travel fostered international feminism. Fredrika Bremer's journey to the United States and England from 1849 to 1851 had special significance. Bremer was initially opposed to women's rights. When she read Harriet Martineau's *Society in America* in 1837, she thought that if women participated in government, they would lose their femininity. But she changed her mind in the course of her travels. Americans prized her favorable impressions of the women's movement in her 1853 memoir, *Homes of the New World*. "After her return from America, her predominating thought was how she might be able to secure liberty and an unrestricted sphere of activity for Swedish women," her sister wrote. "She wanted to see women active in all directions of the world's stage."[15] Befriended by Harriot Hunt and Rebecca and Marcus Spring, who had accompanied Margaret Fuller to Europe in 1846, Bremer maintained an active correspondence with these American radicals after she returned to Sweden. "I have spoken several times before large assemblies," she wrote the Springs in 1854, "and I cannot but thank America and ladies in America to have been able to do so with calm and self-possession. Their example has guided and sustained me. I have thought especially of Lucretia Mott and Rebecca [Spring]."

Visiting England for several months in 1851, Bremer stayed with her translator, reformer Mary Howitt, who introduced her to the young feminists Bessie Rayner Parkes and Barbara Leigh Smith, and their friend, novelist George Eliot. Considering Great Britain the most influential nation in the world, Bremer transmitted American feminist hopes for the future ("when fettered woman shall become perfectly free") to her English acquaintances. She also attempted to enlist women in opposing the

Crimean War of 1854, publishing "Invitation to a Peace Alliance" in the London *Times*. Pitched exclusively at Christians "all over the earth," this sentimental appeal for women to encircle the earth "with a chain of healing, loving energy" had little effect.[16] But Bremer's new view of women's capacities changed conditions in her native land. In 1855 she wrote Harriot Hunt:

> the more I live and see of the world, the more I feel that the elevation of woman to her true character and social position indeed is the question on which depends the true liberation of mankind. I long to learn what you do for the great cause in America and I will tell you by and by what I try to do and want to do for it in Scandinavia.[17]

Bremer's chief contribution to feminism in Sweden came from the work she considered her masterpiece, *Hertha, or the Story of a Soul*. Published in England in 1855 and in Sweden the following year, *Hertha* was the first novel Bremer wrote after she returned from her travels. Hertha's initial situation echoes that of Bremer's unhappy younger years: both begin as homely, unconventional women living under the control of tyrannical, irascible fathers who disparage all they do and deny them any independent action. The novel depicts its heroine's evolution into a powerful, charismatic leader who defies male domination, claims full moral authority for herself and other women, and transforms the lives of those around her through her feminist autonomy and spiritual strength.

Hertha initially rebels when she compares domineering men like her father to slaveholders in the American South—an analogy Bremer first heard used by feminists in the United States. The novel's turning point comes when Hertha falls into a mystical slumber and dreams an internationalist feminist vision. Seeing herself as a winged being, she flies from China, where men bind women's feet to keep them captive, to England, France, and Germany, where an array of social institutions and ideas maintain female subordination. Trapped in homes, cloisters, and bordellos, women confine themselves by believing in their supposed inferiority to men. Opposing the Christian churches' restrictive teachings on women to Jesus' liberating words in the New Testament, Hertha again repeats arguments used by American feminists. The vision ends with Hertha at Yggdrasil, the "world-tree" of Norse mythology, where she hears a chorus of women's voices confirm her independence: "Do not listen to others; follow the inner voice. Your vision will be victorious." Hertha eventually creates a utopian community in which women achieve true equality by gaining an education, working both inside and outside the group home, voting, and becoming lawyers and doctors. Hertha herself ends as a priestly, messianic figure, choosing ten female disciples to promulgate her teachings.[18]

Revolutionary in its portrayal of a female religious authority (Bremer originally gave Hertha twelve disciples but reduced the number to avoid an overt similarity to Jesus), the novel also challenged existing Swedish laws controlling women. Until she was almost forty, Bremer suffered under male guardianship of her finances, which included the income from her successful novels. After her father's death, financial control passed to her wastrel brother, a situation that persisted until Bremer and her sister petitioned the king and a local court for redress. This cumbersome and expensive procedure was still in force when she composed *Hertha*, and Bremer added a fourteen-page appendix to the final Swedish edition of her novel, a call to overturn the guardianship laws. This effort "cannot fail," she argued, because of "the example of other countries, the demands of the age, and an ever-increasing number of voices . . . in our own nation." Reviving debate on the need for a male guardian's approval of a woman's marriage or sale of property, *Hertha* influenced the eventual Swedish reform of 1863 as well as other progressive measures. Bremer lived just long enough to hear the news of parliament's confirmation of new suffrage laws in 1865, which gave women who paid taxes the right to vote in municipal elections.[19]

Hertha had international as well as local influence. American and British writers repeatedly cited Bremer as an example of what a woman could accomplish even under oppressive circumstances. Feminists named their children after Bremer's heroine. For example, in 1855, Mathilde Franziska Anneke gave birth to twin girls and called one of them Hertha; Barbara Leigh Smith Bodichon's protégée, Phoebe Marks, later renamed herself Hertha Ayrton.

Like travel memoirs, novels remained an important medium for international feminism in this era. In addition to *Hertha*, Englishwoman Elizabeth Gaskell's *Ruth* (1853) and American Fanny Fern's *Ruth Hall* (1854) influenced readers in both the United States and Europe. The heroine of *Ruth* is an orphaned seamstress seduced by an aristocrat who bears a child out of wedlock. She raises her son and earns her own living before dying tragically of typhoid. Gaskell was daring to portray a "fallen woman" sympathetically, but her ending paid homage to convention. *Ruth Hall* ventured further. Beginning with the heroine's happy marriage, the crux of the novel comes when Ruth Hall's husband dies, leaving her with no money and three children to raise. Snubbed by her relatives, Hall determines to achieve financial independence by becoming a journalist: "I *can* do it, I *feel* it, I *will* do it." The novel ends triumphantly with the heroine's acquisition of $10,000 in bank stock, with the certificate printed in the book. Published in England as well as the United States, the novel was translated in 1855 into both French and German. Feminists applauded Fern's unconventional story. "The great lesson taught in *Ruth Hall* is that God has given woman sufficient brain and muscle to work out her own destiny unaided and alone," Elizabeth Cady Stanton wrote in the *Una* in 1855.[20]

English poet Elizabeth Barrett Browning, then living happily in Italy, raised similar themes in her 350-page novel in verse, *Aurora Leigh* (1856).

Portraying the struggles and ultimate triumph of a female artist, *Aurora Leigh*, like *Hertha* and *Ruth Hall*, presented an individualistic vision of women's development. All three heroines achieve respect and autonomy "unaided and alone," without important connections to other women like themselves. Hertha and Aurora Leigh, like Charlotte Brontë's Jane Eyre, find true love with men who have learned suffering and humility by being severely injured in fires. Aurora Leigh scorns having her paintings judged "as mere woman's work, / Expressing the comparative respect / Which means the absolute scorn." The poem deals sympathetically with a friend of Leigh's who becomes an unwed mother, but the only overtly feminist character is portrayed as a somewhat comical foreigner: "Delia Dobbs, the lecturer from 'the States' / Upon the 'Woman's Question.'" Although early feminists loved Barrett Browning's writings and she later signed the Englishwomen's petition for a Married Women's Property Act, she lived as an independent abroad, disconnected from international feminism whether in London or Rome.[21]

The five women's rights journals in print during the early 1850s provided even more important validation and information for international feminism. In France, Germany, England, and the United States, feminist editors brought forth a literature supporting their cause under extremely arduous conditions. In France and the German states, governmental repression silenced such efforts by 1852. In Britain and the United States, the pressures of the marketplace made any new journalistic venture difficult. Feminist editors in these freer societies continually complained of the difficulties in signing up enough subscribers to finance their work. But from 1849 to 1855, Mathilde Franziska Anneke, Amelia Bloomer, Paulina Wright Davis, Jeanne Deroin, Louise Otto, and their coworkers managed to produce a women's rights literature that was international in scope and influence.[22] All their journals printed news, correspondence, reports, documents, and fiction from other countries. These publications brought together feminist ideas and strategies, as women learned from each other's opinions and adopted each other's tactics. Topics pursued in individual societies—from marriage rights to dress reform to higher education—benefited from the attention and debate they received in these international forums. The range and influence of these journals was almost certainly greater than we can discern today, since so much of this literature has vanished. Only a single issue of Anneke's German-American women's newspaper survives; other publications now exist only as citations in these few printed works that remain. But the writings that endure testify to the international nature of feminist debate in the middle of the nineteenth century.

Anneke published her feminist journal twice a month from the spring of 1852 until the autumn of 1854. As "the only organ for German women in the Union," her *German Women's Newspaper* naturally drew on both German and American sources, but the one remaining issue—October 15,

1852—displays a wider range. Anneke translated portions of Mary Wollstonecraft's *Vindication of the Rights of Woman* and Margaret Fuller's *Woman in the Nineteenth Century* for her newspaper. She also reprinted the complete text of Jeanne Deroin and Pauline Roland's 1851 prison letter, as well as Ernestine Rose's reply to the Frenchwomen. The front page features a bitter feminist poem, "An Everyday Tale." Written in German by "Emma" and translated into a softer English version by "Julia," its nine stanzas describe the seduction of a "pure," angelic sixteen-year-old orphan girl by a handsome suitor. Abandoned and pregnant, she gives birth and attempts to raise her child. Refused both employment and charity because she is an unwed mother, she "sells her body to save her child," earning her bread as a prostitute, since that is the only way open to her:

> Would you like to see this fallen angel?
> You need only go through the city at night.
> She's still beautiful, but brazen-faced—
> The angel—has become a streetwalker.[23]

By presenting a completely sympathetic portrait of the prostitute as a virtuous woman forced by economic necessity to ply her trade, Anneke contributed to early feminists' questioning and erasure of the social division between the "fallen" and "respectable" women. Mid-nineteenth-century culture contrasted the feminine icon of the angel in the private home to the degraded figure of the prostitute on the public street, who was at best seen as a weak victim and at worst as a vicious degenerate biologically destined for a life of crime. Feminists, in contrast, consistently argued that "the lack of earnings drives women into the arms of prostitution," as Louise Otto asserted, as well as forcing many into loveless marriages. "Why are there so many unhappy marriages, and so few—yes, almost no happy ones?" asked Louise Dittmar in 1849. "We believe we can briefly answer this question: the cause is the *economic* and *political* dependence of women." Feminists also began to criticize legal standards in general for favoring men, especially rich men. Discussing the case in which a fourteen-year-old maid servant had been raped by a thirty-year-old surgeon in his office, a correspondent from England wrote *Opinion des femmes* that the judge "found *that it was doubtful* that the young girl had opposed the accused's actions with *strong enough resistance*" to constitute rape. "They do not admit that rape is facilitated by intimidation nor that it can happen to a person who is ignorant, physically weak, or very innocent, as is the case here." Contrasting the same court's sentencing an elderly woman to six months at hard labor for stealing 3 ½ lbs. of mutton to the surgeon's acquittal, the piece vividly demonstrated the law's bias against poor women.[24]

Feminists in Britain, France, and the United States condemned laws and circumstances that made a husband "either the conscious or unconscious despot of his household," as Harriet Taylor Mill wrote. Some of the most extensive analyses of the wrongs of marriage, however, came from Germany, where Louise Dittmar published essays on the subject in both her feminist journal, *Social Reform*, and the 1850 anthology she edited, *The Essence of Marriage, Along with Some Essays about Women's Social Reform.*[25] Arguing that under current economic and legal conditions, "she is nothing, he is everything," Dittmar used wife beating to demonstrate how "men have, by virtue of the laws, put the weapons in their own hands." Dittmar maintained that state support for higher education and better job training as well as a transformation of the existing laws was essential for such reform. She also argued that women must first work for their rights themselves by "standing on our own two feet, following our own inclinations, and answering our own demands." Self-assertion was essential. "Conjugal equality, the law of the new marriage, exists only where the wife, by her work or by her character, feels herself to be independent," Pauline Roland wrote in 1851.[26]

A number of men active in international feminism divested themselves of the privileges the law gave them over their wives. In 1850, dissident German minister Johannes Ronge published a "model charter" giving identical marriage vows for husband and wife in a reformed German Catholic ceremony, which he probably used when he married his Hamburg parishioner, Bertha Meyer Traun, just after their emigration to London the next year. English philosopher John Stuart Mill "put on record a formal protest against the existing laws of marriage" and "made a solemn promise never in any case or under any circumstances to use them" in his 1851 marriage to Harriet Taylor. When Lucy Stone and Henry Blackwell married in 1855, they wrote a formal "Marriage Protest" against "rules and customs which are unworthy of the name, since they violate justice, the essence of all law." Stone retained her maiden name and numerous U.S. newspapers published the couple's statement.[27]

Arguing that marriage without equality became "legalized prostitution," as Elizabeth Cady Stanton called it in 1861, early feminists spoke out both against the "slave market" that they thought prevailed in courtship and society's prejudice against prostitutes. "I have good authority for saying that more than half of the prostitutes of our towns are driven to that course of life by necessity," Abby Price declared to the First National Woman's Rights Convention in Worcester (1850). "M. Duchatelet [the French doctor], in his investigation in Paris, established this fact in the clearest manner." "I could read you pages from the London *Morning Chronicle*, on the Metropolitan Poor," she continued. "Is it not time to throw open to women, equal resources with men, for obtaining honest employment?"[28]

Like Anneke's *Women's Newspaper*, Jeanne Deroin's *Women's Almanack* was aimed at specific groups of women—the French feminists Deroin left behind when she was forced into exile, her fellow refugees from Europe, and the English allies of her new homeland—but it also had a wider purview. Published annually from 1852 to 1854, the *Women's Almanack* used a variety of international sources to further the work Deroin had pursued full-time since 1848. Despite the increasingly conservative nature of the French revolutionary government after the spring elections of 1848, Deroin, Roland, and other French feminists had continued to fight for their cause. In February 1849, Deroin revived the monthly *Women's Opinion*, which had been forced to suspend publication the previous August. Specifically directed against those who sought to limit women of all classes to domesticity, *Women's Opinion* especially challenged the increasingly popular theories of the French socialist P. J. Proudhon, who asserted that women were essentially different from men and that the female sex had to choose between being housewives or prostitutes. Mocking Proudhon's argument that women lacked the "necessary organs" to be legislators, Deroin explained that prostitution resulted from women's oppression, poverty, and ignorance. Only female participation could truly reform society:

> You ask what will be the mission of woman outside the family? She will help you in reestablishing order in the large, badly administered household which we call the state, and will substitute a just apportionment of the fruits of labor for the permanent theft of the hard work of the proletariat.[29]

In 1851, Pauline Roland published "Does Woman Have the Right to Liberty?" a detailed refutation of Proudhon written while she was in prison; in 1855, Jenny d'Héricourt continued the battle. Repudiating Proudhon's statement that he considered "the sort of crusade that is being carried on at this time by a few estimable ladies in both hemispheres in behalf of the prerogatives of their sex" as "an infatuation that proceeds precisely from the infirmity of the sex and its incapacity to understand and govern itself," d'Héricourt likened the struggles of feminists to those of abolitionists and revolutionaries: "slaves, citizens, blacks, and women, are born for liberty and equality."[30]

This debate rapidly became international. D'Héricourt published her articles in the French freethought organ *Philosophical and Religious Review* (which also printed her interview with Ernestine Rose) and a liberal Turin journal, *La ragione* (Reason). "You have put our country on fire," the Italian editor wrote d'Héricourt, "young men and women are for you." Reading d'Héricourt's article in the French *Review*, English feminist Bessie Rayner Parkes decided to translate it for George Jacob Holyoake's British freethought journal, the *Reasoner*. D'Héricourt's 1860 French book on the subject, *The Emancipated Woman: A Reply to Monsieurs Michelet, Proudhon, etc.* appeared in an American edition four years later.[31]

Feminists' actions, as well as their writings, received international publicity. In April 1849, Jeanne Deroin took advantage of a loophole in

French law that barred women from voting but did not specifically forbid them from running for office. Presenting herself as a candidate for the National Assembly, she proclaimed on her election banners and broadsides that "a legislative assembly entirely composed of men is as incompetent to make laws for a society composed of men and women as an assembly entirely composed of the privileged would be to discuss the interests of workers, or an assembly of capitalists to uphold the honor of the nation."[32]

American women learned about Deroin's candidacy at the 1851 Worcester National Women's Rights Convention, where Unitarian minister William Henry Channing praised Roland for attempting to vote in 1848 and Deroin for claiming women's right to run for office. Deroin's example may have had some influence on Elizabeth Cady Stanton's 1866 decision to stand for Congress as an Independent, the first women to do so. (She garnered only twenty-four votes.) Although there is no evidence of contact between them through the years, Stanton looked up Deroin when she traveled to London in 1882. The sixty-seven-year-old Stanton found the seventy-seven-year-old Deroin "a little, dried-up woman, though her face beams with intelligence," living "in great poverty and obscurity in Shepherd's Bush."[33]

Deroin described her campaign in the prison letters she sent to women in England and the United States, which were printed in the widely distributed American convention *Proceedings*, a radical English newspaper, the *Northern Star*, and Anneke's German-American *Women's Newspaper*. Louise Otto published two articles about Deroin in her German *Women's Newspaper* in 1851, quoting extensively from the Frenchwoman's campaign literature in the first one.[34] Such international support may have encouraged Deroin to continue her labors despite a crushing electoral defeat: she received only fifteen votes; George Sand got forty.

Deroin and Roland's most ambitious undertaking began in the autumn of 1849, when they defied the government's ban on women's involvement in politics by founding a federation of worker's cooperative associations. The resulting umbrella organization, the Union of Associations, drew on Flora Tristan's plan for a Workers Union as well as other socialist attempts to establish "the republic in the workplace." Linking women and peace, Deroin argued that they could save men from the "vicious circle" of senseless violence. Socialist bank notes would bond workers to farmers, as well as one association to another, simultaneously providing both "liberation and conciliation: the first step toward a peaceful solution" of the problem of poverty.[35] The union attracted 104 workers groups, which joined together in October 1849. About a quarter of them were female, representing seamstresses, linen workers, midwives, and teachers.[36]

It was for this organizing that Deroin and Roland were arrested, along with forty-seven men and seven other women, at the end of May 1850. Tried in November, Deroin and Roland were sentenced to six months in the Saint Lazare prison for women, for holding a political meeting unauthorized by the government. It was near the end of their term that they sent their letters to their "sisters" in America and England.

Upon her release, Deroin immediately resumed her feminist activities. "Two hours after I left Saint Lazare on July 2, 1851, I was at the office of the newspaper *La République* to prepare a protest on behalf of women against the limitations of the suffrage," she wrote in a public letter printed in a number of left-wing journals.[37] But the times were against her. In December, the president of the republic, Louis-Napoleon Bonaparte, launched a successful coup d'état and established himself as emperor. In February 1852, Pauline Roland was rearrested and convicted for supposedly fomenting an "insurrection." This second prison term led to her death later that year. Deroin published her first *Women's Almanack* in Paris early in 1852 to "call attention" to "the right of women to liberty and complete social equality," the reorganization of labor (a socialist demand), and the abolition of the death penalty. The police seized most of this printing and in August Deroin went into permanent exile.

Deroin's last important contribution to feminism was the *Women's Almanack*. Throughout its three-year run, it published an array of international news and articles. The first year carried pieces on the American antislavery movement and a recent peace congress in London (which excluded female delegates), in addition to its lead article on the U.S. women's rights convention and an essay on international dress reform. Mentioning American women who had recently worn the new bloomer costume in London, the article surveyed cultures in which women did not wear dresses, like China, India, Circassia, and Russian Georgia, as well as ancient Greece and Rome. The author concluded with a report from Germany that women were beginning to wear the reformed dress there, which had the advantage of allowing them "to walk freely . . . instead of dragging through the mud and dust."[38]

The second issue of 1853 was even more international than the first. Completely bilingual in English and French, printed both in London and the Channel Island of Jersey, where Victor Hugo and other French exiles lived, Deroin's *Almanack* looked to "societies of women" which "have been organized in France, in America, and in England" for hope and confirmation. She featured a letter of support from Anne Knight, who wrote that "a kind Providence . . . is impelling the hearts of Women in America, France, Germany, and England to come to the army of brave warriors and battle for the truth, in the upper, as well as the lower walks of life."

The bulk of this issue was devoted to a section entitled the "Ability of Women for All Professions."[39] Here Deroin ranged widely, using examples from around the world to prove her case. A Polish woman doctor and a French female botanist as well as Hunt, Blackwell, and other recent women graduates of U.S. medical colleges demonstrated women's fitness for science and medicine. Italian female musicians, French painter Rosa Bonheur, and American author Harriet Beecher Stowe illustrated women's talents in literature and the arts. Antoinette Brown, the first female minister ordained in the United States, English lecturer Caroline Dexter, and a young Frenchwoman who pleaded a civil case respectively proved women's fitness for theology, public speaking, and the law. The Scots "She Captain" Betsy Miller, who sailed a brigantine in British waters for twenty years, showed women's ability as navigators and naval commanders. Finally, the "corps of 5 or 6000 courageous and intrepid Amazons" who guarded the king of Dahomey in West Africa displayed female heroism and courage, although their feats raised difficult issues for the pacifist editor of the *Women's Almanack*. The issue concluded sadly, with a lengthy account by Deroin of Roland's death and the publication of a number of Roland's last letters.

The 1854 *Almanack*, although again published in both Jersey and London, appeared only in French. This issue featured the activities of the American Shaker community, the educated female factory workers of Lowell, Massachusetts, temperance organizations, and the U.S. Society of Non-Resistance, which opposed slavery, war, and political participation in the current corrupt system. The English Vegetarian Society and the Society for the Protection of Animals received notice, as well as the French Society for Pure Love. "These societies have our complete sympathy," Deroin wrote. "Through these different associations which are connected by the same spirit the cause of women . . . will lead to the transformation of the world."[40]

Deroin's *Almanack* reached feminists in the United States as well as in Europe. "Pauline Roland, and Jeanie Duroine [sic.] have published in Paris a Woman's Rights Almanac," Paulina Wright Davis's feminist journal the *Una* announced in April 1853. "It contains some 60 or 70 pages of reading matter—short, forcibly written articles, noticing all the principle features of the movement, both at home and in this country. We have seen but one copy, and had only time to read the article upon our Conventions, and one upon dress reform in the United States—commending it fully and entirely."

In November the American journal reprinted Roland's letters from the second year of Deroin's *Almanack*; subsequent articles were also drawn from the Frenchwoman's pages.[41] From its first issue of February 1853 the *Una* (named after the heroine signifying truth in Edmund Spenser's *The Faerie Queen*) consciously served as an international feminist forum. "We shall not confine ourselves to any locality, set, sect, class or caste, for we hold to the solidarity of the race and believe that if one member suffers, all suffer, and that the highest is made to atone for the lowest," began Davis's first editorial. These expansive, universalist sentiments pervaded the *Una* throughout its two-and-a-half-year run.

Paulina Wright Davis, long active in abolitionism and women's rights, believed that "women have been too well, and too long satisfied with

Ladies' Books, Ladies' Magazines, and Miscellanies," and she saw her monthly publication as "one paper which will give a correct history" of the women's movement's "progress, and be a faithful exponent of its principles."[42] Drawing on her extensive European connections, Davis regularly printed letters from correspondents abroad. Pieces from France came primarily from visiting Americans, since censorship prevented direct contact. "Please send the Una to me sometimes," one U.S. visitor wrote Davis from Paris in 1855. "I doubt if it would be allowed to enter France, but I wish that you would attempt it; it might fall on good soil if I never saw it."[43] Davis solicited a letter for her third issue from Marion Reid in Edinburgh; her first and second numbers published letters from the Englishwoman Marianne Finch.

Finch toured the eastern United States in 1851. Like Bremer, she became a convert to feminism during her travels and published an account of the process. Impressed with "the importance attached to the education of the people" in the United States, she justified women's "communicating to the people the results of their knowledge and experience. . . . For doing this I heard them praised or condemned, according to the feelings or prejudices of the speaker," she added. "But what is an American woman to do? Like the women of older countries, she is excluded from public and active life."[44] Meeting a number of U.S. abolitionists and women's rights advocates, Finch came to believe that although women and men were not identical, "*both* sexes" should have "the same advantages in education, the same choice in employments, and the same power in choosing their lawmaking governors." She severely criticized British "anti-woman's-rights men" for their inconsistency in admiring Queen Victoria while depriving "any English woman of her political existence on account of *her sex*, yet so it is." Meeting both Paulina Wright Davis and Boston doctor Harriot Hunt, she remained in correspondence with them for a number of years. "Her work should have been reprinted in this country," Hunt wrote in 1856. "The woman movement pleased her very much. I enjoy her correspondence; she is wide awake on reform, and is one whose spirit breaks down time and space."[45]

Davis reprinted Finch's letter to the 1851 Worcester Convention in the first issue of the *Una*; the second carried a more recent letter from the Englishwoman criticizing the prejudice that allowed "two single women [Harriet Martineau and Eliza Lynn]" to supply "political knowledge to the nation through two London daily papers, and yet they are not considered capable of exercising the elective franchise." Finch also reported some progress from Russia, where the "Duchess of Leuchtenberg has just been chosen to preside over the Imperial Academy of Sciences."[46] Other letters to the *Una* from England came from an anonymous but militant "friend of the cause," who sent detailed information about Anne Knight's Women's Elevation League and her proposed journal, the *Woman's Advocate*, as well

as criticizing the majority of women who opposed feminism. "We constantly hear weak minded women say they are quite satisfied with their
present position," this Englishwoman wrote in 1853,

> They have no desire to have a vote, to come forward in public, or to do any-
> thing towards getting an independent living. They always remind me of lit-
> tle canaries, who have been caged and fed all their lives. You give them their
> liberty [and] the poor things are overwhelmed, and with fluttering wings and
> palpitating heart, they fly back to their prison-house, and cling to its bars
> 'till some kind hand opens the door; when they rush in . . . and offer up a
> song of thankfulness.[47]

The *Una* also transmitted socialist ideas to its American readers. In this
period, socialism remained linked to feminism, even in the increasingly
capitalist United States. "My eyes turn longingly to 'the Association' as a
truer mode of life," Stanton wrote Davis in 1852. "All our talk about wom-
ans rights is mere moonshine, so long as we are bound by the present
social system." Stanton was primarily concerned with the problems caused
by "the isolated household," but in her *Una*, Davis regularly applied
socialist values to the situation of American women. On a "piercing cold"
streetcar trip, Davis was given a seat by "a gentleman," while a poor
woman carrying two children received none and remained crouching by
an open door. Davis told her readers that "it was not our womanhood
which procured this seat, but our soft, warm cloak and furs." "Women are
divided into two classes," she continued. "One class indeed are the idols of
men, their play things, their pets, their household divinities . . . but alas!
the contrast which poverty marks. The *poor* woman is not out of her sphere
sawing wood, picking rags in the gutters, peddling fish in the street, in
short doing any hard drudgery which will give her a subsistence."
Maintaining that fortunately there existed a third class of "'strong
minded women' who will not consent to be slaves or toys," Davis repeatedly linked socialist themes to feminist demands.[48] Mirroring arguments
made by European socialists like Deroin and Roland, Anneke and Otto,
the *Una* asserted that charity was no solution to poverty. "We want asso-
ciative, attractive, and incorporated labor," Davis wrote in 1855. "Do not
the very wrongs to which we have alluded [women's lack of rights, the
meagerness of their earnings] call for the radical, thorough reorganization
of society?"[49]
Reporting sporadically on feminism's fortunes in Europe, the *Una*
maintained especially close contact with Britain. The May 1853 issue featured a full-page announcement for the *Woman's Advocate*, a proposed
"monthly paper" to be published by the Woman's Elevation League.
Founded by six women, among them Anne Knight and dress reform lecturer Caroline Dexter, as well as four men, the league proposed "to
awaken the women of England from their lethargy by public meetings,
lectures, etc." working for "the social, moral, professional, pecuniary, and

political elevation of women." This "affords an opportunity to the Friends of Humanity to evince their willingness *to aid the cause*, by filling up the accompanying form, or by inclosing Postage-stamps to the Secretaries, the Receipt of which will be announced in different Newspapers," Davis added.[50]

The league and its newspaper never materialized, and feminism's relative lack of progress in Britain led Davis and other Americans to contrast their efforts for women's rights to the mother country's conservatism. Printing two long articles deploring a piece by Englishwoman Eliza Cook, which argued that emancipated American women would be bad wives, worse housekeepers, and suffer from ill health and general unhappiness, Davis criticized Cook's entire argument as "so essentially English, so unamerican, so dead." In response to an 1853 statement made by Lord Palmerston, then British Home Secretary, that women should be educated so they could be better wives and mothers, the *Una* asserted that "this will do for an English lord, but we demand to be educated because we are human beings . . . not because we are the *appendages* of man in any of our life relations."[51]

Feminist editors in the 1850s generally erred on the side of optimism, trying to maintain their own hopes and those of their readers by accentuating gains and ignoring setbacks. Davis corresponded with English editor G. J. Holyoake, who printed a letter in the *Reasoner* from the American "editress," as he styled her, announcing that the *Una* "will be the first paper owned, printed, and edited by women in this country." At the end of 1855, the *Reasoner* reported that "eight young women (the first eight out of a hundred who applied) have been employed [as printers on the *Una*] for two months, and all remain at their cases, satisfied themselves, and perfectly satisfying their employers."[52] By the time this letter appeared in print, however, the *Una* had ceased publication.

Feminists in both America and Europe repeatedly tried to employ female typesetters and printers, believing this job ideal for women, but they met with massive opposition from male workers. In France, Britain, and the United States, lower-paid women worked as strikebreakers in the printing industry during the 1850s and 1860s. This lack of class solidarity among women, combined with the antifeminism of most men, led to the organization of male trade unions that excluded women from printer's jobs into the twentieth century.[53] Mathilde Franziska Anneke used Milwaukee women to set type for the first issues of her *German Women's Newspaper*, but three months later male printers organized a trade union to prevent such female competition. Amelia Bloomer faced a similar problem with her *Lily* when she tried to use women printers in Ohio, but she was able to share presses with another newspaper and employ "four women and three men working together peaceably and harmoniously."[54]

These American efforts may have influenced developments in England. British feminists read the *Una*, and in 1857, Bessie Parkes, Barbara Leigh

Smith, Anna Jameson and others raised the money to purchase an
Edinburgh newspaper, the *Waverley.*[55] After publishing three issues as a
feminist weekly in January 1858, Parkes as editor in chief transformed the
publication into the monthly *English Woman's Journal*, which began its
six-year run in March. In November 1859, Parkes invested in a printing
press and type and trained her young associate, Emily Faithfull, to work
as a typesetter. Faithfull's Victoria Press, which eventually employed sixteen women, opened in January 1860. Printing other magazines and
books in addition to the *English Woman's Journal*, the all-female Victoria
Press remained in business until 1899. When Faithfull visited the United
States in 1872–1873, she was greeted by Elizabeth Cady Stanton and
Lucretia Mott.[56]

The American magazine the *Lily* also crossed the Atlantic. Originally
designed to be a journal "Devoted to Temperance and Literature," the *Lily*
soon dedicated itself to women's rights in general. "Some of our gentleman readers are a little troubled lest we should injure ourself and our
paper by saying too much on behalf of the rights and interests of our own
sex," Bloomer wrote in April 1850. "Our readers must bear in mind that
the *Lily* is a woman's paper, and one of its objects as stated in our prospec-
tus is, *to open a medium through which woman's thoughts and aspirations might
be developed.*"[57]

The *Lily* increasingly concentrated on dress reform. A December 1849
article attributed the "new costume" to the English actress Fanny Kemble,
a recent divorcée living in Massachusetts:

> There has been a great cry raised by gentlemen from all quarters, about the
> male attire which Fanny Kemble is said to have adopted; and their fears
> seem to be excited, lest the ladies are going to contest their exclusive right to
> wear pantaloons. It turns out, however, that the so much talked of 'men's
> clothes' which Mrs. Kemble has been guilty of putting on, is nothing more
> nor less than a loose flowing dress falling a little below the knees, and loose
> pantaloons or drawers confined to the ankle by a band or cord.

Similar costumes had been worn in American communes since the
1820s. Both women and men at Owen's New Harmony dressed in wide
trousers and tunics. When Fredrika Bremer visited the New Jersey
Phalanstery with Rebecca and Marcus Spring in 1849, she noted that the
wife of the community's leader "wore a short dress and pantaloons, which
were very becoming to her fine and picturesque figure, and besides which,
were well calculated for walking through wet fields and woods."[58]

Proponents of dress reform tried to separate themselves from the few
women of their era who openly dressed as men. The *Lily* criticized Helene
Maria Weber, the German woman who had written the 1850 Worcester
convention about wearing men's clothing, just as the *English Woman's
Journal* later criticized American doctor Mary Walker for her "trouser-
wearing." "We agree" with Weber "as far as the *right* to wear such a dress

goes, and in regard to its utility," the *Lily* wrote in 1851. "But we have no desire to follow her example. We think something may be substituted far prettier than the common coat and vest, and high crowned hat worn by men; there is a stiffness about them unsuited to a lady's taste." Eager to improve the cumbersome dress of their own day, with its massive skirts, corseted waist, and tightly constructed bodice, feminists asserted that being female did not require wearing unhealthy and constrictive clothing. "Although God created us women," began a June 1851 article, "He did not command us to wear long petticoats or to girt our vital organs."[59]

Early in 1851 a number of upstate New York feminists began wearing what soon came to be called the bloomer costume. Elizabeth Cady Stanton, her cousin Elizabeth Smith Miller, and Amelia Bloomer were among the first, followed shortly by Susan B. Anthony, Lucy Stone, Sarah Grimké, and Angelina Grimké Weld. The costume attracted instant and unwelcome public attention. During the New York City Women's Rights Convention of 1853, Anthony and Stone went out at noon to mail a letter, wearing short skirts and trousers. "Gradually we noticed we were being encircled," Stone remembered,

> A wall of men and boys at last shut us in, so that to go on or to go back was impossible. There we stood. The crowd was a good-natured one. They laughed at us. They made faces at us. They said impertinent things, and they would not let us out. Every moment brought added numbers, who peered over to see what attracted the crowd.

The police eventually rescued the women. The *Lily* reported that a similar scene had occurred in London two years earlier, when an American went to the Crystal Palace in a bloomer costume but attracted such a large crowd that "the police found themselves quite inadequate to the task of dispersing the crowd and had to beg her to retire."[60]

The public's fascination arose not because the costume revealed a woman's figure (it was far more modest than contemporary fashions) but from the titillation caused by crossing the boundary between the sexes. Women who wore pants, even under skirts, were routinely accused of wanting to be men, to "wear the pants" symbolically as well as literally. Contemporary opinion routinely equated men's clothing with men's rights and a spate of cartoons, songs, plays, and even chinaware portrayed women appropriating both male clothing and male privileges, including smoking, military service, voting, and governing. The English *Saturday Review* headed an 1857 article opposing women's rights "Bloomeriana," and the *Una* printed an item in 1855 that the Illinois House of Representatives had passed a resolution that "a fine of $100 be hereafter imposed on any lady who shall lecture in public, in any part of the State, without first putting on gentleman's apparel." Men "cannot get up a picture of a woman's rights meeting . . . but they must put cigars and pipes in our mouths, make us sit cross-legged, or hoist our feet above their legitimate positions," American feminist Frances Gage complained to the *Lily*.[61]

Given such difficulties, early feminists tended to project both the origin and the wearing of the reformed costume on foreigners or other nations, as Jeanne Deroin had in her 1852 *Women's Almanack* when she asserted that the costume was seen on some women in Germany. In 1846, German feminist Louise Aston testified that she herself had not put on trousers in Berlin but had been "confused with a traveling Englishwoman who wore men's clothes to restaurants." However, Aston's denial did not prevent her expulsion from the city. "We learn from foreign papers that [bloomers] are being worn to some extent by the fashionables in England, Ireland, and Spain," the *Lily* wrote in 1851 with little factual basis. "All that is wanting to make the fashion take in this country, is for patterns to be sent back to us from England and France; and from present indications the time is not far distant when this will be done."[62]

Asserting that women in other societies wore pants justified the practice at home. Louise Otto began a long debate in the pages of her *Women's Newspaper* on the topic in 1851 by announcing that the costume had been worn "by a great number of women in New York for over a year," as well as by women in London and Paris. The fact that the subject was being taken seriously in the United States, England, and France justified its discussion in Germany, and Otto devoted a series of articles to "Bloomerismus" throughout the last two years of her journal's run.[63]

Primarily concerned with German news, Otto's weekly also functioned as an international organ both within the German territories and abroad. Since the German states did not unify during the revolution, Otto's *Women's Newspaper*, which reported on developments throughout the German-speaking world from 1849 to 1852, linked feminists both at home and in exile. Producing a prorevolutionary women's rights newspaper in Germany during these years was an amazing feat. In 1850, the state of Saxony, in which she published, passed a law forbidding women to be editors. Rapidly nicknamed the "Lex Otto" (since by then other German female editors had ceased publishing), the law failed to silence Otto, who moved her entire operation to the more liberal state of Thuringia.

The law against women directing journals was part of the severe repression enacted in the German states after 1849. Much of the legislation forcibly removed women from public life: in March 1850 a Prussian law forbade "women, students, and pupils" from attending any meeting at which politics was discussed; it remained on the books until 1908. The Austrian empire passed a similar law and set a tone of brutality and harshness for the counterrevolution late in 1848 by executing liberal editor Robert Blum, who had first published Otto's articles. "Here where everything now again lies in heavy chains . . . our entire movement seems to me only a small light, a small tempest within the whole great slavery of German subjection," a female democrat wrote Otto from Vienna in June

1850. Repression fell as harshly on women as men: female associations were disbanded and the wearing of revolutionary colors was forbidden, as were public funerals for revolutionaries and the decoration of their graves. A handbook for the German political police, published in Dresden in 1855, gave descriptions of "dangerous women," including Louise Otto, as well as providing information about the sentences given to those captured. "Wunderlich, Wilhelmina, serving maid from Weida, a fighter on the barricades, taken prisoner, sentenced to life imprisonment, and to six years hard labor beginning in 1850," read a typical entry.[64]

The 1850s in Germany were called "the silent time," when feminists "whispered about the past," Otto later wrote. Under these circumstances, continuing to publish until 1852 took courage and persistence: Otto's *Women's Newspaper* became the longest-lived revolutionary institution within German territory. Women's letters testified to the journal's importance. "I had become completely resigned," a "Woman Worker" wrote in 1849. "I will always remember the day when I was so happy to read the *Women's Newspaper* for the first time as the day of my spiritual salvation!"[65]

Otto's regular column, "A Look Around," reported on activities in the various German states as well as from abroad, where the German exile community grew rapidly. As repression stifled dissent in Germany, America became the focus of hopes for progress and reform. "So you seek in the West a new fatherland," went Otto's poem "Emigration." "With lasting peace, unity, and freedom. / Here the evil years draw nigh, full of blood and pain, / But there Germany's new age will triumph unbroken!" Otto also published the resolutions passed by an 1850 women's rights convention in Ohio, which detailed women's claims not only to the vote but to equal treatment in general. Asserting that current laws about women were "only a modified slave code," the piece ended by demanding that women "no longer be compelled to pay taxes from their scanty wages to support the maintenance of men who receive $8 a day for the presumption of making laws for themselves and women."[66]

The plight of poor female workers remained a major concern of Otto's. The pages of the *Women's Newspaper* are filled with announcements, letters, articles, and poems about women's cooperative labor associations, which sought to alleviate female poverty by buying goods in bulk, eliminating middlemen, charging enough to provide workers with decent incomes, and enlisting female consumers to buy only from such groups.[67] Otto also regularly printed news about democratic women's associations and the free congregations. The pages of her journal constitute the only source for the chief attempt to form a German women's movement during these years. The *Women's Newspaper* proposed an Association of German Women, which would unite the free religion women's associations, first regionally and then nationally. This Central Association met in Hamburg (1849) and Nuremburg (1850), but the general national meeting scheduled for 1854 never took place because of "the current reigning reaction."[68]

In addition to linking German feminists, socialists, democrats, and free religionists, Otto also published a great deal of information about what was soon to become a chief German export of the 1848 revolution—the progressive reform of education. Although early feminists admired the work of Swiss educator Johann Heinrich Pestalozzi and French minister Jean Frédéric Oberlin (Flora Tristan praised him; Anne Knight settled in the village where he died; Americans named their first coeducational and interracial college after him), it was the dispersal of German revolutionaries in the 1850s that transmitted the invention of the kindergarten to England and America. As conceived by radical brothers Friedrich and Karl Froebel, kindergartens challenged existing traditionalist German primary education, which segregated children along class and religious lines and were taught by male clergy. The new kindergartens, in contrast, fostered religious toleration and cooperative behavior, often had democratic admissions policies, and were staffed by women, including young, unmarried female teachers. Developed by the Free Religion movement in the late 1840s, kindergartens sought to educate children for a progressive, democratic-socialist future. In 1851 the reactionary Prussian government outlawed them as "a part of Froebel's socialist system, which is calculated on training children for atheism," and in 1854 it reimposed religious control on schools and banned single women from teaching.[69]

German exiles like Johannes Ronge and Bertha Meyer Traun Ronge founded kindergartens in their new homes. Publishing an English guide "for the use of Mothers, Nurses, and Infant Teachers" in 1855, the Ronges ran their Hampstead kindergarten (established in 1851) successfully throughout the decade and sponsored a second nursery school, which opened in Manchester in 1857. Bertha Ronge's sister, Margrethe Meyer Schurz, who emigrated with her husband, Carl Schurz, to the United States, opened one in Watertown, Wisconsin, in 1856. Elizabeth Peabody, also influenced by German reformers, established a kindergarten in Boston in 1861. Kindergartens transformed nursery school education in both the United States and Britain, cultivating a liberal approach to child rearing that allowed children relative freedom and creativity. "The interesting Readers children now have were unknown sixty years ago," Elizabeth Cady Stanton wrote in her 1898 memoir, in which she criticized the "Puritan ideas" that had darkened her early years, "We did not reach the temple of knowledge by the flowery paths of ease in which our descendants now walk."[70]

Early feminists put great hope in education and helped found schools and colleges as well as kindergartens to implement their ideas. Angelina Grimké Weld, Theodore Weld, and Sarah Grimké, with financial support from Marcus Spring, ran a progressive school at the New Jersey Phalanstery, later called the Raritan Bay Union, in the 1850s. Two of Stanton's sons and a granddaughter of the Motts attended. Barbara Leigh Smith Bodichon, who visited the school in 1858, wrote, "I never saw such a satisfactory group of young people in my life." Before her marriage, Bodichon herself had financed the coeductional, progressive Portman Hall School in London in 1854. Attended by children from a variety of social classes, including Riciotti Garibaldi, son of the Italian revolutionary, the school sought to transform its pupils' lives.[71] Leigh Smith's friend Bessie Rayner Parkes published her most radically feminist work on education in 1854. Her *Remarks on the Education of Girls* advocated "gymnasia for women, somewhat similar to that mentioned by Miss Bremer" and cited Elizabeth Blackwell's New York lectures on the physical education of girls to strengthen her case. In addition to physical training, Parkes thought "women should be able to study anything," especially "the Science of Social and Political Economy" pioneered by Harriet Martineau twenty years earlier. The goal of education was both to enable women to make better marriages and to do any work "they deem themselves fitted for."[72]

Advanced secondary schools and colleges to train teachers were especially important, since hardly any institutions existed to provide higher education for women. The Freethinking Hamburg Women's Association founded one of the most revolutionary establishments in 1850. Mingling Christians and Jews, the Hamburg College for the Female Sex offered teaching seminars on the kindergarten and elementary school level, as well as standard academic subjects. Two-thirds of the board of directors were female, but the faculty was entirely male. "When I retired to my room the first evening, I felt that I had found the true way to a new life," wrote German feminist Malwida von Meysenbug, who studied there. "Sometimes a grandmother, mother, and granddaughter" sat together at a lecture. Internal dissension, external repression, and rumors that the college "represented a hotbed of demagogery in which revolutionary plans were formed under cover of education" forced the institution to close after two years. "The experiment in any event had been made, the result was perfect," von Meysenbug wrote optimistically. "We did not doubt that many of those who had seen its first incarnation in our school would see its complete triumph, if not in Europe, then certainly in the New World."[73]

London was the site of another feminist attempt to provide higher education: Elizabeth Reid's Bedford College for Women, which opened in 1849. Reid, who had welcomed the American delegates to the World Anti-Slavery Convention in London in 1840, wrote that "a college for Women, or something like it, has been my dream from childhood." Designed in opposition to the conservative Queen's College, which was run by men and aimed at educating governesses, Bedford had an all-female board of governors and a nondenominational policy. Barbara Leigh Smith and her aunt Julia Smith attended briefly, and its example contributed to Bodichon's later founding of Girton College for women at Cambridge University. Lecturing against slavery in Britain in 1859, the African American Sarah Parker Remond found herself "received here as a sister by white women," a welcome which contributed to her decision to complete her education by taking classes at Bedford College during the early 1860s. Returning briefly to the United States after the Civil War, Remond then went back to Europe to attend medical school in Florence.[74]

American feminists in these years put their energies into creating technical educational establishments for women, both in medicine and industrial design. The Worcester convention of 1851 resolved "to promote the higher education of our children at our colleges and institutes of learning, without distinction of sex, challenging the same privileges for our daughters as already accorded our sons, making the public funds available to both," but money was not forthcoming for decades.[75] Instead, women created schools for design in Philadelphia, Boston, and New York City. Mathilde Franziska Anneke printed a long letter describing the Boston establishment in her *German Women's Newspaper* of 1852, and Fredrika Bremer reported in 1851 that she found such institutions "a most cheering sign of the times—of new and better times," for they constituted "the newfound California for women—better than silver and gold!"[76]

Female medical colleges originated because of male resistance to training women doctors. Immediately after Blackwell's graduation, Geneva Medical College refused to admit a second female applicant, stating that "Miss Blackwell's admission was an *experiment*, not intended as a *precedent*." In response, feminists in Philadelphia founded the Female Medical College of Pennsylvania, which began holding classes in October 1850. Louise Otto reported on this college in 1852; she had also printed a piece the previous year on a women's medical college in New York City.[77] The Motts helped raise funds for the Philadelphia institution, and James Mott served on its board. Barbara Bodichon met one of its first graduates, Dr. Elizabeth Cohen, in New Orleans in 1858. Bodichon was "amused" that Cohen wished her nine-year-old daughter to follow in her footsteps. "These Women's Rights women are all on the same tack, longing to make facsimiles of themselves" the Englishwoman wrote in her diary. "I tell them all they are wrong and absurd—have the children to grow up as they will, to be cooks and milliners, soldiers or sailors if they wish it."[78] Her bemusement demonstrated the progress made since the early 1840s: Bodichon assumed—falsely, as it turned out—that girls would soon be able to make such choices.

Attempts to provide higher education for women were the last major effort of the international feminist movement. By the mid-1850s, conservative repression had exiled or silenced the French and the Germans. In 1856—the year he met Ernestine Rose—American poet Walt Whitman added an elegiac section, "To a Foil'd European Revolutionaire," to his *Leaves of Grass.* "The prison, scaffold, garrote, handcuffs, iron necklaces, and lead-balls do their work. . . . Then courage, European revolter, revoltress! For till all ceases neither must you cease," he exhorted.[79] But censorship and prison terms triumphed. The collapse of the European revolutions and the crushing of feminism on the continent contributed to the relative conservatism of the following decades.

In addition, the first international women's movement never created institutions that might have sustained it during these years. In the 1850s American feminists were in the best position to establish an international organization, but they resisted calls to form a permanent National Women's Rights Society in their own country. Fearful of duplicating the bitter feuds that had racked abolitionism and convinced that their movement thrived on "spontaneity" and "agitation," feminists defeated a motion for such an institution at the 1852 convention. Ernestine Rose compared established organizations to "Chinese bandages" and "shackles"; Lucy Stone called them "thumb-screws and soul-screws."[80]

In the absence of any international body, the surviving women's movements in the United States and Britain became increasingly national and conservative. In both societies, lacking the international support that had previously sustained it, radical feminism receded.

The Englishwomen's movement of the late 1850s coalesced around a quintessentially middle-class issue: married women gaining control over their property, which under common law belonged to the husband. Working for property ownership (which included real estate and material possessions) primarily benefited better-off women; the wife's right to her own wages or salary, largely a working-class issue, was deferred for future action. Bodichon, Parkes, Howitt, Reid, Jameson, and their friends organized a committee that delivered a 26,000-signature petition to Parliament in 1856. The House of Commons responded by making divorce slightly easier to obtain; previously every divorce had required a separate act of Parliament. The male legislators reasoned that since happy wives did not need to own property and unhappy wives could now divorce, their work was completed. The Married Women's Property Act was not enacted until 1882.[81]

Following this initial setback, organizers worked more circumspectly. When Bodichon and Parkes founded the *English Woman's Journal* in 1858, they deliberately avoided discussions of marriage, sex, and suffrage so as not to alienate potential sympathizers. The new groups they organized—the Society for Promoting the Employment of Women, the Female Middle-Class Emigration Society, and the Victoria Press—bore no trace of either the socialism or the internationalism of the earlier feminist movement. Working closely with the new National Association for the Promotion of Social Science, the Englishwomen moved slowly, not claiming the right to vote until the late 1860s. Their achievements were considerable, but they differed greatly from the wider goals radical feminists had previously sought. International contacts dwindled to those with Americans. The Englishwomen's movement wrote Lucretia

Mott in the late 1850s (Bodichon had been delighted with Mott's enthusiasm for women's rights when she met the Quaker feminist on her
American honeymoon), but a correspondence did not ensue.[82]

The U.S. women's rights movement itself ran out of steam in the years
just before the Civil War, in part because of the disappearance of the international radicalism that had helped fuel it. Increasingly dramatic conflicts
over the issue of slavery in the late 1850s persuaded many feminists that
ending black bondage should take precedence over women's rights. The
outbreak of hostilities in 1861 convinced Stanton and Anthony to halt
feminist activities in order to devote full attention to the U.S. war effort.
Although they thought women's war work and patriotic support for the
Union would lead to political gains once the war ended, these did not
materialize. The National Women's Loyal League they organized in 1863
proceeded conservatively, appealing for women to aid the cause, but
chiefly in their traditional roles as wives and mothers. However important
its contributions to the Union victory, the nation's male leaders rewarded
them only with flowery rhetoric.

Divisions arising from the Civil War and its aftermath fractured the old
coalition. The success of warfare in abolishing slavery shook the faith of
radical pacifists like Lucretia Mott, while encouraging the entry into public work of a new generation of women who had been reared on military
discipline and bifurcated gender roles. The question of how to respond to
the fact that suffrage had been granted to formerly enslaved men, but not
to women of any race or condition, divided American feminists for
decades. Stone and Blackwell supported "the black man's vote," while
Stanton and Anthony campaigned against it, leaving Mott, Rose, and others with an agenda broader than suffrage on the margins.[83]

In 1865, the Motts were approached by their son-in-law and one of
Garrison's sons, who wanted them to contribute funds to the new journal
they were founding, the *Nation*. "I told [my son-in-law] it was objected,
that Woman was ignored in their organization," Mott wrote her sister,

> He was rather taken aback, said—"if there seemed a necessity for women he
> thought they would be admitted"—to which the impetuous reply was
> "seemed a necessity!! for one half the Nation to act with you"! and the larger
> half too we might say—so many men slain. You ought to have been here—
> He couldn't ask James with quite so good a grace for $1000—He *did* ask tho'
> but I guess he will not get anything like so much from him.[84]

It was the *Nation*'s narrow view of women's role, however, and the
forces of nationalism that triumphed. By the 1860s, even the resurgent
socialist movements in France and Germany followed Proudhon's logic
and automatically excluded women. The most influential feminist book
published in France during the 1850s was Juliette Adam's *Idées anti-proud-
honiennes*, which both in its title and its content acknowledged the triumph

of antifeminist socialism.[85] Although the Marxist International Working Man's Association (formed in 1864) included a lone female representative on its general council, most members called for women's return to their "rightful work" of home and family.[86] In the last quarter of the nineteenth century, continental European women's movements divided into two hostile rival groups: middle-class suffrage organizations and socialist parties arguing that only revolution would liberate women of the working class.

In many important ways, the first international women's movement was connected to the wider hopes that sparked the revolutions of 1848. In the decades before that explosion, the divisions between middle class and working class, between democracy and socialism, and even between women and men seemed possible to overcome. The defeat of these revolutions was also the defeat of these expansive dreams. By the mid-1850s, it was clear that the earlier coalitions had fissioned, perhaps irredeemably.

When women's movements revived, in the late 1860s, they were nationally oriented and far more cautious than their predecessors. The new French feminist organizations concentrated on education and marriage reform. Louise Otto's General German Women's Association of 1865 also focused on education, leaving more controversial issues like the vote for later decades. Instead of the expansive motto of her 1849 *Women's Newspaper*—"I enlist female citizens in the realm of freedom"—she substituted the less threatening "Women want to be human beings and share the laurel wreath of work and victory." Americans, for their part, narrowed the wide range of feminist topics raised between 1830 and 1860 to the single goal of electoral rights. The activists of the first international women's movement and their wide-ranging feminist demands were chiefly remembered in the torrent of antifeminist cartoons and writings produced throughout the remainder of the nineteenth century.

But we should not underestimate the impact of these pioneers. The very amount of criticism and ridicule they unleashed testifies to the power of their movement, as do the harsh laws against female political participation enacted in France, Germany, and Austria. Challenging some of the most ancient traditions of Western culture, they awoke fears and hostility that still confront feminist demands.

The early feminists themselves were convinced that time was on their side and that the future would come to appreciate their efforts. "Calling no man master, she is sure of her reward," the Boston Anti-Slavery Society wrote in a tribute to the abolitionist Abby Kelley. "The gratification of the few—the malignant scorn of the many—the blessings of coming generations." In two hundred years, Louise Otto wrote, German women would "smile good-humoredly" at the problems of the current age. Angelina Grimké Weld assured Elizabeth Cady Stanton, "The very truths you are now contending for, will, in fifty years, be so embedded in public opinion that no one need say one word in their defense."[87] In the mid-1860s, Barbara Bodichon told her friend Emily Davies, "You will go up and vote upon crutches, and I shall come out of my grave and vote in my winding sheet." In 1919, when British women over thirty finally gained the suffrage, Bodichon had been dead for almost thirty years, but the eighty-eight-year-old Davies walked to the polls to cast her ballot.[88]

Their defeat in their own day should not dim the importance of their legacy. Although a great deal of what these early feminists envisioned has been achieved, much remains to be done. They inspire us to complete this revolution.

Notes

∽

Introduction

1. I encountered this letter in Miriam Schneir's anthology, *Feminism: The Essential Historical Writings* (1972; reprint, New York: Random House, 1994), pp. 91–92.

2. *Proceedings of the Woman's Rights Convention held at the Broadway Tabernacle, in the City of New York, on Tues. & Wed., Sept. 6th & 7th, 1853* (New York: Fowler & Wells, 1853), p. 83.

3. Louise Dittmar, *Das Wesen der Ehe nebst einigen Aufsätzen über die soziale Reform der Frauen* (Leipzig: Otto Wiegand, 1849), pp. 115, 47–63.

4. Harriet Taylor Mill, "Enfranchisement of Women," in *Sexual Equality: Writings by John Stuart Mill, Harriet Taylor Mill, and Helen Taylor*, ed. Ann P. Robson and John M. Robson (Toronto: University of Toronto Press, 1994), p. 192.

5. *Proceedings . . . Broadway Tabernacle, 1853*, pp. 4–5.

Chapter One

1. *L'Opinion des femmes* 4 (May 1849), p. 4.

2. *Gazette des tribunaux*, 13 November 1850, p. 3. Deroin's biographer, Adrien Ranvier, possessed an autograph letter of Deroin's from 1880 in which she detailed this incident. Unfortunately many of the papers Ranvier used have disappeared and the only source for some of them is his article. Adrian Ranvier, "Une Féministe de 1848: Jeanne Deroin," in *La Révolution de 1848: Bulletin de la Société d'histoire de la révolution de 1848*, 4 (1907–1908): 420 n. 1.

3. The English letter can be found in *Northern Star*, 14 June 1851, p. 1. The American letter is in *The Proceedings of the Woman's Rights Convention, Held at Worcester, October 15 and 16, 1851* (New York: Fowler & Wells, 1852), pp. 32–35. When Elizabeth Cady Stanton, Susan B. Anthony, and Matilda Joslyn Gage reprinted it in their *History of Woman Suffrage*, vol. 1: 1848–1861 (New York: Fowler & Wells, 1881); reprint, New York: Arno *New York Times*, 1969, pp. 234–237, they toned down the punctuation by removing exclamation points, underlinings, and capital letters.

4. Deroin's election banner with Knight's English translation pasted on it is in the Anne Knight Papers, MS box W, folder 6, Friends House, London. Knight's letter to the Sheffield women, Anne Knight to Mrs. Rooke, 21 January 1851, is the first letter in the Autograph Letter Collection: Women's Suffrage, 1851–1894, the Fawcett Library, London. The House of Lords petition, submitted 13 February 1851, is in the *Journals of the House of Lords*, vol. 83, p. 23.

5. Rose's speech is not in the convention *Proceedings*. It was retrieved by Yuri Suhl from contemporary newspapers, which transcribed it. Yuri Suhl, *Ernestine L. Rose: Women's Rights Pioneer*, 2d ed. (New York: Biblio, 1990), p. 112.

6. *Proceedings of the Woman's Rights Convention Held at Worcester October 23 and 24, 1850* (Boston: Prentiss & Sawyer, 1851), p. 7, 15.

7. Mill got his information from Horace Greeley's *New York Tribune*. Mill-Taylor Papers, London School of Economics, vol. L, no.38, John Stuart Mill to Harriet Taylor [1850?]. The letter is printed in F. A. Hayek, *John Stuart Mill and Harriet Taylor: Their Correspondence and Subsequent Marriage* (London: Routledge & Kegan Paul, 1951), pp. 166–167.

8. Harriet Taylor Mill, "Enfranchisement of Women," in *Sexual Equality: Writings by John Stuart Mill, Harriet Taylor Mill, and Helen Taylor*, ed. Ann P. Robson and John M. Robson (Toronto: University of Toronto Press, 1994), pp. 192, 202–203.

9. Louise Otto, *Frauen-Zeitung*, 23 August 1851, pp. 227–228; 28 December 1851, pp. 358–359.

10. Barbara Leigh Smith Bodichon, *An American Diary, 1857–1858*, ed. Joseph W. Reed Jr. (London: Routledge & Kegan Paul, 1972), p. 140.

11. *The London Journal of Flora Tristan or the Aristocracy and the Working Class of England*, trans. Jean Hawkes (London: Virago, 1982) pp. 68–69. Tristan's book appeared four years before Friedrich Engels's *Condition of the Working Class in England*.

12. Ibid., pp. 71–72.

13. Suzanne Voilquin, *Mémoires d'une saint-simonienne en Russie(1839–1896)*, ed. Maïté Albistur and Daniel Armogathe (Paris: Edition des femmes, 1977), p. 15. For women and men in Saint-Simonianism, see Claire Goldberg Moses and Leslie Wahl Rabine, *Feminism, Socialism, and French Romanticism* (Bloomington: Indiana University Press, 1993), pp. 17–84.

14. "Otto Stern," *Unser Planet* 27 (February 1843), p. 106, cited in Ruth-Ellen Boetscher Joeres, *Die Anfänge der deutschen Frauenbewegung: Louise Otto-Peters* (Frankfurt am Main: Fischer Taschenbuch Verlag, 1983), p.71.

15. From *Der Mensch und sein Gott in und ausser dem Christenthum*, cited in Ruth-Ellen Boetscher Joeres, "Spirit in Struggle: The Radical Vision of Louise Dittmar," in *Out of Line / Ausgefallen: The Paradox of Marginality in the Writings of Nineteenth-Century German Women*, ed. Ruth-Ellen Boetcher Joeres and Marianne Burkhard (Rodopi: Amsterdam, 1989), p. 295. The congregations were either Freie Gemeinde (free congregations), i.e., Protestant in origin, or Deutschkatholik (German Catholic), i.e., Catholic but not Roman. I am calling them all free congregations, since that term describes them accurately.

16. Catherine M. Prelinger, *Charity, Challenge, and Change: Religious Dimensions of the Mid-Nineteenth-Century Women's Movement in Germany* (Westport, Conn.: Greenwood, 1987), pp. 80, 92. On the dynamics of feminism and the free congregations, see Sylvia Paletschek, *Frauen und Dissens: Frauen in Deutschkatholizismus und in den freien Gemeinden, 1841–1852* (Göttingen: Vandenhoeck & Ruprecht, 1990) pp. 157–170.

17. Mathilde Franziska Anneke, "Das Weib im Conflict mit den socialen Verhältnisse," 1847. Typescript, Mathilde Franziska Anneke Papers, State Historical Society of Wisconsin, p. 11.

18. Elizabeth Pease to Anne Warren Weston, 24 June 1841, Boston Public Library, Manuscript Division, Anti-Slavery Collection, Ms.A.9.2, vol. 15, pt. 1, no. 50.

19. Harriet Taylor to W. J. Fox, 10 May 1848, reprinted in Hayek, *John Stuart Mill*, p. 123. For women in Chartism, see Dorothy Thompson, *The Chartists: Popular Politics in the Industrial Revolution* (New York: Pantheon, 1984), chap. 7; and Jutta Schwartzkopf, *Women in the Chartist Movement* (New York: St. Martin's, 1991).

20. Anne Knight to Maria Weston Chapman, 4 August 1840, Boston Public Library, Manuscript Division, Anti-Slavery Collection Ms.A.9.2, vol. 13, p. 49.

21. For a thoughtful discussion of the impact of the 1840 convention on American and British women, see Kathryn Kish Sklar, "'Women Who Speak for an Entire Nation': American and British Women at the World Anti-Slavery Convention, London, 1840," in *The Abolitionist Sisterhood: Women's Political Culture in Antebellum America*, ed. Jean Fagan Yellin and John C. Van Horne (Ithaca, N.Y.: Cornell University Press, 1994), pp. 301–333.

22. For this argument about the American women's movement, see Blanche Glassman Hersh, *The Slavery of Sex: Feminist-Abolitionists in America* (Urbana: University of Illinois Press, 1978), p. 165; for German Catholic internationalism, see Johannes Ronge's 1845 call to "men of Europe and of America" in *The Autobiography and Justification of Johannes Ronge, the German Reformer*, trans. John Lord from the 5th German ed. (London: Chapman Brothers, 1846), pp. 69–70.

23. The first phrase is from an 1845 letter from Knight to William Lloyd Garrison; the second from Knight's letter that same year to Maria Weston Chapman. Boston Public Library, Manuscript Division, Anti-Slavery Collection, Ms.A.1.2, vol. 15, p. 39; Ms.A.9.2, vol. 21, p. 70.

24. Louise Otto, letter to the *Sächsische Vaterlandsblätter*, 23 November 1843, pp. 811–813; reprinted in Ruth-Ellen Boetcher Joeres, *Die Anfänge der deutschen*

Frauenbewegung: Louise Otto-Peters (Frankfurt am Main: Fischer Taschenbuch Verlag, 1983), pp. 75–76.

25. *The London Journal of Flora Tristan*, pp. 253–257; Wilhelm Schulte, "Mathilde Franziska Anneke," *Westfälische Lebensbilder*, vol. 8 (Münster: Aschendorffische Verlag, 1958), p. 130.

26. *Lucretia Mott: Her Complete Speeches and Sermons*, ed. Dana Greene (New York: Edwin Mellen, 1980) p. 28.

27. Gerhard K. Friesen, "A Letter from M. F. Anneke: A Forgotten German-American Pioneer in Women's Rights," *Journal of German-American Studies* 12, no. 2 (1977), p. 35.

28. Margaret Fuller, *"These Sad but Glorious Days": Dispatches from Europe, 1846–50*, ed. Larry J. Reynolds and Susan Belasco Smith (New Haven: Yale University Press, 1991), p. 119. For general accounts of the 1848 revolutions, see Priscilla Robertson, *Revolutions of 1848: A Social History* (Princeton: Princeton University Press, 1952); and Jonathan Sperber, *The European Revolutions, 1848–1851* (Cambridge: Cambridge University Press, 1994).

29. Cited in Ute Gerhard, *Unerhört: Die Geschichte der deutschen Frauenbewegung* (Reinbek bei Hamburg: Rowohlt, 1992), p. 15. Both poems, "Klöpplerinnen" (Lacemakers) and "Für Alle" (For all) are reprinted in *Deutsche Dichterinnen: Vom 16. Jahrhundert bis zur Gegenwart* ed. Gisela Brinker-Gabler (Frankfurt am Main: Fischer Taschenbuch Verlag, 1978), pp. 208–210. "Für Alle" appears in German and in an English translation that differs from mine in *The Defiant Muse: German Feminist Poems from the Middle Ages to the Present*, ed. Susan L. Cocalis (New York: Feminist Press, 1986), pp. 55–59.

30. Anne Knight, printed letter to Richard Cobden, M.P., 13 August 1850, in Tracts, vol. O, folder 229–230, Friends House, London.

31. Malwida von Meysenbug, *Memoiren einer Idealisten* (Berlin: Schuster & Loeffler, 1881), 1:140ff.

32. Louise Otto, "Adresse eines Mädchens," *Leipziger Arbeiter-Zeitung*, 20 May 1848, reprinted in *Frauenemanzipation im deutschen Vormärz*, ed. Renate Möhrmann (Stuttgart: Philipp Reclam, 1978), pp. 199–202; the assessment of its significance is from Gerhard, *Unerhört*, p. 51.

33. Claire Goldberg Moses, *French Feminism in the Nineteenth Century* (Albany: State University of New York Press, 1984), pp. 128–129; the phrase about the Vésuviennes is from their constitution, printed in Paris, 1848, and reprinted in Maïté Albistur and Daniel Armogathe, eds., *Le grief des femmes: Anthologie de textes féministes du môyen age à nos jours*, 2 vols. (Poitiers: Editions Hier et Demain, 1978), 1:296. There is some question whether this group was legitimate or was organized by men to parody women's efforts.

34. Julia Smith to Julia Garnett Pertz in Berlin, 23 March and 4 April 1848, cited in Helen Heineman, *Restless Angels: The Friendship of Six Victorian Women* (Athens: Ohio University Press, 1983), p. 163.

35. He wrote in French. Cited in Larry J. Reynolds, *European Revolutions and the American Literary Renaissance* (New Haven: Yale University Press, 1988), p. 3. I

have drawn on Reynolds for some material in the next paragraphs; I disagree with him, however, about the impact of the revolutions on Seneca Falls.

36. Mott, *Complete Speeches and Sermons* p. 75.

37. Used by Marion Reid as the epigraph to *A Plea for Woman* (1843; reprint, Edinburgh: Polygon, 1988).

38. Robert Darnton, *The Kiss of Lamourette: Reflections in Cultural History* (New York: Norton, 1990), p. 19.

39. Lucretia Mott, letter to *Liberator*, 24 August 1848, cited in Margaret Hope Bacon, *Valiant Friend: The Life of Lucretia Mott* (New York: Walker, 1980), p. 125.

40. Stanton did not reprint this speech in her later *History of Woman Suffrage* (1881), in which she toned down revolutionary aspects of the meeting and considerably increased her own importance to the early American movement. For Stanton's self-aggrandizement, see Nancy Gale Isenberg, *Sex and Citizenship in Antebellum America* (Chapel Hill: University of North Carolina Press, 1998), chap. 1. Stanton's speech is reprinted in Karlyn Kohrs Campbell, *Man Can Not Speak for Her* (New York: Praeger, 1989), 2: 42–70.

41. Cited in Stanton, Anthony, and Gage, *History of Woman Suffrage*, 1: 805.

42. Louise Otto, *Frauen-Zeitung*, 2 November 1851, p. 297.

43. "Les Femmes médicins," *Opinion des femmes*, 5 (June 1849), p. 5.

44. Bessie Rayner Parkes to Kate Jeavons, 8 March 1849, Parkes Papers, Girton College Library, B.R. Parkes vol. 6, p. 52.

45. Marianne Finch, *An Englishwoman's Experience in America* (London: Richard Bentley, 1853), p. 215.

46. *Proceedings of the Woman's Rights Convention, Held at Syracuse, Sept. 8th, 9th and 10th, 1852* (Syracuse: J. E. Masters, 1852), p. 19.

47. *Una*, 1 February 1853, p. 1.

48. Ibid., 1 April 1853, p. 48; 1 June 1853, p. 77.

49. Finch, *Englishwoman's Experience*, pp. 209–210.

50. For Fuller, see Bell Gale Chevigny, "To the Edges of Ideology: Margaret Fuller's Centrifugal Evolution," *American Quarterly* 38 (Summer 1986), pp. 173–201.

51. *Mary Howitt: An Autobiography*, ed. Margaret Howitt (London: Wm. Isbister, 1889), 2: 85. Margaret Howitt was Mary Howitt's daughter.

52. Fredrika Bremer, *Homes of the New World: Impressions of America*, Trans. Mary Howitt (New York: Harper, 1863), 2: 456.

53. On d'Héricourt, see Karen Offen, "A Nineteenth-Century French Feminist Rediscovered: Jenny P. d'Héricourt 1809–1875," *Signs: Journal of Women in Culture and Society* 13, no. 1 (Autumn 1987), pp. 144–158; on Mikhailov, Richard Stites, "M. L. Mikhailov and the Emergence of the Woman Question in Russia," Canadian Slavic Studies 3, no. 2 (Summer 1969), pp. 178–199.

54. Madame d'Héricourt, *A Woman's Philosophy of Woman; or Woman Affranchised* (New York: Carleton, 1864), p. xiv.

55. *Proceedings . . . Syracuse, 1852*, p. 63.

56. Harriet Martineau, *Autobiography*, 2 vols., ed. and with memorials by Maria Weston Chapman (Boston: Houghton Mifflin, 1877) 1: 332; written in 1855. The Bremer quotation is from Adolph B. Benson, "Fredrika Bremer's Unpublished Letters to the Downings," *Scandinavian Letters and Notes* 11, no.8 (November 1931), p. 6. Helene Marie Weber Letter, *Proceedings of the Woman's Rights Convention . . . 1850*, p. 79.

57. Louise Otto, *Frauenleben im Deutschen Reich: Erinnerungen aus der Vergangenheit mit Hinweis auf Gegenwart und Zukunft*, with introduction by Ruth Bleckwenn (1876; reprint Köln: Verlag M. Hüttermann, Paderborn, 1988), pp. 86, 143; Fredrika Bremer, *England in 1851 or Sketches of a Tour in England*, trans. L.A.H. (Boulogne: Merridew, 1853), p. 38.

58. Fredrika Bremer, *The Homes of the New World; Impressions of America*, trans. Mary Howitt (New York: Harper, 1853), 2:173.

59. The letter, Anne Knight to Maria Weston Chapman, is at the Boston Public Library, Manuscript Division, Anti-Slavery Collection, Ms.A.9.2, vol. 13, p. 49. It was reprinted in the Sixth Annual Report of the Glasgow Emancipation Society for 1840 and in William Lloyd Garrison's *The Liberator*.

60. Martineau, *Autobiography*, 2: 366.

61. For an envelope with three stickers, see Anne Knight to Hannah Webb, 6 April 1847, Boston Public Library, Manuscript Division, Anti-Slavery Collection, Ms.A.1.2, vol. 12, p. 119. Webb's husband, Richard, a Dublin reformer, printed the labels for Knight.

62. Bremer, *England in 1851*, p. 57.

63. Malwida von Meysenbug, *Memoiren einer Idealistin* (Berlin: Schuster & Loeffler, 1881), 1: 261.

64. The phrase is President John Tyler's, uttered in 1844. Cited in John W. Dodds, *The Age of Paradox: A Biography of England, 1841–1851* (London: Victor Gollancz, 1953), p. 230. The Atlantic cable was laid in August 1858, but it worked for only three weeks. The next, successful, attempt was made in 1866. On the international development of the telegraph in the 1840s, see Jerome Blum, *In the Beginning: The Advent of the Modern Age, Europe in the 1840s* (New York: Scribner's, 1994), pp. 32–34.

65. Mott, *Complete Speeches and Sermons*, pp. 244–245.

66. Robson and Robson, *Sexual Equality*, p. 184.

67. George Sand, *My Life*, trans. Dan Hofstadter (New York: Harper & Row, 1979), p. 161. Adapted by Dan Hofstadter.

68. Otto wrote this article under her "half pseudonym," Otto Stern. In *Unser Planet*, 27 February, 1843 p. 108, cited in Boetscher Joeres, *Anfänge* p. 72.

69. Helene Menzzer, cited in Paletschek, *Frauen und Dissens*: p. 176.

70. Emma Coe in *Proceedings . . . Worcester 1851*, pp. 107–108.

71. Louise Otto, *Frauen-Zeitung*, 27 April 1850, p. 248.

72. Ernestine Rose, *Boston Investigator*, 21 November 1856, p. 1.

73. Jeanne Deroin, *Almanach des femmes. Seconde année. Women's Almanack for 1853, in the English and French Languages* (London: James Watson; Jersey: Universal Printing Establishment, 1853), p. 14.

74. For this argument applied to women's public speaking, see Campbell, *Man Can Not Speak for Her* 1: 11. For Anneke's life, see Maria Wagner, *Mathilde Franziska Anneke in Selbstzeugnisse und Dokumenten* (Frankfurt am Main: Fischer Taschenbuch Verlag, 1980).

75. Friesen, "Letter from M.F. Anneke," p. 35.

76. *Proceedings of the Woman's Rights Convention, New York, 1853*, pp. 88–89.

77. Cited in Hester Burton, *Barbara Bodichon, 1827–1891* (London: John Murray, 1949), p. 33. For the argument that travel radicalized both women, see Diane Mary Chase Worzala, "The Langham Place Circle: The Beginnings of the Organized Women's Movement in England, 1854–1870" Ph.D. diss., University of Wisconsin, 1982), p. 312.

78. [Bessie Rayner Parkes], *Remarks on the Education of Girls* (London: John Chapman, 1854), p. 21.

79. *Proceedings of the Seventh National Woman's Rights Convention, held in New York City, November 25 and 26, 1856* (New York: Edward O. Jenkins, 1856), p. 35.

80. Mathilde Franziska Anneke, speech to the May anniversary of the American Equal Rights Association, 1869, in Stanton, Anthony, and Gage, *History of Woman Suffrage*, 2: 392.

81. Editorial by George Julian Harney, *The Friend of the People*, 7 February 1852, p. 1. Harney published letters from Anne Knight.

82. Bodichon, *American Diary, 1857–1858*, pp. 130–131. See also Elisabeth Griffith, *In Her Own Right: The Life of Elizabeth Cady Stanton* (New York: Oxford University Press, 1984), p. 91.

83. For this argument, see Worzala, "Langham Place Circle," pp. 124ff.

84. Anne Knight, *Diary*, Anne Knight Papers, MS vol. S486, Friends House, London.

85. *Proceedings . . . Broadway Tabernacle, 1856*, p. 77.

Chapter Two

1. Anne Taylor Gilbert to Anne Knight, 26 February 1849, Anne Knight Papers, Temporary MSS 725/5/35, Friends House, London. For a discussion of this interchange, see Leonore Davidoff and Catherine Hall, *Family Fortunes: Men and Women of the English Middle Class, 1780–1850* (Chicago: University of Chicago Press, 1987), pp. 452–454.

2. For Gilbert's life, see Davidoff and Hall, *Family Fortunes*, passim. They reprint her poems "Remonstrance" and "My Mother" as appendix 1. Also see Claire Midgley, *Women against Slavery: The British Campaigns, 1780–1870* (London: Routledge, 1992), pp. 73–74, 166.

3. Davidoff and Hall, *Family Fortunes*, pp. 66, 455, 457.

4. *Life, Letters, and Posthumous Works of Fredrika Bremer*, ed. Charlotte Bremer [Quiding], trans. Fredr. Milow (New York: Hurd & Houghton, 1868), pp. 82–83. Charlotte Bremer was Frederika's sister.

5. Louise Otto, *Frauenleben im Deutschen Reich: Erinnerungen aus der Vergangenheit mit Hinweis auf Gegenwart und Zukunft* (1876; reprint, Köln: Verlag M. Hüttermann, Paderborn, 1988), p. 15.

6. From John Lawson, *History of North Carolina* (1714), in *Second to None: A Documentary History of American Women*, vol.1, *From the Sixteenth Century to 1865*, ed. Ruth Barnes Moynihan, Cynthia Russett, and Laurie Crumpacker (Lincoln: University of Nebraska Press, 1993), p. 106. Hereafter called *Second to None.*

7. For this subject in England, see Bridget Hill, *Women, Work, and Sexual Politics in Eighteenth-Century England* (Oxford: Basil Blackwell, 1989), chap. 4, "The Undermining of the Family Economy." For the United States, see Gerda Lerner, "The Lady and the Mill Girl: Changes in the Status of Women in the Age of Jackson," in *The Majority Finds Its Past* (New York: Oxford University Press, 1979), pp. 15–30.

8. Cited in Amice Lee, *Laurels and Rosemary: The Life of William and Mary Howitt* (London: Oxford University Press, 1955), p. 126.

9. *The Education of Fanny Lewald: An Autobiography*, translated and annotated by Hanna Ballin Lewis (Albany: State University of New York Press, 1992), pp. 86–87.

10. Louise Otto saw this as the chief cause of German women's discontent in 1876. Otto, *Frauenleben*, pp. 144ff. For this process in England, see Ann Oakley, *Woman's Work: The Housewife, Past and Present* (New York: Vintage, 1976); for the United States, see Glenna Matthews, *Just a Housewife: The Rise and Fall of Domesticity in America* (New York: Oxford University Press, 1987).

11. For England and France, see Louise A. Tilly and Joan W. Scott, *Women, Work, and Family* (New York: Holt, Rinehart & Winston, 1978), pp. 82–83; for the United States, see Faye E. Dudden, *Serving Women: Household Service in Nineteenth-Century America* (Middletown, Conn.: Wesleyan University Press, 1983).

12. For an analysis of this phenomenon in the Nord district of France, see Bonnie G. Smith, *Ladies of the Leisure Class: The Bourgeoises of Northern France in the Nineteenth Century* (Princeton: Princeton University Press, 1981), chaps. 3–4.

13. Cited in Catherine Hall, *White, Male and Middle-Class: Explorations in Feminism and History* (New York: Routledge, 1992), pp. 103–104.

14. From Mrs. A. J. Graves, *Woman in America: Being an Examination into the Moral and Intellectual Condition of American Female Society*, in *Root of Bitterness: Documents of the Social History of American Women*, ed. Nancy F. Cott (New York: Dutton, 1972), p. 147.

15. Cited in Karin Hausen, "Family and Role-Division: The Polarisation of Sexual Stereotypes in the Nineteenth Century-An Aspect of the Disassociation of Work and Family Life," in *The German Family: Essays on the Social History of the Family in Nineteenth- and Twentieth-Century Germany*, ed. Richard J. Evans and W. R. Lee (London: Croon Helm, 1981), p. 64.

16. Wet nurses were most common in royal families, in plantation households of the southern United States, and in France.

17. Bremer, ed., *Life, Letters, and Posthumous Works*, p. 3.

18. Thomas Jefferson to Anne Willing Bingham, May 11, 1788, printed in *Second to None*, 1: 184–185.

19. Cited by G. P. Gooch in the introduction to *The Memoirs of Catherine the Great*, trans. Moura Budberg, ed. Dominique Maroger (New York: Collier, 1961), p. x. On Marie Antoinette, see Lynn Hunt, "The Many Bodies of Marie Antoinette: Political Pornography and the Problem of the Feminine in the French Revolution," in *Eroticism and the Body Politic*, ed. Lynn Hunt (Baltimore, Md.: Johns Hopkins University Press, 1991), pp. 108–130.

20. She wrote this in 1822. Cited in Barbara Corrado Pope, "Revolution and Retreat: Upper-Class French Women after 1789," in *Women, War, and Revolution*, ed. Carol R. Berkin and Clara M. Lovett (New York: Holmes & Meier, 1980), p. 229.

On how the Amazon has functioned in Western culture, see Abby Wettan Kleinbaum, *The War against the Amazons* (New York: McGraw-Hill, 1983).

21. On this subject, see Joan B. Landes, *Women and the Public Sphere in the Age of the French Revolution* (Ithaca, N.Y.: Cornell University Press, 1988); and Isabel V. Hull, "'Sexualität' und bürgerliche Gesellschaft," in *Bürgerinnen und Bürger: Geschlechterverhältnisse im 19. Jahrhundert*, ed. Ute Frevert (Göttingen: Vandenhoeck & Ruprecht, 1988), pp. 49–66.

22. Samuel Johnson to John Taylor, 18 August 1763, in *The Letters of Samuel Johnson*, ed. Bruce Redford (Princeton: Princeton University Press, 1992), 1: 228.

23. Cited in Geneviève Fraisse, *Reason's Muse: Sexual Difference and the Birth of Democracy* [France], trans. Jane Marie Todd (Chicago: University of Chicago Press, 1994), p. 23.

24. Lafayette was on his American tour. Cited in Mary P. Ryan, *Women in Public: Between Banners and Ballots, 1825–1880* [United States] (Baltimore, Md.: Johns Hopkins University Press, 1990), p. 27. For this subject in the United States, see ibid., chap. 1; for France, Landes, *Women and the Public Sphere*; for England, Catherine Hall, "Private Persons versus Public Someones: Class, Gender and Politics in England, 1780–1850," in Hall, *White, Male and Middle Class*, pp. 151–171.

25. Cited in Germaine Greer, *The Obstacle Race* (New York: Farrar, Straus & Giroux, 1979), p. 259.

26. For this argument, see Richard Wortman, "The Russian Empress as Mother," in *The Family in Imperial Russia*, ed. David L. Ransel (Urbana: University of Illinois Press, 1978), pp. 60–61.

27. From "To the Queen," March 1851. This was Tennyson's first poem as poet laureate of England. For "superlative chastity," which was Lord William Russell's comment, and Victoria's symbolizing a new era, see Stanley Weintraub, *Victoria: An Intimate Biography* (New York: Dutton, 1988), pp. 120, 102.

28. For Victoria's presentation of herself, see Elizabeth Longford, *Queen Victoria: Born to Succeed* (New York: Pyramid, 1966), especially chap. 33, "The Jubilee Bonnet."

29. Mrs. Keith of Ravelston, cited in Maurice J. Quinlan, *Victorian Prelude: A History of English Manners, 1700–1830* (New York: Columbia University Press, 1941), p. 1.

30. On this subject, see Barbara Corrado Pope, "Angels in the Devil's Workshop: Leisured and Charitable Women in Nineteenth-Century England and France," in *Becoming Visible: Women in European History*, ed. Renate Bridenthal and Claudia Koonz (Boston: Houghton Mifflin, 1977), pp. 296–324. This article is not in the subsequent editions of *Becoming Visible*.

31. For this reaction in England, see Mary Poovey, *Uneven Developments: The Ideological Work of Gender in Mid-Victorian England* (Chicago: University of Chicago Press, 1988), p. 9 and passim; for Europe, especially Germany, see George L. Mosse, *Nationalism and Sexuality: Middle-Class Morality and Sexual Norms in Modern Europe* (Madison: University of Wisconsin Press, 1985); for the United States, see Ruth H. Bloch, "The Gendered Meanings of Virtue in Revolutionary America," *Signs: Journal of Women in Culture and Society* 13, no. 1 (Autumn 1987), pp. 37–58.

32. Mme. [Albertine Adrienne] Necker de Saussure, *The Study of the Life of Woman* (1838; reprint, Philadelphia: Lea & Blanchard, 1844) p. 217.

For this phenomenon in France, see Margaret H. Darrow, "French Noblewomen and the New Domesticity, 1750–1850," *Feminist Studies* 5, no. 1 (Spring 1979), pp. 41–65; and Barbara Corrado Pope, "Revolution and Retreat: Upper-Class French Women After 1789," in *Women, War, and Revolution*, ed. Carol R. Berkin and Clara M. Lovett (New York: Holmes & Meier, 1980), pp. 215–235.

33. Jean-Jacques Rousseau, *Emile*, trans. Barbara Foxley (London: Everyman's Library, 1974), pp. 350, 370. For Rousseau's ideas about women, see Susan Moller Okin, *Women in Western Political Thought* (Princeton: Princeton University Press, 1977), pt. 3: "Rousseau," pp. 99–196; and Barbara Corrado Pope, "The Influence of Rousseau's Ideology of Domesticity," in *Connecting Spheres: Women in the Western World, 1500 to the Present*, ed. Marilyn J. Boxer and Jean H. Quataert (New York: Oxford University Press, 1987), pp. 136–145.

34. Cited in Fraisse, *Reason's Muse*, p. 14.

35. For Rousseau, see Landes, *Women and the Public Sphere*, p. 85. The phrases from Tennyson's *The Princess: A Medley* (London, 1847) are in bk. 5, lines 435–441.

36. Hausen, "Family and Role-Division," pp. 57–58.

37. For the United States, see Barbara Welter, "The Cult of True Womanhood, 1800–1860," in *Dimity Convictions: The American Woman in the Nineteenth Century* (Athens: Ohio University Press, 1976), pp. 21–41; for England and France, Pope, "Angels in the Devil's Workshop," pp. 302–311, for Germany, Mosse, *Nationalism and Sexuality*, chap. 1.

38. Sarah Stickney Ellis, *Women of England* (1839), cited in Janet Horowitz Murray, *Strong-Minded Women and Other Lost Voices from Nineteenth Century England* (New York: Pantheon, 1982), p. 102.

39. Reprinted in Mary Beth Norton, ed., *Major Problems in American Women's History: Documents and Essays* (Lexington, Mass.: Heath, 1989), pp. 114–116. Rousseau's statement is in *Julie, or the New Heloise*, trans. Barbara Foxley (1760; reprint, London: Everyman's Library, 1975), p. 325.

40. Cited in Murray, *Strong-Minded Women*, pp. 24–26.

41. For the United States, see Ann Douglas, *The Feminization of American Culture* (New York: Alfred A. Knopf, 1977), pt. 1; for Europe, J. Michael Phayer, *Sexual Liberation and Religion in Nineteenth-Century Europe* (London: Croon Helm, 1977).

42. For the angel in the house in France, see Laura S. Strumingher, "L'Ange de la Maison: Mothers and Daughters in Nineteenth-Century France," *International Journal of Women's Studies* 2, no. 1 (January-February 1979), pp. 51–61; for the United States, Welter, "True Womanhood"; and Harvey Green, *The Light of the Home: An Intimate View of the Lives of Women in Victorian America* (1983); for England, France, and and the United States, Erna Olafson Hellerstein, Leslie Parker Hume, and Karen M. Offen, eds., *Victorian Women: A Documentary Account of Women's Lives in Nineteenth-Century England, France, and the United States* (Stanford, Calif.: Stanford University Press, 1981), pp. 134–140, for part of Patmore's "The Angel in the House."

43. Coventry Patmore, *The Angel in the House*, vol. 1, *The Betrothal* (Boston: Ticknor & Fields, 1857), pp. 147, 69.

44. Josephine G. Butler, *Autobiography*, ed. G.A.W. (London, 1911), p. 31.

45. Fanny Lewald, "Für und wieder die Frauen," in *Freiheit des Herzens: Lebensgeschichte—Briefe—Erinnerungen*, ed. Günter de Bruyn und Gerhard Wolf (1870; reprint, Frankfurt am Main: Ullstein Taschenbücher, 1992), p. 276.

46. For George Sand, see André Maurois, *Lélia: The Life of George Sand*, trans. Gerard Hopkins (New York: Harper, 1953), p. 74. For Mrs. Ellis, *Wives of England*, see Murray, *Strong-Minded Women*, pp. 125–126; and Pope, "Angels in the Devil's Workshop," p. 310.

47. Patmore, *Angel in the House*, 1: 94.

48. Hellerstein et. al., *Victorian Women*, p. 97.

49. Bremer, *Life, Letters, and Posthumous Works*, p. 51

50. M. V. Hughes, *A London Girl of the 1880s*, vol. 2 of *A London Family, 1870–1900* (1946; reprint, Oxford: Oxford University Press, 1978), p. 241.

51. Nancy Coffey Heffernan and Ann Page Stecker, *Sisters of Fortune* (Hanover, N.H.: University Press of New England, 1993), pp. 43, 127.

52. For England, see Hall, *Family Fortunes*, pp. 397–415; for Germany, Karin Hausen, "'Eine Ulme für das schwanke Efeu': Ehepaare im Bildungsbürgertum. Ideale und Wirklichkeit im späten 18. und 19. Jahrhundert," in Frevert, *Bürgerinnen und Bürger*, pp. 85–117.

53. Pastoral letter of the Congregational ministers of Massachusetts, reprinted in *Second to None*, 1: 251–252.

54. Dr. Michael Ryan, *A Manual of Midwifery*, 4th ed. (1841), cited in *Women from Birth to Death: The Female Life Cycle in Britain 1830–1914*, ed. Pat Jalland and John Hooper, (Brighton, UK.: Harvester, 1986), p. 20.

55. Jules Michelet, *Love*, cited in *Women, the Family, and Freedom: The Debate in Documents*, vol. 1, *1750–1880*, ed. Susan Groag Bell and Karen M. Offen (Stanford, Calif.: Stanford University Press, 1983), p. 338.

56. E. G. Tilt, *On the Preservation of the Health of Women* (1851), cited in Jalland and Hooper, *Women*, p. 33.

57. Virginia Woolf, "Professions for Women," in *Women and Writing*, by Virginia Woolf, ed. Michèle Barrett (New York: Harcourt Brace Jovanovich, 1979), p. 59.

58. Cited in *Second to None*, 1: 252. For Sarah and Angelina Grimké, see Gerda Lerner, *The Grimké Sisters from South Carolina: Rebels against Slavery* (Boston: Houghton Mifflin, 1967), p. 227.

59. Italics in the original. Cited in *Second to None*, 1: 252–253.

Chapter Three

1. Yuri Suhl, *Ernestine L. Rose: Women's Rights Pioneer*, 2d ed. (New York: Biblio, 1990), pp. 1, i.

2. "Mrs. Ernestine Rose in London," *The Reasoner*, 2 November 1856, p. 139.

3. Jenny P. d'Héricourt, "Madame Rose," *La Revue Philosophique et Religieuse* (1856), 5: 129–139. D'Héricourt's other articles about Rose, published in Italy and the United States, are drawn from this article. Thanks to Karen Offen for help with this point. Besides d'Héricourt's article, the only other contemporary source for Rose's early life is L. E. Barnard, "Ernestine L. Rose," in *History of Woman Suffrage*, vol. 1, *1848–1881*, ed. Elizabeth Cady Stanton, Susan B. Anthony, and Matilda Joslyn Gage (1881; reprint, New York: Arno *New York Times*, 1969), pp. 95–100. For background on Rose's early years, see Suhl, *Ernestine L. Rose*, 1–34.

4. Ernestine Rose, letter, *Boston Investigator*, 26 November 1856, p. 1; d'Héricourt, "Madame Rose," p. 129.

5. D'Héricourt, "Madame Rose," p. 131; Barnard, "Ernestine L. Rose," p. 95; Suhl, *Ernestine L. Rose*, p. 10.

6. D'Héricourt, "Madame Rose," pp. 132–33.

7. For one example of Rose's use of the incident at conventions, see *Proceedings of the National Women's Rights Convention held in Cleveland, Ohio on October 5th, 6th & 7th, 1853* (Cleveland: Grey, Beardsley, Spear, 1854), p. 104. The statement about revealing other women's aptitudes is from an article d'Héricourt wrote in 1856 against the misogynistic views of French socialist P.-J. Proudhon. The English feminist Bessie Rayner Parkes arranged for its translation into English and its publication in *The Reasoner*, 8 March 1857, p. 1. D'Héricourt included it in her *La Femme affranchi* (Bruxelles et Paris: A. Lacroix, Van Meenen & Cie., 1860), 1: 133.

8. D'Héricourt, *La Femme affranchi*, p. 133; Barnard, "Ernestine L. Rose," pp. 95–96.

9. *The London Journal of Flora Tristan 1842 or the Aristocracy and the Working Class of England*, trans. Jean Hawkes (London: Virago Press, 1982), p. 19. By the time she wrote her London journal, Tristan had also traveled to Peru, so her judgment of London was based on a knowledge of Lima as well as of Paris.

10. Tristan, *London Journal*, p. 17. First published in 1840, the journal was based on four trips Tristan took to England, from 1826 to 1839. Rose left no testimony from her years in London in the 1830s about the city; for her 1856 visit, see her letters in the *Boston Investigator*, 6 August 1856, p. 1, and 13 August 1856, p. 1.

11. Cited in Barbara Taylor, *Eve and the New Jerusalem: Socialism and Feminism in the Nineteenth Century* (New York: Pantheon, 1983), p. xii. This is the chief work on women and Owenism.

12. Owen, cited in Taylor, *Eve*, p. 42. Lucretia Mott to Richard and Hannah Webb, 25 February 1842, Boston Public Library, Manuscript Division, Anti-Slavery Collection Ms. A.1.2., vol. 12.2, p. 34, p. 7 of the letter.

13. The names were used interchangeably throughout this era and well into the late nineteenth century.

14. From the *Albany Morning Express*, cited in Suhl, *Ernestine L. Rose*, p. 32.

15. Robert Owen, *The New Moral World*, cited in Suhl, *Ernestine L. Rose*, p. 33.

16. For Owen and feminism, see Taylor, *Eve*, pp. 40ff. For the Owenite communities and women in England, see Taylor, *Eve*, ch. 8, pp. 238–260; for the United States, Carol A. Kolmarten, *Women in Utopia: The Ideology of Gender in the American Owenite Communities* (Bloomington: Indiana University Press, 1990).

17. D'Héricourt, "Madame Rose," p. 134.

18. Ibid., p. 135.

19. Italics in the original. *Proceedings of the Seventh National Woman's Rights Convention, held in New York City at the Broadway Tabernacle on Tuesday & Wednesday, November 25 & 26, 1856* (New York: Edward O. Jenkins, 1856), p. 77.

20. Sixteen of the core twenty were born between these dates. Two were older: Quakers Anne Knight (1786–1862) and Lucretia Mott (1793–1880). Two were younger: the English friends Barbara Leigh Smith Bodichon (1827–1891) and Bessie Rayner Parkes Belloc (1829–1925).

21. Jeanne Deroin, letter to the editor of *La Liberté*, *La Voix des femmes*, 19 April 1848, p. 2. For a discussion of French women's use in 1848 of women from the first French revolution, see Laura S. Strumingher, "Looking Back: Women of 1848 and the Revolutionary Heritage of 1789," in *Women and Politics in the Age of the Democratic Revolution*, ed. Harriet B. Applewhite and Darline G. Levy (Ann Arbor: University of Michigan Press, 1990), pp. 259–285.

22. Madame Suzanne V_____ [Voilquin], *Souvenirs d'une Fille du Peuple ou la Saint-simonienne en Egypte* (Paris: Chez E. Sauzet, 1866), pp. 18–19. For an English translation of parts of this memoir, see Claire Goldberg Moses and Leslie Wahl Rabine, *Feminism, Socialism, and French Romanticism* (Bloomington: Indiana University Press, 1993), pp. 147–177.

23. For Rose, Suhl, *Ernestine L. Rose*, p. 112; Elizabeth Cady Stanton, "Speech at Seneca Falls Convention, July 19, 1848," in *Man Can Not Speak for Her*, vol. 2, *Texts*, ed. Karlyn Kohrs Campbell (New York: Praeger, 1989), pp. 63–70. "Tinga" was Nzinga Mbande (1582–1663).

24. Margaret Fuller, *Woman in the Nineteenth Century* (1855; reprint, New York: Norton, 1971), pp. 93–94.

25. Cited in J. Christopher Herold, *Mistress to an Age: A Life of Madame de Staël* (New York: Time-Life Books, 1958), p. 575.

26. Elizabeth Cady Stanton to Elizabeth Smith Miller, 20 June 1853, printed in Theodore Stanton and Harriot Stanton Blatch, eds., *Elizabeth Cady*

Stanton As Revealed in Her Letters, Diary, and Reminiscences (New York: Harper, 1922), 2: 53. Stanton had just finished reading Lydia Maria Child's 1847 biography of de Staël. See also Caroline H. Dall, "Madame de Staël," *Una*, November 1853, pp. 172–173. For de Staël's influence on Margaret Fuller, see Paula Blanchard, "*Corinne* and the 'Yankee Corinna': Mme. de Staël and Margaret Fuller," in *Woman as Mediatrix: Essays on Nineteenth-Century European Women Writers*, ed. Avriel H. Goldberger (Westport, Conn.: Greenwood, 1987), pp. 39–46.

27. Elizabeth Barrett Browning, *Aurora Leigh: A Poem* (Chicago: Academy, 1979), p. 24. First published in 1856; this edition printed from the 1864 edition.

28. Stanton, Anthony, and Gage, *History of Woman Suffrage*, vol. 1, dedication.

29. *Lucretia Mott: Her Complete Speeches and Sermons*, ed. Dana Greene (New York: Edwin Mellen, 1980), p. 270; Tristan, *London Journal*, p. 253.

30. "Profession de Foi de Melle Jenny De Roin," by Jeanne Deroin, in *De la liberté des femmes: "Lettres de dames" au Globe (1831–1832)*, ed. Michèle Riot-Sarcey (Paris: côté-femmes, 1992), pp. 128–129. Hereafter called Deroin.

31. Italics in the original. From the second feminist journal Otto edited, *Neue Bahnen* (1888), cited in Ruth-Ellen Boetcher Joeres, *Die Anfänge der deutschen Frauenbewegung: Louise Otto-Peters* (Frankfurt am Main: Fischer Taschenbuch Verlag, 1983), pp. 47–48.

32. Barbara Leigh Smith Bodichon letter to Helen Taylor (Harriet Taylor Mill's daughter), 3 August 1869, London School of Economics, Mill-Taylor Collection, vol. 12. Some of Bodichon's letters to Emily Davies date the moment from her visit to Ben at his college in 1851. Barbara Leigh Smith Bodichon to Emily Davies, 1868, Girton College Archives, cited in Sheila R. Herstein, *A Mid-Victorian Feminist, Barbara Leigh Smith Bodichon* (New Haven: Yale University Press, 1985), pp. 171ff.

33. Elizabeth Cady Stanton, *Eighty Years and More: Reminiscences, 1815–1897* (1898; reprint, New York: Schocken, 1971), pp. 20, 23.

34. For other U.S. examples, see Blanche Glassman Hersh, *The Slavery of Sex: Feminist-Abolitionists in America* (Urbana: University of Illinois Press, 1978), p. 134.

35. From "Madame Jenny P. d'Héricourt" in *The Agitator*, Chicago, 1 May 1869, reprinted in Karen Offen, "A Nineteenth-Century French Feminist Rediscovered: Jenny P. D'Héricourt, 1809–1875," *Signs: Journal of Women in Culture and Society* 13, no. 1 (Autumn 1987), p. 151.

36. Paulina Wright Davis manuscript, folder 7D, pp. 13–17, Paulina Wright Davis Papers, Vassar College Library.

37. Reprinted in Stanton, Anthony, and Gage, *History of Woman Suffrage*, 1: 853.

38. For this argument about U.S. feminists, see Hersh, *The Slavery of Sex*, chap. 7, "'A Partnership of Equals': The Role of Husbands in the Women's Movement," pp. 228–251.

39. D'Héricourt, "Madame Rose," pp. 138–139; Barnard, "Ernestine L. Rose," p. 98; Suhl, *Ernestine L. Rose*, p. 268. The friend was Charles Bradlaugh, the English atheist and women's rights supporter.

40. Margaret Hope Bacon, *Valiant Friend: The Life of Lucretia Mott* (New York: Walker, 1980), pp. 30–31. Quotation cited in *Margaret Hope Bacon, Mothers of Feminism: The Story of Quaker Women in America* (New York: Harper & Row, 1989), p. 112.

41. Gerhard K. Friesen, "A Letter from M. F. Anneke: A Forgotten German-American Pioneer in Women's Rights," *Journal of German-American Studies* 12, no.2 (1977), p. 35.

42. For Bremer's decision not to marry, see *Brita K. Stendahl, The Education of a Self-Made Woman: Fredrika Bremer, 1801–1865* (Lewiston, N.Y.: Edwin Mellen, 1994), chaps. 1, 5. For von Meysenbug, her *Memoiren einer Idealistin* (Berlin: Schuster & Loeffler, 1881), 1: 219–220. There is an English translation that is virtually complete for her life up to 1860; for this passage, see Malwida von Meysenbug, *Memoirs: Rebel in Bombazine*, trans. Elsa von Meysenbug Lyons, ed. Mildred Adams (New York: Norton, 1936), p. 111. For Roland, Edith Thomas, *Pauline Roland: Socialisme et Féminisme au XIXe Siècle* (Paris: Marcel Rivière, 1956), passim.

43. Carl Schurz became a U.S. senator and political reform leader; this passage is from his memoirs, reprinted in Gerlinde Hummel-Haasis, ed., *Schwestern zerreist eure Kettern: Zeugnisse zur Geschichte der Frauen in der Revolution von 1848/49* (Munich: Deutscher Taschenbuch Verlag, 1982), p. 234. The hostile description is on pages 234–235.

44. Italics in the original. Mariannne Finch, *An Englishwoman's Experience in America* (London: Richard Bentley, 1853), p. 209.

45. Pauline Wright Davis to Elizabeth Cady Stanton, 12 December 1852, Elizabeth Cady Stanton Papers, Manuscript Division, Library of Congress, reel 1.

46. For Sand and gender, see Donna Dickenson, *George Sand: A Brave Man—The Most Womanly Woman* (Oxford: Berg Publishers, 1988). Barrett's two sonnets, "A Desire" and "A Recognition," from her *Poems* (1844), are reprinted in Elaine Hedges and Ingrid Wendt, *In Her Own Image: Women Working in the Arts* (New York: Feminist Press, 1980), p. 226.

47. For this topic, see Carroll Smith-Rosenberg, "The Female World of Love and Ritual: Relations between Women in Nineteenth-Century America," in her *Disorderly Conduct: Visions of Gender in Victorian America* (New York: Oxford University Press, 1986), pp. 53–76 and Lillian Faderman, *Surpassing the Love of Men: Romantic Friendship and Love between Women from the Renaissance to the Present* (New York: William Morrow, 1981).

48. Cited in *Biographical Notes in Commemoration of Fritz Anneke and Mathilde Franziska Anneke*, by Henriette M. Heinzen with Hertha Anneke Sanne (the surviving twin, named for Fredrika Bremer's heroine and then 85), 1940, p. 148, Mathilde Franziska Anneke Papers, State Historical Society of Wisconsin. Much of Booth's correspondence with the Annekes and theirs with each other during these years is printed in Maria Wagner, *Mathilde Franziska Anneke in*

Selbstzeugnissen und Dokumenten (Frankfurt am Main: Fischer Taschenbuch Verlag, 1980), pp. 97–221.

49. For this argument, see Jane Rendall, "Friendship and Politics: Barbara Leigh Smith Bodichon (1827–91) and Bessie Rayner Parkes (1829–1925)," in *Sexuality and Subordination: Interdisciplinary Studies of Gender in the Nineteenth Century*, ed. Susan Mendus and Jane Rendall (London: Routledge, 1989), pp. 136–170. The quotation is on p. 150.

50. The phrase is George Eliot's (*Letters*, 2: 45). Cited in Jacquie Matthews, "Barbara Bodichon: Integrity in Diversity," in *Feminist Theorists: Three Centuries of Women's Intellectual Traditions*, ed. Dale Spender (London: Women's Press, 1983), p. 92.

51. Parkes Papers, Girton College, Cambridge, U.K., Bessie Rayner Parkes Diary, November 1, 1849, Parkes Papers, vol. 1, 4, 11; Barbara Leigh Smith to Bessie Rayner Parkes, c. 1849, vol. 5, 166.

52. Cited in Hester Burton, *Barbara Bodichon, 1827–1891* (London: John Murray, 1949), p. 92.

53. Dr. Elizabeth Blackwell, *Pioneer Work in Opening the Medical Profession to Women: Autobiographical Sketches* (1895; reprint, New York: Schocken, 1977), p. 175. The poem is "To E.B." in B. R. Parkes, *Poems* (London: John Chapman, 1852), p. 94. The letter is Bessie Rayner Parkes to Barbara Leigh Smith, 15 April 1852, Parkes Papers, Girton College, Cambridge, U.K., vol. 5, 62.

54. Channing's 1819 sermon on the ordination of Jared Sparks is the classic statement of Unitarianism in this era. It is reprinted in H. Shelton Smith, Robert T. Handy, and Lefferts A. Loetscher, *American Christianity: An Historical Interpretation with Representative Documents* (New York: Scribner's, 1960), pp. 493–502.

55. Bessie Rayner Parkes to Barbara Leigh Smith, 1849, Parkes Papers, Girton College, Cambridge, Bessie Rayner Parkes, vol. 5, 33.

56. Lucretia Mott, sermon, Cherry Street Meeting, Philadelphia, September 16, 1849, in *Complete Speeches and Sermons*, p. 101.

57. Barbara Leigh Smith Bodichon, *An American Diary: 1857–1858*, ed. Joseph W. Reed Jr. (London: Routledge and Kegan Paul, 1972), p. 158.

58. Deroin, p. 129.

59. For this argument in the United States, see Martha Tomhave Blauvelt, "Women and Revivalism," in *Women and Religion in America*, vol. 1, *The Nineteenth Century*, Rosemary Radford Ruether and Rosemary Skinner Keller (New York: Harper & Row, 1982), pp. 1–9; for the New Jersey girl, p. 16; for Rush, p. 3. Statistical evidence in England does not exist on female churchgoing, but impressionistic testimony points to the same growing predominance of women there. See *Religion in the Lives of English Women, 1760–1930*, ed. Gail Malmgreen (London: Croon Helm, 1986), pp. 2–3. For France and Germany, see J. Michael Phayer, *Sexual Liberation and Religion in Nineteenth-Century Europe* (London: Croon Helm, 1977).

60. For this subject, see Nathan O. Hatch, *The Democratization of American Christianity* (New Haven: Yale University Press, 1989), pp. 3–8.

61. Cited in Walter L. Arnstein, "Queen Victoria and Religion," *Religion in the Lives of English Women*, ed. Malmgreen, p. 90.

62. Cited in Phayer, *Sexual Liberation*, p. 95.

63. Voilquin, *Souvenirs*, p. 3.

64. G. J. Holyoake, *The History of the Last Trial by Jury for Atheism in England* (London, 1850); Infidel Society material cited in Suhl, *Ernestine L. Rose*, p. 85.

65. Mazzini stated this in the presence of Garibaldi, who replied, "I am an atheist. Have I then no sense of duty?" "Ah," replied Mazzini, "You imbibed a sense of duty with your mother's milk." This anecdote, reported by Holyoake, is cited in Priscilla Robertson, *Revolutions of 1848: A Social History* (Princeton: Princeton University Press, 1952), p. 366.

66. Italics in the original. Jenny D'Héricourt, "Mrs. Ernestine L. Rose," *Boston Investigator*, December 8, 1869, p. 4.

67. The book was Harriet Martineau and Henry G. Atkinson, *Letters on the Laws of Man's Nature and Development* (London, 1851). *Mary Howitt: An Autobiography*, ed. Margaret Howitt, 2 vols. (London: Wm. Isbister, 1889), 2: 69; Margaret Howitt was Mary Howitt's daughter. Edward Quillinan to Henry Crabbe Robinson, March 14-April 28, 1851, cited in Valerie Kossew Pichanick, *Harriet Martineau: The Woman and Her Work, 1802–76* (Ann Arbor: University of Michigan Press, 1980), p. 190.

68. For Aston's account of this incident, see Germaine Goetzinger, *Für die Selbstwirklichung der Frau: Louise Aston* (Frankfurt am Main: Fischer Taschenbuch Verlag, 1983), p. 69. Mathilde Franziska Anneke, "Das Weib im Conflict mit den social Verhaeltnissen," typescript, Mathilde Franziska Anneke Papers, State Historical Society of Wisconsin, p. 11.

69. Italics in the original. Von Meysenbug, *Idealistin*, 1: 172–173.

70. Louise Dittmar, *Vier Zeitfragen* (Offenbach am Main: Gustav André, 1847), p. 23.

71. *Life, Letters, and Posthumous Works of Fredrika Bremer*, ed. Charlotte Bremer, trans. Fredr. Milow (New York: Hurd & Houghton, 1868), p. 133.

72. Cited in Stendahl, *Education of a Self-Made Woman*, p. 174. François de Fénélon (1651–1715) was a French archbishop and educator; William Ellery Channing (1780–1842), an influential U.S. Unitarian minister; François de Sales, a sixteenth-century French cleric; Hermann Francke (1663–1727) a pietist German minister; Hildebrand a medieval German hero; Martin Luther (1483–1536), leader of the German Reformation; George Washington (1732–1799), first president of the United States, represented republicanism. Alexandre Vinet (1797–1847) was a Swiss Protestant minister; St. Birgetta (1303–1373), a visionary who is the patron saint of Sweden; Florence Nightingale, (1820–1910) the English nursing reformer and hospital administrator. All the above were Christian; Laotze, Zarathustra, Buddha, Socrates, and Spinoza represented Eastern religions, philosophy, and in Spinoza's case, either Judaism or pantheism.

73. Von Meysenbug, *Idealisten*, 1: 173.

Chapter Four

1. The piece is reprinted in Richard K.P. Pankhurst, *The Saint Simonians, Mill and Carlyle: A Preface to Modern Thought* (London: Sidgwick & Jackson, 1957), pp. 109–111.

2. For a more recent translation of this "Appel aux Femmes," see Claire Goldberg Moses and Leslie Wahl Rabine, *Feminism, Socialism, and French Romanticism* (Bloomington: Indiana University Press, 1993), pp. 282–284. Thanks to Claire Moses for sharing her copy of the original French document with me.

3. Moses and Rabine, *Feminism*, pp. 282–283.

4. Such novels included Flora Tristan's *Méphis, ou le roman d'un prolétaire* (1838), Louise Aston's *Aus dem Leben einer Frau* (1847), and Louise Otto's *Schloss und Fabrik* (1847). Generally, the novels feminists read were written by authors not active in the international socialist movement, like Charlotte Brontë and George Sand. These works are discussed in chapter 6.

5. Désirée Véret to Charles Fourier, 29 October 1833, in Michèle Riot-Sarcey, "Lettres de Charles Fourier et de Désirée Véret: Une correspondance inédite," *Cahiers Charles Fourier* 6 (1995), p. 5.

6. *First Feminists* is the title of Moira Ferguson's anthology of British women writers, 1578–1799 (Bloomington: Indiana University Press, 1985). For an expanded version of this argument, see Bonnie S. Anderson and Judith P. Zinsser, *A History of Their Own: Women in Europe from Prehistory to the Present* (New York: Oxford University Press, 2000), 2: 333–349.

7. Judith Sargent Murray's "On the Equality of the Sexes," which appeared under her pen name, Constantia, was published in the Boston *Massachusetts Magazine* in 1790; Theodor von Hippel's *On Improving the Civic Status of Women* (*Uber die bürgerliche Verbesserung der Weiber*) in Berlin in 1792. Other major feminist treatises of the 1790s include the Marquis de Condorcet's *Admission of Women to Civic Rights* (1790) as well as the works of Wollstonecraft and Gouges discussed below.

8. Mary Wollstonecraft, *A Vindication of the Rights of Woman*, ed. Carol H. Poston (1792; reprint, New York: Norton, 1975), pp. 5–6.

9. Lucretia Mott to Elizabeth Cady Stanton, 16 March 1855, Elizabeth Cady Stanton Papers, Manuscript Division, Library of Congress, reel 1; Wilhelm Schulte, "Mathilde Franziska Anneke," *Westfälische Lebensbilder* (Münster: Aschendorffische Verlag, 1958), 8: 130.

10. *Almanach des femmes. Seconde année. Women's Almanack for 1853, in the English and French Languages* (London: James Watson; Jersey: Universal Printing Establishment, 1853), p. 12.

11. Gouges's *Declaration of the Rights of Woman* is reprinted in Darline Gay Levy, Harriet Branson Applewhite, and Mary Durham Johnson, *Women in Revolutionary Paris, 1789–1795* (Urbana: University of Illinois Press, 1979), pp. 87–96; for the Assembly's law against women's clubs, pp. 216–217. On the Society of

Revolutionary Republican Women, see Margaret George, "The 'World Historical Defeat' of the Républicaines-Révolutionaires," *Science and Society* 40, no. 4 (Winter 1976–1977), pp. 410–437.

12. Mary Wollstonecraft, *Maria or the Wrongs of Woman*, introduction by Moira Ferguson (1798; reprint, New York: Norton, 1975), p. 27.

13. Jeanne Deroin, "Profession de Foi de Melle Jenny De Roin," in *De la liberté des femmes: "Lettres de dames" au Globe (1831–1832)*, ed. Michèle Riot-Sarcey (Paris: côté-femmes, 1992), p. 129. Hereafter called "Profession de Foi."

14. Cited in William Thompson, *Appeal of One Half the Human Race, Women, against the Pretensions of the Other Half, Men, to Retain Them in Political, and Thence in Civil and Domestic Slavery* (1825; reprint, London: Virago, 1983), p. 9. Hereafter called *Appeal*.

15. Reprinted in Ruth Barnes Moynihan, Cynthia Russett, and Laurie Crumpacker, eds., *Second to None: A Documentary History of American Women*, vol. 1: *From the 16th Century to 1865* (Lincoln: University of Nebraska Press, 1993), p. 204.

16. Shelley, "The Revolt of Islam," canto 2, stanza 43, line 1. Thanks to Scarlett Freund for help in finding this line.

17. Italics in the original. Cited in Jonathan Beecher, *Charles Fourier: The Visionary and His World* (Berkeley: University of California Press, 1986), p. 208.

18. Cited in Richard K.P. Pankhurst, "Anna Wheeler: A Pioneer Socialist and Feminist," *Political Quarterly* 25 (1954), p. 133. For Wheeler's life, see "Anna Wheeler," pp. 132–143; Margaret McFadden, "Anna Doyle Wheeler (1785–1848): Philosopher, Socialist, Feminist," *Hypatia* 4, no. 1 (Spring 1989), pp. 91–101; and Barbara Taylor, *Eve and the New Jerusalem: Socialism and Feminism in the Nineteenth Century* (New York: Pantheon, 1983), pp. 59–64.

19. From the preface to *Peregrinations of a Pariah* (1838) in Moses and Rabine, *Feminism*, p. 211.

20. "Profession de Foi," p. 133.

21. *Appeal*, p. xxx.

22. Ibid.

23. Moses and Rabine, *Feminism*, p. 283.

24. The Harriet Martineau quotation is from her *History of the Thirty Years' Peace* (1849), cited in Pankhurst, *Saint-Simonians*, p. 1; for Marx, p. ix; for Mill, pp. 147–150. The Mill quotation is from his *Autobiography*, in John Stuart Mill, *Collected Works*, 1: 175, cited in Gail Tulloch, *Mill and Sexual Equality* (Hemel Hempstead: Harvester Wheatsheaf, 1989), p. 22.

25. Karl Marx and Friedrich Engels, *The Manifesto of the Communist Party*, end of section 3. Also see Friedrich Engels, *Socialism: Utopian and Scientific* (1880).

26. Deroin, "Profession de Foi," p. 116.

27. *Appeal*, pp. xxii, xxi.

28. *Appeal*, p. 132.

29. *Appeal*, pp. 56, 65, 67, 64–65.

30. *Appeal*, pp. 200, 187; Pankhurst, *Saint-Simonians*, pp. 94–95.

31. Cited in Taylor, *Eve*, p. 60. The friend was James Elishama "Shepherd" Smith, coeditor of the *The Crisis*.

32. Anna Wheeler, "Rights of Women," *The British Co-operator*, 1: 1.

33. Taylor, *Eve*, p. 67

34. A. J. G. Perkins and Theresa Wolfson, *Frances Wright, Free Enquirer: The Study of a Temperament* (New York: Harper, 1939), p. 53. For Wright's life, see this biography, which is not completely reliable: Celia Morris Eckhardt, *Fanny Wright: Rebel in America* (Cambridge: Harvard University Press, 1984); and Carol A. Kolmerten, *Women in Utopia: The Ideology of Gender in the American Owenite Communities* (Bloomington: Indiana University Press, 1990), chap. 4, "Frances Wright: A Woman in Utopia," pp. 111–141.

35. Cited in Arthur Bestor, *Backwoods Utopias: The Sectarian Origins and the Owenite Phase of Communitarian Socialism in America, 1663–1829*, 2d enl. ed. (Philadelphia: University of Pennsylvania Press, 1957), p. 222. For Owenite communities in the United States, see Kolmerten's *Women in Utopia* and J. F. C. Harrison, *Robert Owen and the Owenites in Britain and America: The Quest for the New Moral World* (London: Routledge & Kegan Paul, 1969).

36. From the Indianapolis *Indiana Journal*, 14 November 1826, cited in Bestor, *Backwoods Utopias*, p. 223.

37. Frances Trollope, *Domestic Manners of the Americans*, cited in Perkins and Wolfson, *Frances Wright*, p. 213.

38. Cited in Kolmerten, *Women in Utopia*, p. 113; cited in Perkins & Wolfson, *Frances Wright*, p. 193.

39. Madison cited in Eckhardt, *Fanny Wright*, p. 166; the Martineau quotation is from an obituary she wrote about herself in 1855, when Martineau thought she was dying (she lived until 1876). First published in Harriet Martineau, *Autobiography*, 2 vols., edited and with memorials by Maria Weston Chapman (Boston: Houghton Mifflin, 1877), pp. 415–427; reprinted in Gayle Graham Yates, *Harriet Martineau on Women* (New Brunswick, N.J.: Rutgers University Press, 1985), p. 41.

40. For Crandall, see Moynihan, Russett, and Crumpacker, eds., *Second to None*, 1: 318.

41. James Mott, *Three Months in Great Britain* (Philadelphia: J. Miller M'Kim, 1841), p. 64. Josephine Brown cited in *We Are Your Sisters: Black Women in the Nineteenth Century*, ed. Dorothy Sterling (New York: Norton, 1984), p. 146.

42. Mary Shelley was Mary Wollstonecraft Godwin's posthumous daughter and the poet Percy Bysshe Shelley's widow. The letter is cited in Eckhardt, *Fanny Wright*, p. 151.

43. From the *Biography, Notes, and Political Letters of Frances Wright D'Arusmont* (New York: John Windt, 1844), pp. 29–30, reprinted in Frances Wright D'Arusmont, *Life, Letters, and Lectures 1834/1844* (New York: Arno, 1972). For the boarding schools, see her speech "Of Existing Evils and the Remedy" (Philadelphia, 1829), reprinted in this volume, pp. 101–116.

44. For Dale Owen and Wright's advocacy of contraception, see Angus McLaren, *Birth Control in Nineteenth Century England* (New York: Holmes & Meier, 1978), pp. 53ff, 85.

45. Rose was describing Wright to the American poet Walt Whitman, who had heard Wright lecture in New York City in 1829 when he was a boy of ten. Walt Whitman, *Notebooks and Unpublished Prose Manuscripts*, ed. Edward F. Grier (New York: New York University Press, 1984), 1: 344.

46. Elizabeth Barrett Browning, *Aurora Leigh* (1856; reprint, Chicago: Academy Chicago, 1979), book 7, p. 266; Barrett Browning cited by Gardner B. Taplin in the introduction, p. xx.

47. Cited in Maclaren, *Birth Control*, p. 102 n. 25. For one example of Wright's example used to threaten other women, see Valerie Kossew Pichanick, *Harriet Martineau: The Woman and Her Work, 1802–1876* (Ann Arbor: University of Michigan Press, 1980), p. 100.

48. Gerhard K. Friesen, "A Letter from M. F. Anneke: A Forgotten German-American Pioneer in Women's Rights," *Journal of German-American Studies* 12, no. 2 (1977), p. 35.

49. Cited in Kolmerten, *Women in Utopia*, p. 140.

50. Louise Aston, "An George Sand," in *Frauenemanzipation im deutschen Vormärz: Texte und Dokumente*, ed. Renate Möhrmann (Stuttgart: Philipp Reclam, 1978), p. 61; Ashurst cited in Kathryn Gleadle, *The Early Feminists: Radical Unitarians and the Emergence of the Women's Rights Movement, 1831–51* [England] (New York: St. Martin's, 1995), p. 61.

51. Moncure Daniel Conway, cited in Diane Mary Chase Worzala, "The Langham Place Circle: The Beginnings of the Organized Women's Movement in England, 1854–1870" (Ph.D. diss., University of Wisconsin, 1982), p. 80.

52. Sand's letter to the editors of *Voix des femmes* was published in *La Réforme* and is reprinted in Adrien Ranvier, "Une Féministe de 1848: Jeanne Deroin," *La Révolution de 1848: Bulletin de la Société d'histoire de la révolution de 1848*, vol. 4 (1907–1908), p. 332; Sand's pamphlet about the *Académie* was "Pourquoi les Femmes à l'Académie?"

53. Taylor, *Eve*, p. 62.

54. Letter to M. Jullien, cited in Taylor, *Eve*, p. 61.

55. Ernestine Rose, letter to the *Boston Investigator*, 15 October 1856, p. 1; for the impact of the Revolution of 1830 on the Saint-Simonians, see Moses and Rabine, *Feminism*, pp. 20–21.

56. "L'homme et la femme, voilà l'individu social." For a discussion of this topic, see Marguerite Thibert, *Le Féminisme dans le socialisme français de 1830 à 1850* (Paris: Marcel Giard, 1926), pp. 8–9.

57. Cited in Thibert, *Féminisme*, p. 63.

58. Pankhurst, *Saint-Simonians*, pp. 109–110.

59. Suzanne Voilquin, *Memories of a Daughter of the People*, reprinted in Moses and Rabine, *Feminism*, p. 164. For similar testimony from Deroin, see her "Profession de Foi," p. 133, cited above.

60. Martineau, *Autobiography*, 1: 334. Also see her article "The Martyr Age of the United States," originally published in the *Westminster Review* and reprinted in 1839; Lucretia Mott, *Her Complete Speeches and Sermons*, ed. Dana Greene (New York: Edwin Mellen, 1980), p. 270.

61. Pankhurst, *Saint-Simonians*, p. 23.

62. Riot-Sarcey, *De la liberté des femmes*, p. 71.

63. Moses and Rabine, *Feminism*, pp. 35ff.; Claire Démar, *My Law of the Future*, reprinted in Moses and Rabine, *Feminism*, p. 179.

64. *Tribune des femmes* 1, no. 1, pp. 6–8, reprinted in Moses and Rabine, *Feminism*, pp. 286–287.

65. Démar, *My Law of the Future*, reprinted in Moses and Rabine, *Feminism*, p. 179; *Tribune des femmes*, p. 291.

66. *Tribune des femmes*, pp. 303, 296.

67. Deroin, "Profession de Foi," p. 135; *Tribune des femmes*, p. 296.

68. Cited in Ruth-Ellen Boetscher Joeres, *Die Anfänge der deutschen Frauenbewegung: Louise Otto-Peters* (Frankfurt am Main: Fischer Taschenbuch Verlag, 1983), p. 86.

69. *Turning the World Upside Down: The Anti-Slavery Convention of American Women*, introduction by Dorothy Sterling (1837; reprint, New York: Feminist Press at the City University of New York, 1987), p. 21.

70. Theodore Stanton and Harriot Stanton Blatch, eds., *Elizabeth Cady Stanton As Revealed in Her Letters, Diary, and Reminiscences* (New York: Harper, 1922), 2: 15–6.

71. Pankurst, *Saint-Simonians*, p. 109. Wheeler and Thompson's *Appeal* argued that socialism would emancipate women. For Désirée Véret's use of this phrase, see *Tribune des femmes*, p. 289.

72. *Tribune des femmes*, p. 316.

73. *Tribune des femmes*, pp. 290, 315.

74. *Tribune des femmes*, pp. 284, 288–289.

75. C.B. [Catherine Barmby], *The Apostle, and Chronicle of the Communist Church*, 1 August 1848, p. 5; Louise Otto, "My Program as a Contributer to a Women's Newspaper" in *Das Wesen der Ehe*, ed. Louise Dittmar (Leipzig: Verlag Otto Wiegand, 1849), p. 20; reprinted in Möhrmann, *Frauenemanzipation im deutschen Vormärz*, p. 198. Thanks to Dagmar Herzog for sharing her copy of the original with me.

76. *Tribune des femmes*, pp. 321, 323–327.

77. *My Law of the Future*, p. 203.

78. Anne Knight, *Diary*, Anne Knight Papers, Library of the Society of Friends, Friends House, London, MS vol. S486. The most complete collection of her labels, including some in French, is pasted into Knight's copy of Marion Reid's *A Plea for Woman*, also in the Knight Papers. For this label in the United States, see Anne Knight to Hannah Webb, April 6, 1847, Ms.A.1.2, vol. 12.1, p. 119, Anti-Slavery Collection, Manuscript Division, Boston Public Library. For Knight ordering a thousand "labels (various colors)" from the Dublin printer Richard Webb, see the previous letter in this volume, Anne Knight to Hannah Webb (Richard was her husband), 12 October 1841, Ms.A.1.2, vol. 12.1, p. 118.

79. Theodore Stanton, *Reminiscences of Rosa Bonheur* (New York: D. Appleton, 1910), p. 61. Thanks to Laura Cannistraci for sharing this reference with me.

Chapter Five

1. Louise Otto, "Programm," *Frauen-Zeitung*, 21 April 1849, p. 1. Reprinted in *"Dem Reich der Freiheit werb' ich Bürgerinnen": Die Frauen-Zeitung von Louise Otto*, ed. Ute Gerhard, Elisabeth Hannover Drück, and Romina Schmitter (Frankfurt am Main: Syndikat, 1980), pp. 39–41.

2. Louise Otto-Peters, *Das Erste Vierteljahrhundert des allgemeinen deutschen Frauenvereins* (Leipzig: Moritz Schäfer, 1890), p. 1.

3. Otto Stern [Louise Otto], "Zur Frauenemancipation", *Unser Planet: Blätter für Unterhaltung, Literatur, Kunst, und Theater*, ed. Ernst Keil, 28 (February 1843), pp. 107. Portions of this article are reprinted in Ruth-Ellen Boetcher Joeres, *Die Anfänge der deutschen Frauenbewegung: Louise Otto-Peters* (Frankfurt am Main: Fischer Taschenbuch Verlag, 1983), pp. 71–73.

4. Cited in Amice Lee, *Laurels and Rosemary: The Life of William and Mary Howitt* (London: Oxford University Press, 1955), p. 146. The Howitts lived in Heidelberg from 1840 to 1843.

5. Reprinted in Karlyn Kohrs Campbell, *Man Can Not Speak for Her* (New York: Praeger Publishers, 1989), 2: 43. For another example, see Harriet Martineau, *How to Observe Manners and Morals* (1838), cited in Gayle Graham Yates, *Harriet Martineau on Women* (New Brunswick, N.J.: Rutgers University Press, 1985), p. 61.

6. Otto Stern, "Zur Frauenemancipation," p. 108; Boetcher Joeres, *Anfänge*, p. 73.

7. Louise Otto, letter to *Sächsischen Vaterlandsblätter*, ed. Robert Blum, September 1843, reprinted in Boetcher Joeres, *Anfänge*, p. 76; see also, pp. 39, 48, 63. The visitor was German author Karl Albrecht, who thought "it would be difficult to find a man who could do two such different things as reading and knitting at once—reading and smoking, maybe."

8. Louise Dittmar, *Vier Zeitfragen* (Offenbach am Main: Gustav André, 1847), p. 25.

9. Louise Otto, *Frauenleben im Deutschen Reich: Erinnerungen aus der Vergangenheit mit Hinweis auf Gegenwart und Zukunft* (1876; reprint, Köln: Verlag M. Hüttermann, Paderborn, 1988), p. 183.

10. For the equation of women's writing with prostitution, see Dorothy Mermin, *Godiva's Ride: Women of Letters in England, 1830–1880* (Bloomington: Indiana University Press, 1993), p. xiv; for Hawthorne, Louise Hall Tharp, *The Peabody Sisters of Salem* (1950; reprint, Boston: Little, Brown, 1988), p. 161.

11. Cited in Dorothy Mermin, *Elizabeth Barrett Browning: The Origins of a New Poetry* (Chicago: University of Chicago Press, 1989), p. 1.

12. Elizabeth Cady Stanton to John Greenleaf Whittier, in *Elizabeth Cady Stanton As Revealed in Her Letters, Diary, and Reminiscences*, ed. Theodore Stanton and Harriot Stanton Blatch (New York: Harper, 1922), 2: 14

13. Margaret Fuller, *Woman in the Nineteenth Century* (1845; reprint, New York: Norton, 1971), p. 30.

14. Boetcher Joeres, *Anfänge*, pp. 35, 57. The diary no longer exists.

15. Cited in Barbara Bardes and Suzanne Gossett, *Declarations of Independence: Women and Political Power in Nineteenth-Century American Fiction* (New Brunswick, N.J.: Rutgers University Press, 1990), p. 5.

16. *Douglas Jerrold's Shilling Magazine*, cited in Kathryn Gleadle, *The Early Feminists: Radical Unitarians and the Emergence of the Women's Rights Movement, 1831–51* (New York: St. Martin's, 1995), p. 55.

17. On this subject, see Rachel M. Brownstein, *Becoming a Heroine: Reading about Women in Novels* (New York: Penguin, 1984), passim.

18. Mary Wollstonecraft, *A Vindication of the Rights of Woman*, ed. Carol H. Poston (New York: Norton, 1975), pp. 184–185.

19. Louise Otto, *Frauen-Zeitung*, 31 March 1852, p. 95.

20. The portraits are mentioned in her friend Auguste Scheibe's memoir of Otto, reprinted in Boetcher Joeres, *Anfänge*, p. 136.

21. Cited in Gerlinde Hummel-Haasis, ed., *Schwestern zerreist eure Kettern: Zeugnisse zur Geschichte der Frauen in der Revolution von 1848/9* (München: Deutscher Taschenbuch Verlag, 1982), p. 150. Barrett's sonnets to Sand, "A Desire" and "A Recognition," were both published in 1844. Otto's poem "To George Sand" appeared in her *Frauen-Zeitung*, 2 June 1849, and is partially reprinted in Louise Otto, *Dem Reich der Freiheit werb' ich Bürgerinnen*, p. 85. Other poetic tributes to Sand were written by the Germans Louise Aston and Ida Reinsberg-Düringsfeld. For Sand's influence on English women authors, see Mermin, *Godiva's Ride*, pp. 20, 53; and Patricia Thomson, *George Sand and the Victorians* (New York: Columbia University Press, 1977), passim.

22. George Sand, *Indiana*, trans. Eleanor Hochman (1832; reprint, New York: Signet Classic, 1993), pp. 26 (from the preface to the second edition), 184.

23. Fredrika Bremer, *The Homes of the New World: Impressions of America*, trans. Mary Howitt (New York: Harper & Brothers, 1853), 1: 14.

24. For translations of Bremer's works, including those into Dutch and Russian, see Brita K. Stendahl, *Fredrika Bremer: The Education of a Self-Made Woman, 1801–1865* (Lewiston, N.Y.: Edwin Mellen, 1994), p. 190 n. 1; for Bremer's letter to Sophie Bolander, Stendahl, *Fredrika Bremer*, p. 178.

25. Fredrika Bremer, *Brothers and Sisters*, trans. Mary Howitt (London: Henry Colburn, 1848), 1: 12.

26. For Bremer and Jane Eyre, see Fredrika Bremer, *The Homes of the New World*, 2: 227; for Anthony, see Kathleen Barry, *Susan B. Anthony: A Biography of a Singular Feminist* (New York: New York University Press, 1988), p. 106.

27. Cited in Mary Poovey, *Uneven Developments: The Ideological Work of Gender in Mid-Victorian England* (Chicago: University of Chicago Press, 1988), p. 135.

28. Charlotte Brontë, *Jane Eyre* (London, 1847), chap. 12, p. 141.

29. *Una* 3 (July 1855), p. 104.

30. The article Otto reprinted was by German novelist Fanny Lewald. *Frauen-Zeitung* 1 May 1852, p. 130. Caroline Dall in *Reports on the Laws of New England, Presented to the New England Meeting convened at the Meionan, Spt. 19 & 20, 1855* (Boston), p. 7.

31. From the preface to *Peregrinations of a Pariah*, cited in Màire Cross and Tim Gray, *The Feminism of Flora Tristan* (Oxford: Berg, 1992), p. 27.

32. Harriet Martineau, *Autobiography* (1877; reprint, Boston: Houghton, Mifflin, 1885), 1: 141.

33. *Lily*, 1 November 1849. Other prominent female authors of the era who discarded their early pseudonyms included Charlotte and Emily Brontë, Elizabeth Gaskell, and Louisa May Alcott. Thanks to Linda Grasso for help with this point.

34. Louise Otto, Letter to *Sächsichen Vaterlandsblätter*, cited in Boetcher Joeres, *Anfänge*, pp. 74–77.

35. Otto Stern, "Zur Frauenemancipation," p. 107; Boetcher Joeres, *Anfänge*, p. 72.

36. Otto Stern, "Zur Frauenemancipation," p. 108; Boetcher Joeres, *Anfänge*, p. 73.

37. Lucretia Mott, "Discourse on Woman," in *Lucretia Mott: Her Complete Speeches and Sermons*, ed. Dana Greene (New York: Edwin Mellen, 1980), p. 148. The paragraph concluded, "True, nature has made a difference in her configuration, her physical strength, her voice, &c.—and we ask no change, we are satisfied with nature. But how has neglect and mismanagement increased this difference!"

38. Sarah Grimké to Elizabeth Pease, 11 February 1842, in Clare Taylor, *British and American Abolitionists: An Episode in Transatlantic Understanding* (Edinburgh: Edinburgh University Press, 1974), p. 163.

39. For illuminating discussions of this topic among the Saint-Simonian New Women, see Claire Goldberg Moses, "Debating the Present, Writing the Past: 'Feminism' in French History and Historiography," *Radical History Review* 52 (1992), pp. 79–94; and "'Equality' and 'Difference' in Historical Perspective: A Comparative Examination of the Feminisms of French Revolutionaries and Utopian Socialists," in *Rebel Daughters: Women and the French Revolution*, ed. Sara E. Melzer and Leslie W. Rabine (New York: Oxford University Press, 1992), pp. 231–254. For one example of Rose's use of this argument, see the *Proceedings of the National Women's Rights Convention, held at Cleveland, Ohio on Oct. 5th, 6th, and 7th, 1853* (Cleveland: Grey, Beardsley, Spear, 1854), p. 36. For Jeanne Deroin, letter to *Le Peuple*, April 1849, cited in Adrien Ranvier, "Une Féministe de 1848: Jeanne Deroin," *La Révolution de 1848: Bulletin de la Société d'histoire de la révolution de 1848*, 4 (1907–1908): 337.

40. Louise Otto, *Frauen-Zeitung*, 23 November 1851, p. 321.

41. Otto Stern, "Zur Frauenemanczipation," p. 107; Boetcher Joeres, *Anfänge*, p. 72.

42. *Société pour l'emancipation des femmes: Manifeste*, (March 16, 1848), p. 1. Thanks to Michèle Riot-Sarcey for sending me a copy of this document.

43. For the Saint-Simonian women, see Claire Goldberg Moses, *French Feminism in the Nineteenth Century* (Albany: State University of New York Press, 1984), p. 133; For the Owenites, see Barbara Taylor, *Eve and the New Jerusalem: Socialism and Feminism in the Nineteenth Century* (New York: Pantheon, 1983), pp. 183–216; the quotation is on p. 208 and is by James Elishema Smith. For a similar argument

about Germany, see Dagmar Herzog, *Intimacy and Exclusion: Religious Politics in Pre-Revolutionary Baden* (Princeton: Princeton University Press, 1996), chap. 3 "(Wo)Men's Emancipation and Women's Difference," pp. 85–110.

44. Madame Suzanne V_____ [Voilquin], *Souvenirs d'une fille du peuple ou la Saint-simonienne en Egypte* (Paris: Chez E. Sauzet, 1866), pp. 127–128.

45. For Roland, see Edith Thomas, *Pauline Roland: Socialisme et féminisme au XIXe siècle* (Paris: Marcel Rivière, 1956), p. 172; for Rose, see Yuri Suhl, *Ernestine L. Rose: Women's Rights Pioneer*, 2d ed. (New York: Biblio, 1990), pp. 194–195.

46. Paulina Wright Davis, "Emancipated Women," *Una*, June 1854, p. 280.

47. Anna Schepeler-Lette and Jenny Hirsch, "Germany," in *The Woman Question in Europe: A Series of Original Essays*, ed. Theodore Stanton (1884; reprint, New York: Source Book, 1970), p. 140.

48. Mrs. John Sandford, *Woman in Her Social and Domestic Character* (Boston: Otis, Broaders, 1842), p.15.

49. Cited in E. J. Hobsbawm, *The Age of Revolution: Europe 1789–1848* (London: Weidenfeld & Nicholson, 1962), p. 132.

50. *The London Journal of Flora Tristan 1842 or the Aristocracy and the Working Class of England*, translated, annotated, and introduced by Jean Hawkes (1842; reprint, London: Virago, 1982), pp. 89, 178.

51. Harriet Martineau, *Life in the Sickroom*, pp. 78–79, cited in R. K. Webb, *Harriet Martineau: A Radical Victorian* (London: Heineman, 1960), p. 211.

52. Fredrika Bremer, *England in 1851 or Sketches of a Tour in England*, trans. L.A.H. (Boulogne: Merridew, 1853), p. 55.

53. Macaulay and Emerson cited in Jerome Blum, *In the Beginning: The Advent of the Modern Age, Europe in the 1840s* (New York: Scribner's, 1994), pp. 88–89.

54. James Mott, *Three Months in Great Britain* (Philadelphia: J. Miller M'Kim, 1841), pp. 13–14.

55. For the views of English progressives about the United States in this period, see Frank Thistlethwaite, *America and the Atlantic Community: Anglo-American Aspects, 1790–1850* (New York: Harper & Row, 1959), pp. 40ff. William Lloyd Garrison to Helen Garrison, 29 June 1840, printed in Taylor, *British and American Abolitionists*, p. 93.

56. Harriet Martineau, *Retrospect of Western Travel* (New York: Charles Lohman, 1838), 2: 147–148. For a similar appraisal of the United States in this era, see Alexis de Tocqueville, *Democracy in America*, trans. George Lawrence, ed. J. P. Mayer (1855; reprint, New York: HarperPerennial, 1988), pp. 9–11, 340–362, 612–614. Convinced that U.S. equality and democracy represented the hopeful future of humanity's development, Tocqueville found African-American slavery a troubling remnant of the past. He also considered Americans "impatient of the slightest criticism and insatiable for praise. . . . [the most] obnoxious or boastful form of patriotism." Tocqueville visited the United States in 1831–1832, a few years before Martineau.

57. Priscilla Robertson, *Revolutions of 1848: A Social History* (Princeton: Princeton University Press, 1952), p. 296 n. 1.

58. Bessie Rayner Parkes to Barbara Leigh Smith, 25 June 1847, Bessie Rayner Parkes Papers, vol. 10; Ernestine Rose, *Boston Investigator*, 8 October 1856, p. 1.

59. From a declaration of the Luxembourg Commission, 28 February 1848, reprinted in *1848 in France*, ed. Roger Price (Ithaca, N.Y.: Cornell University Press, 1975), p. 69.

60. Cited in J. G. Legge, *Rhyme and Revolution in Germany: A Study in German History, Life, Literature, and Character, 1813–1850* (London: Constable, 1918), p. 193.

61. Schepeler-Lette and Hirsch in Theodore Stanton, *Woman Question in Europe*, p. 140.

62. For Freiligrath, see Legge, *Rhyme and Revolution*, p. 145; for Otto, Ute Gerhard, *Unerhört: Die Geschichte der Deutschen Frauenbewegung* (Reinbek bei Hamburg: Rowohlt, 1990), p. 42.

63. From "Wrongs of Woman—Hypocrisies of Men," *Douglas Jerrold's Weekly Newspaper*, 23 October 1847, p. 1337, cited in Gleadle, *Early Feminists*, p. 123.

64. For Olympe de Gouges, see her *The Declaration of the Rights of Woman*, reprinted in Darline Gay Levy, Harriet Branson Applewhite, and Mary Durham Johnson, *Women in Revolutionary Paris, 1789–1795* (Urbana: University of Illinois Press, 1979), pp. 93, 96. For Mary Wollstonecraft, *A Vindication of the Rights of Woman*, ed. Carol H. Poston (1792; reprint, New York: Norton, 1975), p. 35. For Hippel, Theodor Gottlieb von Hippel, *On Improving the Status of Women*, trans. and ed. Timothy F. Sellner (1792; reprint, Detroit: Wayne State University Press, 1979), pp. 89–90, 120, 121.

65. Italics in the original. Cited in Claire Midgley, *Women against Slavery: The British Campaigns, 1780–1870* (London: Routledge, 1992), p. 110.

66. Ibid., pp. 65ff.

67. Cited in Deborah Bingham Van Broekhoven, "'Let Your Names Be Enrolled': Method and Ideology in Women's Antislavery Petitioning," in *The Abolitionist Sisterhood: Women's Political Culture in Antebellum America*, ed. Jean Fagan Yellin and John C. Van Horne (Ithaca, N.Y.: Cornell University Press, 1994), p. 188.

68. Moses, *French Feminism*, pp. 104–105, 108.

69. Cited in Maria Weston Chapman, *Memorials of Harriet Martineau* (1877; reprint, Boston: Houghton, Mifflin, 1885), p. 165.

70. Mary Wigham to Maria Weston Chapman, 1 April 1839, in Taylor, *British and American Abolitionists*, p. 69.

71. Maria W. Stewart, "Lecture Delivered at the Franklin Hall, Boston, September 21, 1832," in *Maria W. Stewart: America's First Black Woman Political Writer, Essays and Speeches*, ed. Marilyn Richardson (Bloomington: Indiana University Press, 1987), pp. 39–40.

72. For this overall argument with regard to women in Britain and the United States, see Kathryn Kish Sklar, "'Women Who Speak for an Entire Nation': American and British Women at the World Anti-Slavery Convention, London, 1840," in Yellin and Van Horne, *Abolitionist Sisterhood*, pp. 322ff.

73. Anglina Grimké to William Lloyd Garrison, 30 August 1835, published by Garrison in the *Liberator*. Reprinted in Katherine Du Pre Lumpkin, *The Emancipation of Angelina Grimké* (Chapel Hill: University of North Carolina Press, 1974), p. 84.

74. Cited in James Oliver Horton, "Freedom's Yoke: Gender Conventions among Antebellum Free Blacks," *Feminist Studies* 12, no. 1 (1986), p. 70.

75. See Dana Greene, "Introduction," in Mott, *Complete Speeches and Sermons*, p. 8, for a discussion of this concept's importance for Mott. In 1860, Mott gave a sermon in which she stated: "All we can do, one for another, is to bring each to know the light of truth in the soul. It is pure, holy, unmistakable, and no *ignis fatuus*. Feeling and believing that I would call you all to it." Mott, *Complete Speeches and Sermons*, p. 259.

76. Cited in Blanche Glassman Hersh, *The Slavery of Sex: Feminist-Abolitionists in America* (Urbana: University of Illinois Press, 1978), p. 15; cited in Otelia Cromwell, *Lucretia Mott* (Cambridge: Harvard University Press, 1958), p. 3.

77. Named after the minister Elias Hicks, who emphasized "inner light" over orthodox tradition. Quaker feminists also tended to come from farm villages rather than cities, in which the doctrine of "separate spheres" prevailed. Nancy A. Hewitt, "Feminist Friends: Agrarian Quakers and the Emergence of Woman's Rights in America," *Feminist Studies* 12, no. 1 (1986), pp. 27–49.

78. Ruth Ketring Neurumberger, *The Free Produce Movement: A Quaker Protest against Slavery* (Durham, N.C.: Duke University Press, 1942); for English support for Mott's position, see Mary Lloyd's 1826 letter from London, cited in Margaret Hope Bacon, *Valiant Friend: The Life of Lucretia Mott* (New York: Walker, 1980), p. 42.

79. Cromwell, *Lucretia Mott*, p. 47; cited in Dorothy Sterling, *Lucretia Mott: Gentle Warrior* (Garden City, N.Y.: Doubleday, 1964), p. 81.

80. Cited in Julie Winch, "Philadelphia's Black Female Literary Societies," in Yellin and Van Horne, *Abolitionist Sisterhood*, p. 113.

81. Louise Otto, "Adresse eines Mädchens an den hochverehrten Herrn Minister Oberländer, an die durch ihn berufene Arbeiterkommission und an alle Arbeiter" *Leipziger Arbeiter-Zeitung*, May 1848, reprinted in Renate Möhrmann, *Frauenemanzipation im deutschen Vormärz: Texte und Dokumente* (Stuttgart: Philipp Reclam, 1978), pp. 199–202.

82. *Flora Tristan, Utopian Feminist: Her Travel Diaries and Personal Crusade*, ed. and trans. Doris Beik and Paul Beik (Bloomington: Indiana University Press, 1993), pp. 139–140.

83. D. C. Bloomer, *Life and Writings of Amelia Bloomer* (1895; reprint, New York: Schocken, 1975), p. 159.

84. Queen Victoria, letter, 17 February 1852, cited with similar examples in Françoise Basch, *Relative Creatures: Victorian Women in Society and the Novel*, trans. Anthony Rudolf (New York: Schocken, 1974), p. 285, n. 152; Louise Otto, *Frauenleben im Deutschen Reich*, p. 125.

85. Cited in Bacon, *Lucretia Mott*, p. 73. The proposal was passed 2 January 1837.

86. Lucretia Mott to Abby Kelley, 18 March 1839, Foster Papers, American Antiquarian Society, Worcester, Mass. For European examples of this debate, see Claire Goldberg Moses, "Debating the Present, Writing the Past: 'Feminism' in French History and Historiography," *Radical History Review* 52 (1992), p. 89ff; and Sylvia Paletschek, *Frauen und Dissens: Frauen in Deutschkatholizismus und in den freien Gemeinden, 1841–1852* (Göttingen: Vandenhoeck & Ruprecht, 1990), pp. 226, 231.

Louise Otto was replying to editor Robert Blum's assertion that "women's participation in the life of the state is not just a right but a duty." Gerhard, *Unerhört*, p. 37.

87. From *Turning the World Upside Down: The Anti-Slavery Convention of American Women*, with an introduction by Dorothy Stirling (New York: Feminist Press, 1987), p. 19; a reprint of the 1837 proceedings.

88. Ibid., pp. 12–13.

89. Ibid., pp. 13, 31. The six publications were *An Appeal to the Women of the Nominally Free States*, an *Address to Free Colored Americans*, a *Letter to the Women of Great Britain*, a *Circular to the Female Anti-Slavery Societies in the United States*, a *Letter to Juvenile Anti-Slavery Soceties*, and a *Letter to John Quincy Adams*, who defended women's right to petition. The quotation is from the first pamphlet.

90. Cited in Lumpkin, *Emancipation of Angelina Grimké*, p. 107.

91. Letter to Theodore Weld and John Greenleaf Whittier, cited in Campbell, *Man Can Not Speak for Her*, p. 25.

92. Abby Kelley, cited in Hersh, *Slavery of Sex*, p. 34; Chapman, cited in Jean Fagan Yellin, "Introduction," in Yellin and Van Horne, *Abolitionist Sisterhood*, p. 15; Angelina Grimké, cited in Lumpkin, *Emancipation of Angelina Grimké*, p. 120.

93. Sarah Grimké, *Letters on the Equality of the Sexes and Other Essays*, ed. Elizabeth Ann Bartlett (1837; reprint, New Haven: Yale University Press, 1988), p. 64.

94. Bacon, *Lucretia Mott*, pp. 76–77. On its first evening, the convention transformed itself into a "special meeting," so that women not used to addressing mixed audiences could be more comfortable.

95. For Chapman, see Jean Fagan Yellin, *Women and Sisters: The Antislavery Feminists in American Culture* (New Haven: Yale University Press, 1989), p. 49; for Sarah Grimké, see Lumpkin, *Emancipation of Angelina Grimké*, p. 42; for Angelina Grimké Weld, Lumpkin, *Emancipation of Angelina Grimké*, chap. 4; for Kelley, see *The Proceedings of the Woman's Rights Convention Held at Worcester, October 15 & 16, 1851* (New York: Fowler & Wells, 1852), p. 102.

96. Martineau, *Retrospect of Western Travel*, 2: 67; Thoreau, cited in Cromwell, *Lucretia Mott*, p. 116.

97. Marianne Finch, *An Englishwoman's Experience in America* (London: Richard Bentley, 1853), p. 264.

98. For Philadelphia 1838, see Cromwell, *Lucretia Mott*, p. 58; for Mott's *sangfroid* at the "Mob Convention" of 1853, see *Proceedings of the Woman's Rights Convention held at the Broadway Tabernacle, in the City of New York, on Tues. & Wed., Sept. 6th & 7th, 1853* (New York: Fowler & Wells, 1853), passim.

99. Bacon, *Lucretia Mott*, pp. 75–79; Sterling, *Lucretia Mott*, pp. 100–107.

100. Bessie Rayner Parkes to Barbara Leigh Smith, Girton College, Cambridge, Parkes Papers, Bessie Rayner Parkes, vol. 5, p. 155.

101. Harriet Martineau, *The Martyr Age of the United States* (1839; reprint, New York: Arno *New York Times*, 1969), p. 82, 52.

102. Harriet Martineau, *Society in America*, (1837; reprint, New York: AMS Press, 1966), 1: 199–207.

103. For Mott having read Martineau's *Society in America* and using her to justify women's right to vote, see her "Discourse on Women" in *Complete Speeches and Sermons*, p. 156.

104. Dorothy Sterling, *Ahead of Her Time: Abby Kelley and the Politics of Antislavery* (New York: Norton, 1991), p. 84.

105. Mott was addressing the Pennsylvania Anti-Slavery Society in 1860, shortly after John Brown's execution. Cited in Dorothy Stirling, *Lucretia Mott*, p. 181. On this subject, see Margaret Hope Bacon, "By Moral Force Alone: Antislavery Women and Non-Resistance," in Yellin and Van Horne, *Abolitionist Sisterhood*, pp. 275–297; and Aileen S. Kraditor, *Means and Ends in American Abolitionism: Garrison and His Critics on Strategy and Tactics, 1834–1850* (New York: Pantheon, 1969). Nonresistance later had an impact on Tolstoy and Gandhi.

106. "Abolitionism made easy," Sterling, *Abby Kelley*, p. 96; Whittier in Sterling, *Abby Kelley*, p. 106.

107. The U.S. women were Mary Grew, Abby Kimber, Lucretia Mott, Elizabeth Neall, Sarah Pugh, Abby Southwick, and Emily Winslow. Marion Reid was not related to Elizabeth Reid; Lady Noel Byron was the poet's widow. Sklar in Yellin and Van Horne, *Abolitionist Sisterhood*, pp. 332–333; Midgely, *Women against Slavery*, p. 161ff.

108. "Lucretia Mott to Dear Children," 14 June 1840, pp. 7, 9, Lucretia Mott Papers, Friends Historical Library, Swarthmore College, Mott MSS, box 1.

109. Harriet Martineau's letter was printed in James Mott's *Three Months in Great Britain*, p. 75.

110. Lucretia Mott to Richard and Hannah Webb, 2 April 1841, Boston Public Library, Manuscript Division, Anti-Slavery Collection, Ms. A.1.2, vol. 11, p. 136.

111. Lucretia Mott to Richard and Hannah Webb, 25 February 1842, Boston Public Library, Manuscripts Division, Anti-Slavery Collection, Ms. A.1.2, vol. 12.2, pp. 34, 5.

112. Elizabeth Cady Stanton, *Eighty Years and More: Reminiscences, 1815–1897*, introduction by Gail Parker (1898; reprint, New York: Schocken, 1971), pp. 80ff.

113. R. D. Webb to Maria Weston Chapman, 20 November 1841, printed in Taylor, *British and American Abolitionists*, p. 157.

Chapter Six

1. Lucretia Mott to Richard and Hannah Webb, 25 February-7 March 1842, p. 8, Boston Public Library, Manuscript Division, Anti-Slavery Collection, Ms. A.1.2, vol. 12.2, p. 34.

2. For this interchange, see Otelia Cromwell, *Lucretia Mott* (Cambridge: Harvard University Press, 1958), p. 104; Dorothy Stirling, *Lucretia Mott: Gentle Warrior* (Garden City, N.Y.: Doubleday, 1964), pp. 136–137; *The Letters of Charles Dickens*, vol. 3, *1842–1843*, ed. Madeline House, Graham Storey, and Kathleen Tillotson (Oxford: Clarendon, 1974), pp. 99 n. 1, 357 n. 2; Louise H. Johnson, "The Source of the Chapter on Slavery in Dickens' *American Notes*," *American Literature* 14 (January, 1943), pp. 422–430.

3. *Yankee Notions*, October 1853; cited in the *Journal of Women's History* (frontispiece) 3, no. 3 (Winter 1992).

4. Charles Dickens, *Martin Chuzzlewit* (1843; reprint, New York: Signet Classic, 1965), pp. 308, 320, 398. Mrs. Jellaby appears in *Bleak House*.

5. Cited in Bell Gale Chevigny, *The Woman and the Myth: Margaret Fuller's Life and Writings*, rev. ed. (Boston: Northeastern University Press, 1994), p. 502.

6. For these cartoons and English translations of their captions, see *Daumier: Lib Women (Bluestockings and Socialist Women) (Les bas-bleus et les femmes socialistes)*, ed. Jacqueline Armingeat (Paris: Leon Amiel, 1974), pp. 29, 130. The reference is to the *Gazette des femmes*, edited by Charles Frédéric Herbinot de Mauchamps.

7. For *Judy*, Gary L. Bunker, "Antebellum Caricature and Woman's Sphere," *Journal of Women's History* 3, no. 3 (Winter 1992), p. 39 n. 3; for Poe, Susan Phinney Conrad, *Perish the Thought: Intellectual Women in Romantic America, 1830–1860* (New York: Oxford University Press, 1976), p. 48.

8. *Life, Letters, and Posthumous Works of Fredrika Bremer*, ed. Charlotte Bremer, trans. Fredr. Milow (New York: Hurd & Houghton, 1868), p. 281.

9. Paulina W. Davis, *A History of the National Woman's Rights Movement* (1871; reprint; New York: Source Book Press, 1970), pp. 9–10.

10. Helen Richardson to Anne Knight, 11–13 January 1846, Anne Knight Papers, Friends House, London, MS box W2, 2/2/26.

11. Robert Browning to Elizabeth Barrett, 30 June 1846, *The Letters of Robert Browning and Elizabeth Barrett Browning, 1845–46* (Cambridge: Harvard University Press, 1989), 2: 826.

12. Elizabeth Cady Stanton, *Eighty Years and More: Reminiscences, 1815–1897* (1898; reprint, New York: Schocken, 1971), pp. 147–148.

13. Lucretia Mott to Richard and Hannah Webb, 25 February-7 March 1842, pp. 4–5, Boston Public Library, Manuscript Division, Anti-Slavery Collection, Ms.A.1.2, vol. 12.2, p. 34.

14. Paulina Saxton Wright to Maria Weston Chapman, 29 August 1843, Boston Public Library, Manuscript Division, Anti-Slavery Collection, Ms.A.9.2, vol. 19, p. 23.

15. Elizabeth Reid to Anne and Wendell Phillips, 26 August 1843, Boston Public Library, Manscript Division, Anti-Slavery Collection, Ms.1.2, vol. 13, p. 49.

16. On women in early peace societies, see Jill Liddington, *The Long Road to Greenham Common: Feminism and Anti-Militarism in Britain since 1820* (London: Virago, 1989); and W. H. van der Linden, *The International Peace Movement, 1815–1874* (Amsterdam: Tilleul, 1987). Thanks to Sandi Cooper for lending me

this volume. For Mott, see *Lucretia Mott: Her Complete Speeches and Sermons*, ed. Dana Greene (New York: Edwin Mellen, 1980), p. 49; and the Swarthmore College Peace Collection, which has a peace scroll sent from women in Exeter, England, and Mott's reply. For Wright, the Paulina Wright Davis Papers, folder 4C, pp. 6–7, Vassar College Library.

17. For Niboyet, see Evelyne Lejeune-Resnick, *Femmes et Associations (1830/1880): Vraies démocrates ou dames patronnesses?* (Paris: Editions Publisud, 1991), pp. 100ff. For Knight, Anne Knight Papers, tracts, vol. O, folder 229–230, Friends House, London.

18. Alexander Tyrrell, "'Woman's Mission' and Pressure Group Politics in Britain (1825–60)," *Bulletin of the John Rylands University Library of Manchester* 63, no.1 (Autumn 1980), pp. 215, 222.

19. Cited in Dorothy Thompson, *The Chartists: Popular Politics in the Industrial Revolution* (New York: Pantheon, 1984), chap. 7 "The Women," p. 120. The six points of the charter were universal (male) suffrage, the secret ballot, equal electoral districts, the abolition of property qualifications for members of parliament, payment for members of parliament, and annual parliaments. All except the last were enacted by 1910.

20. Jutta Schwartzkopf, *Women in the Chartist Movement* (New York: St. Martin's, 1991), pp. 185, 89, 245–246.

21. For Tristan, *The London Journal of Flora Tristan 1842 or the Aristocracy and the Working Class of England*, trans. Jean Hawkes (London: Virago, 1982), p. 48; with an introduction and annotations by Jean Hawkes. For Barmby, from a "declaration" printed in the *Communitarian Apostle* (January 1842), cited in Gail Malmgreen, *Neither Bread nor Roses: Utopian Feminists and the English Working Class, 1800–1850* (Brighton, U.K.: John L. Noyce, 1978), pp. 19–20. The last sentence is from Shelley's "Revolt of Islam."

22. For Fourier and the Saint-Simonian New Women, Claire Goldberg Moses and Leslie Wahl Rabine, *Feminism, Socialism, and French Romanticism* (Bloomington: Indiana University Press, 1993), pp. 62–63; for Anne Knight, *Diary*, MS vol. S486, Knight Papers, Friends House, London. Knight copied Fourier's dictum on the position of women in society as the index of civilization into her diary right after a passage from Tristan. For Louise Otto and Fourier, see Louise Otto, letter to the *Sächsischen Vaterlandsblätter*, ed. Robert Blum, September, 1843, reprinted in Ruth-Ellen Boetcher Joeres, *Die Anfänge der deutschen Frauenbewegung: Louise Otto-Peters*, p. 76. For one example of Fourier in early U.S. feminist journals, see "Woman—Civil Rights," *Lily*, 2, no. 4 (April 1850): "When we look back to the history of nations we find that females have been elevated, and their true position approximated just in proportion to the progress of civilization."

23. For a detailed list, see Arthur Bestor, *Backwoods Utopias: The Sectarian Origins and the Owenite Phase of Communitarian Socialism in America, 1663–1829*, 2d enl. ed. (Philadelphia: University of Pennsylvania Press, 1957), pp. 280–282.

24. From the New York *Tribune*, 20 April 1842, cited in Kathryn Manson Tomasek, "Fourierism and Gender in the Habermasian Public Sphere" (unpublished paper, p. 1). Thanks to Prof. Tomasek for sharing her work with me.

25. Carl J. Guarneri, *The Utopian Alternative: Fourierism in Nineteenth-Century America* (Ithaca, N.Y.: Cornell University Press, 1991), pp. 207–209.

26. From her diary, 26 August 1843, cited in Sarah Elbert, *A Hunger for Home: Louisa May Alcott and Little Women* (Philadelphia: Temple University Press, 1984), p. 63.

27. Cited in Tomasek, "Fourierism and Gender," p. 12.

28. Gertrude Sears to Anna Q.T. Parsons, 23 January 1848, cited in Guaneri, *Utopian Alternative*, p. 208.

29. *London Journal of Flora Tristan*, pp. 70, 66–67.

30. James Mott, *Three Months in Great Britain* (Philadelphia: J. Miller M'Kim, 1841), p. 53.

31. For this argument generally, see Guarneri, *Utopian Alternative*, chap. 9, "The Problem of Slavery."

32. Anna Jameson to Ottilie von Goethe, 2 July 1840, in G. H. Needler, ed., *Letters of Anna Jameson to Ottilie von Goethe* (London: Oxford University Press, 1939), p. 126. Ottilie von Goethe was the daughter-in-law of German author Johann Wolfgang von Goethe.

33. Marion Reid, *A Plea for Woman* (1843; reprint, Edinburgh: Polygon, 1988), pp. ix, v. Introduction by Suzanne Ferguson.

34. Ibid., pp. 2, 6.

35. Ibid., pp. 71, 75.

36. Ibid., pp. 6, 14.

37. Ibid., p. 24. For the vote, p. 27: for legislators, p. 63.

38. Ibid., pp. 36, 87.

39. Mott, *Complete Speeches and Sermons*, pp. 49, 91.

40. For Native Americans, see Mott, *Complete Speeches and Sermons*, p. 49; and Margaret Hope Bacon, *Mothers of Feminism: The Story of Quaker Women in America* (New York: Harper & Row, 1989), p. 112; for strikes and wages, Margaret Hope Bacon, *Valiant Friend: The Life of Lucretia Mott* (New York: Walker, 1980), p. 116; for parental nonviolence, Bacon, *Valiant Friend*, p. 117; for "Hindoo women," Mott, *Complete Speeches and Sermons*, pp. 55–56.

41. Lucretia Mott to Richard and Hannah Webb, 25 February-7 March 1842, p. 7, Boston Public Library, Manuscript Division, Anti-Slavery Collection Ms. A.1.2, vol. 12.2, p. 34; James Mott, *Three Months in Great Britain*, p. 48.

42. Cited in Barbara Taylor, *Eve and the New Jerusalem: Socialism and Feminism in the Nineteenth Century* (New York: Pantheon, 1983), p. 260.

43. Catherine Barmby, *The Demand for the Emancipation of Woman, Politically and Socially* in *New Tracts for the Times: or, Warmth, Light, and Food for the Masses*, ed. Goodwyn Barmby (London, 1843), pp. 2–3. This pamphlet is reprinted in *Sources of British Feminism*, vol. 3, *Socialist Feminism*, ed. Marie Mulvey Roberts and Tamae Mizuta (London: Routledge/Thoemmes Press, 1993), pp. 1–19. The introductory notes are not reliable. For Catherine and Goodwyn Barmby and the Communist Church, see Barbara Taylor, *Eve*, pp. 172–182.

44. Reid, *Plea for Women*, chap. 4, "Business and Domestic Duties Compared," and p. 65. Reid's remark that "we have no wish whatever to see women

sitting as representatives" prompted an outburst from Anne Knight in the margin of her copy of *A Plea for Woman*: "The point at issue must be equalization of human privilege if my brother have a right to sit then his sister has the same right." Anne Knight Papers, Friends House, London.

45. Barmby, *Demand*, pp. 4, 10.

46. Ibid., pp. 8, 10.

47. Ibid., pp. 14–15.

48. From Thompson's *Practical Directions for the Speedy and Economical Establishment of Communities* (1830), cited in Richard Pankhurst, *William Thompson, Britain's Pioneer Socialist, Feminist, and Co-operator* (London: Watts, 1954), p. 75; Louise Otto cited in Renate Möhrmann, ed., *Frauenemanzipation im deutschen Vormärz: Texte und Dokumente* (Stuttgart: Philipp Reclam, 1978), p. 53.

49. For Fuller, see Margaret Fuller, *Woman in the Nineteenth Century* (1845; reprint, New York: Norton, 1971), p. 78. For Anne Knight and the White Quakers (who dressed in biblical clothing, did not cut their hair, and practiced free love), see Gail Malmgreen, "Anne Knight and the Radical Subculture," *Quaker History* 71, no. 2 (Fall 1982), p. 110. For Tristan, see *London Journal of Flora Tristan*, p. xxxix.

50. For Tristan's visit to parliament, see *London Journal of Flora Tristan*, pp. 58–64; for her later admiration of O'Connell, Flora Tristan, *The Workers' Union*, trans. with an introduction by Beverly Livingston (Urbana: University of Illinois Press, 1983), pp. 62–66; for Mott's contact with O'Connell, including the text of his letter, James Mott, *Three Months in Britain*, pp. 20–22; for Stanton's, Elizabeth Cady Stanton, *Eighty Years and More: Reminiscences, 1815–1897* (1898; reprint, New York: Schocken, 1971), pp. 89–90. Stanton added, "Could he have looked forward fifty years [to 1890] and have seen the present condition of his unhappy country, he would have known that English greed and selfishness could defeat any policy, however wise and far-seeing."

51. *Flora Tristan, Utopian Feminist: Her Travel Diaries and Personal Crusade*, ed. and trans. Doris Beik and Paul Beik (Bloomington: Indiana University Press, 1993), p. 3.

52. Tristan petitioned the Chamber of Deputies in 1837 for the reinstatement of divorce, which had been legal in France from 1792 to 1816. For Sand and divorce, see Donna Dickenson, *George Sand: A Brave Man—The Most Womanly Woman* (Oxford: Berg, 1989), p. 65ff.

53. Knight copied sections of Tristan's writings into her diary, writing her name in large characters and circling it; Deroin and Roland both subscribed to Tristan's *Workers' Union* and drew many of their ideas for an association of unions and workers' palaces from it; Roland took care of Tristan's daughter after Flora Tristan died. Anne Knight, *Diary*, MS vol. S486, Knight Papers, Friends House, London. For Deroin, Laura S. Strumingher, *The Odyssey of Flora Tristan* (New York: Peter Lang, 1988), pp. 244–245. For Roland, Edith Thomas, *Pauline Roland: Socialisme et Féminisme au XIXe Siècle* (Paris: Marcel Rivière, 1956), p. 139.

54. *London Journal of Flora Tristan*, pp. 1–5 (from the preface to the fourth edition).

55. *London Journal of Flora Tristan*, pp. 80, 82, 244, 253, 257.

56. Tristan, *Workers' Union*, pp. 39, 113ff.

57. Tristan, *Workers' Union*, pp. 76, 125

58. Tristan, *Workers' Union*, pp. 76, 80; *Flora Tristan, Utopian Feminist*, p. 127. Also see S. Joan Moon, "Feminism and Socialism: The Utopian Synthesis of Flora Tristan," in *Socialist Women: European Socialist Feminism in the Nineteenth and Early Twentieth Centuries*, ed. Marilyn J. Boxer and Jean H. Quataert (New York: Elsevier, 1978), pp. 19–50.

59. For a list of the subscribers to the *Workers' Union*, see *The Workers' Union*, trans. and ed. Beverly Livingston, pp. 30–33. Deroin's husband's first name was restored to history by Vaughan Baker Simpson, whom I thank for having shared her work with me. For Tristan's letters, see Stéphane Michaud, ed., *Flora Tristan: Lettres* (Paris: Editions de Seuil, 1980) and *Flora Tristan: La paria et son rêve* (Paris: ENS Editions, 1995). A photograph of the monument is included in the illustrations section of *The London Journal of Flora Tristan*.

60. Cited in Chevigny, *The Woman and the Myth*, pp. 146, 56.

61. Fuller, *Woman in the Nineteenth Century*, p. 99.

62. Margaret Fuller to Caroline Tappen, 16 November 1837, cited in Conrad, *Perish the Thought*, p. 62.

63. The phrase "intimate friendship" is from Martineau's *Autobiography*, published in 1877. The section on Fuller is reprinted in Gayle Graham Yates, ed., *Harriet Martineau on Women* (New Brunswick, N.J.: Rutgers University Press, 1985), pp. 193–195. Fuller's 1837 letter to Martineau is in Chevigny, *The Woman and the Myth*, pp. 117–118; her letter to Chapman, pp. 238–239.

64. Elizabeth Hoar to Hannah L. Chappell, 3 April 1839, cited in Chevigny, *The Woman and the Myth*, pp. 89–90. On the Conversations, Blanchard, *Margaret Fuller*, pp. 146–152, Chevigny, pp. 210–215. Elizabeth Cady Stanton, Susan B. Anthony and Matilda Jocelyn Gage, *History of Woman Suffrage*, vol. 1 *1848–1861*, p. 801, cited in Chevigny, *The Woman and the Myth*, p. 213.

65. Fuller, *Woman in the Nineteenth Century*, pp. 172, 174.

66. Ibid., pp. 116, 150, 153–154.

67. Margaret Fuller to Elizabeth Hoar, 17 March 1847, cited in Chevigny, *The Woman and the Myth*, pp. 361–362.

68. Cited in Margaret Fuller, *"These Sad But Glorious Days": Dispatches from Europe, 1846–1850*, ed. Larry J. Reynolds and Susan Belasco Smith (New Haven: Yale University Press, 1991), p. 14.

69. Elizabeth Barrett Browning to Mary Russell Mitford, from *Letters of Elizabeth Barrett Browning* (New York: Macmillan 1898), 1: 459–460 cited in Chevigny, *The Woman and the Myth*, pp. 413–414. Also see Bell Gale Chevigny, "To the Edges of Ideology: Margaret Fuller's Centrifugal Evolution," *American Quarterly* 38 (Summer 1986), pp. 173–201.

70. For Fuller, see Margaret Fuller, *"These Sad but Glorious Days"* p. 97; for Tristan, see Sandra Dijkstra, *Flora Tristan: Feminism in the Age of George Sand* (London: Pluto, 1992), p. 136. Ruge devoted a chapter in his *Zwei Jahre im Paris* (1846) to Tristan's Worker's Union and transmitted her ideas to Karl Marx.

71. Cited in Ingeborg Drewitz, "Bettina von Arnim-A Portrait," in *New German Critique* vol. 27 (Fall 1982), p. 120.

72. Cited in Sylvia Paletschek, *Frauen und Dissens: Frauen in Deutschkatholizismus und in den freien Gemeinde, 1841–1852* (Göttingen: Vandenhoeck & Ruprecht, 1990): Ronge, p. 161; Otto, p. 236.

73. For Ronge's appeal for international support, see *The Autobiography and Justification of Johannes Ronge, the German Reformer*, trans. John Lord from the 5th German ed. (London: Chapman Brothers, 1846), especially pp. 69–70; for Ronge's use of Fourier, see Paletschek, *Frauen und Dissens*, p. 155.

74. Paletschek, *Frauen und Dissens*, p. 244ff; Malwida von Meysenbug, *Memoiren einer Idealistin* (Berlin: Schuster & Loeffler, 1881), 1: 198. Meysenbug also gave up a pension that required her to swear that she was Protestant; the free congregation did not qualify her.

75. Paletschek, *Frauen und Dissens*, pp. 163, 172. The German word "Mündigkeit," which I have translated as "adult status," means the ability to function without a legal guardian.

76. Cited in Catherine M. Prelinger, *Charity, Challenge, and Change: Religious Dimensions of the Mid-Nineteenth-Century Women's Movement in Germany* (Westport, Conn.: Greenwood, 1987), p. 80.

77. Aston cited in Möhrmann, *Frauenemanzipation*, p. 71; Keil from the *Wandelstern 3* (January 1845), pp. 58–59, cited in Ruth-Ellen Boetcher Joeres, "Louise Otto and Her Journals: A Chapter in Nineteenth-Century German Feminism," *Internationales Archiv für Sozialgeschichte der deutschen Literatur* 4 (1979), pp. 105–106.

78. Cited in Germaine Goetzinger, *Für die Selbstwirklichung der Frau: Louise Aston* (Frankfurt am Main: Fischer Taschenbuch Verlag, 1983), pp. 103–104.

79. Mathilde Franziska [Anneke], *Das Weib im Conflict mit den socialen Verhältnisse*, pp. 5, 14, written in the winter of 1846–1847. This document exists only as a typescript in the Mathilde Franziska Anneke Papers, State Historical Society of Wisconsin.

80. Louise Dittmar, *Vier Zeitfragen* (Offenbach am Main: Gustav André, 1847), p. 6.

81. For Ronge, Dagmar Herzog, *Intimacy and Exclusion: Religious Politics in Pre-Revolutionary Baden* (Princeton: Princeton University Press, 1996) p. 97. Thanks to Dagmar Herzog for letting me read this work in manuscript. Otto cited in Möhrmann, *Frauenmanzipation*, pp. 58–59. For this poem in German and an English translation that differs from mine, see Susan Cocalis, ed., *The Defiant Muse: German Feminist Poems from the Middle Ages to the Present* (New York: Feminist Press, 1986), pp. 55–59.

82. Cited in Paletschek, *Frauen und Dissens*, p. 176.

Chapter Seven

1. Louise Aston, *Aus dem Leben einer Frau*, p. 133, cited in Louise Aston, *Ein Lesebuch: Gedichte, Romane, Schriften in Auswahl (1846–1849)*, ed. Karlheinz Fingerhut (Stuttgart: Hans-Dieter Heinz Akademischer Verlag, 1983), p. 154. Thanks to Jörg Thurow for sending me this book.

2. Margaret Fuller, *"These Sad But Glorious Days": Dispatches from Europe, 1846–1850*, ed. Larry J. Reynolds and Susan Belasco Smith (New Haven: Yale University Press), pp. 164–165. For other warnings, see pp. 119, 146, 154.

3. From John 4:35. The full verse goes "Say not ye, there are yet four months and then cometh the harvest. Behold I say unto you, Lift up your eyes, and look on the fields for they are white already to harvest." Thanks to Paul Williams for identifying this reference. For Mott's use of this verse, see *Lucretia Mott: Her Complete Speeches and Sermons*, ed. Dana Greene (New York: Edwin Mellen, 1980), pp. 31, 55.

4. For Ireland, see Jonathan Sperber, *The European Revolutions, 1848–1851* (Cambridge: Cambridge University Press, 1994), p. 242. In Ireland, there was one police officer for every 500 inhabitants, in France, one for 2,000, in Prussia, one for 7,000. Louise Otto, "Die Teilnahme der weiblichen Welt am Staatsleben" reprinted in Renate Möhrmann, ed., *Frauenemanzipation im deutschen Vormärz: Texte und Dokumente* (Stuttgart: Philipp Reclam, 1978), p. 51.

5. Alexis de Tocqueville, *Recollections*, trans. George Lawrence, ed. J. P. Meyer and A. P. Kerr (Garden City, N.Y.: Doubleday, 1971), pp. 16–17.

6. Cited in Hester Burton, *Barbara Bodichon 1827–1891*, p. 78. Leigh Smith visited Vesuvius in 1855. Her painting of the sight is reproduced as plate 27, "Barbara Leigh Smith Bodichon, Artist and Activist," by Pam Hirsch, in *Women in the Victorian Art World*, ed. Clarissa Campbell Orr (Manchester, U.K.: Manchester University Press, 1995), p. 175.

7. For Italy, Priscilla Robertson, *Revolutions of 1848: A Social History* (Princeton: Princeton University Press, 1952), p. 323. For Lewald, Fanny Lewald, *Freiheit des Herzens: Lebensgeschichte, Briefe, Errinerungen*, ed. Günter de Bruyn and Gerhard Wolf (Frankfurt am Main: Ullstein Taschenbücher, 1992), p. 239. For Bremer, Fredrika Bremer, *England in 1851 or Sketches of a Tour in England*, trans. L.A.H. (Boulogne: Merridew, 1853), p. 27.

8. Robertson, *Revolutions of 1848*, p. 7.

9. Fuller, *"Sad but Glorious Days,"* p. 207.

10. For women fighting on the barricades, *Les révolutions de 1848: l'Europe des images*, vol. 2, *Le printemps des peuples* (Paris: Assemblée Nationale, 1998), pp. 18, 24; and Gerlinde Hummel-Haasis, *Schwestern zerreist eure Kettern: Zeugnisse zur Geschichte der Frauen in der Revolution von 1848/49* (München: Deutscher Taschenbuch Verlag, 1982), p. 328. For the women at the national workshops, *La Révolution Française de 1848 à travers les affiches officielles du gouvernement provisoire* (Paris: Kiosque de l'Assemblée Nationale, 1998), p. 7. For early 1848 illustrations of revolutionary women as victims of street fighting, see Roger Price, ed., *1848 in*

France, trans. C. N. Smith (Ithaca, N.Y.: Cornell University Press, 1975), p. 25.

11. Cited in Carola Lipp, "Liebe, Krieg und Revolution: Geschlechter-beziehung und Nationalismus", in *Schimpfende Weiber und patriotische Jungfrauen: Frauen im Vormärz und in der Revolution 1848/49*, ed. Carola Lipp (Moos & Baden-Baden: Elster Verlag, 1986), p. 353. Thanks to Marion Kaplan for lending me this book.

12. For illustrations of this, see *Les révolutions de 1848: l'Europe des images*, vol. 1, *Une république nouvelle*, cover, pp. 70–71, 78–80, 125–131; vol. 2, *Le printemps des peuples*, pp. 59–63.

13. Cited in Gudrun Wittig, *"Nicht nur im stillen Kreis des Hauses": Frauenbewe-gung in Revolution und nachrevolutionärer Zeit, 1848–76* (Hamburg: Ergebnisse Ver-lag, 1986), frontispiece quotation.

14. Anne Knight Diary, Knight Papers, Friends House, London. The letter was also signed by "A. François," a woman whose identity is not known.

15. Anne Knight, *Letter to Lord Brougham, Result of an Interview at Meurice's Hotel, Paris, 4th month 14, 1849* (Holborn: Johnson & Co., Printers, 1849), in Tracts, vol. O, folder 229–230, Friends House London; Malwida von Meysenbug, *Memoiren einer Idealistin* (Berlin: Schuster & Loeffler, 1881), 1: 140–141; *The Com-plete Poems of Emily Dickinson*, ed. Thomas H. Johnson (Boston: Little, Brown, 1960), p. 694, poem no. 1705. The poem is undated.

16. For the cartoon, which appeared in the satiric journal *Silhouette* on March 24, 1848, see Laura S. Strumingher, "The Vésuviennes: Images of Women War-riors in 1848 and Their Significance for French History," *History of European Ideas* 8, nos. 4–5 (1987), p. 454; for the account of the Vésuviennes, *La Voix des femmes*, 28 March 1848, p. 3.

17. *La Voix des femmes*, 20 March 1848, p. 4. Also see Armelle Le Bras-Chopard, "Pierre Leroux et l'égalité des sexes," in *Femmes dans la Cité 1815–1871*, ed. Alain Corbin, Jacqueline Lalouette, and Michèle Riot-Sarcey (Grâne: Créaphis, 1997), p. 447.

18. Cited in Michèle Riot-Sarcey, *La démocratie à l'épreuve des femmes: Trois fig-ures critiques du pouvoir, 1830–1848* (Paris: Albin Michel, 1994), p. 186.

19. Cited in Riot-Sarcey, *La démocratie*, p. 189.

20. *La Voix des femmes*, 20 March 1848, p. 1.

21. *La Voix des femmes*, 20 March 1848, pp. 3–4; 22 March 1848, pp. 1–2; 23 March 1848, p. 3. The text is in French both in *La Voix des femmes* and on Knight's label. For a sample of this label, see Knight's copy of Marion Reid's *A Plea for Woman* (1843), Anne Knight Papers, Library of the Society of Friends, Friends House, London. The label is pasted onto the back cover.

22. Louise Otto, *Frauen-Zeitung* 19 May 1849, reprinted in *"Dem Reich der Freiheit werb' ich Bürgerinnen": Die Frauen-Zeitung von Louise Otto*, ed. Ute Ger-hard, Elisabeth Hannover-Drück, and Romina Schmitter (Frankfurt am Main: Syndikat, 1979), p. 70. This volume reprints an edited version of the first two years of Otto's newspaper.

23. For Kemble, see *Lily*, 1 December 1849, p. 1; for Stanton, who still wrote under her "Sunflower" pseudonym, see *Lily*, 1 December 1849.

24. Madame d'Héricourt, *A Woman's Philosophy of Woman; or Woman Affranchised* (New York: Carleton, 1864), p. 171.

25. Adrien Ranvier, "Une Féministe de 1848: Jeanne Deroin," *La Révolution de 1848: Bulletin de la Société d'histoire de la révolution de 1848*, 4 (1907–1908): 324; *La Voix des femmes*, 26 March 1848, p. 1.

26. From *Les femmes électeurs et éligibles, 1848*, in *Le grief des femmes: Anthologie de textes féministes du môyen age à nos jours*, ed. Maïté Albistur and Daniel Armogathe (Poitiers: Editions Hier et Demain, 1978), 1: 280.

27. Jeanne Deroin, "A Ceux qui nous méconnaissant," *La Voix des femmes*, 10 April 1848, p. 2.

28. For Otto, Möhrmann, *Frauenemanzipation*, p. 199. For Otto having written the text in March, see Ute Gerhard, "Uber die Anfänge der deutschen Frauenbewegung um 1848: Frauenpresse, Frauenpolitik, und Frauenvereine" in *Frauen suchen ihre Geschichte: Historische Studien zum 19. und 20. Jahrhundert*, ed. Karin Hausen (München: Verlag C. H. Beck, 1983), p. 199.

29. *La Voix des femmes*, 27 March 1848, p. 4.

30. Emma Willard, "Letter to DuPont de l'Eure on the Political Position of Women," *American Literary Magazine* 2, no. 4 (April 1848), p. 248. Thanks to Karen Offen for informing me about this letter and sending me a copy.

31. Anne Knight, *Letter to Lord Brougham*.

32. Jeanne Deroin, letter to *La Liberté*, cited in Ranvier, "Feministe de 1848," pp. 326–327; for Stanton, Karlyn Kohrs Campbell, *Man Can Not Speak for Her*, vol. 2, *Texts* (New York: Praeger, 1989), pp. 42, 57.

33. Reprinted in Susan Groag Bell and Karen M. Offen, *Women, the Family, and Freedom: The Debate in Documents*, vol. 1, *1750–1880* (Stanford, Calif.: Stanford University Press, 1983), p. 166.

34. Jeanne Deroin, *Cours de droit social pour les Femmes* (Paris: 1848), pp. 3, 8. For an extended version of this argument, see Joan Scott, "The Duties of the Citizen: Jeanne Deroin in the Revolution of 1848," in *Only Paradoxes to Offer: French Feminists and the Rights of Man* (Cambridge: Harvard University Press, 1996), pp. 70–77. French feminists who had formerly been Saint-Simonian New Women, like Pauline Roland and Suzanne Voilquin, were more likely to use the argument from motherhood than feminists in other nations.

35. Jeanne Deroin, *Lettre d'une femme à M. Athanase Coquerel* (Paris: Imprimarie de Lacour, 1848); Jeanne Deroin, "Mission de la femme dans le present et dans l'avenir," *Opinion des Femmes*, 10 March 1849, reprinted in *Women, the Family, and Freedom: The Debate in Documents*, vol. 1, *1750–1880*, ed. Susan Groag Bell and Karen M. Offen (Stanford, Calif.: Stanford University Press, 1983), p. 262. Translation by Karen M. Offen.

36. For Otto, see Möhrmann, *Frauenemanzipation*, pp. 201–202; for Deroin, "Aux Citoyens Membres de la commission du banquet commemoratif de la Révolution de février, et Aux Représentants de la Montagne," 29 February 1849, Bibliothèque Historique de la Ville de Paris, NA MS. 111, no. 162. For another example of fraternity coming first, see Deroin, *Cours de droit social*, (Paris: 1848), pp. 1–2.

37. For the general argument about sisterhood, see Keith E. Melder,

Beginnings of Sisterhood: The American Woman's Rights Movement, 1800–1850 (New York: Schocken, 1977); and Carol Lasser, "'Let Us Be Sisters Forever': The Sororal Model of Nineteenth-Century Female Friendship," *Signs* 14, no. 1, (Autumn 1988), pp. 158–181.

38. Otto's novel was *Römisch und Deutsch*. For this citation, thanks to Michaela Tomaschewsky for sending me the relevant pages of her Ph.D. dissertation, "Malwida Von Meysenbug and the Cult of Humanism" (University of Illinois, 1993). For Leigh Smith, Diane Mary Chase Worzala, "The Langham Place Circle: The Beginnings of the Organized Women's Movement in England, 1854–1870" (Ph.D. diss., University of Wisconsin, 1982), p. 70; for the antislavery women, Jean Fagan Yellin, *Women and Sisters: The Antislavery Feminists in American Culture* (New Haven: Yale University Press, 1989).

39. Otto in Möhrmann, *Frauenemanzipation*, p. 199; Jeanne Deroin in *La Voix des femmes* 10 April 1848, p. 2.

40. Jeanne Deroin, *Cours de droit*, p. 3. For the same argument made in 1837 by Sarah Grimké, see her *Letters on the Equality of the Sexes and Other Essays*, ed. Elizabeth Ann Bartlett (New Haven: Yale University Press, 1988), pp. 55–56. Grimké concluded her letter on women's "Condition in Some Parts of Europe and America" by writing, "The page of history teems with woman's wrongs, and it is wet with woman's tears.—For the sake of my degraded sex everywhere, and for the sake of my brethren, who suffer just in proportion as they place woman lower in the scale of creation than man, lower than her Creator placed her, I entreat my sisters to arise in all the majesty of moral power, in all the dignity of immortal beings, and plant themselves, side by side, on the platform of human rights, with man, to whom they were designed to be companions, equals and helpers in every good word and work."

41. Cited in Ronald G. Walters, *American Reformers, 1815–1860* (New York: Hill & Wang, 1978), p. ix.

42. Brita K. Stendahl, *Fredrika Bremer: The Education of a Self-Made Woman, 1801–1865* (Lewiston, N.Y.: Edwin Mellen, 1994), pp. 70, 80.

43. Anne Knight, *Lettre à Monsieur Coquerel* (Paris: July, 1848); Lucretia Mott, *Speeches and Sermons*, p. 141. From Mott's 1849 *Discourse on Woman*, reprinted in the United States and Britain.

44. [Frances Wright], *England the Civilizer: Her History Developed in Its Principles; with Reference to the Civilizational History of Modern Europe (America Inclusive) and with a View to the Denouement of the Difficulties of the Hour by a Woman* (London: Simpkin, Marshall, 1848), pp. 384, 427, 470. For Anthony and Stanton reading this work, Celia Morris Eckhardt, *Fanny Wright: Rebel in America* (Cambridge: Harvard University Press, 1984), p. 282.

45. On this subject, see Lucette Czyba, "From Daumier to Flaubert: Caricatures of Feminism in the 1840s and 1848," in *Femmes d'esprit: Women in Daumier's Caricature*, ed. Kirsten Powell and Elizabeth C. Childs (Hanover, N.H.: University Press of New England, 1990), pp. 87–104. *La Liberté* is cited in Ranvier's article on Deroin, p. 326.

46. For Sand's nomination, *La Voix des femmes*, 6 April 1848; for Sand's repudiation, *La Voix des femmes*, 10 April 1848.

47. For the Breton delegate, Price, *1848 in France*, p. 89; for Considérant, Claire Goldberg Moses, *French Feminism in the Nineteenth Century* (Albany: State University of New York Press, 1984), pp. 141–142.

48. This is the letter that Anne Knight had a friend copy into her diary shortly before her death in 1862. Knight Papers, Friends House, London.

49. Jeanne Deroin, *Lettre d'une femme à M. Athanase Coquerel* (Paris: Imprimarie de Lacour, 1848); Anne Knight, *To Athanius Coquerel Paris 7 mo., 1848* is at Friends House, London in Tracts, vol. O, folder 229–230. The U.S. minister was Lindley Murray Hoag; the English one, Benjamin Parsons, and they are identified by Knight in footnotes. A slightly different version of this letter is reprinted in Bell and Offen, *Women*, 1: 250–251.

50. *La Politique des Femmes*, 25 June 1848, p. 2. Thanks to Michèle Riot-Sarcey for sending me a copy of this issue.

51. Fuller, *"Sad but Glorious Days,"* p. 230. Fuller had recently discovered she was pregnant, which also contributed to her decision to remain abroad.

52. For New York, Elliott Shore, Ken Fones-Wolf, and James P. Danky, eds., *The German-American Radical Press: The Shaping of a Left Political Culture, 1850–1940* (Urbana: University of Illinois Press, 1992), p. 10; for the French poster, *Les révolutions de 1848: l'Europe des images*, 2: 63.

53. For the newspapers, letter from J. Gordon Bennett to Emile de Girardin, Archives Nationales 113AP 1; for Mott, *Complete Speeches and Sermons*, p. 72.

54. Mott, *Complete Speeches and Sermons*, pp. 75, 78.

55. Lucretia Mott to Edmund Quincy, 24 August 1848, published in *The Liberator*, 6 October 1848, cited in Margaret Hope Bacon, *Valiant Friend: The Life of Lucretia Mott* (New York: Walker, 1980), p. 125.

56. From Stanton's eulogy of Mott in 1880, reprinted in Elizabeth Cady Stanton, Susan B. Anthony, and Matilda Joslyn Gage, eds., *History of Woman Suffrage*, vol. 1, *1848–1861* (1881; reprint, New York: Arno *New York Times*, 1969), p. 422.

57. Elizabeth Cady Stanton, *Eighty Years and More: Reminiscences, 1815–1897* (New York: Schocken, 1971), p. 147; Stanton cited in Elisabeth Griffith, *In Her Own Right: The Life of Elizabeth Cady Stanton* (New York: Oxford University Press, 1984), p. 51. For Douglass, Nancy A. Hewitt, "American Women in 1848: Woman's Rights in Comparative Perspective," *American Historical Association*, January, 1998, p. 4. Thanks to Nancy Hewitt for sending me this paper. For Stanton on "the first woman's rights convention," see Elizabeth Cady Stanton to Elizabeth W. McClintock (Mary Ann's daughter), 14[?] July 1848, printed in Ann D. Gordon, ed., *The Selected Papers of Elizabeth Cady Stanton and Susan B. Anthony*, vol. 1: *In The School of Anti-Slavery, 1840–1866* (New Brunswick, N.J.: Rutgers University Press, 1997), p. 69.

58. *Report of the Woman's Rights Convention held at Seneca Falls, N.Y., July 19 and 20, 1848* (Rochester: John Dick at the North Star Office, 1848).

59. For a detailed analysis of these networks, of which legal reform, the Free Soil party, and the dissident Congregational Quakers were paramount, see Judith Wellman, "The Seneca Falls Women's Rights Convention: A Study of Social Networks," *Journal of Women's History* 3, no. 1 (Spring 1991), pp. 9–37.

60. *Proceedings of the Woman's Rights Convention held at the Broadway Tabernacle, in the City of New York, on Tues. & Wed., Sept. 6th & 7th, 1853* (New York: Fowler & Wells, 1853), p. 17.

61. Cited in Nancy A. Hewitt, "Feminist Friends: Agrarian Quakers and the Emergence of Woman's Rights in America," *Feminist Studies* 12, no. 1 (Spring 1986), pp. 39–40.

62. *Proceedings of the Woman's Rights Convention, held at the Unitarian Church, Rochester, N.Y., August 2, 1848 to Consider the Rights of Woman, Politically, Religiously, and Industrially*, rev. by Mrs. Amy Post (New York: Robert J. Johnston, 1870), pp. 3, 11, 15; Nancy A. Hewitt, *Women's Activism and Social Change: Rochester, New York, 1822–1872* (Ithaca, N.Y.: Cornell University Press, 1984), p. 42ff.

63. Cited in Stanton, Anthony, and Gage, *History of Woman Suffrage*, 1: 805.

64. The speech was printed only once in the nineteenth century, in 1870, when an enlarged version the *Proceedings* of the Seneca Falls Convention was published in New York. It is reprinted in Campbell, *Man Can Not Speak for Her*, 2: 42–70. Mott's reference to Stanton's "*great* speech," which urges her to give it on the second day at Seneca Falls, so that James Mott and the other men can hear it, is from a 16 July 1848 letter printed in Gordon, *Selected Papers*, 1:74. In this volume, Ann D. Gordon argues that Stanton did not deliver this speech until September in Waterloo, New York; she also repeated it at Farmington in October (see pp. 94, 127). I believe this is a misreading of the evidence. For Stanton giving the speech at Rochester, see Griffith, *In Her Own Right*, p. 59. The 1848 *Proceedings* of both Seneca Falls and Rochester refer to speeches by Mott and Stanton but do not give their texts.

65. Stanton told her audience that this was the first time she had spoken in public; in 1842, however, Lucretia Mott wrote Richard and Hannah Webb that Stanton had addressed an audience of about 100 women on temperance: "She infused her speech with a homeopathic dose of woman's rights and does the same in many private conversations." Lucretia Mott to Richard and Hannah Webb, 25 February–March 7, 1842, Boston Public Library, Manuscript Division, Anti-Slavery Collection, Ms. A.1.2, vol. 12.2, p. 34; p. 5 of the letter.

66. Campbell, *Man Can Not Speak for Her*, 2: 42–45, 64–65, 47. "Tinga" was Nzinga Mbande (1582–1663).

67. Ibid., 2: 54, 56–57, 69, 70.

68. Lucretia Mott to Hannah and Richard Webb, 10 September 1848, Boston Public Library, Manuscript Division, Anti-Slavery Collection, Ms. A.1.2, vol. 18, p. 34.

69. Lucretia Mott to Elizabeth Cady Stanton, 3 October 1848, Library of Congress, Manuscript Division, Elizabeth Cady Stanton Papers, General Correspondence, reel 1.

70. Bessie Rayner Parkes, "Helen's Answer," in *Summer Sketches, and other Poems* (London: John Chapman, 1854), p. 38.

71. G. J. Holyoake, "Hints to the Advocates on the Rights of Women," *Reasoner* 11 August 1847, pp. 429, 434–435. The other journal was *People's Press.* Also, George Jacob Holyoake, *Sixty Years of an Agitator's Life* (London: T. Fisher Unwin, 1892), 1: 225.

72. Eliot cited in Rosemary Ashton, *Little Germany: German Refugees in Victorian Britain* (Oxford: Oxford University Press, 1989), p. 248; George Eliot to John Sibree, 8 March 1848, *Letters of George Eliot,* ed. Gordon S. Haight (New Haven: Yale University Press, 1954), 1: 256.

73. *The Times* (London), 11 April 1848, p. 1.

74. From Tennyson's *The Princess,* conclusion, lines 59, 62–65, 70–71. Although Tennyson first published *The Princess* in 1847, he kept adding to it; this section was written in 1850 or 1851.

75. For the cartoon, see *Les révolutions de 1848: l'Europe des images,* vol. 2, *Le printemps des peuples,* p. 62. Anna Jameson to Ottilie von Goethe, 25 April 1848, in Needler, *Letters of Anna Jameson to Ottilie von Goethe,* p. 161. Jameson's 1845 treatise on women, *The Relative Position of Mothers and Governesses,* was republished as *Women's Mission and Women's Position.* For her life, see Clara Thomas, *Love and Work Enough: The Life of Anna Jameson* (Toronto: University of Toronto Press, 1967).

76. Disraeli's speech is reprinted in Ray Strachey, *The Cause: A Short History of the Women's Movement in Great Britain* (1928; reprint, London: Virago, 1978), p. 43. Disraeli argued that "in a country governed by a woman, where you allow women to form part of the estates of the Realm—Peeresses in their own right for example—where you allow women not only to hold land but to be ladies of the manor and to hold legal courts—where a woman by law may be a church warden and overseer of the poor—I do not see, where she has as much to do with State and Church, on what reasons, if you come to right, she has not the right to vote." For Knight's attempt to make contact with the younger feminists, see Bessie Rayner Parkes to Barbara Leigh Smith, 2 April 1850, Parkes Papers, B. R. Parkes Vol. 5, 45, Girton College, Cambridge, England.

77. For Otto's address to the Worker's Commission, see Möhrmann, *Frauenemanzipation,* p. 199; for her editorial, *"Dem Reich der Freiheit werb' ich Bargerinnen:" Die Frauen-Zeitung von Louise Otto,* p. 39. Her "address" was written during the spring and first published on 20 May 1848 in the *Leipziger Arbeiter-Zeitung.* Gerhard, *Unerhört,* p. 51.

78. Von Meysenbug, *Idealisten,* 1: 141–143.

79. For Fröbel, see Hummel-Haasis, *Schwestern,* p. 125. For Amalie Struve, see her *Errinerungen aus den badischen Freiheitskämpfen* (Hamburg, 1850), as well as Anna Blos, *Frauen der deutschen Revolution, 1848* (Dresden: Verlag Kaden & Comp., 1928), chap. 8; and Dagmar Herzog, "Amalie Dusar Struve," in *Encyclopedia of the 1848 Revolutions,* ed. James Chastain (New York: Garland, 1995). Thanks to Dagmar Herzog for sending me this entry in manuscript.

80. Mathilde Franziska Anneke, *Mutterland: Memoiren einer Frau aus dem badisch-pfälzischen Feldzuge 1848/49* (1853; reprint, Münster: Tende, 1982), p. 10.

81. For a contemporary illustration of such a parade in Berlin in color, see *Les révolutions de 1848: l'Europe des images*, vol. 2, *Le printemps des peuples*, p. 62; for Mainz, see Hummel-Haasis, *Schwestern*, pp. 116–117.

82. Meysenbug, *Idealisten*, 1: 70–71. For a print and description of Philipp Veit's painting of Germania, see George L. Mosse, *Nationalism and Sexuality: Middle-Class Morality and Sexual Norms in Modern Europe* (Madison: University of Wisconsin Press, 1985), p. 18. For the Austrian parliament, Gabriella Hauch, *Frau Biedermeier auf den Barrikaden: Frauenleben in der Wiener Revolution 1848* (Vienna: Gesellschaftskritik, 1990), p.101.

83. For Otto, see Ruth-Ellen Boetcher Joeres, *Die Anfänge der deutschen Frauenbewegung: Louise Otto-Peters* (Frankfurt am Main: Fischer, 1983) p. 100. For the kindergarten teachers, see Catherine M. Prelinger, *Charity, Challenge, and Change: Religious Dimensions of the Mid-Nineteenth-Century Women's Movement in Germany* (Westport, Conn.: Greenwood, 1987), pp. 91–93. Information on Democratic Women's Associations drawn from Wittig, *Nicht nur im Stillen Kreis*, pp. 120–130. For Perin and the Viennese Association, see Hummel-Haasis, *Schwestern*, pp. 240–258.

84. For Perin, see Hummel-Hassis, *Schwestern*, p. 252. For Anneke, see Maria Wagner, *Mathilde Franziska Anneke in Selbstzeugnissen und Dokumenten* (Frankfurt am Main: Fischer Taschenbuch Verlag, 1980), p. 40.

85. Hummel-Haasis, *Schwestern*, pp. 198–199.

Chapter Eight

1. *Proceedings of the National Women's Rights Convention, held at Cleveland, Ohio on Oct. 5th, 6th, & 7th, 1853* (Cleveland: Gray, Beardsley, Spear, & Co., 1854), pp. 57–58. Mott paraphrased Hugo; for his words, which are used here, see Claire Goldberg Moses, *French Feminism in the Nineteenth Century* (Albany: State University of New York Press, 1984), p. 149.

2. *Proceedings of the Woman's Rights Convention held at the Broadway Tabernacle, in the City of New York, on Tues. & Wed., Sept. 6th and 7th, 1853* (New York: Fowler & Wells, 1853), pp. 17–18. For Stone's appearance, see Andrea Moore Kerr, *Lucy Stone: Speaking Out for Equality* (New Brunswick, N.J.: Rutgers University Press, 1992), p. 71.

3. Jeanne Deroin, ed. *Almanach des femmes pour 1852* (Paris: Chez l'Editeur, 1852), p. 14. The author identified herself only as "Anna."

4. Fredrika Bremer, *The Homes of the New World; Impressions of America*, trans. Mary Howitt, 2 vols. (New York: Harper, 1853), 2: 615–616.

5. *Proceedings of the Tenth National Woman's Rights Convention, held at the Cooper Institute, New York City, May 10th & 11th, 1860* (Boston: Yerrinton & Garrison, 1860), p. 10.

6. Gerhard K. Friesen, "A Letter from M. F. Anneke: A Forgotten German-American Pioneer in Women's Rights," *Journal of German-American Studies*, 12, no. 2 (1977), p. 36.

7. The statement about conventions reaching out to "the Old and the New World" is from Paulina W. Davis, *A History of the National Woman's Rights Movement* (New York: Journeyman's Press, 1871), p. 5, reprinted as a New York Times Source Book in 1970. The statement about writing letters is from a manuscript of a speech by Davis, "On the Renting of a Hall for Women's Rights Meetings," pp. 9–10, Paulina Wright Davis Papers, Vassar College. For Anneke's words, *Proceedings . . . New York City, 1853*, p. 89.

8. *Proceedings . . . New York City, 1853*, pp. 76–77.

9. Weber's letter was printed in *The Proceedings of the Woman's Rights Convention Held at Worcester, October 23 & 24, 1850* (Boston: Prentice & Sawyer, 1851), pp. 76–79. It was not discussed at the meeting because, although the organizers thought the subject of "woman's dress" "all important," they did not think there was time to deal with it sufficiently at this first convention and they also disagreed with Weber's solution of wearing men's clothing. Martineau's, Deroin and Roland's, and Spring's letters are in *The Proceedings of the Woman's Rights Convention Held at Worcester, October 15 & 16, 1851* (New York: Fowler & Wells, 1852) on pp. 13–16, 32–35, and 102–103 respectively. Reid's letter is in *The Proceedings of the Woman's Rights Convention, Held at Syracuse, September 8th, 9th, & 10th, 1852* (Syracuse, N.Y.: Masters, 1852), pp. 10–12.

10. Harriet Taylor Mill, "Enfranchisement of Women," reprinted in *Sexual Equality: Writings by John Stuart Mill, Harriet Taylor Mill, and Helen Taylor*, ed. Ann P. Robson and John M. Robson (Toronto: University of Toronto Press, 1994), p. 203. For the importance of Mill's article in the United States, see Evelyn L. Pugh, "John Stuart Mill, Harriet Taylor, and Women's Rights in America," *Canadian Journal of History*, 13, no. 3 (December, 1978), pp. 423–442; for Martineau, *Proceedings . . . 1851*, p. 13.

11. *Proceedings . . . Cleveland, 1853*, p. 56.

12. Paulina Wright Davis, *Una*, vol. 1, no. 2, (March 1853), pp. 24–25.

13. See Dr. Elizabeth Blackwell, *Pioneer Work in Opening the Medical Profession to Women: Autobiographical Sketches* (1875; reprint, New York: Schocken, 1977); Elinor Rice Hays, *Those Extraordinary Blackwells: The Story of a Journey to a Better World* (New York: Harcourt, Brace & World, 1967), and Jo Manton, *Elizabeth Garrett Anderson* (New York: Dutton, 1965).

14. For Bremer and Hunt, see Bremer, *Homes of the New World*, 1: 93; and Harriot K. Hunt, M.D., *Glances and Glimpses; or Fifty Years Social, including Twenty Years Professional Life* (1856; reprint, New York: Source Book Press, 1970), pp. 235–237; for Finch and Hunt, see Hunt, *Glances and Glimpses*, p. 217; for Bodichon and Hunt, see Barbara Leigh Smith Bodichon, *An American Diary, 1857–8*, ed. from the MS by Joseph W. Reed Jr. (London: Routledge & Kegan Paul, 1972), pp. 154–157, 160. For Hunt on Worcester, Hunt, *Glances and Glimpses*, pp. 249–250.

15. Signe Alice Rooth, *Seeress of the Northland: Fredrika Bremer's American Journey 1849–1851* (Philadelphia: American Swedish Historical Foundation, 1955), p. 17; Charlotte Bremer, ed., *Life, Letters and Posthumous Works of Fredrika Bremer*, trans. Fredr. Milow (New York: Hurd & Houghton, 1868), pp. 85, 88.

16. Fredrika Bremer to Marcus and Rebecca Spring, 18 January 1854, cited in Rooth, *Seeress*, p. 136. For Parkes's view of Bremer, see Bessie Rayner Parkes to Elizabeth Priestley Parkes [her mother] 16 October 1851, Bessie Rayner Parkes Papers, vol. II 3/3, Girton College, Cambridge. For Eliot's view of Bremer, see *The George Eliot Letters*, ed. Gordon S. Haight (New Haven: Yale University Press, 1954), vol. I, p. 365ff. Bremer's comment is from her *England in 1851 or Sketches of a Tour in England*, trans. L.A.H. (Boulogne, Merridew, 1853), p. 121. The call for an international peace alliance is in the London *Times*, 28 August 1854, p. 5. It reads in part: "Sisters then, whom we do not know as yet, but in whose existence we believe and hope, here and there among the ancient kingdoms of Asia, the steppes of Siberia, or in the Imperial cities of Russia; sisters of the western countries of Europe, who have lighted and guided us a long time by your bright example; and you, sisters in that vast new land beyond the Atlantic Ocean . . . give us your hands!"

17. Bremer to Hunt, cited in Rooth, *Seeress*, pp. 135–136.

18. This account of the Swedish version of *Hertha*, which is far longer and more complex than the English version, is drawn from Brita K. Stendahl, *Fredrika Bremer: The Education of a Self-Made Woman, 1801–1865* (Lewiston, N.Y.: Edwin Mellen Press, 1994) and private correspondence with the author.

19. Greta Wieselgren, "Romanen Herthas betydelse för myndighetsreformen 1858" (The importance of the novel *Hertha* for the legal majority reforms of 1858) in *Fredrika Bremer ute och hemma* (*Fredrika Bremer abroad and at Home*) Birgitta Holm, ed., (Uppsala, Sweden: Almqvist & Wiksell Tryckeri, 1987), pp. 95, 103, 115. Thanks to Barry Jacobs for translating this article for me.

20. Information on *Ruth Hall* drawn from Joyce W. Warren, *Fanny Fern: An Independent Woman* (New Brunswick, N.J.: Rutgers University Press, 1992), chap. 8. Thanks to Linda Grasso for help with this section.

21. Elizabeth Barrett Browning, *Aurora Leigh: A Poem*, (1856; reprint, Chicago: Academy, 1979), bk. 2, p. 45, bk. 5, p. 176. Also see Dorothy Mermin, *Elizabeth Barrett Browning: The Origins of a New Poetry* (Chicago: University of Chicago Press, 1989), chap. 7.

22. In addition to Bloomer's *Lily* and Davis's *Una*, two other U.S. women's rights journals appeared in the early 1850s: *The Genius of Liberty*, edited by Elizabeth A. Aldrich in Cincinnati from 1851 to 1853 and *The Pioneer and Women's Advocate*, edited by Anne W. Spencer in East Greenwich, Rhode Island. Neither had an international dimension. The same is true of two slightly later U.S. journals: Anne McDowell's *The Woman's Advocate* of Philadelphia, 1855–1856, which later merged with the *Woman's Temperance Paper* and was published until 1858, and Dr. Lydia Sayer Hasbrouck's *The Sibyl*, published in Middletown, New York from 1856 to 1864. On this subject, see *The Radical Women's Press of the 1850s*, ed. Ann Russo and Charis Kramarae,(New York: Routledge, 1991); and Martha M.

Solomon, ed., *A Voice of Their Own: The Woman Suffrage Press, 1840–1910* (Tuscaloosa: University of Alabama Press, 1991).

23. Mathilde Franziska Anneke, *Deutsche Frauen-Zeitung*, 15 October 1852, p. 49. This is my translation, which is truer to the German original than the English version printed in the newspaper. This sole remaining issue is at the American Antiquarian Society, Worcester, Massachusetts.

24. Louise Otto, "Mein Programm als Mitarbeiterin einer Frauenzeitung" in *Das Wesen der Ehe nebst einigen Aufsätzen über die sociale Reform der Frauen*, ed. Louise Dittmar (Leipzig: Otto Wigand, 1849), p. 20. Thanks to Dagmar Herzog for sending me a copy of this work. Louise Dittmar, "Das Wesen der Ehe" in the anthology just cited, p. 48. *Opinion des femmes*, 5 (June, 1849), p. 5.

25. For Harriet Taylor Mill, see Robson and Robson, eds., *Sexual Equality*, p. 197. For other feminists' views of marriage, see *Lucretia Mott: Her Complete Speeches and Sermons*, ed. Dana Greene (New York: Edwin Mellen, 1980), p. 154, for Deroin and Roland, see *Gazette des Tribunaux* (Court Gazette), 14 November 1850, p. 2; 15 November 1850, p. 2.

26. Dittmar in *Frauenemanzipation im deutschen Vormärz*, ed. Renate Möhrmann, (Stuttgart: Philipp Reclam, 1978), p. 145. Roland cited in Edith Thomas, *Pauline Roland: Socialisme et Féminisme au XIXe Siècle* (Paris: Marcel Rivière, 1956), p. 165.

27. For Ronge, see Catherine M. Prelinger, "Religious Dissent, Women's Rights, and the Hamburger Hochschule für das weibliche Geschlecht in Mid-Nineteenth-century Germany," in *Church History* (March 1976), p. 44. Ronge's charter is in his *Aufruf an die deutschen Männer und Frauen nebst Grundstimmungen der freien Kirche* (Hamburg, 1850). Mill's statement is printed in F. A. Hayek, *John Stuart Mill and Harriet Taylor Mill: Their Correspondence and Subsequent Marriage* (London: Routledge & Kegan Paul, 1951), p. 168; Stone and Blackwell's protest is in Kerr, *Lucy Stone*, pp. 86–87.

28. *Proceedings . . . Worcester, 1850*, pp. 25–26.

29. Jeanne Deroin, *L'Opinion des femmes*, 10 February 1849, pp. 1, 6.

30. Madame [Jenny] d'Héricourt, *A Woman's Philosophy of Women; or Woman Affranchised* (New York: Carleton, 1864), pp. 36–37.

31. For *La ragione*, Karen Offen, "A Nineteenth-Century French Feminist Rediscovered: Jenny P. d'Héricourt, 1809–1875," *Signs: Journal of Women in Culture and Society* 13, no. 1 (Autumn 1987), p. 157. For Parkes and Holyoake, see Bessie Rayner Parkes to Mary Merryweather, 26 January 1857, BRP VI, 72, and G. J. Holyoake to Bessie Rayner Parkes, February, 1857, BRP IX, 122, Parkes Papers, Girton College, Cambridge. The articles appeared in *Reasoner*, 1 March 1857, p. 1; 8 March 1857, p. 1; 15 March 1857, p. 1; 22 March 1857, pp. 1–2.

32. Jeanne Deroin, *L'Opinion des femmes*, 10 April 1849, p. 2.

33. For Stanton's campaign, see Elisabeth Griffith, *In Her Own Right: The Life of Elizabeth Cady Stanton* (New York: Oxford University Press, 1984), pp. 125–126. For Channing, see *Proceedings . . . 1851*, p. 32. For the visit to Deroin, see Stanton's *Diary* for 15 December 1882, printed in Theodore Stanton and Harriot Stanton Blatch, eds., *Elizabeth Cady Stanton as Revealed in Her Letters, Diary, and*

Reminiscences (New York: Harper, 1922), 2: 201. Stanton also looked up Ernestine Rose on this visit.

34. Knight published two letters from Deroin and Roland, both of which mentioned Deroin's campaign. For the first, see *Northern Star*, 14 June 1851, p. 1. For the second, see *Northern Star, and National Trades' Journal* [the paper kept changing its name in these years], 9 August 1851, p. 1. For Otto, see *Frauen-Zeitung*, 23 August 1851, p. 228. The article was written by E. Weller.

35. For associations in general, see Maurice Agulhon, *The Republican Experiment, 1848–1852*, trans. Janet Lloyd (Cambridge: Cambridge University Press, 1983), pp. 115–116. For Deroin's ideas, *L'Opinion des femmes*, June 1849, p. 1; *L'Opinion des femmes*, August 1849, passim, and her *Lettre aux associations sur l'organisation du crédit* (Paris: Gustave Sandré, 1851).

36. Michèle Riot-Sarcey, *La démocratie à l'épreuve des femmes: Trois figures critique du pouvoir, 1830–1848* (Paris: Albin Michel, 1994), pp. 255ff.

37. For the letter as it appeared in *La Presse*, see Archives Nationales, 113AP1; for the letter in *Le Pays*, see Bibliothèque Historique de la Ville de Paris, NA111, no. 164.

38. *Almanach des Femmes pour 1852*, pp. 69–70. The article runs from p. 62 to p. 70. The first portion is signed "Eve," the second, "Clemence."

39. Jeanne Deroin, ed., *Almanach des femmes. Seconde année. Women's Almanack for 1853, in the English and French Languages* (London: James Watson; Jersey: Universal Printing Establishment, 1853), pp. 14, 112, 100, 106, 116–162. Hereafter called *Almanach des femmes 1853*.

40. Jeanne Deroin, *Almanach des femmes pour 1854* (Londres: Librairie et Agence de l'Imprimerie Universelle de Jersey; James Watson, 1854), pp. 38–39.

41. Paulina Wright Davis, *Una*, 1, no. 3 (April 1853), p.48; 1, no. 10 (November 1853), pp. 164–166; November 1853, pp. 169–170 reprinted Victor Hugo's elogy of Louise Collet, also printed in Deroin's 1853 *Almanack*; 3, no. 7 (July 1855), p. 110 printed information on the "Amazons of Africa" drawn from Deroin's 1853 *Almanack*.

42. Paulina Wright Davis, *Una*, 1 February 1853, p. 1.

43. Letter from N. E. Clark, M.D., published in *Una*, 3, no. 1 (January 1855), p. 13.

44. Marianne Finch, *An Englishwoman's Experience in America* (London: Richard Bentley, 1853), pp. 16, 73, 79.

45. Finch, *Englishwoman's Experience*, p. 226; Harriot K. Hunt, M.D., *Glances and Glimpses; or Fifty Years Social, including Twenty Years Professional Life* (1856; reprint, New York: Source Book Press, 1970), p. 281.

46. *Una*, 1, no. 2 (March 1853), p. 23.

47. *Una*, 1, no. 3 (April 1853), p. 35.

48. Elizabeth Cady Stanton to Paulina Wright Davis, 6 December 1852, in *The Selected Papers of Elizabeth Cady Stanton and Susan B. Anthony*, vol. 1, *In The School of Anti-Slavery 1840 to 1866*, ed. Ann D. Gordon (New Brunswick, N.J.: Rutgers University Press, 1997), pp. 214–215; Paulina Wright Davis, *Una*, 1, no. 4 (May 1853), pp. 62–63.

49. Paulina Wright Davis, *Una*, 3, no. 2 (February 1855), pp. 24–25.

50. *Una*, 1, no. 5 (June 1853), p. 77. The names of the league's founders are in *Star of Freedom* [originally *Northern Star*], London, 8 May 1852, p. 5.

51. *Una*, 2, no. 6 (June 1854), p. 280; *Una*, 1, no. 9 (October 1853), p. 155.

52. For Davis's letter to Holyoake, see *Reasoner*, 14 December 1853, pp. 396–397; for Holyoake's piece on women printers in the United States, see *Reasoner*, 2 December 1855, p. 288. Holyoake wrote that he based his information on a 29 November 1855 letter from Davis. He also claimed that the *Providence Post* and the Pittsburgh *Daily Dispatch* employed female typesetters.

53. For France, where the issue focused in 1912 on "l'affaire Couriau" when a Lyon union refused a female typesetter membership and expelled her husband, also a typesetter, for employing her, see Charles Sowerwine, *Sisters or Citizens? Women and Socialism in France since 1876* (Cambridge: Cambridge University Press, 1982), pp. 135–136. In Britain, compositors' trade unions excluded women until 1886, and as late as 1926 the English Typographical Society blocked a merger with the Scottish Typographical Association because they had female members. Sheila Lewenhak, *Women and Trade Unions: An Outline History of Women in the British Trade Union Movement* (New York: St. Martin's, 1977), p. 62. For the United States, see Russo and Kramarae, *Radical Women's Press of the 1850s*, pp. 110–112.

54. For Anneke, see Maria Wagner, *Mathilde Franziska Anneke in Selbstzeugnissen und Dokumenten* (Frankfurt am Main: Fischer Taschenbuch Verlag, 1980), p. 76; for Bloomer, see *Lily*, 1 May 1854, p. 69.

55. Parkes worked *Una* into a poem. "Here's the 'Una,' / Chiefly by brave New England women penn'd / In favour of their movement, and the stream / Of good ideas flowing from their midst." She had a character representing herself write to one based on her good friend Barbara Leigh Smith. Parkes went on to criticize *The Una's* name: "It has a most uncomfortable title, / For our plain nation likes plain words and round, / And here some such are needed." Bessie Rayner Parkes, "Helen's Answer," in *Summer Sketches, and Other Poems* (London: John Chapman, 1854), p. 34.

56. On Faithfull and the Victoria Press, see Candida Ann Lacey, ed., *Barbara Leigh Smith Bodichon and the Langham Place Group* (New York: Routledge & Kegan Paul, 1987), pp. 279–291; William E. Fredeman, "Emily Faithfull and the Victoria Press: An Experiment in Sociological Bibliography," *Library*, 5th series, 29, no. 2 (June 1974), pp. 139–164.

57. *Lily* 1, no. 1 (January 1849), p. 1.

58. *Lily* 2, no. 4 (April 1851), p. 30; Carol A. Kolmerten, *Women in Utopia: The Ideology of Gender in the American Owenite Communities* (Bloomington: Indiana University Press, 1990), p. 56; Bremer, *Homes of the New World*, 1: 80.

59. *Lily* 3, no. 5 (May 1851), p. 38; Dr. Mary Walker (1832–1919), who served during the Civil War, wore men's clothing for most of her life. *English Woman's Journal* 16 (January 1867), p. 112. *The Lily* 3, no. 6, (June 1851), p. 46.

60. Cited in Kathleen Barry, *Susan B. Anthony: A Biography of a Singular Feminist* (New York: New York University Press, 1988), p. 81. *Lily* 3, no. 11, (November 1851), p. 83. See also Elizabeth Cady Stanton to Amelia Opie, 30 October 1851,

Elizabeth Cady Stanton Papers, Library of Congress, Manuscript Division, reel 1. I have not been able to corroborate this incident from English sources.

61. Stanton and Blatch, *Elizabeth Cady Stanton*, 2:30; *Una* 3, no. 5 (May 1855), p. 77; *Lily* 4, no. 2 (February 1852), p. 14. Charles Neilson Gattey, *The Bloomer Girls* (London: Femina, 1967), has illustrations of a number of these sources; his reference to an article on the Crystal Palace event in the London *Times*, however, is inaccurate.

62. Aston cited in Möhrmann, *Frauenemanzipation*, p. 79; *Lily* 3, no. 10 (October 1851), p. 79.

63. Louise Otto, *Frauen-Zeitung*, 2 November 1851, pp. 297–298. Other articles on the subject are in issues dated 9 November 1851, pp. 305–307; 16 November 1851, pp. 313–314; 23 November 1851, p. 319; 7 December 1851, pp. 342–343, 14 December 1851, p. 349; 11 January 1852, pp. 5–6; 18 January 1852, pp. 14–15; 4 April 1852, p. 103.

64. The female democrat was Henriette Bock, a Hanau German Catholic and member of a democratic women's association, who wrote to Blum's widow and sent a copy of the letter to Otto. Cited in Sylvia Paletschek, *Frauen und Dissens: Frauen in Deutschkatholizmus und in den freien Gemeinden, 1841–1852* (Göttingen: Vandenhoeck & Ruprecht, 1990), p. 241. Parts of the police handbook are reprinted in Gerlinde Hummel-Haasis, ed., *Schwestern zerreist eure Kettern: Zeugnisse zur Geschichte der Frauen in der Revolution von 1848/49* (München: Deutscher Taschenbuch Verlag, 1982), p. 133.

65. Cited in Ute Gerhard, *Unerhört: Die Geschichte der Deutschen Frauenbewegung* (Reinbek bei Hamburg: Rowohlt, 1990), p. 73. Louise Otto, *Frauen-Zeitung*, 7 July 1849, p. 111 in *"Dem Reich der Freiheit werb' ich Bürgerinnen: Die Frauen-Zeitung von Louise Otto*, ed. Ute Gerhard, Elisabeth Hannover-Dürck, and Romina Schmitter (Frankfurt am Main: Syndikat, 1979).

66. For the poem, see *Louise Otto-Peters: Ihr literarisches und publizistisches Werk*, ed. Johanna Ludwig and Rita Jorek (Leipzig: University of Leipzig Press, 1995), p. 32. *Frauen-Zeitung*, 29 June 1850, reprinted in *Dem Reich der Freiheit*, p. 279.

67. See her article "Für die Arbeiterinnen", *Frauen-Zeitung*, 8 December 1849; 15 December 1849, reprinted in *Dem Reich der Freiheit*, pp. 179–182, 184–187.

68. Paletschek, *Frauen und Dissens*, pp. 223ff.

69. On this subject, see Ann Taylor Allan, *Feminism and Motherhood: Germany, 1800–1914* (New Brunswick, N.J.: Rutgers University Press, 1991), pp. 60ff.; Paletschek, *Frauen und Dissens*, pp. 216ff.; and Catherine M. Prelinger, *Charity, Challenge, and Change: Religious Dimensions of the Mid-Nineteenth-Century Women's Movement in Germany* (Westport, Conn.: Greenwood, 1987).

70. Prelinger, *Charity*, p. 161. Joh. and Bertha Ronge, *A Practical Guide to the English Kinder Garten (Children's Garden) for the use of Mothers, Nurses, and Infant Tenders, Being an Exposition of Froebel's System of Infant Training, accompanied by a great variety of Instructive and Amusing Games, and Industrial and Gymnastic Exercises, also Numerous Songs, Set to Music and Arranged to the Exercises* (London: J. S.

Hodson, 1855). Also see Herr and Madame Ronge, *Addresses on the Kinder Garten System of Elementary Education* (Manchester: Fletcher & Tubbs, 1859) and *Madame Ronge's Kinder Garten Alphabet* (1857), owned by the British Library. For Elizabeth Peabody, Louise Hall Tharpe, *The Peabody Sisters of Salem* (1950; reprint, Boston: Little, Brown and Co., 1988), chap. 25. Elizabeth Cady Stanton, *Eighty Years and More: Reminiscences 1815–1897* (1898; reprint New York: Schocken, 1971), pp. 4,9.

71. Bodichon, *American Diary*, p. 142. On this school, also see ibid., p. 179 n. 162; Marie Marmo Mullaney, "Feminism, Utopianism, and Domesticity: The Career of Rebecca Buffum Spring, 1811–1911," *New Jersey History* 104, nos. 3–4 (Fall-Winter 1986), pp. 1–21; Gerda Lerner, *The Grimké Sisters from South Carolina: Rebels against Slavery* (Boston: Houghton Mifflin, 1967). The school was known as the Belleville School and the Englewood School. For the Portman School, Elizabeth Malleson, *Autobiographical Notes and Letters*, with a memoir by Hope Malleson (London: Printed for private circulation, 1926), pp. 48ff.

72. [Bessie Rayner Parkes], *Remarks on the Education of Girls* (London: John Chapman, 1854), pp. 9, 12, 20.

73. The late Catherine M. Prelinger introduced knowledge of the Hamburger Hochschule to English speakers in her pioneering "Religious Dissent, Women's Rights, and the Hamburger Hochschule für das weibliche Geschlecht in Mid-Nineteenth Century Germany," *Church History* 45 (March 1976), pp. 42–55. Since then, her work has been added to by Paletschek, *Frauen und Dissens*, pp. 215ff. and Elke Kleinau, "Ein (hochschul-)praktischer Versuch—Die 'Hochschule für das weibliche Geschlecht' in Hamburg," in *Geschichte der Mädchen und Frauenbildung*, vol. 2, ed. Elke Kleinau and Claudia Opetz (Frankfurt am Main: Campus, 1996). Jewish women's role has been studied by Sabine Knappe, "Jüdische Frauenorganisationen in Hamburg zwischen Assimilation, jüdischer Identität, und weiblicher Emanzipation während des Kaiserreichs" (master's thesis, University of Hamburg, 1991), sect. 4.3.1. Thanks to Maria Baader for providing me with copies of these last two works. Malwida von Meysenbug, *Memoiren einer Idealistin* (Berlin: Schuster & Loeffler, 1881), 1: 194, 237.

74. Margaret Tuke, *A History of Bedford College for Women, 1849–1937* (London: Oxford University Press, 1939), pp. 3, 36, 78. For Sarah Parker Remond, the younger sister of Charles Lenox Remond who attended the 1840 Anti-Slavery Convention (and refused to take his seat in solidarity with the silenced female delegates), see Sibyl Ventriss Brownlee, "Out of the Abundance of the Heart: Sarah Ann Parker Remond's Quest for Freedom," (Ph.D. diss., University of Massachusetts, 1997) and *We Are Your Sisters: Black Women in the Nineteenth Century*, ed. Dorothy Stirling (New York: Norton, 1984), pp.178–179.

75. *Proceedings . . . Worcester, 1851*, p. 89.

76. Mathilde Franziska Anneke, *Deutscher Frauen-Zeitung*, 15 October 1852, pp. 55–56. Bremer, whose article appeared in a U.S. magazine, is cited in Sarah Allaback, "'Better Than Silver and Gold': Design Schools for Women in America, 1848–1860," *Journal of Women's History* 10, no. 1 (Spring 1998), p. 88.

77. Thomas Neville Bonner, *To the Ends of the Earth: Women's Search for Education in Medicine* (Cambridge: Harvard University Press, 1992), p. 6. Louise Otto, *Frauen-Zeitung*, 24 March 1852, p. 70; 12 April 1851, p. 79.

78. Bodichon, *American Diary*, p. 100. Thanks to Eric Goldstein for helping me identify Elizabeth Cohen, M.D.

79. For Whitman, see Howard E. Hugo, ed., *The Portable Romantic Reader* (New York: Viking, 1960), pp. 514–516.

80. *The Proceedings of the Woman's Rights Convention, Held at Syracuse, Sept. 8th, 9th, & 10th, 1852* (Syracuse, N.Y.: J. E. Masters, 1852), pp. 85ff.

81. For the conservatism of the English women's movement, Diane Mary Chase Worzala, "The Langham Place Circle: The Beginning of the Organized Women's Movement in England, 1854–1879" Ph.D. diss., University of Wisconsin, 1982), pp. 124ff. On property law and marriage legislation in England, see Lee Holcombe, *Wives and Property: Reform of the Married Women's Property Law in Nineteenth-Century England* (Toronto: University of Toronto Press, 1983); and Mary Lyndon Shanley, *Feminism, Marriage, and the Law in Victorian England, 1850–1895* (London: I. B. Tauris, 1989), chap. 1. The 1856 organizing petition is reprinted as appendix 1 in Holcombe, *Wives and Property*, pp. 237–238. Married women received control over their earnings in 1870.

82. Bodichon's account of her visit to Mott is in her *American Diary*, pp. 140–141. An envelope with the Langham Place address—the headquarters of the English women's movement—on it was used by Mott to write to her daughter, Pattie Lord. Mott Manuscripts, box 1, Friends Historical Library, Swarthmore College.

83. On this subject, see Wendy Hamand Venet, *Neither Ballots Nor Bullets: Women Abolitionists and the Civil War* (Charlottesville: University of Virginia Press, 1991). Thanks to Nancy Hewitt for help with this section.

84. Lucretia Mott to Martha Wright, 9 April 1865, Mott Manuscripts, box 2, 1861–66, Friends Historical Library, Swarthmore College, Pennsylvania.

85. For a discussion of this work, see Claire Goldberg Moses, *French Feminism in the Nineteenth Century* (Albany: State University of New York Press, 1984), chap. 7. Thanks to Claire Moses for sending me a copy of Adam's book.

86. Bonnie S. Anderson and Judith P. Zinsser, *A History of Their Own: Women in Europe from Prehistory to the Present*, rev. ed. (New York: Oxford University Press, 2000), 2: 261, 373. The woman was Harriet Law (1831–1897), a married English schoolteacher active in Owenite feminism.

87. For Kelley, see Dorothy Stirling, *Ahead of Her Time: Abby Kelley and the Politics of Anti-Slavery* (New York: Norton, 1991), p. 118. For Otto, see Louise Otto, *Das Recht der Frauen auf Erwerb: Blicke auf das Frauenleben des Gegenwart* (Hamburg, 1866), p. 65. For Stanton, see *Elizabeth Cady Stanton/Susan B Anthony: Correspondence, Writings, Speeches*, ed. Ellen Carol DuBois (New York: Schocken, 1981), p. vii.

88. Bodichon, cited in *American Diary*, p. 52.

Bibliography

∿

Primary Sources

Manuscript Collections

Mathilde Franziska Anneke Papers, State Historical Society of Wisconsin.
Barbara Bodichon Collection, Beinecke Library, Yale University.
Letters to Barbara Leigh Smith Bodichon, MacCrimmon Collection, Fawcett
    Library, London.
Clarkson Manuscripts, British Library.
Paulina Wright Davis Papers, Vassar College.
Jeanne Deroin Papers, Bibliothèque Historique de la Ville de Paris.
Fawcett Library Autograph Letter Collection: Woman's Suffrage, 1851-1894.
Anne Knight Papers, Library of the Society of Friends, Friends House, London.
Lucretia Mott Papers, Friends Historical Library, Swarthmore College.
Parkes Papers, Girton College, Cambridge.
Pauline Roland Papers, Bibliothèque Historique de la Ville de Paris.
Elizabeth Cady Stanton Papers, Library of Congress and Vassar College.

Newspapers and Journals

Mathilde Franziska Anneke, ed. *Deutsche Frauen-Zeitung*, 1852–54
———. *Frauen-Zeitung*, 1848.
Jeanne Deroin, ed. *Almanach des femmes*, 1852–1854.
English Woman's Journal, 1858–1863.
Gazette des tribunaux, 13–15 November, 1850 [Deroin and Roland's trial]
Lily, 1849–1855.

L'Opinion des femmes, 1848–1849.
Louise Otto, *Frauen-Zeitung*, 1849–1852.
La Politique des femmes, 1848.
Una, 1853–1855.
La Voix des femmes, 1848.

Published Documents

Albistur, Maïté, and Daniel Armogathe, eds. *Le Grief des femmes: Anthologie de textes féministes du môyen age à nos jour*. 2 vols. Poitiers: Editions hier et demain, 1978.

Anneke, Mathilde Franziska. *Mutterland: Memoiren einer Frau aus dem badisch-pfälzischen Feldzuge 1848/49*. 1853. Reprint, Münster: Tende, 1982.

Appleton, Jane. "Sequel to the Vision of Bangor in the Twentieth Century," *American Utopias: Fiction*, edited by Arthur O. Lewis, 243–265. New York: Arno, 1971.

Aston, Louise. *Ein Lesebuch: Gedichte, Romane, Schriften in Auswahl (1846–1849)*. Edited by Karlheinz Fingerhut. Stuttgart: Hans-Dieter Heinz Akademischer Verlag, 1983.

Barmby, Catherine. *The Demand for the Emancipation of Woman, Politically and Socially*. In *Sources of British Feminism*. Vol. 3, *The Reformers*. Edited by Marie Mulvey Roberts and Tamae Mizuta. London: Routledge/Thoemmes Press, 1993.

Bauer, Carol, and Lawrence Ritt, eds. *Free and Ennobled: Source Readings in the Development of Victorian Feminism*. Oxford: Pergamon, 1979.

Beik, Doris and Paul Beik, eds. *Flora Tristan, Utopian Feminist: Her Travel Diaries and Personal Crusade*. Bloomington: Indiana University Press, 1993.

Bell, Susan Groag, and Karen M. Offen, eds. *Women, the Family, and Freedom: The Debate in Documents*. Vol. 1, *1750–1880*. Stanford, Calif.: Stanford University Press, 1983.

Benson, Adolph B. "Fredrika Bremer's Unpublished Letters to the Downings." *Scandinavian Letters and Notes* 11, no. 8 (November 1931), 8 parts.

Blackwell, Dr. Elizabeth. *Pioneer Work in Opening the Medical Profession to Women: Autobiographical Sketches*. 1895. Reprint, New York: Schocken, 1977.

Bloomer, D. C. *Life and Writings of Amelia Bloomer*. 1895. Reprint, New York: Schocken, 1975.

Bodichon, Barbara Leigh Smith. *An American Diary, 1857–1858*. Edited by Joseph W. Reed Jr. London: Routledge & Kegan Paul, 1972.

Bodichon, Mrs. *Reasons for the Enfranchisement of Women*. London: Social Science Association, 1866.

Böttger, Fritz, ed. *Frauen im Aufbruch: Frauenbriefe aus dem Vormärz und der Revolution von 1848*. Darmstadt: Hermann Luchterhand Verlag, 1979.

Bremer, Fredrika. *England in 1851 or Sketches of a Tour in England*. Translated by L.A.H. Boulogne: Merridew, 1853.

Life, Letters, and Posthumous Works of Fredrika Bremer. Edited by Charlotte Bremer. Translated by Fredr. Milow. New York: Hurd & Houghton, 1868.

Bremer, Fredrika. *Homes of the New World: Impressions of America*. Translated by Mary Howitt. 2 vols. New York: Harper, 1853.

Brinker-Gabler, Gisela, ed. *Deutsche Dichterinnen: Vom 16. Jahrhundert bis zur Gegenwart*. Frankfurt am Main: Fischer Taschenbuch Verlag, 1978.

Browning, Elizabeth Barrett. *Aurora Leigh: A Poem*. Introduction by Gardner B. Taplin. 1856. Reprint, Chicago: Academy, 1979.

Bulgar, Raymonde Albertine. *Lettres à Julie Victoire Daubié (1824–1874): La première bachelière de France et sons temps*. New York: Peter Lang, 1992.

Chapman, Maria Weston. *Memorials of Harriet Martineau*. Boston: Houghton Mifflin, 1885.

Cocalis, Susan, ed. *The Defiant Muse: German Feminist Poems from the Middle Ages to the Present*. New York: Feminist Press, 1986.

Dall, Mrs. *Historical Pictures Retouch'd*. Boston: Walker, Wise, 1860.

Dall, Caroline H. *"Woman's Right to Labor"; or, Low Wages and Hard Work: In Three Lectures*. Boston: Walker, Wise, 1860.

Daubié, Julie-Victoire. *La femme pauvre au dix-neuvième siècle*. 3 vols. 1870. Reprint, Paris: côté-femmes, 1993.

Davis, Paulina W. *A History of the National Woman's Rights Movement*. 1871. Reprint, New York: Source Book Press, 1970.

Deroin, Jeanne. *Cours de droit social pour les femmes*. Paris, 1848.

———. *Du Célibat*. Paris: Chez Tous Les Marchands de Nouveautés, 1851.

———. *Lettre aux associations sur l'organisation du crédit*. Paris: Gustave Sandré, 1851.

———. *Lettre d'une femme à M. Athanase Coquerel*. Paris: Imprimarie de Lacour, 1848.

———. et al. *Association fraternelles des démocrates socialistes des deux sexes, pour l'affranchissement politique et social des femmes*. Paris: A. Lacour et Comp., 1849.

———. et al. *Solidarité*. Paris: Société pour la propagation et la réalisation de la Science sociale, 1848.

Dittmar, Louise. *Vier Zeitfragen*. Offenbach: Gustav André, 1847.

Dittmar, Louise. *Das Wesen der Ehe*. Leipzig: Otto Wiegand, 1850.

Dittmar, Louise. *Das Wesen der Ehe nebst einigen Aufsätzen über die soziale Reform der Frauen*. Leipzig: Otto Wiegand, 1849.

DuBois, Ellen Carol, ed. *Elizabeth Cady Stanton/Susan B. Anthony: Correspondence, Writings, Speeches*. New York: Schocken, 1981.

Eminent Women of the Age; Being Narratives of the Lives and Deeds of the Most Prominent Women of the Present Generation. 1869. Reprint, New York: Arno, 1974.

Erskine, Mrs. Steuart, ed. *Anna Jameson: Letters and Friendships*. London: T. Fisher Unwin, 1915.

Finch, Marianne. *An Englishwoman's Experience in America*. London: Richard Bentley, 1853.

Friesen, Gerhard K. "A Letter from M. F. Anneke: A Forgotten German-American Pioneer in Women's Rights." *Journal of German-American Studies* 12, no. 2 (1977), pp. 34–44.

Fuller, Margaret. *"These Sad but Glorious Days": Dispatches from Europe, 1846–1850*. Edited by Larry J. Reynolds and Susan Belasco Smith. New Haven: Yale University Press, 1991.

Fuller, Margaret. *Woman in the Nineteenth Century and Kindred Papers relating to the Sphere, Condition, and Duties of Woman*. Edited by Arthur B. Fuller. 1855. Reprint, New York: Norton, 1971.

Geiger, Ruth-Esther, and Sigrid Weigel, eds. *Sind das noch Damen: Vom gelehrten Frauenzimmer-Journal zum feministischen Journalismus*. München: Frauenbuchverlag, 1981.

Greene, Dana, ed. *Lucretia Mott: Her Complete Speeches and Sermons*. New York: Edwin Mellen, 1980.

Grimké, Sarah. *Letters on the Equality of the Sexes and Other Essays*. Edited by Elizabeth Ann Bartlett. New Haven: Yale University Press, 1988.

Haight, Gordon, ed. *The George Eliot Letters*. Vols. 1–3. New Haven: Yale University Press, 1954.

Hale, Sarah Josepha. *Woman's Record*. 1855. Reprint, New York: Source Book Press, 1970.

Hallowell, Anna Davis, ed. *Life and Letters of James and Lucretia Mott*. Boston: Houghton Mifflin, 1884.

Hayek, F. A. *John Stuart Mill and Harriet Taylor: Their Correspondence and Subsequent Marriage*. London: Routledge & Kegan Paul, 1951.

Hellerstein, Erna Olafson, Leslie Parker Hume, and Karen M. Offen, eds. *Victorian Women: A Documentary History of Women's Lives in Nineteenth-Century England, France, and the United States*. Stanford, Calif.: Stanford University Press, 1981.

Helsinger, Elizabeth K., Robin Lauterbach Sheets, and William Veeder. *The Woman Question: Society and Literature in Britain and America, 1837–1883*. 3 vols. New York: Garland, 1983.

d'Héricourt, Jenny P. "La Bible et la Question des Femmes." *Revue Philosophique et Religieuse*, 1857, 6: 16–34.

———. "Madame Rose," *Revue Philosophique et Religieuse*, 1856, 5: 129–139.

———. *La Femme affranchi*. 2 vols. Bruxelles and Paris: A. Lacroix, Van Meenen, 1860.

d'Héricourt, Madame. *A Woman's Philosophy of Woman, or Woman Affranchised*. New York: Carleton, 1864.

Holyoake, G. J. "Hints to the Advocates on the Rights of Women." *The Reasoner*, 11 August 1847, pp. 429–437.

Holyoake, George Jacob. *Sixty Years of an Agitator's Life*. 2 vols. London: T. Fisher Unwin, 1892.

Howitt, Margaret. *Twelve Months with Fredrika Bremer in Sweden*. 2 vols. London: Jackson, Walford, & Hodder, 1866.

Mary Howitt: An Autobiography. Edited by Margaret Howitt. 2 vols. London: Wm. Isbister, 1889.

Hummel-Haasis, Gerlinde, ed. *Schwestern zerreist eure Kettern: Zeugnisse zur Geschichte der Frauen in der Revolution von 1848/49*. München: Deutscher Taschenbuch Verlag, 1982.

Hunt, Harriot K., M.D. *Glances and Glimpses; Or Fifty Years Social, including Twenty Years Professional Life*. 1856. Reprint, New York: Source Book Press, 1970.

Knight, Anne. *Mary Grey: A Tale for Little Girls*. London: Harvey & Darnton, 1831.

Lacey, Candida Ann, ed. *Barbara Leigh Smith Bodichon and the Langham Place Group*. New York: Routledge & Kegan Paul, 1987.

Lefrançais, Pauline Roland, Perot. *L'Association des instituteurs, institutrices et professeurs socialistes*. Paris: Imprimarie Schneider, 1849.

[Lefrançais, Roland, Perot]. *Programme d'éducation*. Paris: Perot, 1849.

Lewald, Fanny. *Freiheit des Herzens: Lebensgeschichte—Briefe—Erinnerungen*. Edited by Günter de Bruyn and Gerhard Wolf. Frankfurt am Main: Ullstein Taschenbücher, 1992

Lewis, Hanna Ballin, trans. *The Education of Fanny Lewald: An autobiography*. Albany: State University of New York Press, 1992. With notes by Hanna Ballin Lewis.

Louise Otto-Peters: Ihr literarisches und publizistisches Werk. Catalogued by Johanna Ludwig and Rita Jorick. Leipzig: Leipzig University Press, 1995.

Malleson, Elizabeth. *Autobiographical Notes and Letters*. Printed for private circulation, 1926.

Martineau, Harriet. *Autobiography*. 2 vols. Edited by Maria Weston Chapman. Boston: Houghton Mifflin, 1877.

———. *The Martyr Age of the United States*. 1839. Reprint, New York: Arno, 1969.

———. *Society in America*. 3 vols. 1837. Reprint, New York: AMS Press, 1966.

von Meysenbug, Malwida. *Memoiren einer Idealistin*. 2 vols. Berlin: Schuster & Loeffler, 1881.

Möhrmann, Renate, ed. *Frauenemanzipation im deutschen Vormärz: Texte und Dokumente*. Stuttgart: Philipp Reclam, 1978.

Mott, James. *Three Months in Great Britain*. Philadelphia: J. Miller M'Kim, 1841.

Moynihan, Ruth Barnes, Cynthia Russet, and Laurie Crumpacker, eds. *Second to None: A Documentary History of American Women*. Vol. 1, *From the Sixteenth Century to 1865*. Lincoln: University of Nebraska Press, 1993.

Narrative of Sojourner Truth. 1878. Reprint, New York: Arno, 1968.

Necker de Saussure, Mme. *The Study of the Life of Woman*. Philadelphia: Lea & Blanchard, 1844.

Needler, G. H., ed. *Letters of Anna Jameson to Ottilie von Goethe*. London: Oxford University Press, 1939.

Nightingale, Florence. *Cassandra*. 1852. Reprint, Old Westbury, N.Y.: Feminist Press, 1979.

Norton, Caroline. *Caroline Norton's Defense: English Laws for Women in the Nineteenth Century*. Introduction by Joan Huddleston. Chicago: Academy Chicago, 1982.

Otto, Louise. *Frauenleben im Deutschen Reich: Erinnerungen aus der Vergangenheit mit Hinweis auf Gegenwart und Zukunft*. 1876. Reprint, Köln: Verlag M. Hütterman, Paderborn, 1988.

———. *"Dem Reich der Freiheit werb' ich Bürgerinnen": Die Frauen-Zeitung von Louise Otto*. Edited by Ute Gerhard, Elisabeth Hannover-Drück, and Romina Schmitter. Frankfurt am Main: Syndikat, 1979.

Otto-Peters, Louise. *Das Erste Vierteljahrhundert des allgemeinen deutschen Frauenvereins*. Leipzig: Moritz Schäfer, 1890.

Parkes, Bessie Rayner. *Essays on Woman's Work*. London: Alexander Strahan, 1865.

Parkes, B. R. *Poems*. London: J. Chapman, 1852.

[Parkes, Bessie Rayner]. *Remarks on the Education of Girls*. London: John Chapman, 1854.

Parkes, Bessie Rayner. *Summer Sketches, and other Poems*. London: John Chapman, 1854.

———. *Vignettes: Twelve Biographical Sketches*. London: Alexander Strahan, 1866.

Proceedings of the Woman's Rights Convention, held at the Unitarian Church, Rochester, N.Y. August 2, 1848, To Consider the Rights of Woman, Politically, Religiously and Industrially. Rochester, N.Y.: John Dick, 1848.

The Proceedings of the Woman's Rights Convention Held at Worcester, October 23 & 24, 1850. Boston: Prentiss & Sawyer, 1851.

The Proceedings of the Woman's Rights Convention Held at Worcester, October 15 & 16, 1851. New York: Fowler & Wells, 1852.

The Proceedings of the Woman's Rights Convention, Held at Syracuse, September 8, 9, & 10, 1852. Syracuse: J. E. Masters, 1852

Proceedings of the Woman's Rights Convention held at the Broadway Tabernacle, in the City of New York, on Tues. & Wed., Sept. 6th & 7th, 1853. New York: Fowler & Wells, 1853.

Proceedings of the National Women's Rights Convention, held at Cleveland, Ohio on Oct. 5th, 6th, & 7th, 1853. Cleveland: Gray, Beardsley, Spear, 1854.

Proceedings of the Seventh National Woman's Rights Convention, held in New York City at the Broadway Tabernacle on Tues. & Wed., Nov. 25 & 26, 1856. New York: Edward O. Jenkins, 1856.

Proceedings of the Ninth National Woman's Rights Convention Held in New York City, Thursday, May 12, 1859. Rochester: A. Strong, 1859.

Proceedings of the Tenth National Woman's Rights Convention, held at the Cooper Institute, New York City, May 10th & 11th, 1860. Boston: Yerrinton & Garrison, 1860.

Pulszky, Francis, and Theresa Pulszky. *White, Red, Black: Sketches of Society in the United States during the Visit of Their Guest*. 3 vols. 1853. Reprint, New York: Negro Universities Press, 1968.

Reed, W. S. *The Beauties of Bloomerism*. London: Ackermann, 1852.

Reid, Marion. *A Plea for Woman*. 1843. Reprint, Edinburgh: Polygon, 1988.

Reports on the Laws of New England [about women], *Presented to the New England Meeting convened at the Meionan, Sept. 19 & 20, 1855.* Boston, 1855.

Richardson, Marilyn, ed. *Maria W. Stewart: America's First Black Woman Political Writer, Essays and Speeches.* Bloomington: Indiana University Press, 1987.

Riot-Sarcey, Michèle, ed. *De la liberté des femmes: "Lettres de Dames" au Globe (1831–1832).* Paris: Côté-femmes, 1992.

———. "Lettres de Charles Fourier et de Désirée Véret: Une correspondance inédite," *Cahiers Charles Fourier* 6 (1995), pp. 3–14.

Ripley, C. Peter, Roy E. Finkenbine, Michael F. Hembree, and Donald Yacavone, eds. *Witness for Freedom: African American Voices on Race, Slavery, and Emancipation.* Chapel Hill: University of North Carolina Press, 1993.

Robson, Ann P., and John M. Robson, eds. *Sexual Equality: Writings by John Stuart Mill, Harriet Taylor Mill, and Helen Taylor.* Toronto: University of Toronto Press, 1994.

Roland, Pauline. "La Femme a-t-elle droit à la liberté?" *Almanach des corporations nouvelles, 1852,* pp. 93–99. Paris: Au Bureau de la Société de *La Presse du Travail,* 1851.

Ronge, Herr and Madame. *Addresses on the Kinder Garten System of Elementary Education.* Manchester: Fletcher & Tubbs, 1859.

Ronge, Joh., and Bertha Ronge. *A Practical Guide to the English Kindergarten.* London: J. S. Hodson, 1855.

Rose, Ernestine L. *A Defence of Atheism.* Boston: J. P. Mendum, 1889.

Russo, Ann, and Cheris Kramarae, eds. *The Radical Women's Press of the 1850s.* New York: Routledge, 1991.

Sams, Henry W., ed. *Autobiography of Brook Farm.* Englewood Cliffs, N.J.: Prentice-Hall, 1958.

Sand, George. *My Life.* Translated by Dan Hofstadter. New York: Harper & Row, 1979. Originally published in 1855.

[Smith, Barbara Leigh]. *A Brief Summary, in Plain Language, of the Most Important Laws Concerning Women: Together with a Few Observations Thereon.* London: Holyoake, 1854.

Smith, Barbara Leigh. *Women and Work.* London: Bosworth & Harrison, 1857.

Société pour l'Emancipation des Femmes. *Manifeste.* Paris: Imprimerie de A. Guyot, 1848.

Spender, Dale, ed. *The Education Papers: Women's Quest for Equality in Britain, 1850–1912.* New York: Routledge & Kegan Paul, 1987.

Stanton, Elizabeth Cady. *Eighty Years and More: Reminiscences, 1815–1897.* 1898. Reprint, New York: Schocken, 1971.

Stanton, Elizabeth Cady, Susan B. Anthony, and Matilda Joslyn Gage, eds. *History of Woman Suffrage.* Vol. 1, *1848–1861.* Vol. 2, *1861–1876.* 1882. Reprint, New York: Arno, 1969.

The Selected Papers of Elizabeth Cady Stanton and Susan B. Anthony. Vol. 1, *In the School of Anti-Slavery, 1840 to 1866.* Edited by Ann D. Gordon. New Brunswick, N.J.: Rutgers University Press, 1997.

Stanton, Henry B. *Sketches of Reforms and Reformers of Great Britain and Ireland.* New York: John Wiley, 1849.

Stanton, Theodore, ed. *The Woman Question in Europe: A Series of Original Essays.* 1884. Reprint, New York: Source Book, 1970.

Stanton, Theodore, and Harriot Stanton Blatch, eds. *Elizabeth Cady Stanton As Revealed in Her Letters, Diary, and Reminiscences.* 2 vols. New York: Harper, 1922.

Stirling, Dorothy, ed. *Turning the World Upside Down: The Anti-Slavery Convention of American Women Held in New York City, May 9–12, 1837.* New York: Feminist Press, 1987.

————. *We Are Your Sisters: Black Women in the Nineteenth Century.* New York: Norton, 1984.

Stoehr, Taylor. *Free Love in America: A Documentary History.* New York: AMS Press, 1979.

Taylor, Clare. *British and American Abolitionists: An Episode in Transatlantic Understanding.* Edinburgh: Edinburgh University Press, 1974.

Thompson, William. *Appeal of one Half the Human Race, Women, Against the Pretensions of the Other Half, Men, To Retain Them in Political, and Thence in Civil and Domestic Slavery.* 1825. Reprint, London: Virago, 1983.

Tolles, Frederick B., ed. *Slavery and "The Woman Question": Lucretia Mott's Diary of Her Visit to Great Britain to Attend the World's Anti-Slavery Convention of 1840.* Haverford, Pa.: Friends' Historical Association, 1952.

Tristan, Flora. *Lettres.* Edited by Stéphane Michaud. Paris: Editions de Seuil, 1980.

Hawkes, Jean, trans. *The London Journal of Flora Tristan.* With an Introduction by Jean Hawkes. London: Virago, 1982. Originally published in 1840.

Tristan, Flora. *The Workers' Union.* Translated by Beverly Livingston. Urbana: University of Illinois Press, 1983.

Voilquin, Suzanne. *Mémoires d'une saint-simonienne en russie (1839–1846).* Edited by Maïté Albistur and Daniel Armogathe. Paris: Des femmes, 1977.

V———[oilquin], Madame Suzanne. *Souvenirs d'une Fille du Peuple ou la Saint-Simonienne en Egypte.* Paris: Chez E. Sauzet, 1866.

Wagner, Maria. *Mathilde Franziska Anneke in Selbstzeugnissen und Dokumenten.* Frankfurt am Main: Fischer Taschenbuch Verlag, 1980.

[Wright, Frances]. *England the Civilizer.* London: Simpkin, Marshall, 1848.

Wright D'Arusmont, Frances. *Life, Letters, and Lectures.* 1834, 1844. Reprint, New York: Arno, 1972.

Yates, Gayle Graham, ed. *Harriet Martineau on Women.* New Brunswick, N.J.: Rutgers University Press, 1985.

Secondary Sources

Adler, Laure. *A l'aube du féminisme: Les premières journalistes (1830–1850).* Paris: Payot, 1979.

Agulhon, Maurice. *The Republican Experiment, 1848–1852.* Translated by Janet Lloyd. Cambridge: Cambridge University Press, 1983.

Allen, Ann Taylor. *Feminism and Motherhood: Germany, 1800–1914.* New Brunswick, N.J.: Rutgers University Press, 1991.

Ashton, Rosemary. *Little Germany: German Refugees in Victorian Britain.* Oxford: Oxford University Press, 1989.

Bacon, Margaret Hope. *Mothers of Feminism: The Story of Quaker Women in America.* New York: Harper & Row, 1989.

———. *Valiant Friend: The Life of Lucretia Mott.* New York: Walker, 1980.

Banks, Olive. *Becoming A Feminist: The Social Origins of "First Wave" Feminism.* Brighton: Wheatsheaf, 1986.

———. *The Biographical Dictionary of British Feminists.* Vol. 1, *1800–1930.* New York: New York University Press, 1985.

———. *Faces of Feminism: A Study of Feminism as a Social Movement.* New York: St. Martin's, 1981.

Bardes, Barbara, and Suzanne Gossett, *Declarations of Independence: Women and Political Power in Nineteenth-Century American Fiction.* New Brunswick, N.J.: Rutgers University Press, 1990.

Barry, Kathleen. *Susan B. Anthony: A Biography of a Singular Feminist.* New York: New York University Press, 1988.

Basch, Françoise. *Rebelles Américaines au XIXe Siècle: Mariage, amour libre et politique.* Paris: Méridiens Klincksieck, 1990.

Beecher, Jonathan. *Charles Fourier: The Visionary and His World.* Berkeley: University of California Press, 1986.

Belloc Lowndes, Mrs. *"I, Too, Have Lived in Arcadia": A Record of Love and Childhood.* London: Macmillan, 1941. The author, Marie Adelaide Belloc Lowndes, is the daughter of Bessie Rayner Parkes.

Berg, Barbara J. *The Remembered Gate: Origins of American Feminism.* Oxford: Oxford University Press, 1980.

Bestor, Arthur. *Backwoods Utopias: The Sectarian Origins and the Owenite Phase of Communitarian Socialism in America, 1663–1829.* 2d enl. ed. Philadelphia: University of Pennsylvania Press, 1957.

Bidelman, Patrick K. *Pariahs Stand Up! The Founding of the Liberal Feminist Movement in France, 1858–1889.* Westport, Conn.: Greenwood, 1982.

Blackett, R. J. M. *Building an Antislavery Wall: Black Americans in the Atlantic Abolitionist Movement, 1830–1860.* Baton Rouge: Louisiana State University Press, 1983.

Blake, Catriona. *The Charge of the Parasols: Women's Entry to the Medical Profession.* London: Women's Press, 1990.

Blanchard, Paula. *Margaret Fuller: From Transcendentalism to Revolution.* Reading, Mass.: Addison-Wesley, 1987.

Blos, Anna. *Frauen der deutschen Revolution 1848.* Dresden: Verlag Kaden, 1928.

Blum, Jerome. *In the Beginning: The Advent of the Modern Age, Europe in the 1840s.* New York: Scribner's, 1994.

Boetcher Joeres, Ruth-Ellen. *Die Anfänge der deutschen Frauenbewegung: Louise Otto-Peters.* Frankfurt am Main: Fischer Taschenbuch Verlag, 1983.

————. "Louise Otto and Her Journals: A Chapter in Nineteenth-Century German Feminism." *Internationales Archiv für Sozialgeschichte der deutschen Literatur* 4 (1979), pp. 100–129.

Boetcher Joeres, Ruth-Ellen, and Marianne Burkhard, eds. *Out of Line/Ausgefallen: The Paradox of Marginality in the Writings of Nineteenth-Century German Women.* Rodopi: Amsterdam, 1989.

Bogin, Ruth. "Sarah Parker Remond: Black Abolitionist from Salem." *Black Women in United States History*, edited by Darlene Clark Hine, 1: 135–166. Brooklyn, N.Y.: Carlson, 1990.

Bolt, Christine. *The Women's Movements in the United States and Britain from the 1790s to the 1920s.* Amherst: University of Massachusetts Press, 1993.

Bonner, Thomas. *To the Ends of the Earth: Women's Search for Education in Medicine.* Cambridge: Harvard University Press, 1992.

Bortolotti, Franca Pieroni. *Alle origini del movimento femminile in Italia, 1848–1892.* Turin: Giulio Einaudi, 1963.

Bradbrook, M. C. "Barbara Bodichon, George Eliot, and the Limits of Feminism." In *Women and Literature, 1779–1982: The Collected Papers of Murial Bradbrook*, 2: 49–68. Sussex: Harvester Press, 1982.

Brownlee, Sibyl Ventriss. "Out of the Abundance of the Heart: Sarah Ann Parker Remond's Quest for Freedom." Ph.D. diss., University of Massachusetts, 1997.

Bunker, Gary L. "Antebellum Caricature and Woman's Sphere." *Journal of Women's History* 3, no. 3 (Winter 1992), pp. 6–43.

Burton, Hester. *Barbara Bodichon, 1827–1891.* London: John Murray, 1949.

Caine, Barbara. "Feminism, Suffrage and the Nineteenth-Century English Women's Movement." *Women's Studies International Forum*, 5, no. 6 (1982), pp. 537–550.

————. *Victorian Feminists.* Oxford: Oxford University Press, 1992.

Campbell, Karlyn Kohrs. *Man Can Not Speak for Her: A Critical Study of Feminist Rhetoric with Texts.* 2 vols. New York: Praeger, 1989.

Chafetz, Janet Saltzman, and Anthony Gary Dworkin. *Female Revolt: Women's Movements in World and Historical Perspective.* Totowa, N.J.: Rowman & Allanheld, 1986.

Chevigny, Bell Gale. "To the Edges of Ideology: Margaret Fuller's Centrifugal Evolution," *American Quarterly* 38 (Summer 1986), pp. 173–201.

————. *The Woman and the Myth: Margaret Fuller's Life and Writings.* Rev. ed. Boston: Northeastern University Press, 1994.

Clark, Elizabeth. "Religion, Rights, and Difference in the Early Woman's Rights Movement." *Wisconsin Women's Law Journal* 3 (1987), pp. 29–57.

Clinton, Catherine. *The Other Civil War: American Women in the Nineteenth Century.* New York: Hill & Wang, 1984.

Conrad, Susan Phinney. *Perish the Thought: Intellectual Women in Romantic America, 1830–1860.* New York: Oxford University Press, 1976.

Corbin, Alain, Jacqueline Lalouette, and Michèle Riot-Sarcey, eds. *Femmes dans la Cité, 1815–1871.* Grâne, France: Créaphis, 1997.

Cromwell, Otelia. *Lucretia Mott*. Cambridge: Harvard University Press, 1958.

Cross, Máire, and Tim Gray. *The Feminism of Flora Tristan*. Oxford, U.K.: Berg, 1992.

Daley, Caroline, and Melanie Nolan, eds. *Suffrage and Beyond: International Feminist Perspectives*. Australia: Pluto; New Zealand: Aukland University Press, 1994.

Davidoff, Leonore, and Catherine Hall. *Family Fortunes: Men and Women of the English Middle Class, 1780–1850*. Chicago: University of Chicago Press, 1987.

Dickenson, Donna. *George Sand: A Brave Man—The Most Womanly Woman*. Oxford, U.K.: Berg, 1989.

Dijkstra, Sandra. *Flora Tristan: Feminism in the Age of George Sand*. London: Pluto, 1992.

DuBois, Ellen Carol. *Feminism and Suffrage: The Emergence of an Independent Women's Movement in America, 1848–1866*. Ithaca, N.Y.: Cornell University Press, 1978.

———. "The Radicalism of the Woman Suffrage Movement: Notes toward the Reconstruction of Nineteenth-Century Feminism," *Feminist Studies* 3 (Fall 1975), pp. 63–71.

Eckhardt, Celia Morris. *Fanny Wright: Rebel in America*. Cambridge: Harvard University Press, 1984.

Elbert, Sarah. *A Hunger for Home: Louisa May Alcott and Little Women*. Philadelphia: Temple University Press, 1984.

Engel, Barbara Alpern. *Mothers and Daughters: Women of the Intelligensia in Nineteenth-Century Russia*. Cambridge: Cambridge University Press, 1983.

Frevert, Ute, ed. *Bürgerinnen und Bürger: Geschlechterverhältnisse im 19. Jahrhundert*. Göttingen: Vandenhoeck & Ruprecht, 1988.

———. *Women in German History: From Bourgeois Emancipation to Sexual Liberation*. Translated by Stuart McKinnon-Evans with Terry Bond and Barbara Norden. Oxford, U.K.: Berg, 1989.

Frow, Ruth, and Edmund Frow, eds. *Political Women, 1800–1850*. London: Pluto, 1989.

Gattey, Charles Neilson. *The Bloomer Girls*. London: Femina, 1967.

Gerhard, Ute. "Über die Anfänge der deutschen Frauenbewegung um 1848: Frauenpresse, Frauenpolitik, Frauenvereine." In Karin Hausen, ed. *Frauen suchen ihre Geschichte*, pp. 196–220. München: Verlag C.H. Beck, 1983.

———. *Unerhört: Die Geschichte der Deutschen Frauenbewegung*. Reinbek bei Hamburg: Rowohlt, 1990.

Giddings, Paula. *When and Where I Enter: The Impact of Black Women on Race and Sex in America*. New York: William Morrow, 1984.

Ginzberg, Lori D. *Women and the Work of Benevolence: Morality, Politics, and Class in the Nineteenth-Century United States*. New Haven: Yale University Press, 1990.

Gleadle, Kathryn. *The Early Feminists: Radical Unitarians and the Emergence of the Women's Rights Movement, 1831–1851*. New York: St. Martin's, 1995.

Goetzinger, Germaine. *Für die Selbstwirklichung der Frau: Louise Aston*. Frankfurt am Main: Fischer Taschenbuch Verlag, 1983.

Griffith, Elisabeth. *In Her Own Right: The Life of Elizabeth Cady Stanton*. New York: Oxford University Press, 1984.

Groult, Benoîte. *Pauline Roland ou comment la liberté vint aux femmes*. Paris: Editions Robert Laffont, 1991.

Guarneri, Carl J. *The Utopian Alternative: Fourierism in Nineteenth-Century America*. Ithaca, N.Y.: Cornell University Press, 1991.

Hansen, Debra Gold. *Strained Sisterhood: Gender and Class in the Boston Female Anti-Slavery Society*. Amherst: University of Massachusetts Press, 1993.

Harrison, J. F. C. *Robert Owen and the Owenites in Britain and America: The Quest for the New Moral World*. London: Routledge & Kegan Paul, 1969.

Hauch, Gabriella. *Frau Biedermeier auf den Barrikaden: Frauenleben in der Wiener Revolution 1848*. (Vienna: Verlag für Gesellschaftskritik, 1990.

Hays, Elinor Rice. *Those Extraordinary Blackwells: The Story of a Journey to a Better World*. New York: Harcourt, Brace & World, 1967.

Hersh, Blanche Glassman. *The Slavery of Sex: Feminist-Abolitionists in America*. Urbana: University of Illinois Press, 1978.

Herstein, Sheila R. *A Mid-Victorian Feminist: Barbara Leigh Smith Bodichon*. New Haven: Yale University Press, 1985.

Herzog, Dagmar. *Intimacy and Exclusion: Religious Politics in Pre-Revolutionary Baden*. Princeton: Princeton University Press, 1996.

Hewitt, Nancy A. "Feminist Friends: Agrarian Quakers and the Emergence of Women's Rights in America." *Feminist Studies* 12, no. 1 (Spring 1986), pp. 27–49.

———. *Women's Activism and Social Change: Rochester, New York, 1822–1872*. Ithaca: Cornell University Press, 1984.

Hirsch, Pam. *Barbara Leigh Smith Bodichon: Feminist, Artist, and Rebel*. London: Chatto, 1998.

Hoffert, Sylvia D. *When Hens Crow: The Woman's Rights Movement in Antebellum America*. Bloomington: University of Indiana Press, 1995.

Holcombe, Lee. *Wives and Property: Reform of the Married Women's Property Law in Nineteenth-Century England*. Toronto: University of Toronto Press, 1983.

Holm, Birgitta, ed. *Fredrika Bremer ute och hemma*. Uppsala: Almqvist & Wiksell Tryckeri, 1987.

Horton, James Oliver. "Freedom's Yoke: Gender Conventions among Antebellum Free Blacks." *Feminist Studies* 12, no. 1 (Spring 1986), pp. 51–76.

Isenberg, Nancy Gale. *Sex and Citizenship in Antebellum America*. Chapel Hill: University of North Carolina Press, 1998.

Jeffrey, Julie Roy. *The Great Silent Army of Abolitionism: Ordinary Women in the Anti-Slavery Movement*. Chapel Hill: University of North Carolina Press, 1998.

Kerr, Andrea Moore. *Lucy Stone: Speaking Out for Equality*. New Brunswick, N.J.: Rutgers University Press, 1992.

Kolmerten, Carol A. *Ernestine Rose in America*. Syracuse, N.Y.: Syracuse University Press, 1998.

————. *Women in Utopia: The Ideology of Gender in the American Owenite Communities*. Bloomington: Indiana University Press, 1990.

Kraditor, Aileen S. *Means and Ends in American Abolitionism: Garrison and His Critics on Strategy and Tactics, 1834–1850*. New York: Pantheon, 1969.

Leach, William. *True Love and Perfect Union: The Feminist Reform of Sex and Society*. New York: Basic, 1980.

Lee, Amice. *Laurels and Rosemary: The Life of William and Mary Howitt*. London: Oxford University Press, 1955.

Lejeune-Resnick, Evelyne. *Femmes et associations (1830/1880): Vraies démocrates ou dames patronnesses?* Paris: Editions Publisud, 1991.

Lerner, Gerda. *The Grimké Sisters from South Carolina: Rebels against Slavery*. Boston: Houghton Mifflin, 1967.

Levine, Philippa. *Feminist Lives in Victorian England: Private Roles and Public Commitment*. Oxford: Basil Blackwell, 1990.

————. *Victorian Feminism, 1850–1900*. Tallahassee: Florida State University Press, 1987.

Liddington, Jill. *The Long Road to Greenham Common: Feminism and Anti-Militarism in Britain since 1820*. London: Virago, 1989.

Lindholm, Marika. "Swedish Feminism, 1835–1945: A Conservative Revolution." *Journal of Historical Sociology* 4, no. 2 (June 1991), pp. 121–142.

Lipp, Carola, ed. *Schimpfende Weiber und patriotische Jungfrauen: Frauen im Vormärz und in der Revolution 1848/49*. Moos & Baden-Baden: Elster Verlag, 1986.

Malmgreen, Gail. "Anne Knight and the Radical Subculture." *Quaker History* 71, no. 2 (Fall 1982), pp. 100–113.

————. *Neither Bread nor Roses: Utopian Feminists and the English Working Class, 1800–1850*. Brighton, U.K.: John L. Noyce, 1978.

Mason, Michael. *The Making of Victorian Sexual Attitudes*. Oxford: Oxford University Press, 1994.

Matthews, Jacqui. "Barbara Bodichon: Integrity in Diversity." In *Feminist Theorists: Three Centuries of Women's Intellectual Tradition*s, ed. Dale Spender, pp. 90–123. London: Women's Press, 1983.

McFadden, Margaret. "Anna Doyle Wheeler (1785–1848): Philosopher, Socialist, Feminist." *Hypatia*, 4, no. 1 (Spring 1989), pp. 91–101.

Melder, Keith E. *Beginnings of Sisterhood: The American Woman's Rights Movement, 1800–1850*. New York: Schocken, 1977.

Melzer, Sara E. and Leslie W. Rabine, eds. *Rebel Daughters: Women and the French Revolution*. New York: Oxford University Press, 1992.

Mermin, Dorothy. *Elizabeth Barrett Browning: The Origins of a New Poetry*. Chicago: University of Chicago Press, 1989.

————. *Godiva's Ride: Women of Letters in England, 1830–1880*. Bloomington: Indiana University Press, 1993.

Midgley, Claire. *Women against Slavery: The British Campaigns, 1780–1870.* London: Routledge, 1992.

Möhrmann, Renate. *Die andere Frau: Emanzipationsansätze deutscher Schriftstellerinnen im Vorfeld der Actundvierziger-Revolution.* Stuttgart: J. B. Metzler, 1977.

Moon, S. Joan. "Feminism and Socialism: The Utopian Synthesis of Flora Tristan." In *Socialist Women: European Socialist Feminism in the Nineteenth and Early Twentieth Centuries,* edited by Marilyn J. Boxer and Jean H. Quataert, pp. 19–50. New York: Elsevier, 1978.

Moses, Claire Goldberg. "Debating the Present, Writing the Past: 'Feminism' in French History and Historiography." *Radical History Review* 52 (1992), pp. 79–94.

———. *French Feminism in the Nineteenth Century.* Albany: State University of New York Press, 1984.

———. "Saint-Simonian Men/Saint-Simonian Women: The Transformation of Feminist Thought in 1830s France." *Journal of Modern History* 54 (June 1982), pp. 240–267.

Moses, Clare Goldberg and Leslie Wahl Rabine. *Feminism, Socialism, and French Romanticism.* Bloomington: Indiana University Press, 1993.

Mosse, George L. *Nationalism and Sexuality: Middle-Class Morality and Sexual Norms in Modern Europe.* Madison: University of Wisconsin Press, 1985.

Mullaney, Marie Marmo. "Feminism, Utopianism, and Domesticity: The Career of Rebecca Buffum Spring, 1811–1911." *New Jersey History* 104, no. 3–4 (Fall-Winter 1986), pp. 1–21.

Nueremberger, Ruth Ketring. *The Free Produce Movement: A Quaker Protest against Slavery.* Durham, N.C.: Duke University Press, 1942.

Offen, Karen. "Contextualizing the Theory and Practice of Feminism in Nineteenth-Century Europe (1789–1914)." In *Becoming Visible: Women in European History,* edited by Renate Bridenthal, Susan Stuard, and Merry E. Wiesner, pp. 327–356. 3d ed. Boston: Houghton Mifflin, 1998.

———. "Ernest Legouvé and the Doctrine of 'Equality in Difference' for Women: A Case Study of Male Feminism in Nineteenth-Century French Thought." *Journal of Modern History,* 58, no. 2 (June 1986), pp. 452–484.

———. "A Nineteenth-Century French Feminist Rediscovered: Jenny P. d'Héricourt 1809–1875." *Signs: Journal of Women in Culture and Society* 13, no. 1 (Autumn 1987), pp. 144–158.

———. "On the French Origin of the Words *Feminism* and *Feminist.*" *Feminist Issues* 8, no. 2 (Fall 1988), pp. 45–51.

Paletschek, Sylvia. *Frauen und Dissens: Frauen in Deutschkatholizismus und in den freien Gemeinden, 1841–1852.* Göttingen: Vandenhoeck & Ruprecht, 1990.

Pankhurst, Richard K.P., "Anna Wheeler: A Pioneer Socialist and Feminist." *Political Quarterly* 25 (1954), pp. 132–143.

———. *The Saint-Simonians, Mill, and Carlyle: A Preface to Modern Thought.* London: Sidgwick & Jackson, 1957.

———. *William Thompson: Britain's Pioneer Socialist, Feminist, and Co-operator.* London: Watts, 1954.

Pichanik, Valerie Kossew. *Harriet Martineau: The Woman and Her Work, 1802–76.* Ann Arbor: University of Michigan Press, 1980.

Prelinger, Catherine M. *Charity, Challenge, and Change: Religious Dimensions of the Mid-Nineteenth-Century Women's Movement in Germany.* Westport, Conn.: Greenwood, 1987.

———. "Religious Dissent, Women's Rights, and the Hamburger Hochschule für das weibliche Geschlecht in Mid-Nineteenth Century Germany," *Church History* 45 (March 1976), pp. 42–55.

Pugh, Evelyn L. "Florence Nightingale and J. S. Mill Debate Women's Rights." *Journal of British Studies* 21, no. 2 (Spring 1982), pp. 118–138.

———. "John Stuart Mill, Harriet Taylor, and Women's Rights in America, 1850–1873." *Canadian Journal of History* 13, no. 3 (December 1978), pp. 423–442.

Ranvier, Adrien. "Une Féministe de 1848: Jeanne Deroin." *La Révolution de 1848: Bulletin de la Société d'histoire de la révolution de 1848*, 4 (1907–1908): 317–355, 421–430, 480–498.

Rendall, Jane, ed. *Equal or Different: Women's Politics, 1800– 1914.* Oxford: Basil Blackwell, 1987.

———. "Friendship and Politics: Barbara Leigh Smith Bodichon (1827–1891) and Bessie Rayner Parkes (1829–1925)." *Sexuality and Subordination: Interdisciplinary Studies of Gender in the Nineteenth Century*, edited by Susan Mendus and Jane Rendall, pp. 136–170. London: Routledge, 1989.

———. *The Origins of Modern Feminism in Britain, France and the United States, 1780–1860.* New York: Schocken, 1984.

Reynolds, Larry J. *European Revolutions and the American Literary Renaissance.* New Haven: Yale University Press, 1988.

Riot-Sarcey, Michèle. *La démocratie à l'épreuve des femmes: Trois figures critiques du pouvoir, 1830–1848.* Paris: Albin Michel, 1994. The three figures discussed are Jeanne Deroin, Eugnie Niboyet, and Désirée Véret.

Robertson, Priscilla. *Revolutions of 1848: A Social History.* Princeton, N.J.: Princeton University Press, 1952.

Rooth, Signe Alice. *Seeress of the Northland: Fredrika Bremer's American Journey, 1849–1851.* Philadelphia: American Swedish Historical Foundation, 1955.

Rose, Phyllis. *Parallel Lives: Five Victorian Marriages.* New York: Knopf, 1983.

Ryan, Mary P. *Women in Public: Between Banners and Ballots, 1825–1880.* Baltimore, Md.: Johns Hopkins University Press, 1990.

Schnetzler, Barbara. *Die frühe amerikanische Frauenbewegung und ihre Kontakte mit Europa (1836–1869).* Bern: Herbert Lang, 1971.

Schulte, Wilhelm. "Mathilde Franziska Anneke." *Westfälische Lebensbilder* 8 (1958), pp. 120–138.

Schwartzkopf, Jutta. *Women in the Chartist Movement.* New York: St. Martin's, 1991.

Scott, Joan. *Only Paradoxes to Offer: French Feminists and the Rights of Man*. Cambridge: Harvard University Press, 1996.

Shanley, Mary Lyndon. *Feminism, Marriage, and the Law in Victorian England, 1850–1895*. Princeton: Princeton University Press, 1989.

Siemann, Wolfram. *Die deutsche Revolution von 1848/49*. Frankfurt am Main: Edition Suhrkamp, 1985.

Smith-Rosenberg, Carroll. *Disorderly Conduct: Visions of Gender in Victorian America*. New York: Oxford University Press, 1985.

Solomon, Martha M., ed. *A Voice of Their Own: The Woman Suffrage Press, 1840–1910*. Tuscaloosa: University of Alabama Press, 1991.

Sperber, Jonathan. *The European Revolutions, 1848–1851*. Cambridge: Cambridge University Press, 1994.

———. *Rhineland Radicals: The Democratic Movement and the Revolution of 1848–1849*. Princeton: Princeton University Press, 1991.

Spurlock, John C. *Free Love: Marriage and Middle-Class Radicalism in America, 1825–1860*. New York: New York University Press, 1988.

Stendahl, Brita K. *Fredrika Bremer: The Education of a Self-Made Woman 1801–1865*. Lewiston, N.Y.: Edwin Mellen, 1994.

Sterling, Dorothy. *Ahead of Her Time: Abby Kelley and the Politics of Antislavery*. New York: Norton, 1991.

———. *Lucretia Mott: Gentle Warrior*. Garden City, N.Y.: Doubleday, 1964.

Stites, Richard. "M. L. Mikhailov and the Emergence of the Woman Question in Russia." *Canadian Slavic Studies* 3, no. 2 (Summer 1969), pp. 178–199.

———. *The Women's Liberation Movement in Russia: Feminism, Nihilism, and Bolshevism, 1860–1930*. Princeton: Princeton University Press, 1978.

Stoddart, Anna M. *Elizabeth Pease Nichol*. London: J. M. Dent, 1899.

Struminger, Laura S. "Looking Back: Women of 1848 and the Revolutionary Heritage of 1789." In *Women and Politics in the Age of Democratic Revolution*, edited by Harriet B. Applewhite and Darline G. Levy, pp. 259–285. Ann Arbor: University of Michigan Press, 1990.

———. *The Odyssey of Flora Tristan*. New York: Peter Lang, 1988.

———. "The Vésuviennes: Images of Women Warriors in 1848 and Their Significance for French History." *History of European Ideas* 8, nos. 4–5 (1987), pp. 451–488.

Suhl, Yuri. *Ernestine L. Rose: Women's Rights Pioneer*. 2d ed. New York: Biblio, 1990.

Taylor, Barbara. *Eve and the New Jerusalem: Socialism and Feminism in the Nineteenth Century*. New York: Pantheon, 1983.

Thibert, Marguerite. *Le Féminisme dans le Socialisme Français de 1830 à 1850*. Paris: Marcel Giard, 1926.

———. "Pauline Roland: Une apôtre socialiste de 1848." *La Révolution de 1848* 22 (1925–1926), pp. 478–502, 524–540.

Thistlethwaite, Frank. *America and the Atlantic Community: Anglo-American Aspects, 1790–1850*. New York: Harper & Row, 1959.

Thomas, Clara. *Love and Work Enough: The Life of Anna Jameson*. Toronto: University of Toronto Press, 1978.

Bibliography 275

Thomas, Edith. *Pauline Roland: Socialisme et féminisme au XIXe siècle*. Paris: Marcel Rivière, 1956.
Thomas, John L. *The Liberator: William Lloyd Garrison*. Boston: Little, Brown, 1963.
Thompson, Dorothy. *The Chartists: Popular Politics in the Industrial Revolution*. New York: Pantheon, 1984.
Tuke, Margaret J. *A History of Bedford College for Women, 1849–1937*. London: Oxford University Press, 1939.
Tulloch, Gail. *Mill and Sexual Equality*. Hemel Hempstead: Harvester Wheatsheaf, 1989.
Tyrrell, Alexander. "'Woman's Mission' and Pressure Group Politics in Britain (1825–60)," *Bulletin of the John Rylands University Library of Manchester* 63, no. 1 (Autumn 1980), pp. 194–230.
Venet, Wendy Hammand. *Neither Ballots Nor Bullets: Women Abolitionists and the Civil War*. Charlottesville: University Press of Virginia, 1991.
Wagner, Maria. "A German Writer and Feminist in Nineteenth-Century America." In *Beyond the Eternal Feminine: Critical Essays on Women and German Literature*, edited by Susan L. Cocalis and Kay Goodman, pp. 159–175. Stuttgart: Akademischer Verlag Hans-Dieter Heinz, 1982.
Webb, R. K. *Harriet Martineau: A Radical Victorian*. London: Heineman, 1960.
Wellman, Judith. "The Seneca Falls Women's Rights Convention: A Study of Social Networks." *Journal of Women's History* 3, no. 1 (Spring 1991), pp. 9–37.
Welter, Barbara. *Dimity Convictions: The American Woman in the Nineteenth Century*. Athens: Ohio University Press, 1976.
Wittig, Gudrun. *"Nicht nur im stillen Kreis des Hauses": Frauenbewegung in Revolution und nach revolutionärer Zeit, 1848–76*. Hamburg: Ergebnisse Verlag, 1986.
Worzala, Diane Mary Chase. "The Langham Place Circle: The Beginnings of the Organized Women's Movement in England, 1854–1870." Ph.D. diss., University of Wisconsin, 1982.
Yee, Shirley J. *Black Women Abolitionists: A Study in Activism, 1828–1860*. Knoxville: University of Tennesee Press, 1992.
Yellin, Jean Fagan, and John C. Van Horne, eds. *The Abolitionist Sisterhood: Women's Political Culture in Antebellum America*. Ithaca, N.Y.: Cornell University Press, 1994.
———. *Women and Sisters: The Antislavery Feminists in American Culture*. New Haven: Yale University Press, 1989.
Zucker, A. E., ed. *The Forty-Eighters: Political Refugees of the German Revolution of 1848*. New York: Columbia University Press, 1950.
Zucker, Stanley. *Kathinka Zitz-Halein and Female Civic Activism in Mid-Nineteenth Century Germany*. Carbondale: Southern Illinois University Press, 1991.

Index

〜

Page numbers in *italics* indicate photographs or illustrations.